Wind Crossing Grasses

风吹草木动：来自黄河长江的诗

Edited and Translated by Wang Ping
Introduction by Wang Ping and Gary Snyder

KIN 詩 SHIP
PRESS

Wind Crossing Grasses: Poems from China's Dragon Rivers
An Anthology of Contemporary Chinese Poetry from the Yellow and Yangtze Rivers
Compilation, Editing, Translation, and Photography

Published by Kinship Poetry Press, St. Paul, MN
www.kinshippoetry.com

First Edition, 2026
ISBN 978-1-970902-02-0
Library of Congress Control Number: 2026931763

All photos by Wang Ping unless otherwise indicated
Cover design by Ping Wang, Jacquelyn Song, and Jiang Zijun
Interior design by Jacquelyn Song and Ping Wang
Copy Editing: Jacquelyn Song, Jeff Lambert
Advisory Editor: Paul Hoover
Art by Jin Lingzi
Additional photos by Mo Fei

Attributions

Many of the poems from *Wind Crossing Grasses: Poems from China's Dragon Rivers* have appeared in the following magazines:

Poetry Magazine, July - August 2025, a 40-page folio with introduction and poems
Hanging Loose Press, 2025
New American Writing, 2023, 2024, 2025
Café Review, 2023, special edition on Chinese poets
Spoke 8, 2023, special folio on Chinese poets from the anthology
Granta, 2022

This anthology is dedicated to the Yellow and Yangtze – my Father and Mother Rivers.
They run in my veins wherever I wander.

– Wang Ping

Table of Contents

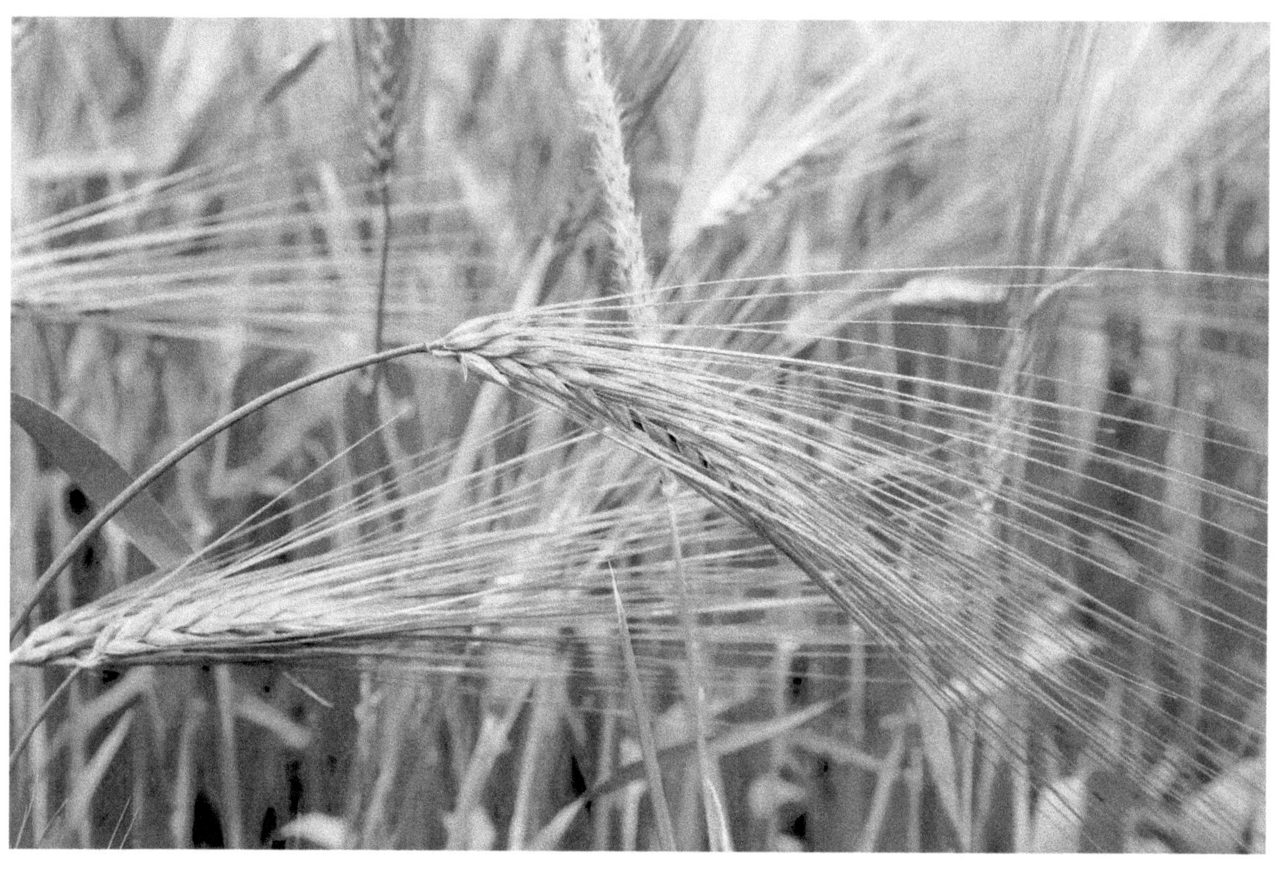

"If you want me again look for me under your boot-soles."

– Walt Whitman

When the Wind Blows
An Introduction by Wang Ping & Gary Snyder

From the Qinghai-Tibet Plateau, a wind blows. With it flow two great rivers—the Yellow and the Yangtze, twin dragons of China. They carve through the high roof of the earth, the gorges of Sichuan and Yunnan, the Loess Plateau, Mongolia's steppes, and fertile deltas before merging with the Bohai Sea and East China Sea.

Everything moves with the wind: grasses, trees, rivers, mountains, emotions, poetry, civilizations. It shakes, awakens, and transforms the earth. It carries soil, seeds, life, and death across continents, sculpting loess, deserts, grasslands, and fields. It is the qi of earth and sky—stirring roots, lifting typhoons, guiding birds from pole to pole. It makes souls yearn beyond the flesh. It awakens poets to sing to swaying trees and dancing rivers.

The Chinese call the wind—*feng* (风), qi, force, poetry.

Chinese poetry grows from this wind. Each poem carries the soil of its birth village, the ripple of its birth river, the scent of the cities where poets live, work, and love, and the mountains that stand as their backbones. A poem is not just a poem, but history, memory, home. Each word beckons the reader: This is my home, my memory. Enter gently, and let our wind and qi enrich your world.

The first Chinese anthology 《诗经》 (*shijing*, 11th century BCE) is divided into three sections: 风 雅颂 (Feng, Ya, Song—Wind, Elegance, Grace). The first section, Feng, gathered poems sung by peasants and soldiers in ancient China—their sorrow, love, and hope, which still run in the veins of every Chinese person today.

The poets in this anthology are rooted along the Yellow and Yangtze Rivers, their songs flying from the Qinghai Plateau all the way to the seas, mapping the land and waterscapes of China. Mo Fei's poems of the 24 Solar Terms follow the sun, providing a timescape for this anthology as it travels through four seasons, from 立春 (*lichun*, Start of Spring) to 大寒 (*dahan*, Major Cold), completing a full cycle.

The Yellow and Yangtze share one source: Sanjiangyuan, the Three-River Headwaters on the Qinghai-Tibet Plateau. The Yellow River flows through nine provinces: Qinghai, Sichuan, Gansu, Ningxia, Inner Mongolia, Shanxi, Shaanxi, Henan, and Shandong. The Yangtze flows through eleven: Qinghai, Sichuan, Xizang (Tibet), Yunnan, Chongqing, Hubei, Hunan, Jiangxi, Anhui, Jiangsu, and Shanghai. They run parallel across China like twin dragons of Chinese civilization, bringing fortune and ruin, joy and grief, agriculture and industry, harvest and flood, commerce and war, life and death. They birthed the multifaceted civilizations of China: yin and yang, dreamy and pragmatic, stoic and joyful, hardworking and playful, living in awe and harmony with earth, sky, and cosmos.

This anthology begins with the Yellow Dragon, meeting poets from the nine provinces along its path. Then it returns to the headwaters of the Yangtze, encountering poets downstream—from the high plateau to Jiangnan, the Yangtze Delta, then to Shanghai and the East China Sea.

The Yellow and Yangtze flow around the clock of sun and moon. Chinese poets follow the movement of rivers and mountains. Their poems pause this constant flow of time and water, offering us a glimpse into the wonder of China—its land and waters, its history, and all its living things, blossoming and fruiting in the seed of each poem.

Three millennia ago, Confucius walked these waters, gathering feng—songs—for the Shijing. Today, we follow the dragon rivers to collect new winds from this ancient land.

This anthology also collects new songs from China's west and north—Tibet, Qinghai, Gansu, Ningxia, Mongolia—where wind and altitude strip away desire, ambition, power, and other noises of the human world. As the roof of the earth, Asia's water tower, and the gateway to China's west, east, and south, the Upper Reaches of the Yellow and Yangtze have profoundly shaped Chinese poetry and music. The wind and water from sky, mountains, rivers, the Gobi, and grasslands stir the hearts of poets and pull the translator's heartstrings. Something happens when we stand on the mountain, so close to the sky, so deep in the river, so free in the wind, so far from desire… The land restores us as human, as animal, as grass, as life. The only things that matter are how to breathe—one breath at a time; how to walk—one step at a time; how to live— truly and happily.

That's what a poet is—
A gust of wind, a blade of grass,
Tying sky and earth together with words.

Let's flow with the two dragon rivers. Let the wind and poems carry us into the heart of China.

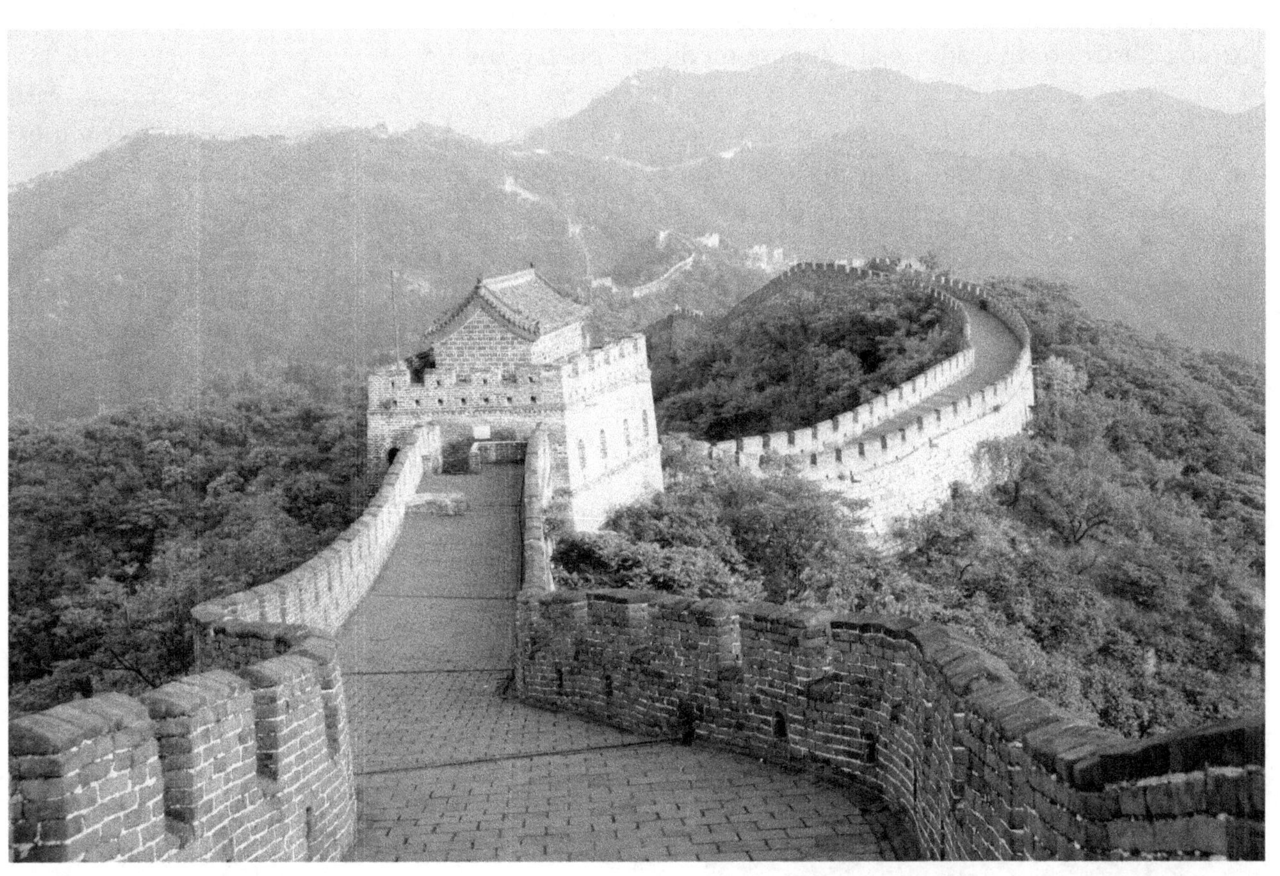

24 Solar Terms
Three Poems by Mo Fei

If you want to meet **Mo Fei**, follow leaves of grass, blooming flowers, fallen tree leaves. You'll find him bending over each bud, flower, fruit, at each change of the season. Mo Fei's poems follow the 24 Solar Terms, a method of timekeeping made in the Shang Dynasty. For five thousand years, the terms have been used for agriculture, weather observation, climate change, astrology, astronomy, traditional Chinese medicine, poetry and art.

His poems use the 24 Solar Terms, which trace the 360-degree rotation of the earth. Mo Fei uses the terms as clocks to mark season's changes. They provide a time-map while the two dragon rivers offer a roadmap for the landscape of Chinese history and poetry.

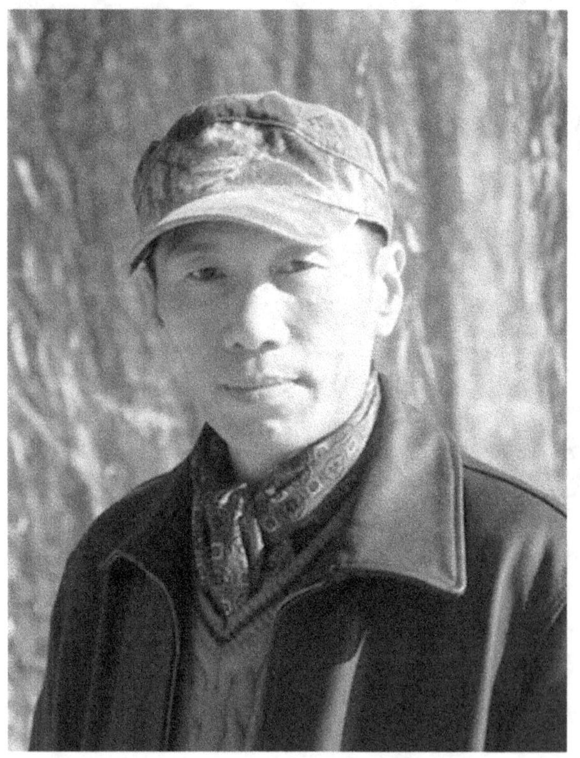

Born in Beijing in 1960, Mo Fei has worked all his life as a gardener in Beijing Zizuyuan Botanical Garden. He photographed all of the wildlife there, then began photographing every plant, flower, fruit and tree that appeared in the work of ancient Chinese poet Qu Yuan (屈原) in *The Book of Songs* (11-7th century BCE), and in the *Compmendium of Materia Medica* (1518 — 1593) by Ming Dynasty physician and writer Li Shizhen (李時珍).

 In 2018, Beijing University Press published *When Wind Blows, Grass and Trees Dance* (风吹草木动)— an anthology of his poetry and photography, following the 24 Solar Terms and the cycles of plants, seasons, rivers and mountains along the Yellow and Yangtze Rivers.

Mo Fei has also authored many other books, including *Words and Things* (词与物：人文科学的考古学), *Mo Fei Short Poems* (莫非短诗), and *I Think You Are Here* (我想你在这里).

立春

春天不肯来而且那么远，于是我讨好春天
枣树更高了好像不是枣树，我讨好枣树

云朵的翅膀可以飞到无影无踪，那么
我讨好云朵。提着大海的篮子来到岸上

我讨好火车。然后我一路讨好雨水和柚子
好像柚子不够大也不够甜，讨好柠檬蜜柑

我讨好春天的时候，正月没有问我为什么
没有讨好粮食和青菜，为什么没有讨好

那些宝座，而去讨好瓦缝里的龙葵和苋兰
不够结实的房顶依旧讨好风。看看太阳

不用讨好谁，诅咒太阳的人也依旧被照耀
像黑夜讨好大地的寂静，我讨好几粒蚕豆

Start of Spring

Spring is still far away, so I court spring.
Date trees seem taller but bear no fruit,
so I court the trees

Clouds float away till nothing remains, so I
court clouds. I go to the shore, carrying
the sea in my basket

I court the train, then rain and grapefruit
along the way. Grapefruit is not sweet enough,
so I court lemons and tangerines

I court spring. The first frost never asks me
why I never court grains or vegetables, why
I never try to court

Kings and queens, but worship
orchids and nightshades between the tiles.
Fragile roofs still court the wind.

But look at the sun. It never courts anyone,
shining on those who curse it, like night
courting earth, like me courting horse beans

雨水就是我们的种子

雨水就是我们的种子，词语和蛇的种子
向下生长一直向下，乔木和大地有了着落

有了隆重的云朵，为的是把天空给空出来
种子可以飞苋兰可以绕。星辰可以照耀

黑夜的航行，树叶的船在树上等风吹
太阳可以升起，接送青草和堇菜的种子

你在荒野和大道的中央，等气候不等天气
等万物转折不等万物等你。等万物吩咐

雨水流淌玫瑰发芽，雨水流淌玫瑰开花
在时间的前后，就在我们屋檐的前后滴答

雨的种子串起雨的帘幕，你透过来看啊
到处是雨的种子，才有去年和来年的萝藦

Rain Is Our Seed

Rain is our seed, for language and snakes
It grows downward, root for trees and earth

Clouds make room in the sky so seeds can
Fly, stars shine, orchids circle and climb

Sailing at night, leaves waiting for the wind
to blow. The sun is ready to rise, to meet
seeds of grass and viola

Standing in the fields and roads, waiting for
climate but not weather, waiting for things
to change, for the order of the world

Rain is falling, roses are sprouting, rain
falling, roses blooming. Time drips and
drops, in front of and behind our house

Rain strings its seeds to make a rain curtain.
Come and look at these seeds, making
luomo grow last year and next year

时间开花了

仿佛白露之后满院的桂香。影子说话
虎尾草说话，树上的葫芦提起来不出声

出声就会拽我们笑我们。时间开花了
结果在前面，又惊又喜却只有一次

风声响彻屋顶。干干净净的字句
隐去了两片树叶。田垄上的野莴苣

不知道摇晃的玉米为什么。不知道秋天
从哪一天开始。荞麦和高粱在山两边

鸟儿们知道收成怎么样。只有你来过
从雨的滴答里清点新的事物。白露之后

大地上的工作行将结束。造拱圈的人
用不上石头，而石头配得上每一块废墟

Time Is Blossoming

Sweet olives bloom after first frost. Shadows
chat with tiger-tail grass, but the gourds
stay silent, picked from the trees

Talking gourds may mock us. Time blossoms,
fruit before flowers. This surprise
delights us only once

Wind blows on the roof. Clean words hide
last leaves. Wild lettuces don't know why

Corns shake. No one knows when
autumn starts. Sorghum and buckwheat
grow on each side of the mountain

Birds know how good the harvest is.
They come to count new things in the
dripping rain. After the first frost

The work on earth will end. Stonehenge
makers no longer need stones, but they still
match each piece of the ruins

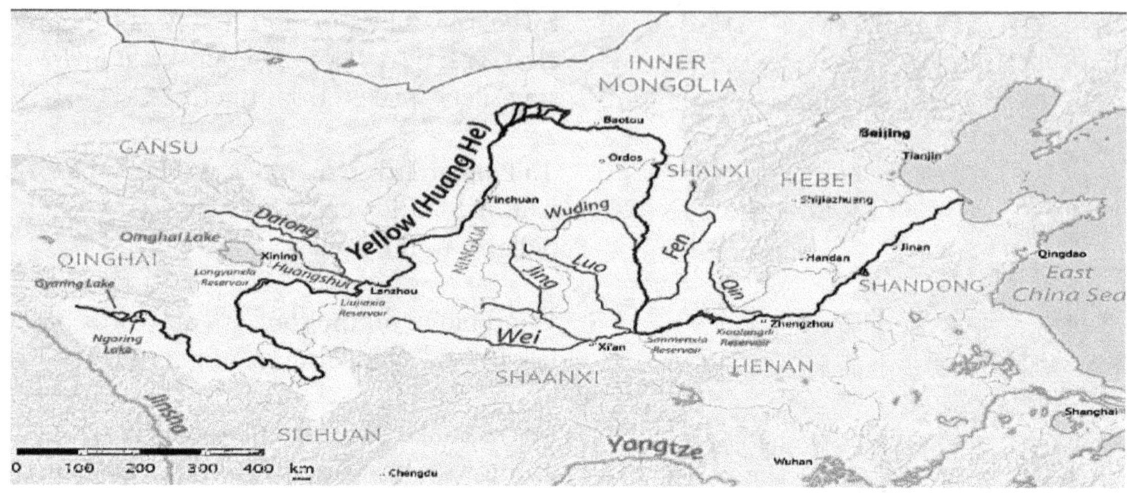

Born in the Bayan Har Mountains (Qinghai-Tibet Plateau), the Yellow River (*huanghe*, 黄河) is China's second-longest river—and its most relentless. It carves through nine provinces, carrying 40% of China's loess, the fine yellow soil eroded from the Loess Plateau. Each year, it dumps 1.6 billion tons of silt into the Bohai Sea, building a delta that expands and drowns with every flood.

This is the river that shaped Chinese characters—"几" (jī), a leg striding across the land; and "龙" (*long*), a dragon coiled in the empire's heart. More than water and sediment, the Yellow River is memory in motion. Its sharp bends twist like a dragon's flow—a zigzag of sorrows, hopes, dreams, and triumphs that forged China's civilization.

On its southward turn, the river and its tributaries slice through the thickest loess deposits on Earth, gathering immense silt. This lifts the riverbed 13–16 feet above the land, earning it the name "the hanging river"—a constant flood threat. Between 608 BCE and 1938 CE, the Yellow River breached its levees 26 times, shifted course, and flooded over 1,500 times, causing millions of deaths and countless refugees. Thus, it is also called "China's Sorrow."

Yet this river also nurtured fertile plains that cradled China's earliest civilizations: the Yangshao

(5000–3000 BCE) and Longshan (3200–1850 BCE). For millennia, the Chinese have wandered with its cycles, carrying their roots in songs, stories, poetry, and memory—always tied to their "old home" along the Yellow River.

The river's restless spirit inspired poets like Li Bai, Du Fu, Li Qingzhao, Lu You, and Wang Anshi, as well as modern voices such as Jidi Majia, He Zhong, Axin, Ye Zhou, and Zhai Yongming—from its upper reaches, through Inner Mongolia's great bend, to its delta. They roamed with the river, felt its pulse, and sang of its sorrow and joy, leaving timeless treasures:

Wang Zhihuan (王之涣)
No need to climb higher—
the whole river hangs from heaven.

Li Bai (李白)
The Yellow River rises from white clouds,
charging seaward like an exiled god.

Li Qingzhao (李清照)
I fear the little skiff at Twin Creek
Could never carry such a weight of sorrow.

This anthology introduces new poets of the Yellow Dragon, singing as brilliantly as the ancients.

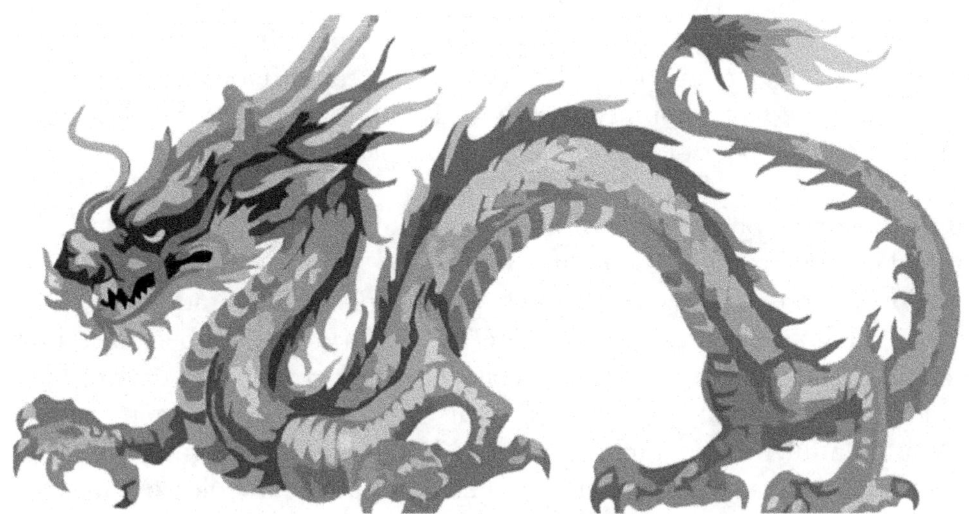

The Yellow Dragon is a symbol of the Yellow River and China

Qinghai (青海): The "Blue Sea" of Geological Wonders and Cultural Crossroads

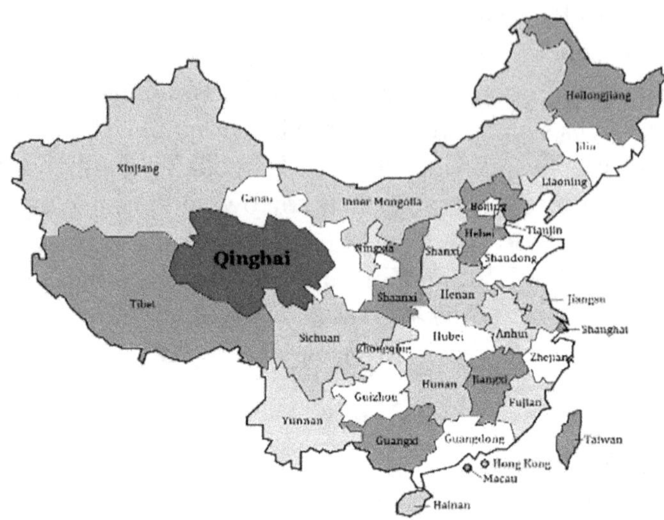

Qinghai's dramatic landscapes are shaped by the collision of tectonic plates, earning it the nickname "Roof of the World" (*shijie wuji*, 世界屋脊). Its geological formations include Hoh Xil Natural Reserve, a UNESCO World Heritage Site known as the world's highest plateau; Qaidam Basin, the Mars-esque "Salt Lake Capital" of China, containing 70% of the country's lithium reserves; Qinghai Lake, the largest lake in the country, sacred for Tibetan Buddhists; and Sanjiangyuan, the "Three-River Source," which feeds into the Yangtze, Yellow, and Mekong Rivers, sustaining the livelihoods of over one billion people downstream.

Historically, Qinghai was a pivotal corridor of the Silk Road's Southern Route, linking Tibet, Central Asia, and China. From the 4th to 7th century, the area was predominated by the Tuyuhun Kingdom, whose nomadic rulers left behind gold, artifacts, and tombs still being excavated around Qinghai Lake today. In the late 7th century, Qinghai became a battleground for the Tibetan and Tang Dynasties. Nowadays, its 37 ethnic groups weave a tapestry of traditions. Tibetan nomad culture is renowned for its gesar bards (epic singers) and thangka schools. Hui Muslim influence remains deeply rooted in the halal food and architecture, blending Chinese and Arabic customs to create delicacies like hand-pulled noodles and marvels like Xining's Dongguan Mosque. And, quite notably, Mongolian traditions shape the way of life, from Kumbum Monestary, a major Gelugpa Buddhist center under Mongol patronage, to the Haixi Prefecture Nadam Fair, a traditional festival with wrestling, archery, and horse-racing.

Qinghai balances development and ecology——its solar and wind farms power eastern China, while its grasslands combat desertification. Yet its people, from yak herders to lithium miners, share a resilience as vast as the plateau itself. Nurtured by its diverse origins, Qinghai is a place of poetry and spirituality: it hosts the the Qinghai International Poetry Festival, founded by Yi poet Jidi Majia, which draws writers from across the world to its "land of sky and silence."

To know Qinghai is to walk its high-altitude deserts, taste butter tea in a black yak-hair tent, or hear a Tibetan monk's low chant echo across a frozen lake. As Jidi Majia wrote: "Here, the sky is so close, you can touch the gods with your fingertips."

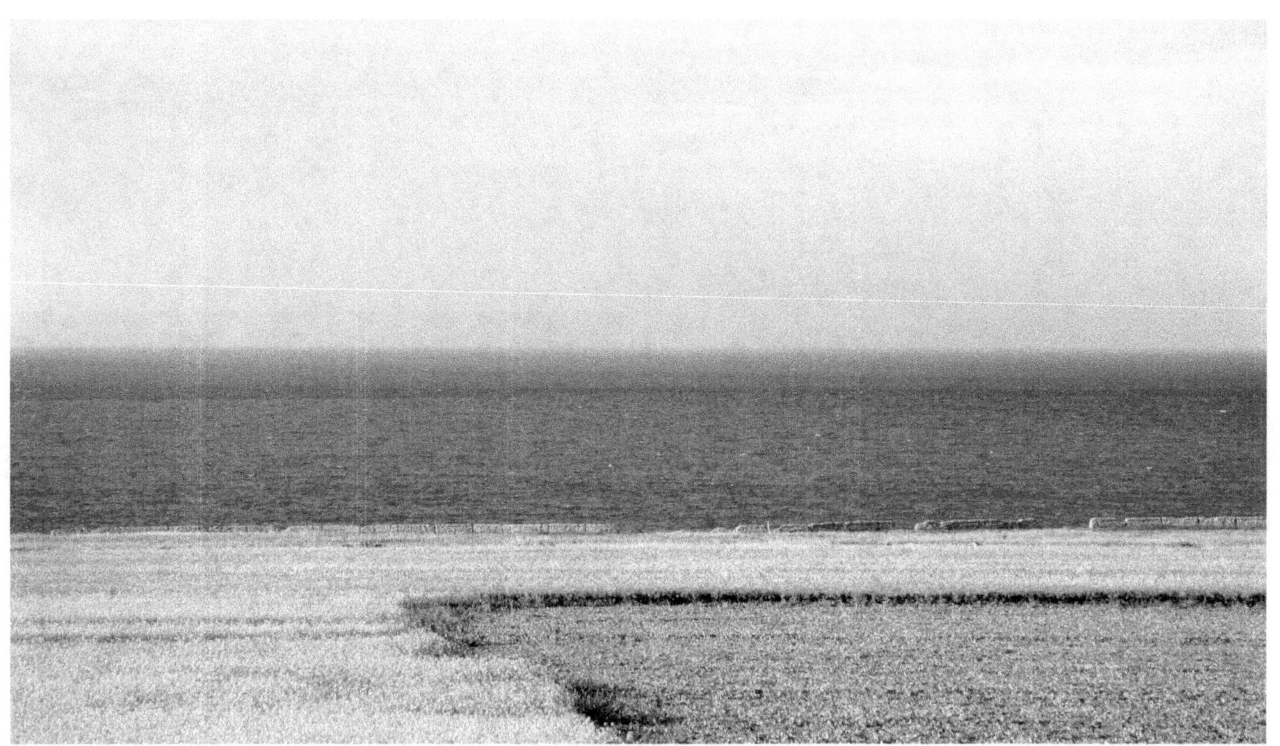

Qinghai Lake

Jidi Majia (吉狄马加) is a Yi poet born in 1961 in Liangshan, Sichuan. He spent much of his life in Qinghai as a celebrated writer and the President of the Qinghai Writers' Association. His works include *Songs of First Love* (初恋之歌), *Dreams of a Yi* (彝人的梦), *Rome's Sun* (罗马的太阳), *Jidimajia Selected Poems* (吉狄马加诗选), and *Forgotten Words* (被遗忘的词语), among others. He has received numerous accolades, including the National Poetry Award and the National Ethnic Poetry Award.

I first met Jidi Majia at the 2013 Qinghai Poetry Festival near the Headwaters of the Yellow River. There, I translated and recited his poems alongside him, accompanied by Grammy-winning musician Alex Wand. After the event, we feasted on hand-pulled lamb—a famed Tibetan-Mongolian dish—and sang loudly into the night, fueled by rounds of *baijiu* (rice wine).

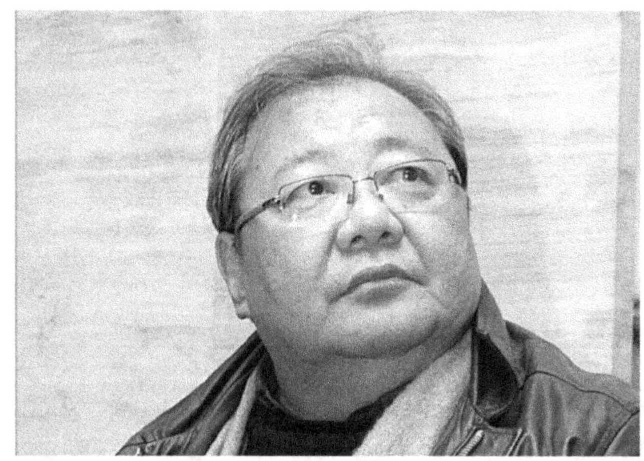

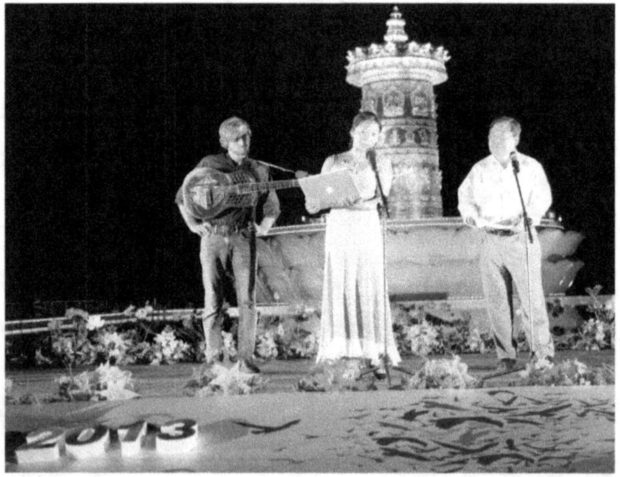

Jidimajia read poetry with Alex and Ping, 2003

天涯海角

刚刚离开了繁忙的码头
又来到一个陌生的车站
一生中我们就这样追寻着时间
或许是因为旅途被无数次的重复
其实人类从来就没有一个所谓的终点
可以告诉你，
我是一个游牧民族的儿子
我相信爱情和死亡是一种方式
而这一切都只会发生在途中

At the End of the Earth

After leaving a busy dock
we come to a new railway station
We chase time like this all our lives
The journey seems to repeat itself
Our destiny is forever beyond our reach
Let me tell you,
I am a Nomad's son
Love and death are ways of living
And everything happens along the path

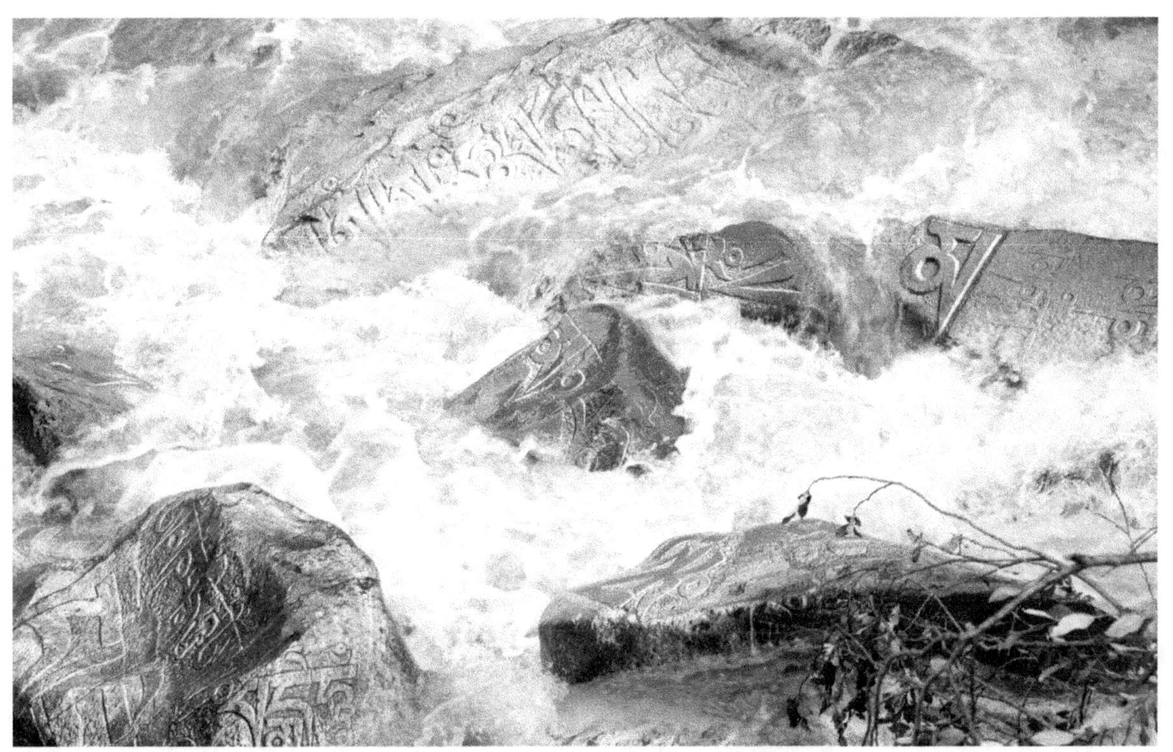

Prayer rocks in running water

鹿回头

传说一只鹿子被猎人追杀，无路可逃站在悬崖上，正当猎人要射杀时，鹿子猛然回头变成
了一个美丽的姑娘，最终猎人和姑娘结成了夫妻．
这是一个启示
对于这个世界，对于所有的种族
这是一个美丽的故事
但愿这个故事，发生在非洲，发生在波黑，发生在车臣
但愿这个故事发生在以色列，发生在巴勒斯坦，发生在
任何一个有着阴谋和屠杀的地方
但愿人类不要在最绝望的时候
才出现生命和爱情的奇迹

When a Deer Looks Back

A hunter chased a deer to the edge of a cliff. When the hunter was about to shoot the deer, it
suddenly looked back, changing into a beautiful girl. They married and lived happily ever after.
This is an enlightenment
for this world, for each race
This is a beautiful story
May it happen in Africa, Bosnia-Herzegovina and Chechnya
May it happen in Israel, Palestine
Wherever massacres brew and happen
Let the miracle of life and love live
Before mankind sinks into despair

感恩

我们出生的时候
只有一种方式
而我们怎样敲开死亡之门
却千差万别
当我们谈到土地
无论是哪一个种族
都会在自己的灵魂中
找到父亲和母亲的影子
是大地赐予了我们生命
让人类的子孙
在她永恒的摇篮中繁衍生息
是大地给了我们语言
让我们的诗歌
传遍了这个古老而又年轻的世界
当我们仰望璀璨的星空
躺在大地的胸膛
那时我们的思绪
会随着秋天的风儿
飞到很远很远的地方
大地啊，不知道这是为什么？
往往在这样的时刻
我的内心充满着从未有过的不安
人的一生都在向大自然索取
而我们的奉献更是微不足道
我想到大海退潮的盐碱之地
有一种冬枣树傲然而生
尽管土地是如此的贫瘠
但它的果实却压断了枝头
这是对大地养育之恩的回报人类啊，
当我们走过它们的身旁
请举手向它们致以深深的敬意！

Gratitude

We have only one way
To be born
But have many paths
To arrive at the door of death
When we talk about the earth
We always find our parents'
Shadows flickering in our souls
No matter what race we belong to
The earth gave us life
Allowing us to live
In her cradle
The land gave us languages
Allowing our poetry
To spread across this old and young world
We lie on the earth, looking up at the stars
Our thoughts drift up
With the autumn wind
I don't know why
This moment fills my heart
With anxiety
We ask so much from nature
We give back so little
I remember the winter jujube tree
Standing on the salty mud
After the tide receded
Its branches thick with fruits
As if giving thanks to
The land that is so poor and harsh
But still allows it to live
So, as we pass by, we raise our hands
To salute the tree and its jujubes

看不见的波动

有一种东西，在我
出生之前 它就存在着
如同空气和阳光
有一种东西，在血液之中奔流
但是用一句话 的确很难说清楚
有一种东西，早就潜藏在
意识的最深处
回想起来却有模糊
有一种东西，虽然不属于现实
但我完全相信
鹰是我们的父亲
而祖先走过的路
肯定还是白色
有一种东西，恐怕已经成了永恒
时间稍微一长
就是望着终日相依的群山
自己的双眼也会潮湿
有一种东西，让我默认
万物都有灵魂，人死了
安息在土地和天空之间
有一种东西，似乎永远不会消失
如果作为一个彝人
你还活在世上！

The Invisible Waves

Something has been alive in me
Before I was born
Like air and sunlight
Something has been running in my blood
But it can't be explained with a few words
Something has been living
In the depths of our mind
When we try to recall, it becomes vague
Something doesn't belong to this world
But I believe
The eagle is our father
And the road our ancestors walked
remains white.
Something might have become eternal
My eyes get wet
Whenever I watch mountains
Leaning upon each other
Something makes me believe
Everything has a spirit, the dead
Resting between earth and sky
Something seems never to go away
Like being the son of Yi people
Like being alive!

致布拖少女

你细长的脖子
能赛过阿呷查莫鸟*的
美丽颈项
你的眼睛是湖水倒映的星光
你的前额如同金子
浮悬着蜜蜂的记忆
你高高的银质领箍
是一块网织的悬岩
你神奇多姿的裙裾
在黄昏退潮的时候
为夜的来临尽情摆浪
你那光滑的肌肤
恰似初夏的风穿越撒满松针的幽谷
然后悄悄地掠过母羊的腹部
你的呼吸回旋如梦幻
万物在你的鼻息下
摇动一颗颗金色的晨露
你的笑声
起伏就像天上的云雀
可以断定
因为你的舞步
山脉的每一次碰撞
牛角的每一次冲动
都预示着秋天的成熟

* 阿呷查莫鸟是大凉山一种以脖颈长和美著称的
鸟。

To a Young Girl in Butuo

Your long slender neck
looks more beautiful than an Axia Chamo
Your eyes look like stars
mirrored on the lake
Your forehead looks like gold
Floating in sweet memories
Your tall silver hoop
hangs like a knitted cliff
Your colorful skirt sways wondrously
with the receding tide at dusk
to greet the night's arrival
Your skin is smooth like a summer breeze
passing through the pine valley, brushing
past the swollen belly of an ewe
Your breathing circles like a dream
The world sways with your breaths
dripping with morning's dewdrops
Your laughs
rise or fall like a skylark in the sky
I dare to say
because of your dancing steps
mountains collide
bulls clash
and autumn ripens

* Axia Chamo — a beautiful bird, dwelling in Mt.
Daliang, famous for its long slender neck.

Sichuan (四川): Mountains, Rivers & Poetry Without End

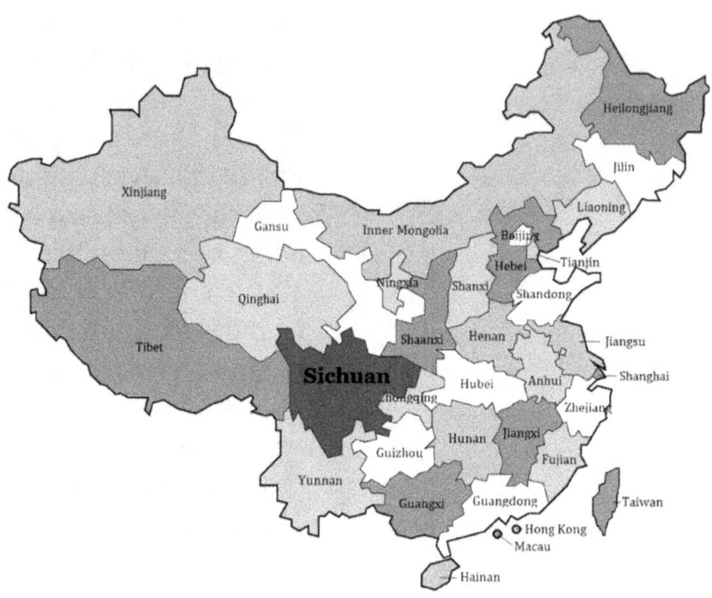

The literal meaning of Sichuan is "four plains in the basin." It is surrounded by mountain ranges and borders Tibet, Qinghai, Gansu, Shaanxi, Chongqing, Guizhou, and Yunnan. The Chengdu Plain is home to the world's oldest operational irrigation system, Dujiangyan (built in 251 BCE), which is still in use today.

Major rivers flow through this province—the Jialing, Jinsha, Min, and Tuo rivers, all tributaries of the Yangtze—bringing biodiversity, beauty, and poetic inspiration to the landscape. The basin of Sichuan sustains rivers, cultures, and life in all forms. It serves as a refuge for species such as the ginkgo tree, the dawn redwood, the giant panda, and the Yangtze sturgeon, protecting them from extinction during the Ice Age.

Fifty-six ethnic groups, including the Yi, Tibetan, Miao, Mongolian, and others, coexist in harmony here. With its 5,000-year history of Ba-Shu culture, the basin has produced countless poets, writers, and politicians. Over the centuries, poets have journeyed through these gorges and rivers, leaving behind some of the most beautiful verses in Chinese literature: Qu Yuan's "Nine Songs" and "Mountain Spirits," Li Bai's "Crying Gibbons," and Du Fu's "Song of My Thatched Roof Destroyed by Autumn Winds."

Sichuan is also home to the Shudao, ancient mountain roads connecting Shaanxi and Sichuan, built and maintained since the 4th century BCE. These historic paths consist of planks supported by wooden or stone beams, anchored into holes carved into cliff faces along the Yangtze and other rivers. Their engineering complexity remains astonishing even by modern standards.

Every time I return to China, I travel along the Yangtze, from Shanghai all the way to Lhasa. Chengdu is always a mandatory stop—to savor its tongue-numbing hotpot and meet some of modern China's greatest poets, such as Zhai Yongming, Aku Wuwu, and others.

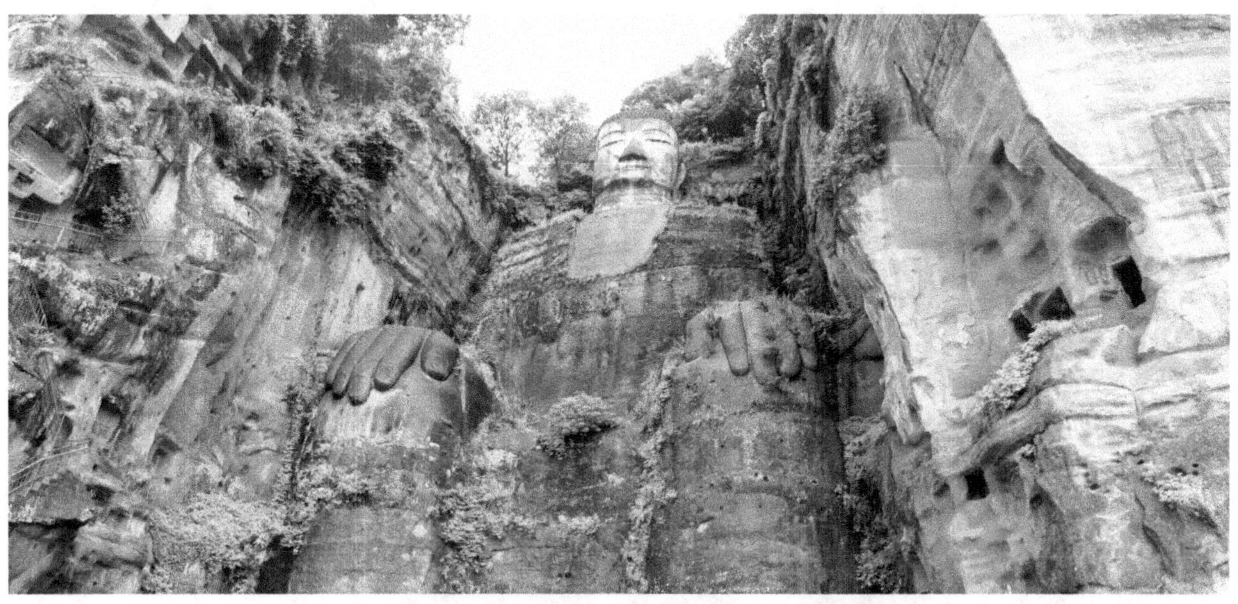

Sichuan's famous Leshan Buddha (71 meters tall), built at the confluence of
Min and Dadu Rivers from 713 - 803 CE.

Zhai Yongming (翟永明), born in 1955, is one of China's most distinguished contemporary poets, celebrated for her evocative and introspective verse. Her two groundbreaking poetry series, *Life in This World* (人间笔记) and *Designs of Death* (死亡的设计), mark her as a vital voice in modern Chinese literature. Her published collections, *Women* (女人), *Above All the Roses* (在所有玫瑰之上), *Collected Poems of Zhai Yongming* (翟永明诗选), and *Plain Songs in the Dark Night* (黑夜里的素歌) reflect her profound engagement with themes of identity, femininity, and existential inquiry.

Internationally recognized, Zhai has been invited to literary conferences and poetry festivals across Europe, and her work has been translated into numerous languages. In 2012, Zephyr Press released *The Changing Room*, a selection of her poems translated by Andrea Lingenfelter, further broadening her global readership.

I first met Zhai Yongming in New York City in the early 1990s, during her time living in SoHo with her then-husband. Their loft became a vibrant gathering place for Chinese artists and writers, where we held salons—reading poetry, debating ideas, and exploring the city's galleries together. Though she eventually returned to Chengdu, her creative evolution continued, her poetry deepening in both thematic scope and stylistic mastery. Today, her work remains as expansive and resonant as ever, a testament to her enduring literary vision.

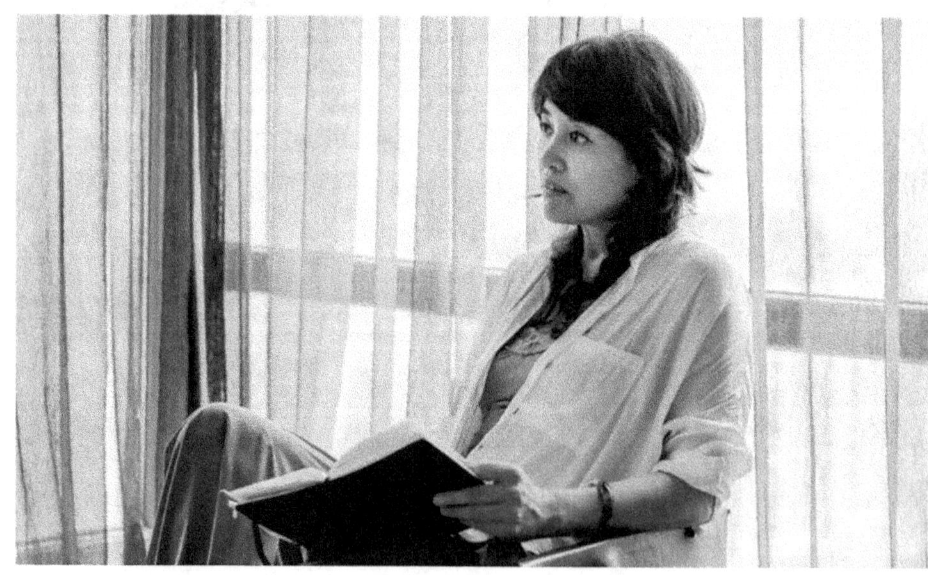

老虎与羚羊

半夜 有人在我耳边说：
我醒了，你们还在沉睡

世界像老虎 在梦里
追着你追着你
世界的万物都像老虎
它们一起追赶你这只
细脚踵的羚羊
永恒的天敌绝不放过你
即使在梦中 即使在虚空

早上 2021 大年初一
我慢慢读着马雁的诗
细嚼慢咽地把那些词语吞下
然后拧亮台灯 打开手机显示屏
那是我的面孔还是老虎的面孔？
老虎念着诗 而我动着嘴唇
她也是这样一颗一颗
吐出星星的瑰丽吗？

她也是这样被追赶着
被躯使着 被抓挠着
直至跌入黑暗？
她在黑暗中醒来
还是我在明亮中逝去？
那只老虎斜刺里冲出
抓住你 那只利爪
不！那是锋利的刀刃
刺进你的肉体
你被一缕透明的锋芒
一片一片剖开 化作光晕

星星就是这样亘古永久地
吐出一颗又一颗　　瑰丽

注：2021，大年初一，为白夜录读马雁
诗有感。

Tiger and Gazelle

Midnight, someone whispered at my ear:
I'm awake, but you're still sleeping

The world runs, a tiger chasing you
on and on in your dreams
Everything in the world is like this tiger
chasing you together, thin-legged gazelle
Your eternal predators, even
in a dream, in empty space

Dawn 2021, first day of the Spring Festival
I was reading Ma Yan's poems, slowly
chewing each word swallowing sentences
I turned on the lamp. The face in my phone:
Was it me or a tiger?
The tiger was reciting a poem
I was moving my mouth
Was she spitting stars, one by one, dazzling?

Was she being chased like this,
captured, vanished
in the abyss?
Did she wake up in the dark
Or was it me, who died in light?
That tiger leapt out of the corner
to catch me with its sharp claws
No! It's a knife
Plunged into your flesh
Slicing you into pieces

This is how stars spit eternity
One by one   dazzling

Note: poem after Ma Yan, on the Chinese
New Year's Day, 2021

关于雏妓的一次报道

雏妓又被称作漂亮宝贝
她穿着花边蕾丝小衣
大腿已是撩人
她的妈妈比她更美丽
她们像姐妹 "其中一个像羚羊
男人都喜欢这样的宝贝
宝贝也喜欢对着镜头的感觉
我看见的雏妓却不是这样
她十二岁 瘦小而且穿着肮脏
眼睛却能装下一个世界
或者 根本已装不下哪怕一滴眼泪
她的爸爸是农民 年轻
但头发已花白
她的爸爸花了三个月
一步一步地去寻找他
失踪了的宝贝
雏妓的三个月
算起来快一百多天
三百多个男人
这可不是简单数
她一直不明白为什么
那么多老的，丑的，脏的男人
要趴在她的肚子上
她也不明白这类事情本来的模样
只知道她的身体
变轻变空 被取走某些东西
雏妓又被认为美丽无脑
关于这些她一概不知
她只在夜里计算
她的算术本上有三百多个
无名无姓 无地无址的形体
他们合起来称作消费者
那些数字像墓地里的古老符号

Report on a Child Prostitute

A child prostitute is called a babe
She wears lace lingerie
Thighs already enticing
Her mother, even prettier
But she's the "gazelle" of all the sisters…
Men love such a babe, and she loves
to gaze at herself in the mirror
Not the child I saw
Twelve, thin, dirty
An entire world filled up her eyes
Leaving no room for a tear
Her father is a young peasant
But his hair has turned gray
In the past three months
As he walked from city to city
Searching for his babe
Three months
Almost one hundred days
More than three hundred men
Not an easy figure for a child
She couldn't understand
Why these old, ugly, filthy men
Climbed on her stomach
She had no idea why her body
Became lighter and emptier
Why some parts were missing
She didn't know, as a pretty babe
She's not supposed to have a brain
At night she adds in her math book
The number, three hundred men
Who have no name nor address
But together, become one body
devouring her and the number,
like a symbol on an old grave

太阳出来以前 消失了
看报纸时我一直在想：
不能为这个写诗
不能把诗变成这样
不能把诗嚼得嘎嘣直响
不能把词敲成牙齿 去反复啃咬
那些病 那些手术
那些与十二岁加在一起的统计数字
刮伤我的眼球
（这是视网膜的明暗交接地带）
一切全表明：都是无用的
都是无人关心的伤害
都是每一天的数据 它们
正在创造出某些人一生的悲哀
部分地 她只是一张新闻照片
这有一个"照片""新闻照片"。
十二岁 与别的女孩站在一起
你看不出 她少一个卵巢
一般来说 那只是报道
每天 我们的眼睛收集
成千上万的资讯
现在讲到"眼睛"了，这个器官。
它们控制着消费者的欢愉
它们一掠而过 "它"也如此
信息量 热线 和国际视点
像巨大的麻布 抹去了
一个人卑微的伤痛
我们这些人 看了也就看了
它被揉皱
塞进黑铁桶里

evaporating before the sunrise.
Reading the newspaper, I tell myself:
I must not write a poem for this
Must not turn this into poetry
Must not tear these words
Or grind my teeth to chew out
The disease, the surgery
And the number that heaped
Upon a twelve-year-old child
Poetry, bandage, photo, memory
Are scratching my eyes
(border between dark and light in my retina)
Numbers are useless
No one cares about the damage
These are just daily facts
That ruin someone's life quietly
Her twelve-year-old body is nothing
But a news photo when she stands
Next to other children
You can't tell she's missing an ovary
Our eyes pick her up as a piece of news
With tons of other information
That controls our pleasure as a consumer
They sweep us by, just as the news
About the babe
Hotlines of information and global
Perspectives have erased a girl's humble
Pain like a giant rag
We've read it
The paper is crumbled then trashed
Into a dark steel can

太空垃圾

我被国际空间站的宇航员
推入太空 从此
无人问津 从此
我在你们头顶持续运行

每130分钟 我将绕地球一圈
每130分钟 我诉说寂寞无边
每130分钟 我身边多了相同的废物
每130分钟 我看见太空加倍拥堵

绕地球一圈 滴答 哼哈 嗡嗡
绕地球一圈 翻滚 漂浮 冻结
绕地球一圈 上升 下沉 起舞
绕地球一圈 蓝色 绿色 死寂色

碎片 漆片 粉尘 残骸
固体 液体 晶体 实体
我们将杀死彼此 或者
被无人问津变成杀人犯

当人类探索宇宙的年龄
而我则一遍遍地探索出口
盖子或 黑洞 或穹顶的漏缝——

从什么地方溜出去?
怎样躲避来自另一飞行物的碰撞?
或者 让我在大气层中燃烧成灰烬?
没有一种方法能让我寿终正寝
没有一种 现在还没有

我只能漫天飞舞
与20万件类似的物件一同
跳静止的 慢动作的太空舞
等待下一个舞伴的加入

Space Garbage

From the International Space Station
I was flung into space   Since then
Nobody's asked how I was doing.   Since then
I've been flying over your heads

Every 130 minutes   I circle around the earth
Every 130 minutes   I talk about loneliness
Every 130 minutes   more garbage piles up
Every 130 minutes   space is more crowded

A spin around   ticktock hum buzz
A spin around   flipflop float freeze
A spin around   rise sink dance
The earth spins   blue green dead silence

Shards paint dust wreckage
Solid liquid crystal objects
We shall kill each other or
Nobody cares if we become murderers

Humanity searches for the age of cosmos
I grope for the exit through the cover
black hole or its opening
round and round—

Where can we escape?
How do we dodge another flying object?
Or will I become ash flying in the atmosphere?
No way will allow me to live a normal life
No way at all

I can only float
Dancing the slow stalled space dance
With those 200,000 objects in space
Waiting for the next partner to join me

渴望

今晚所有的光只为你照亮
今晚你是一小块殖民地
久久停留，忧郁从你身体内
渗出，带着细腻的水滴

月亮像一团光洁芬芳的肉体
酣睡，发出诱人的气息
两个白昼夹着一个夜晚
在它们之间，你黑色眼圈
保持着欣喜

怎样的喧嚣堆积成我的身体
无法安慰，感到有某种物体将形成
梦中的墙壁发黑
使你看见三角形泛滥的影子
全身每个毛孔都张开
不可捉摸的意义
星星在夜空毫无人性地闪耀
而你的眼睛装满
来自远古的悲哀和快意

带着心满意足的创痛
你优美的注视中，有着恶魔的力量
使这一刻，成为无法抹掉的记忆

Thirst

Tonight all the light is shining for you
Tonight you are a small colony, stuck in time
melancholy seeping through your body
In tiny droplets

The moon is a flesh, smooth and fragrant
Giving off a seductive smell in her sleep
Sandwiched between two days
You look joyful, despite the dark circles
Around your eyes

My body is made with noises
inconsolable, something is forming inside
The walls darken in the dream
Triangle shadows flood your eyes
Every pore on your body opens
For no reason
Stars twinkle with indifferent lights
Your eyes are loaded with
Ancient sorrow and satisfaction

With pain and content, you gaze
Your grace comes with a demon's force
Making this moment an eternal memory

Gansu (甘肃): A Land of History and Natural Wonders

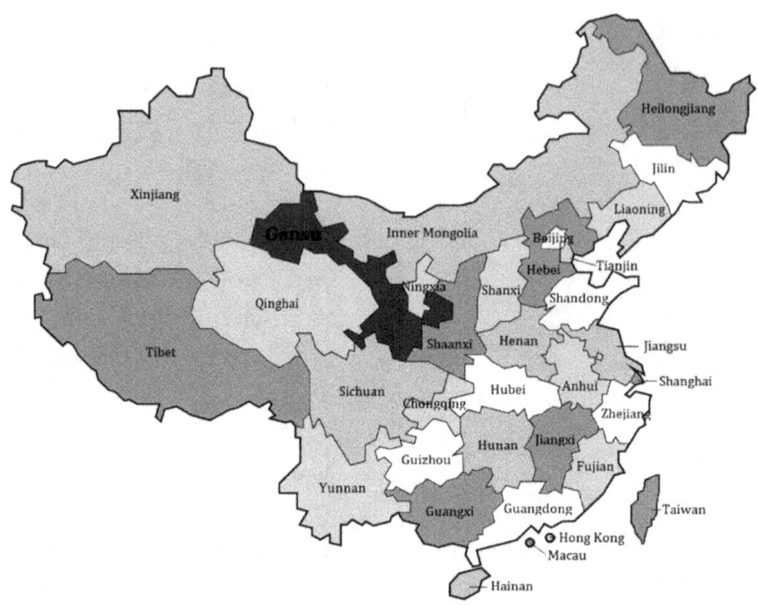

Every visit to Gansu leaves me in awe. This breathtaking land of plateaus, plains, and the Gobi Desert is the ancestral homeland of the poet Li Bai. It borders Xinjiang, Qinghai, Ningxia, Inner Mongolia, Sichuan, and Shaanxi, as well as the country of Mongolia. The Yellow River flows through its capital, Lanzhou, famous for its beef lamian (hand-pulled noodles).

The State of Qin, which originated here, laid the foundation for China's first imperial dynasty. In 221 BCE, Qin Shi Huang unified the warring states and became the first emperor of a unified China. Gansu's strategic importance was further cemented by the Northern Silk Road, which turned the region into a vital hub for trade and cultural exchange. The magnificent Buddhist grotto art of the Mogao Caves stands as a testament to these historical connections.

The Great Wall of China begins at Jiayuguan Pass, initially constructed during the Warring States period and later expanded under Qin Shi Huang in 221 BCE. Qin Shi Huang mobilized 300,000 laborers to extend the wall from Gansu all the way to the Korean border. The wall served not only as a line of defense against invaders, but also as a means of securing trade routes and state control. Travelers were required to obtain an official pass from the government to cross through its gates—a system akin to modern-day passports.

For centuries, poets were banished to this "end of the world"—Li Bai, Du Fu, Wang Wei, Wang Zhihuan… They left behind some of China's most beautiful and haunting verses, echoing the windswept Gobi's sandstorms and their own sorrows. Once they passed Jiayuguan's gates, there was little hope of return.

I arrived at Lanzhou Airport in Winter 2023, eager to explore. But first, I had to learn how to navigate a new world: scanning WeChat to pay for the long-distance bus, rushing with my luggage to the stop. Two hours later, the bus reached Lanzhou, and I realized my suitcase—packed with all my clothes—was still on the luggage cart. I had a long journey ahead, following the Yellow River from Lanzhou all the way to the Yellow Sea in Shandong.

Then, a stranger's kindness turned despair into warmth. The woman I'd befriended on the bus stepped in—using her own ID to book me a hotel, bringing me spare clothes, guiding me through the city. She helped me find a driver to visit the Yellow River's first reservoir. I lost a suitcase of Patagonia gear, but I gained a friend.

That is Gansu: a vast land of raw beauty, profound history, and big hearts.

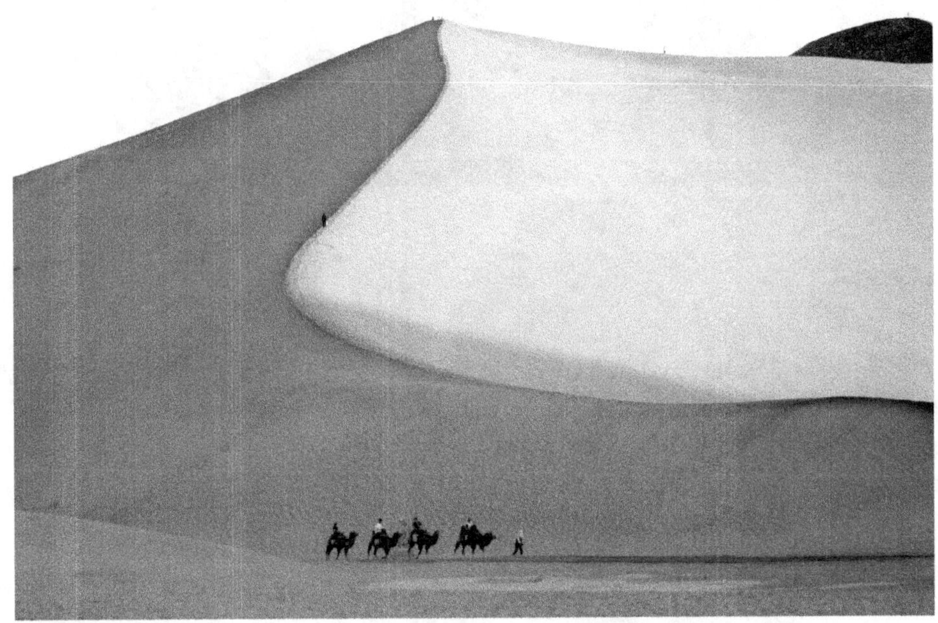

Dunhuang, Gansu

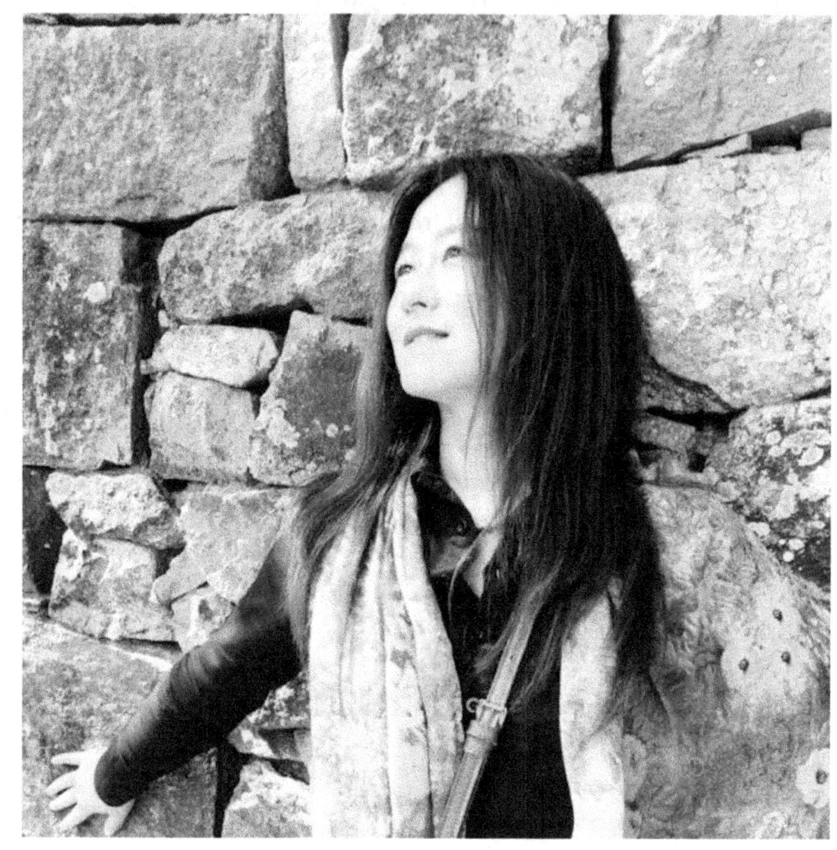

Wu Qianghua (武强华) was born in 1978 in Zhangye, Gansu. Her poetry collections include *38 Degrees North Latitude, Sleeping with Mountains* and others. Her poems appeared in *People's Literature* (人民文学), *Poetry* (诗刊), *The Stars Poetry Journal* (星星诗刊), *Feitian* (飞天), *Poetry Exploration* (诗歌探索), and others.

祁连山

雪，白过它自己的骨头了
白得整座山看起来只有骨头
没有肉。
肉藏在野牦牛的身上
它秘密地穿过山谷时
站在山坡上的那个人
嗅到了山的香味。据说
他三岁时就嗅到过同样的味道
现在他十七岁，像豹子一样
已经不能再等了

Qilian Mountains

Snow, already whiter than its own bones
The whole mountain looks like a bone
No flesh.
All the meat is hidden in yaks' bodies
When they pass the valley quietly
He smells their fragrance from the peak.
He smelled the same fragrance
When he was three years old
Now at 17, strong like a leopard
He no longer wants to wait

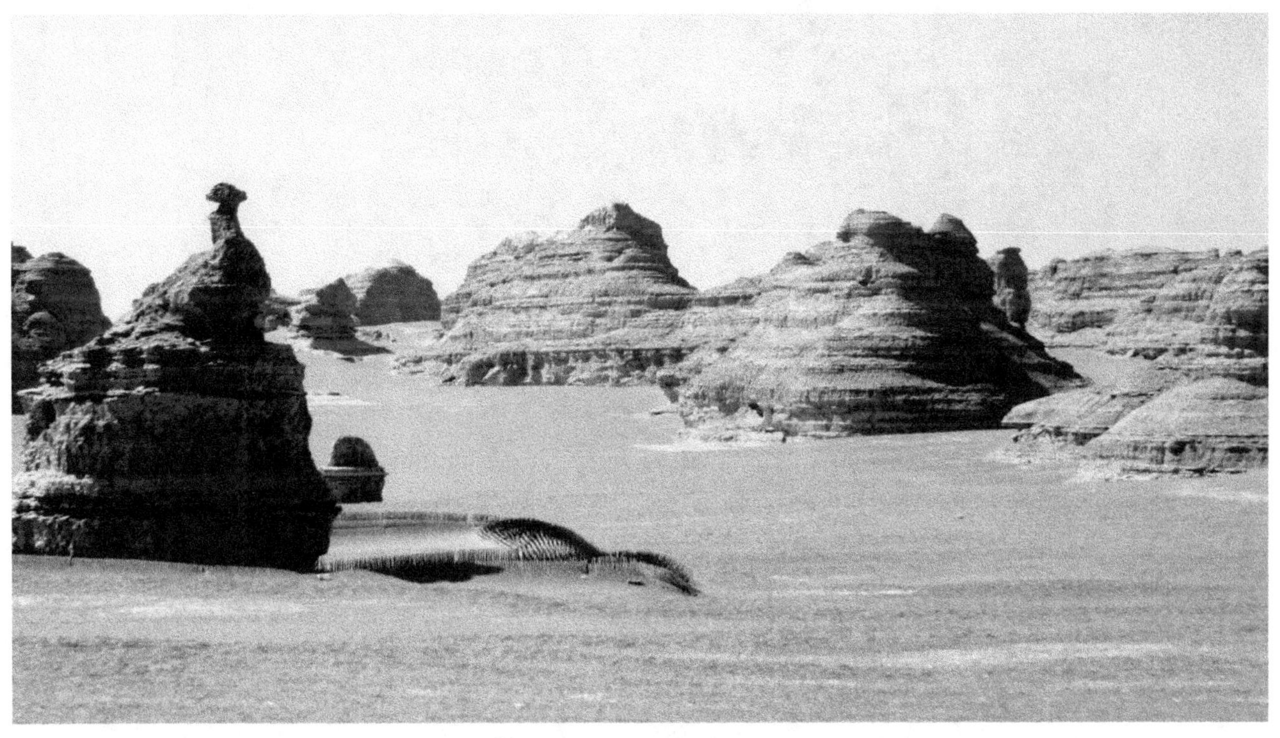

Yadang National Park, Gansu

Ye Zhou (叶舟) (b. 1966, Lanzhou, Gansu Province) is an acclaimed Chinese poet and novelist, known for works such as *Poems from the Borders* (边城诗草), *Selected Poems by Ye Zhou* (叶舟诗选), and *Dunhuang* (敦煌). His major literary honors include the Lu Xun Literary Prize and the Mao Dun Literary Prize.

We met in Lanzhou over a lamb hot pot, at his favorite restaurant, Lamb Gate. "This is the best lamb in the northwest," he said. I smiled and told him people had warned me that Tibet, Qinghai, Gansu, Ningxia, and Inner Mongolia all claim to have the best lamb. We laughed. Ye then recommended where to see the most breathtaking stretch of the Yellow River in Lanzhou—and he was absolutely right.

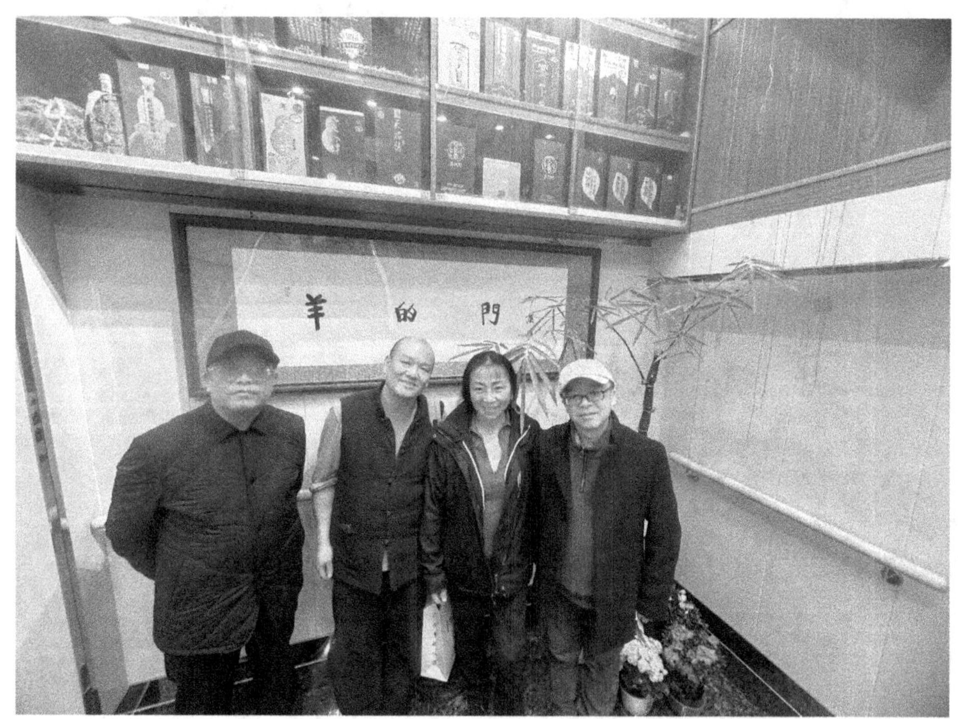

From right: Ye Zhou, Ping, Fan and his friend

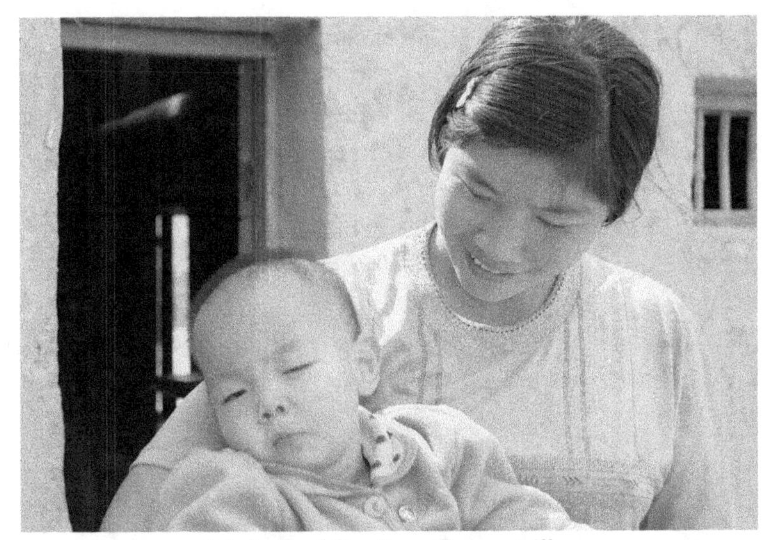

Little Buddha in a Gansu village

叮嘱

将一盏灯送进

石窟，也别忘了
带一把青稞。

将一棵菩提
栽上壁画，也别忘了
供一碗净水。

将一尊佛像请进
敦煌，一定别忘了
养一对羔羊。

菩萨不会走。
可万一走了，这些
就是我们疼痛的拌料。

Please

Please bring a light

Into the grotto cave, please don't forget
To bring a handful of barley.

Please plant a Bodhi tree
On the grotto painting, please don't forget
To offer a bowl of clean water.

Please bring a Buddha's statue
Into Dunhuang, please don't forget
To bring a pair of lambs.

Buddhas don't walk away.
But if they do leave us,
Sorrow stays forever.

怀想

那时候 月亮还朴素 像一块
古老的银子 不吭不响 静待黄昏

那时候的野兽 还有牙齿 微小的
暴力 只用于守住疆土 丰衣足食

那时候 天空麇集了凤凰和鲲鹏
让书生们泪流不止 写光了世上的纸

那时候的大地 只长一种香草
名曰君子 有的人入史 有的凋零

那时候 铁马秋风 河西一带的
炊烟饱满 仿如一匹广阔的丝绸

那时候的汉家宫阙 少年刘彻
白衣胜雪 刚刚打开了一卷羊皮地图

那时候 黄河安澜 却也白发三千
一匹伺伏的鲸鱼 用脊梁拱起了祁连

那时候还有关公与秦琼 亦有忠义
和然诺 事了拂衣去 一般不露痕迹

那时候 没有磨石 刀子一直闪光
拳头上可站人 胳膊上能跑马

那时候的路不长 足够走完一生
谁摸见了地平线 谁就在春天称王

Remembering

Back then, the moon was still simple like
An old tale of silver, sitting quietly for dusk

Back then, animals used teeth
For food and guarding home only

Back then, sky had Kunpeng & phoenixes
Weeping poets used up paper for poetry

Back then, the land grew fragrant herb–
Man of Honor, some in history, some faded away

Back then, steel horses, fall wind, cooking smoke
Spread along the Yellow River like silk

Back then, in the Han Palace, youth Liu Ce opened
a sheepskin map, his robe whiter than snow

Back then, the Yellow was calm, 3000 li of white hair
crouching like a whale, spine lifting Mount Qilian

Back then, Guan Yu and Qin Qiong were loyal.
They needed no return after a fulfilled promise

Back then, swords shone without a grinding stone.
A man could stand on a fist, arms long enough
to let horses gallop

Back then, the path was far enough to fulfill one's life
Whoever touched the horizon became King

万物生长

坐在正午，坐入
今天灿烂的日光下
我比天空明净，比云朵坚定
比一切过往的爱恨
更加温馨。大地生长，青草葳蕤
世上的好儿女们
前赴后继。

爱上每一寸光，爱着
无限的大气和苍茫
我比一本古籍悠久，比一堆
暗夜的篝火晌彻
鹰隼告诉我的每一个好消息，我也将
传递四方。我放还了马，它黝黑的脸
仿如世上的奇迹。

鲜花怒放，时间吹袭
在人生的海拔上，我比一捧雪
比一炉时代的钢铁
更加热烈。我劈下内心的柴，
取出沸腾的心跳
因为，并不是我孤身一人，马不停蹄
走在锦绣的春天。

Everything in Blossom

Sitting alone at noon
Under the blue light
I'm brighter than sky, more solid than clouds
More tender than all the love and hate
From the past. Earth is alive, grass is green,
and good children on Earth
keep coming and going.

I'm in love with every inch of light
Wth the universe, infinite vastness
I'm older than an antique book, louder
than the bonfire crackling in the dark
I spread good news from eagles
To the world's four corners, let go my horse,
its black face, a shining miracle.

Flowers bloom, time blows
On the peak of my life.
My passion is hotter
Than the melting steel and snow.
I split open my boiling heart.
I'm not alone, as I trot
Through this blooming spring

晒太阳的下午

寺院上空的太阳最好，不光
晒我，还晒着
世上的所有佛像；寺院内的
太阳最好，照着蚂蚁
松枝、锦鸡与香火，
也照着一棵菩提树，
光明正大，
没有芥蒂；
寺墙上的太阳最好，像下了
一个冬天的肥雪，
养着这个空空荡荡的人世，
养着青稞和酒；
寺院以外的太阳最好了，它们像
迷了路的羊群，
有的人跌倒，
有的人哭泣，看见了这里
金顶之上的佛光。

Sunning in the Afternoon

The sun over the temple is the best
It warms me and all the Buddhas
On earth: the sun in the temple
Is the best, warming ants
Pines, pheasants and incense,
And the Bodhi tree,
Tall and shining,
Carrying no grudge;
The sun on the temple's walls is the best,
Thick like whole winter's snow,
Nursing this empty world,
Brewing barley wine;
The sun outside the temple is the best
Like sheep losing their way,
Some falling,
Some weeping, and some watching
Buddha's light on the temple's gold steeple.

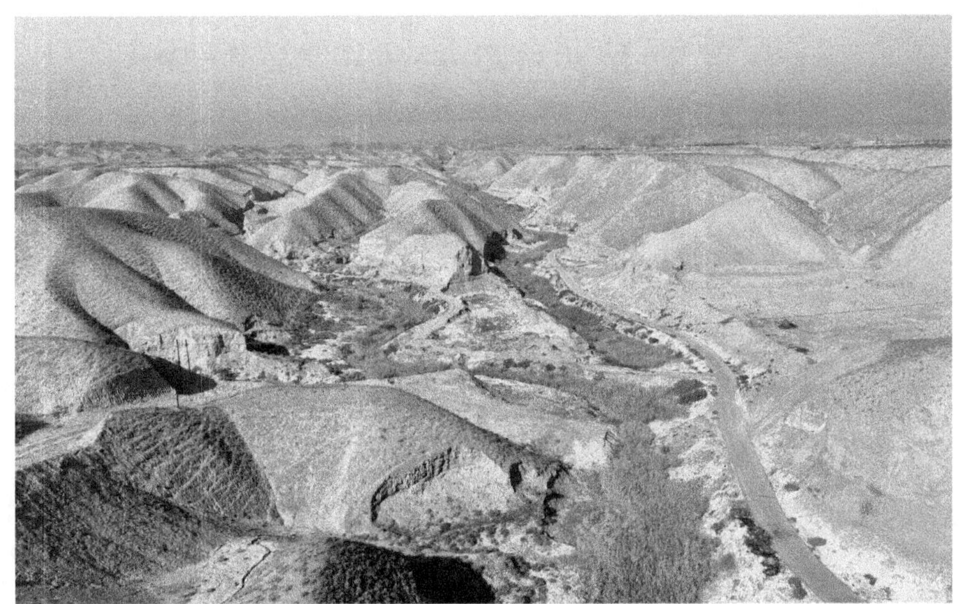

The Yellow River flowing through Gansu

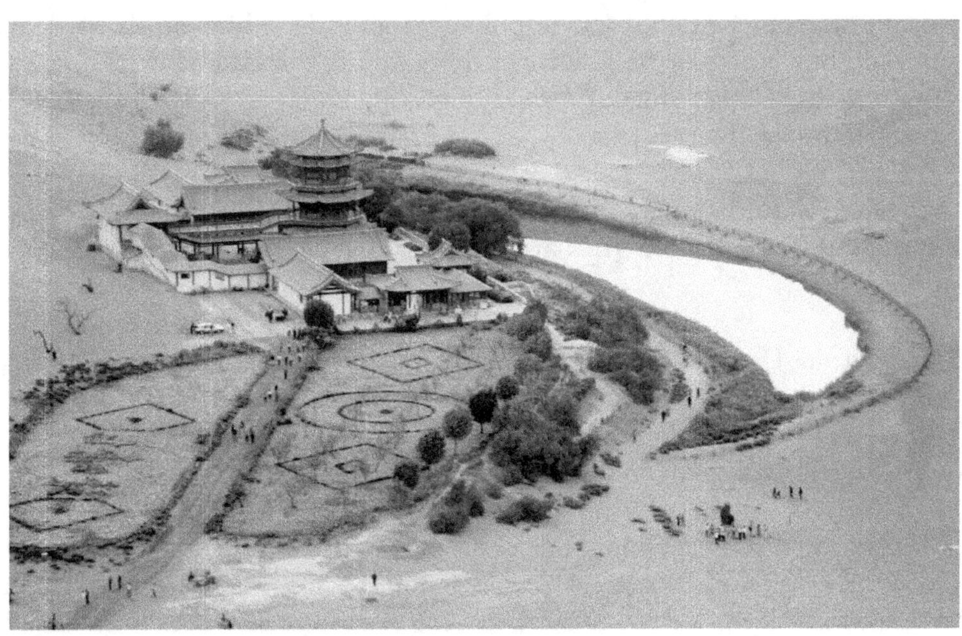

Half-Moon Spring, Dunhuang, Gansu

Ningxia (宁夏): Land of Fish and Rice in the Desert

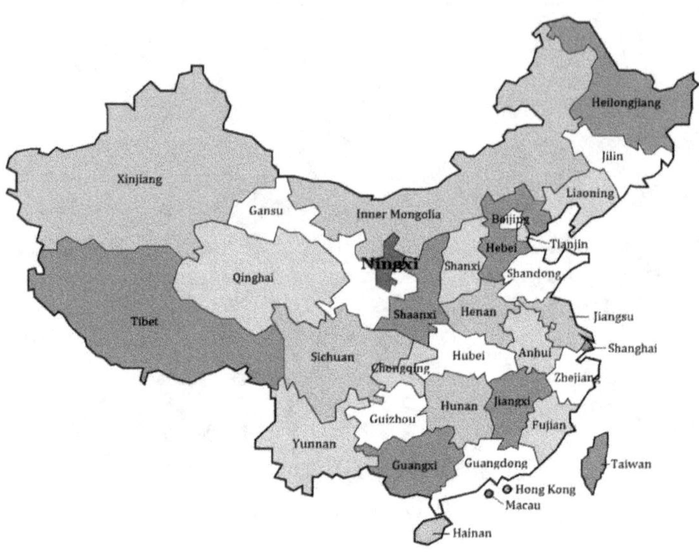

Ningxia, a Hui Autonomous Region, has a population that is 25% Muslim. It borders Gansu, Inner Mongolia, and Shaanxi. The Yellow River flows through its capital, Yinchuan, which translates to "silver plain." This fertile land yields high-quality crops and grass, along with the world's finest goji berries (wolfberries).

This ancient land holds Shuidonggou, China's earliest excavated Paleolithic site, dating back over 30,000 years. Nearby, prehistoric rock art adorns Helan Mountain, watching over modern-day Yinchuan.

After the fall of the Tang Dynasty in 907, the Tangut leader Yuanhao declared himself Emperor of Great Xia (Xixia) and made Yinchuan his capital. Ruling alongside Han Chinese and Tibetan leaders, he fostered a flourishing empire in agriculture, animal husbandry, and culture. The name Ningxia ("Peaceful Xia") emerged from this era.

In 1209, the Mongols attacked Yinchuan, but Great Xia's garrison held out against Genghis Khan's siege for nearly 20 years. In 1227, Genghis Khan died under mysterious circumstances, and soon after, the Mongols massacred the city, erasing the Great Xia Kingdom from history.

Yet Yinchuan endured, as did the Yellow River and the Loess Plateau. Today, the city remains
a hub for the Muslim Hui people, who have long played a vital role in trade between China and
the Middle East.

I arrived in Yinchuan during a winter storm in 2023. With no taxis available at rush hour, I
waited in a noodle shop for two hours until local poets found me a ride to a banquet in a private
restaurant. There, they welcomed me with Ningxia's finest lamb, fish, and poetry.

The next day, two poets took me to the oldest section of the Great Wall of China. Standing atop
the ancient stones, I unfurled prayer flags from the Mississippi, Yangtze, Amazon, Nile, and other
major world rivers. On one side stretched Inner Mongolia's Alxa Desert; on the other
lay Ningxia's driest, more desolate lands, home to China's earliest Paleolithic site. Beneath our
feet lay the world's finest coal, and the road was lined with coal trucks vanishing into the desert.

We found a lone goji berry tree in the desert. As I wrapped it in prayer flags, Hui poet Zang
started singing his poems, and for a moment, it felt as if all the land and river had joined us.
That is Ningxia in my heart—a goji tree in the desert, wrapped in verse, whispering peace and
love into the wind.

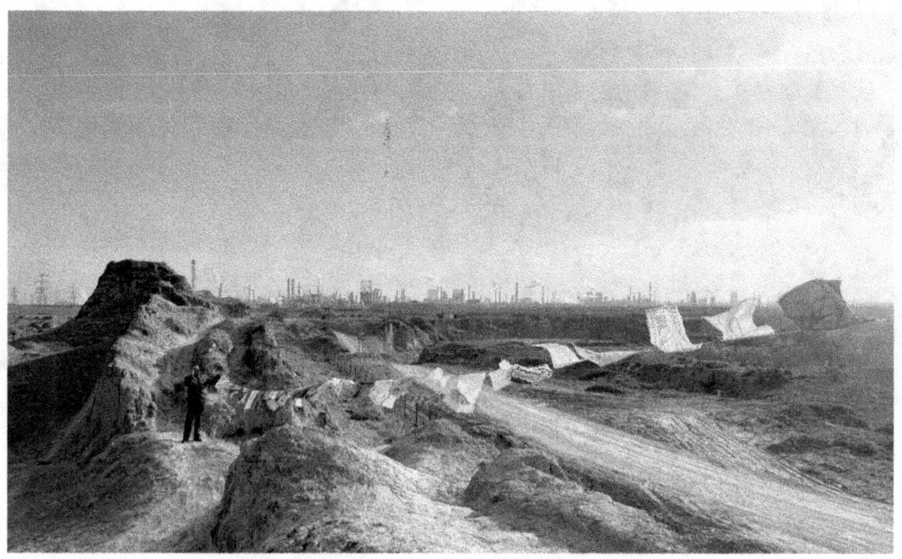

The oldest section of the Great Wall,
built during Qin Dynasty (221-206 BCE), Ordos, Ningxia

A'er (阿尔), born in 1970 in Ningxia, China, is a poet and journalist. His works include *Rilke's Park* (里尔克公园), *History of Yinchuan* (银川史记), and *Secret Garden—Notes of a Wandering Journalist* (秘境之旅：一个记者的采访手记), among others. He currently serves as the secretary of the Ningxia Writers' Association, where he plays an active role in promoting regional literature.

Known for his lyrical and introspective writing, A'er's studio is filled with music and poetry, reflecting his deep engagement with the arts. He contributes greatly to contemporary Chinese literature—particularly in blending poetic sensibility with journalistic observation and his knowledge of both western and eastern music.

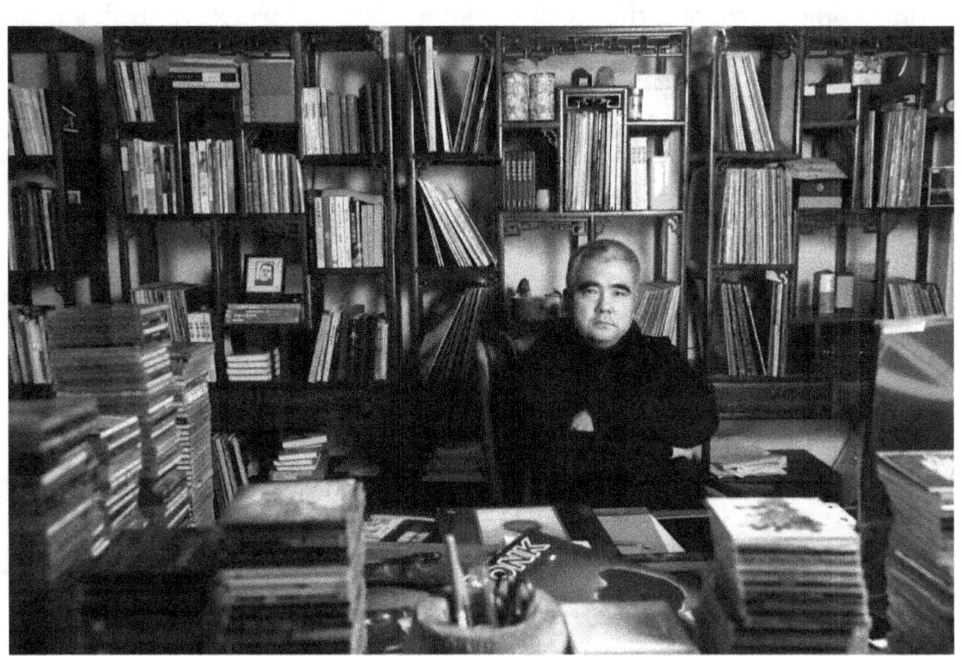

曼德拉岩画记

这一刻是沙漠从云端耸起
沉下的是恒河之旅
那是洗不去的光阴
一个小时代的美好派对
一支雪茄飘出的哈瓦那
曾经还是左派的年月
格瓦拉的伏特加扁酒壶
塞进一张列侬和洋子的美颜照

那时我们多么热爱和平
其实更是在渴望爱情
这一刻便是远去的阿拉善
蒙古高原穿越呼麦的长啸
喝一口六十度的二锅头

雄起的却是那些石头
在山岗上暴晒着自身
这是另一种囚禁似的降临：

明月高挂曼德拉岩画峰顶
就连石头也静默如渺小
而她降临
或者星光和陨石 或者我们已不是
自我的拿铁或者卡布奇若
一柄小勺
正好搅动舌尖的那一粒蜜糖

这似乎是奇异的世界
当石头降临
街角再也没有带刀之徒
他和那些人在黑暗中闪烁
更多的石头将我们和羊群淹没

Rock Painting on the Mandela

It rises from the desert into clouds
It sinks into the river of eternity
Time can't wash away
Its short-lived glory
Like the fragrance of Havana cigar
Or the storm of the leftist's era
Vodka in a flask
A photo of Lennon and Yoko

Oh how we loved peace
No we were just thirsty for love
Like the Alxa in the distance
The Mongolian Steppe passes by us
whistling as I gulp Erguotou

The rocks keep rising
Exposing themselves on the hills
Like locked up prisoners

The moon hangs over
The painting on the Mandela Mountains
The rocks seem quiet
Waiting for the arrival of light, falling stars
We stir our cappuccino
With a spoon
Honey on the tip of tongue

This is a strange world
When rocks arrive
Nobody will carry knives
Glistening in the dark streets
Rocks will drown us and our sheep

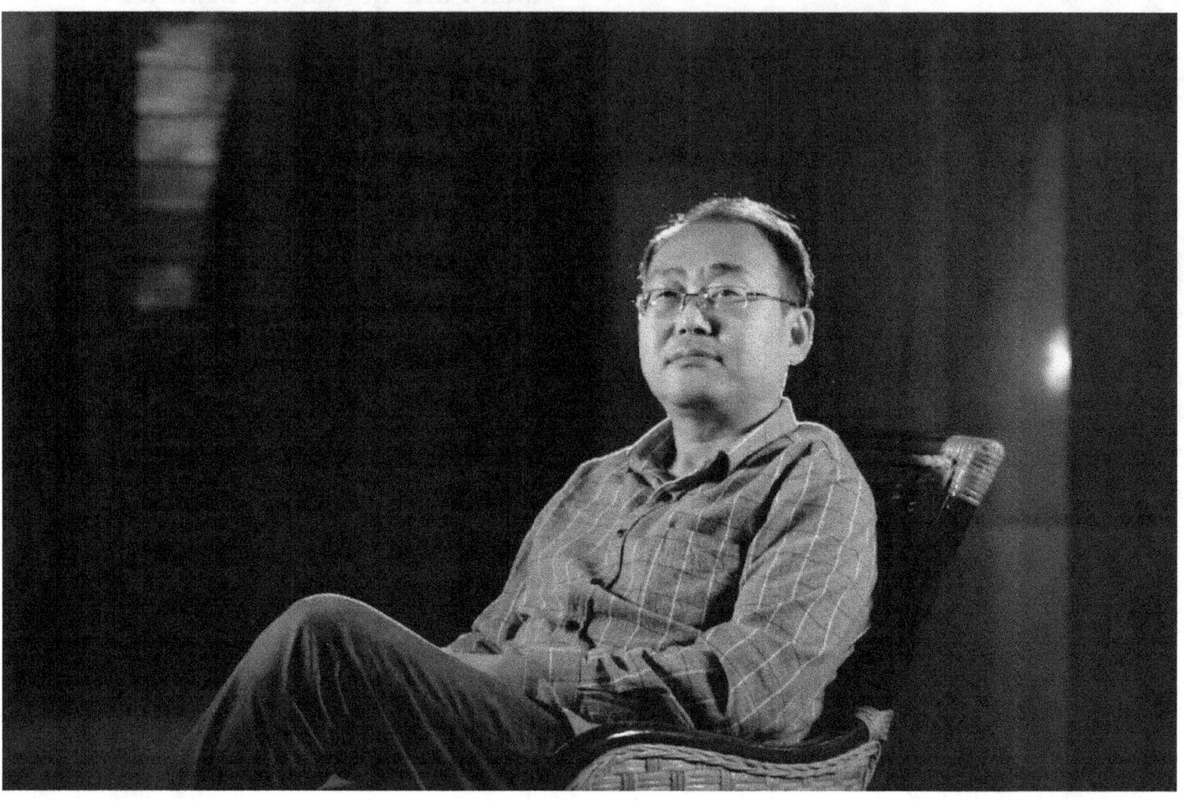

Chi Lechuan (敕勒川) is a poet from Hohhot, Inner Mongolia, named after the famed region celebrated in classical Chinese poetry—now a restored ecological park near his hometown. Formerly an editor at *Grassland* (草原), a literary magazine of Inner Mongolia, he now resides in Ningxia. His published poetry collections include *Subtle Love* (细碎的爱) and others, reflecting his deep connection to the landscapes and cultures of northern China. Though we never met in person, his verses—and the translations that carry them across languages—have opened a window into the land he loves.

伤口

伤口无数，那个咬牙切齿的
肯定不是伤得最深的

有的伤口说出悲伤
有的伤口说出疼痛
有的伤口说出绝望
有的伤口说出无所谓

有的伤口，什么也不说，仿佛它
从没有受过伤，仿佛它知道
沉默，是一个永恒的伤口

Wounds

So many wounds, the one that looks
Most angry is not the deepest cut, for sure

Some wounds speak of sorrow
Some scream pain
Some moan in despair
Some shrug with indifference

Some wounds say nothing
As if they've never been wounded
they know silence is a permanent wound

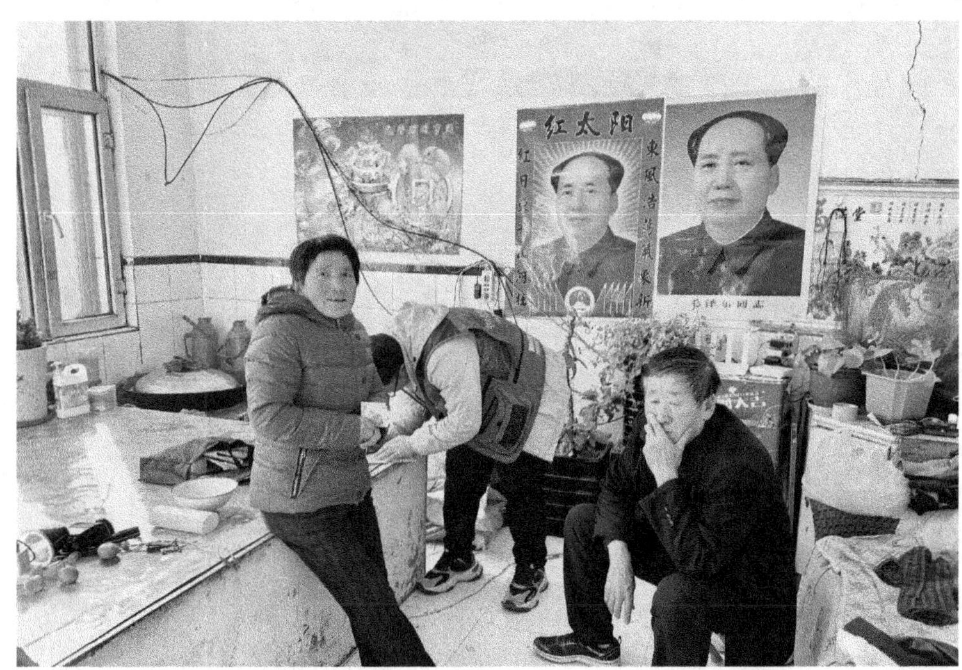

Government visit to help a peasant family

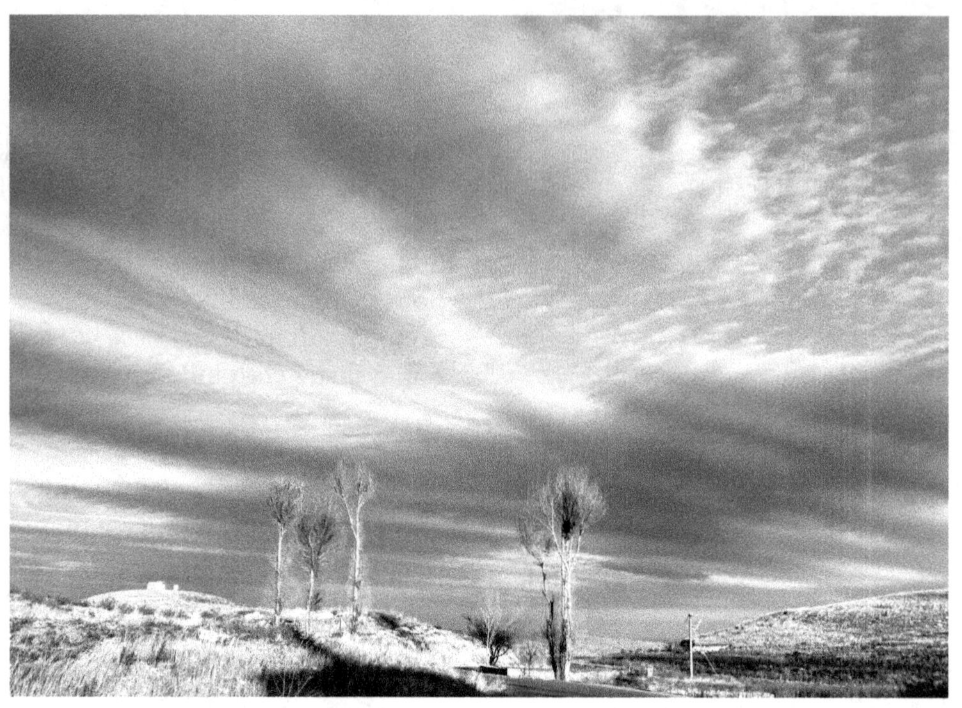

<table>
<tr><td>

邂逅

是八月间的事了，我在草原上
遇到了一棵我认识的小草
它遇到我时一脸哀痛，它向我讲述了
另一棵健壮的草，是怎样转眼就夭折了
"它是那么英俊，充满生气，然而……"
它说着说着就哭了起来，我看见
它流下的眼泪，比我们人类
稠多了

我想安慰它几句，但一个人
怎么能安慰一棵草呢

</td><td>

Encounter

It was August, I was roaming on the grassland
I encountered a tiny blade of grass
With a sad face, it told me its friend,
Strong and healthy, had died suddenly
"It was so handsome, so vital, but…"
It started to cry, its tears
Thicker than human tears
Much thicker.

I wanted to give condolence, but what does
Man know to comfort a blade of grass

</td></tr>
</table>

幸福

把小米淘三遍，淘米的水
用来浇花，南瓜切成小块
像我们的心思一样小
什么也不需要了，加上清水就可以了
让小米和南瓜温暖地交谈
让它们慢慢说出
秋天的黄，泥土的甜
世代相传的秘密……

傍晚如期降临，像命运
三碗小米南瓜粥，静静地放在桌子上
我们像往常一样，谁也没有说话
低下头，看见一种叫幸福的东西
一直冒着热气，还没有凉

Happiness

I washed the millet three times, then watered
my flowers with millet water. Cut the
pumpkin in small cubes, like our thoughts.
Nothing else needed, just water heating
millet and pumpkin,
let them talk about
the fall's yellow color, the soil's sweetness,
the secret passed on…

Dusk has arrived, like our destiny
Three bowls of porridge, millet and pumpkin,
on the table. We sit quietly, as usual
Our heads bent, watching happiness
Steaming away, still warm

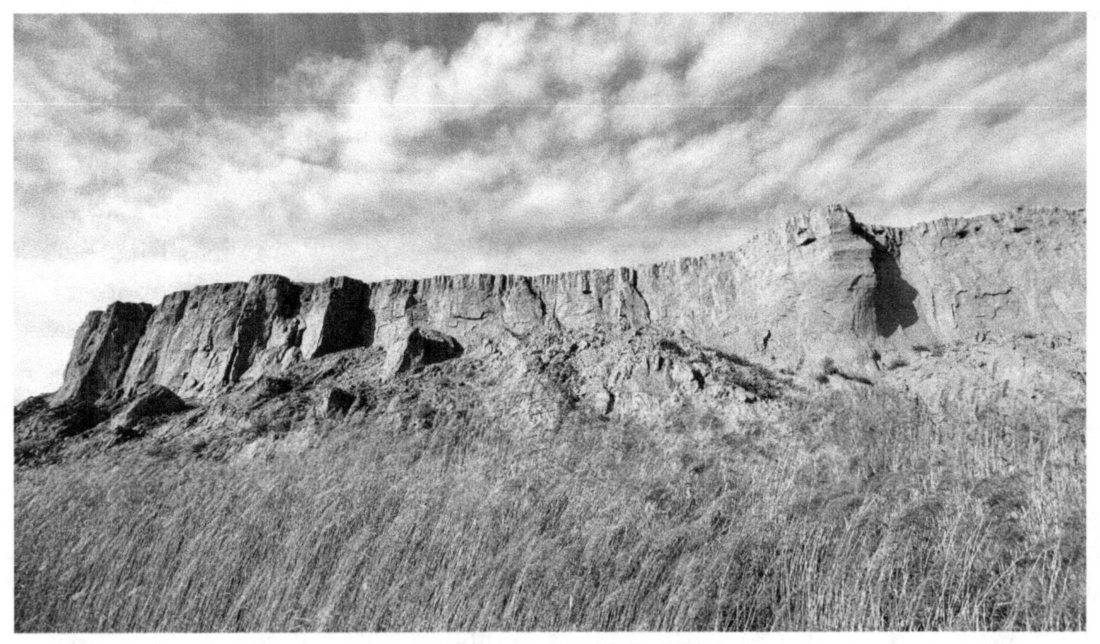

Alxa, Inner Mongolia

母亲盐

朴素，沉默，总是躲在家里
最不起眼的角落
被生活的烟火一再锤炼，让一棵白菜
脱胎换骨，让一枚土豆意味深长……

一粒盐，坚守着永远不变的承诺
永远独自守着生活的咸、苦、涩，把生活
最美的滋味加倍地给你

从不知道恨是什么，给你的永远是爱
是整整一生的牵挂，让家
有一个家的味道——

家的味道，就是母亲的味道，就是一粒盐
历尽世态炎凉后，仍然为你留着
温暖的怀抱

煎熬就不说了，千难万险
也不说了，甚至，一颗破碎的心
一粒盐也从没有说过啊

多少年了，我一直分不清，到底是一粒盐
在母亲的手掌上跳动、闪烁，还是母亲
在一粒盐中蹒跚、劳作……

只知道，母亲的霜发，闪烁着一粒盐
无法言说的
疼痛

一粒盐，从不曾停下忙碌的身影——
那是母亲的爱，住到我们身体里
就再也不会离开

Mother Salt

Simple, silent, always sitting
in the quiet corner of the house
Smoked daily by life's fire, cabbage
adds rich flavors to potatoes…

A grain of salt keeps its promise forever
Guarding tastes of life: salty, bitter, sour
Returning us with double sweetness

It doesn't know how to hate; it gives love
With its heart, so that a home
Has the taste of home—

The taste of home is the taste of mother
a grain of salt, no matter the cold of life
it keeps home warm.

This grain of salt
Never talks about its pain or hardship
Not even its broken heart

All these years, I can't tell, if it's a grain of salt
rolling in mother's palm, or mother
walking, working in a grain of salt…

But I do know, how her hair shimmers like
Grains of salt, like the unspeakable
Pain

A grain of salt, its shadow never stops—
Mother's love, once entering our body
Will never leave us

三匹马在河边饮水

一匹雪白，一匹枣红，一匹黝黑
三匹马在河边饮水

它们此起彼伏地饮着，有一阵子，
它们一起把头伸进河里

仿佛一条河，是从它们口中
流出来似的

它们源远流长的心思
还是那么单纯，清澈，波澜不惊

天色一点点暗淡下来
一个人眼睁睁看着

一条河，被三匹马叼着
消失在暮色中

Three Horses at the Riverbank

One white, one red, one black
Three horses are drinking at the riverbank

They drink at their own pace, some up, some down
Their heads reach the river at the same time

As if a river were flowing
Out of their mouths

As their minds flow from the river source
Still innocent, clear, undisturbed

The sun is setting slowly
A man watches, without blinking

How a river disappears into the night
Held in the mouths of three horses

对于一座山的个人注解

1

我要找一座山做靠山
一抬头，看见苍苍的阴山
——好，就它吧

2

我总是一抬头就看见苍苍的阴山
从我未出生时它就站在那里
不吃不喝，不说不闹，不喜不怒，即使
我多少次登上它的峰顶，它也
没有什么反应

3

我曾经看见一只鹰在它上面反复盘旋
然后
嗖地一下俯冲下来，仿佛阴山
突然伸出一只无形的手，将一只鹰
猛地拽了下来

仿佛，我的心，也被什么
重重地
扯了一下

疼或者痛，都是蔚蓝的

4

有时候，我会用一两个小时的时光，慢慢
地　　走到阴山脚下，偶尔
我会看到一只野兔，从山坡上面
石头一样
滚下

Personal Notes about the Yin Mountain

1

I want to find a mountain to lean on
I look up, see the Yin Mountain Range
—amazing, this is it

2

Every time I look up, I see the magnificence
Standing there before I was born
No food nor drink, talk nor scream, joy nor rage
no matter how many times I climbed its peak
It says and does nothing

3

I once saw an eagle circling on its top
Then
Diving down, as if the Yin Mountain
Reached out her invisible hand, to pull down
The eagle

Something tugged
My heartstrings
Hard

Pain or agony, color is the same: sky blue

4

Sometimes, I take a few hours, walking
Slowly to the foothill, sometimes
I see a rabbit, rolling down
The hill like a
stone

后面　跟着一大群松树、杨树、榆树——
那奔跑的姿势
多么令人羡慕，多么令人惊心动魄——
它们，才是阴山最古老的游牧民族

当然，还有那些石头、风和月光，以及
一匹匹不羁的野草

5
在阴山的一座峰顶上，我目睹了先人们
刻在岩石上的图画，有些我可以认出是牛
是羊，有些，已模糊不清，我深知
那是阴山，故意对我
隐瞒了一些什么

6
据考古学家说，几十万年前
阴山就有人类活动
我还在他们研究发现的
大窑文化遗址上的石器制造场
拣了一枚石头回来，似乎
与别的石头
是有些不同

想一想都是一件令人怦然心动的事啊——
年轻的人类，站在古老的阴山上
眺望着我们

7
还有那些秦长城，斑斑驳驳，仿佛
嶙峋的历史露出了时光的肋骨
一片片青色的石头，像一具具
风干了的尸体，它们
被帝王差遣，又被百姓抛弃，现在
被我的目光仔细辨认——

Followed by forests of pines, birches, elms—
the way they run
stir my heart with awe and envy—
Only they should count as ancient nomads

Of course, don't forget the rocks, wind,
Moonlight, schools of wild running grasses

5
On the peak of the Yin Mountain, I saw my
ancestors' rock paintings,
some resemble oxen and sheep
Some are blurry, unrecognizable, I know
The Yin Mountain is trying to hide

6
Archaeologists say, hundreds of thousands
years ago, there was human activity
On the mountain, I brought home
A stone in the stone weapon fields
Of Dao Yao Culture Ruins
As if this stone is different
From other stones

It is indeed exciting to imagine this—
A young human race watches us
From an old Yin Mountain

7
The Great Wall from the Qin Dynasty peels
Revealing its ribs through jagged history
Its blue slates like bodies
Dried in the wind, used by Emperor Qin
Then abandoned by his people
Now all under my scrutiny—

一株颤抖的小树，从石缝间站起来
仿佛是某一个人的灵魂，把严密的历史
戳了一个窟窿

阵阵山风过后，是历史的窃窃私语

8
作为一座北方的山，很少听说
它有过什么塌方
塌方不是北方山的性格，它像一个胸有成
竹的人　　　　心里，一直有数

它一直坚持着
不让自己摔倒

9
有一年秋天，我和一个朋友
驱车来到阴山深处，满山的金黄
波涛汹涌，让人睁不开眼睛
以至于我把夕阳，也当做了
一枚缓缓落下的树叶，一次一次伸出手
接了又接

想起不久前，我目睹了一片叶子
飘落的全过程
那是一片普通的杨树叶子
先是犹疑、挣扎，然后义无反顾地一跳
一片叶子
在偌大的阴山
缓缓地飘落——

一座山
在飘落

Like a spirit, a trembling sapling
Rises from the slates, poking a hole
Through the sealed history

The wind blows, whispering the past

8
The Yin Mountain in the north rarely
Gives in to landslides
It's not the mountain's character, like a
mature man knows what's inside

It stands still
Never falls

9
One autumn, my friend and I drove
deep into the mountain, gold everywhere
Washing down like waves, blinding me
I thought the setting sun
Was a falling leaf, I tried to catch it
With my hands, over and over

I remember once I witnessed the whole
Journey of a leaf, a common birch leaf,
hesitant first, struggling,
Then a leap of faith
A leaf
Down
Down the vast Yin Mountain

And the whole mountain
Floated together

10
记不得在哪一个冬天，一小片雪
在阴山顶上
经冬未化

整个冬天
一座山睁开亮晶晶的眼
看着我　　　和这个世界

我一直记得，一座山的目光
清澈，悲凉，无辜
而又不知所措

当我艰难地爬上那片雪地，
仿佛是给阴山　　　用生命
嵌上了一粒黑眼珠

11
常常，我会看到一个朝阳般的老人
在阴山脚下跑步，一群山不紧不慢地跟在
身后　他矫健的步伐，暗合了
一座山脉的起伏——
他领着一群大山，在清晨的时光中
慢慢跑向远处

12
一天傍晚，我爬上阴山
就在我爬上山顶的一瞬间
星星和满城的灯火　亮了
仿佛是我
突然拧亮了它们

10
I don't remember which winter, a snowflake
Was frozen all season
On the snowcap

The whole winter, the mountain
Gazed at the world and me
With its shining eyes

I remember its eyes
Clear, sorrowful, innocent
Helpless

I climbed that snowcap
As if adding an eye to the mountain
With my life

11
Sometimes, I see an old man
With morning sun energy
Running at the foot of the Yin, followed
By a mountain range at leisure
His footsteps in sync with
The rolling mountains

12
At dusk, I climbed the Yin Mountain
The moment I reached the peak
all the stars and the city
lit up
As if I switched it on suddenly

13
山中的夜，到底还是有些凉因为凉，那些
狗吠与鸡鸣
便清脆了许多
但是一个老者的喘息，像阴山一样
黑魆魆的，连绵不绝

13
Evening on the mountain is crisp and cold
In the cold, barking dogs, crowing roosters
sound crystal clear
An old man huffs and puffs
Like the dark Yin Mountain

14
没碰见过野生的狼，但听说近些年
在阴山里可以看到，有些
还咬死了老乡的猪和羊
老乡们说，狼咬死了猪和羊也不能打
狼是国家二级保护动物呢
我还知道，狼是狗的祖先

14
I've never seen wild wolves, but heard
They roam on the Yin Mountain, some even
Killed villagers' pigs and sheep
But the villagers won't kill the wolves
They're listed as the most protected animals
I know wolf is dog's ancestor

15
阴山脚下，一点点红
随着我的脚步慢慢放大
走近了才知道，那是一处庙宇
一处几近荒芜的庙宇——
庙的门已经荒芜，断墙上的杂草探头探脑
院子里，几只老鸦仿佛几个闲淡的老僧
我走进去，它们就往天空里挪了挪身子

为我空出了一场梦的地方

15
At the foothill, a little red dot
Growing as I walked closer
I got there, and saw it was a temple
Abandoned—its door collapsed,
Weeds peeking out of the broken wall
In the yard, crows cawing like chatting monks.
I walked in, they moved a few steps to the sky

to make room for my dreams

16
阴山少水，没有大的河，至多
也只是一些小溪，从阴山深处
不紧不慢地流下来

好几次，我蹲在小溪边，看着自己的影子
在溪水里像一只松鼠一样
蹦跳到了山外

16
The Yin Mountain has little water, no rivers,
only a streams from the mountain's deep belly
flowing at leisure

Sometimes I squat by the stream
watching my reflection leap like a squirrel
Out of the mountain

17

每隔几天，我都会去阴山脚下的
那眼泉水旁打一次泉水，我用它
做饭，熬药
这么多年，一座山的血脉
在我的身体里，竟然积聚成了一条黄河

这么多年，不知打回来多少桶水
但一次也没有打回来它们流动的样子
对此，它们也不做过多的解释

真正的长流水，日夜不歇……
我知道,一座山也需要倾诉
也需要一个永恒的倾听者

18

山中日月长，一棵巨大的柳树下，一群人
男男女女，正忙着烧烤，旁边的简易桌上
放着啤酒、饮料和水果，他们穿着时尚，
说话夸张，不时往手里的屏幕上瞥几眼，
忙里偷闲地划拉几下……倒是袅袅娜娜的
炊烟　显出几分古意

就想起，那些在山中踽踽独行的古人，
常常停下脚步弹琴、听风、发呆……
等一封
遥遥无期的家书

19

我也常常停下脚步，但我无琴可弹
在漫无边际的阴山，我只能偶尔听听风、
发发呆，更多时候，我会蹲下来
和那些花花草说说话，无非是问问暖，
嘘嘘寒，说今天的天气真好啊……

17

Every other day, I go fetch spring water
At the foot of the Yin, for tea, meals and
medicine. All these years, the blood stream
Of this mountain has become
The Yellow River running through me

All these years, I've collected many barrels of
water. But I could never bring back her flow
She made no comments about this

True flowing water never stops…I know
Even a mountain needs to tell, needs
A loyal listener

18

In the mountain, days are long, a group of
people are barbecuing under a giant willow
Beer and fruit on the table, dressed in fashion,
chatting loudly, stealing glasses at their cells,
making quick swipes… the only thing
from the past is the cooking smoke

I remember those ancient travelers, alone
In the mountain, pausing to play their zither
Listen to wind, or do nothing,…waiting for a
letter from home, far away

19

I often pause my steps, but I have no zither
On the vast Yin, I can only
Listen to the wind, do nothing, or squat
To greet flowers and grasses, and say
What a lovely day…

黄花、马莲、野菊花……我相信
那是阴山，一年年，不厌其烦
写给我的邀请函，我也相信
在这世上，再也没有比它们
更生动的文字了

20
以前我一抬头就可以看到阴山，现在
我一抬头先看到的是一座座的高楼，它们
像一座座拔地而起的陡崖，横亘在
我和阴山之间

那些崭新的山，的确
比阴山年轻气盛

21
这么多年了，阴山从没有离开过我一步
想一想，还真没有一个人
可以做到这样

好，那就它吧，就让它
在孤独无依的时候
也可以　　　　靠一靠我

22
可阴山怎么会孤独无依呢？阴山
不是一座山，阴山是一群山，一群山
聚在一起，肯定是在商量一些
我们不知道的事情
人有人的事情
山也有山的事情
或许，那些飘荡在阴山顶上的云
就是它们商量的结果吧
群山荡漾，我看见了大海的另一副面孔

Lily, iris, wild chrysanthemum…I believe
They're the annual invitations
From the Yin, I also believe
No language on earth is as vivid
As these flowers

20
I used to see the Yin Mountain whenever
I looked up, now I see high rises only,
Standing like cliffs
Between the Yin and me

Those new mountains
Are younger and full of qi, indeed

21
The Yin Mountain has never left me
All these years, it ever moved a single step
away from me. Nobody has done this

Ah, my mountains
When you feel lonely and helpless
You can lean on me, too

22
But how can the Yin feel lonely or helpless?
She's not just a mountain, but a range—
mountains gathered in discussions, secrets
we humans will never know
Humans have human business
Mountains have mountain business
Maybe, the clouds on their peaks
Are the results of their conference
From the rolling hills, I see an ocean

23
忘了说了，有一次
我和阴山喝酒，喝着喝着
阴山就手舞足蹈起来……

酒后吐真言，但我忘了
阴山对我说了些什么
以后有机会，再好好喝一顿，看看阴山
到底对我说了什么

——那一次，我与阴山
对饮成混沌

23
Oh, forgot to mention, once upon a time
We were drinking together, the Yin and I
Till she got drunk and started dancing…

She told me some secrets, but I forgot
What she said
If we drink again, I'll ask the Yin
what on earth did she tell me that time

——that time, the Yin and I drank
Till we became one

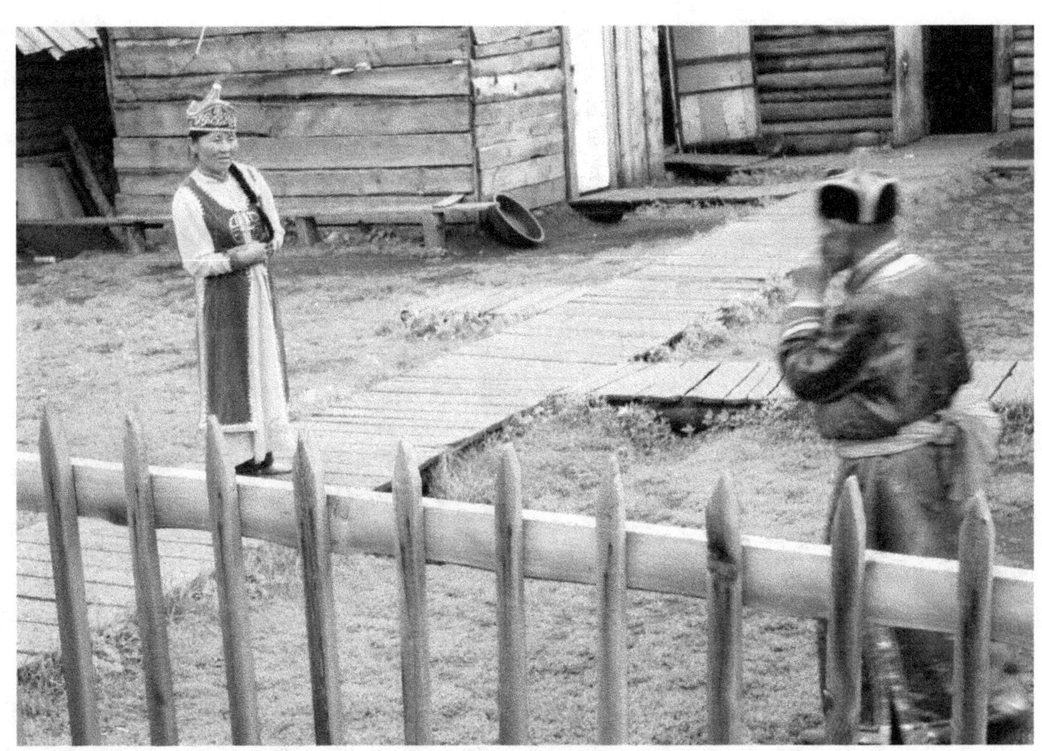

Mongolian musicians playing eagle flute

He Wudong (何武东) is a poet, artist and filmmaker, born in 1969, Yanchi (Salt Lake), Ningxia. His poetry has appeared in *Poetry* (诗刊), *Poetry Monthly* (诗月刊), *The Stars Poetry Journal* (星星诗刊), and *Yangtze River* (扬子江), and has been included in anthologies like *China's Best Poetry 2012* (中国最佳诗选 2012). He is also a multidisciplinary artist—painter, documentary film maker and photographer. His visual work often mirrors the desolate beauty of his homeland, capturing the interplay of light and shadow in the Ningxia Desert.

Despite the harsh poverty of his birthplace—one of China's most economically challenged regions—He Wudong has remained deeply connected to Yanchi. His journeys have taken him to Tibet, Yunnan and beyond, yet he's always returned, dedicating himself to local cultural initiatives, teaching art, and mentoring young poets.

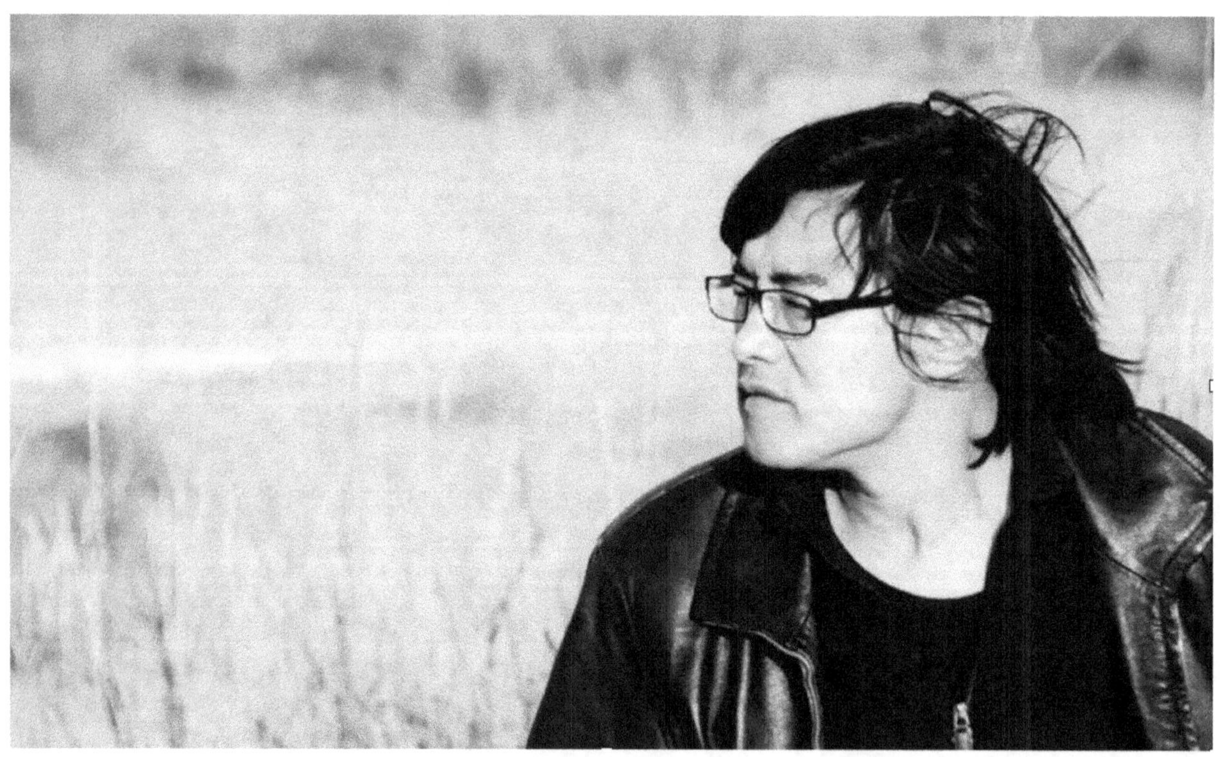

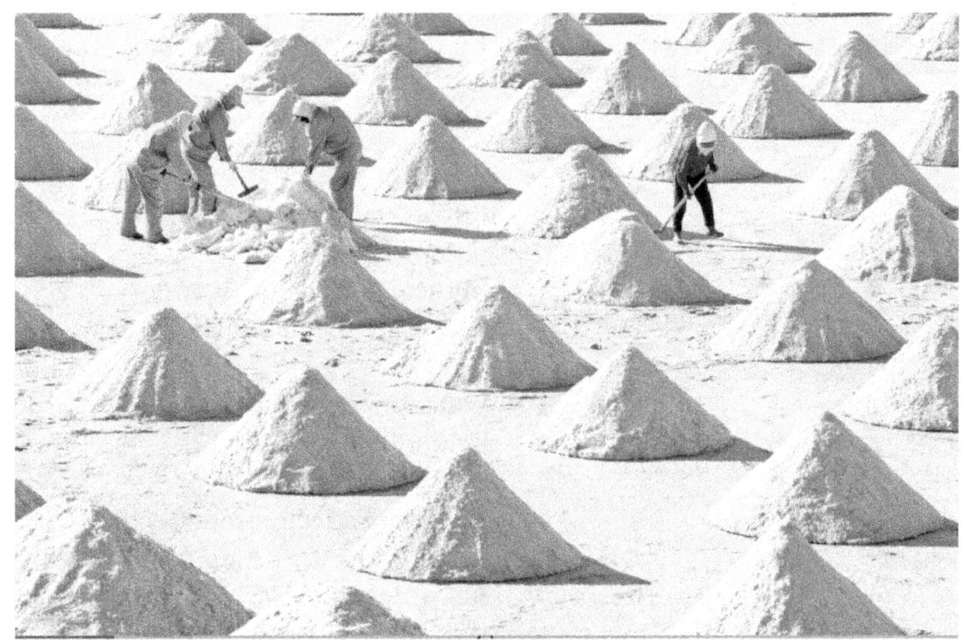

Yanchi, Salt Lake, Ningxia

寂静诗

在辽阔西北以北
今天雪已经下完
刚好够得上我梦的尺度
我走进院子
仰望天空
没有任何星星无缘无故
砸到我脑袋上
除了寂静还是寂静
绵延数公里
让我感觉我的孤独是
离世已久的空旷
它在那儿像一台被遗忘
在后院的老机器
还在那儿独自嗡嗡作响

Solitude

In the north of the Northwest
Snow stopped
Just when it reached my dream
I walked into the yard
Gazed at the sky
No star fell onto my face
From the sky
Only silence everywhere
From far away
My loneliness
Stemmed from past lives
Long ago
A forgotten machine, humming
In the backyard, alone

画像

我给世界画像
我被框在外面

世界中心的那个人
就像核桃般大小

他趴在门扇后
透过圆孔看辽阔星空

然后他消失于我的笔触中
那铁锹翻土的声音

我知道将在我晚年的头顶
持久响起

Portrait

I paint the world
I'm locked outside the frame

In the center of the world
The man appears small like a walnut

Watching stars through a hole
Behind the window

Then he vanishes from my pen
And I know the sound of his digging

Will keep clanking
Into my old age

黑暗诗

黑暗，抬起了我的胳膊
又抬起了我的腿
最后抬起我包裹着纱布的头
来，写一首关于黑暗的诗
我想我从来不知道黑暗是什么样子
当然了，对所谓光明更是
一无所知。我深陷
在城市高大的钢筋混泥土建筑群中
甚至几乎忘记了月亮的颜色
忘记了一条鱼，跃出明亮水面的瞬间
也听不到一串高音
飞出盲人波切利的口中
我低下怀疑的头，被自己绊倒
看，脚踝周围围绕着那么多的黑色
只有微弱的亮光证实了它

A Dark Poem

Night lifts my arms
Then my legs
Then my head, wrapped in gauze
Come, let's write a poem on darkness
But I don't know what it looks like
Of course, I don't know of light
either. I sink deeper
into the city of steel or concrete
forgetting the color of the moon
forgetting how fish leap out of the water
I can't hear the sound
Flying from the blind poet Bocheli
I look down, worrying I'd trip myself
Look, all the darkness surrounding my ankles
only proven by a weak light

Zang Xinhong (藏新宏) was born in 1973 in Yinchuan, Ningxia, and is a Hui Muslim poet. His work has appeared in *Yellow River Literature* (黄河文学), *Liupan Mountain* (六盘山), and other literary journals. Beyond poetry, he is also a music and food critic.

When I visited Ningxia, Zang took me to a coal mine on the border of Inner Mongolia. Together, we climbed the Great Wall of the Qin Dynasty. Later, he led me to his secret spring in the desert, where a lone wild olive tree stands. We wrapped its branches in prayer flags, and Zang promised, "I'll send you pictures of the tree—in snow, in bloom, in fruit."

He kept his word.

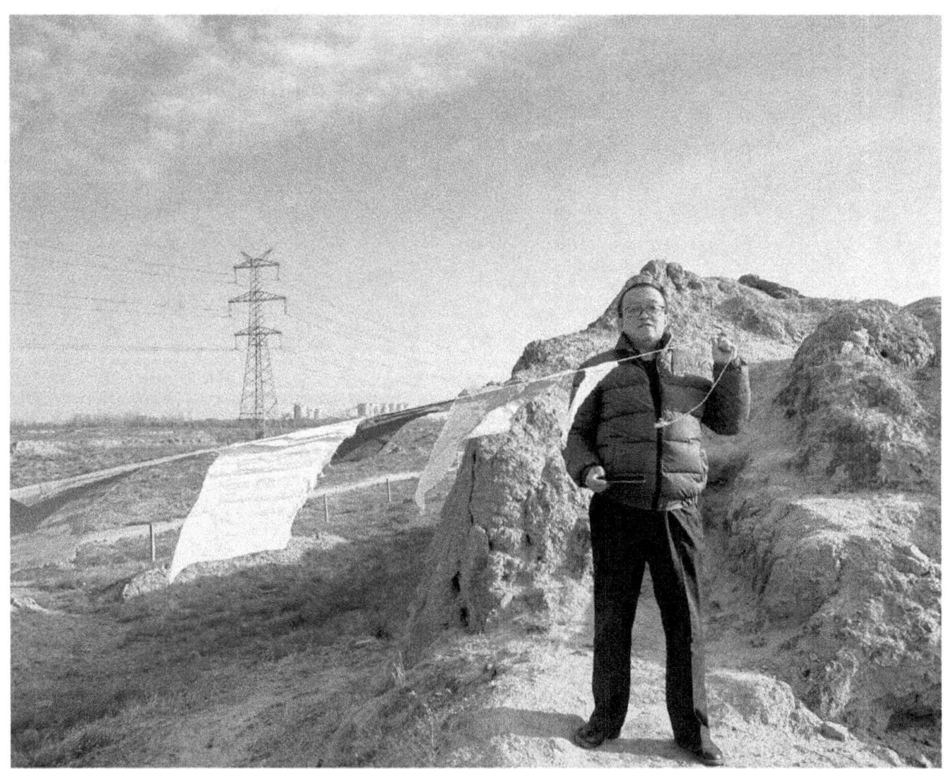

Zang on the oldest section of the Great Wall of China, Alxa, Inner Mongolia

希德尼·奥康娜

狮子和眼镜蛇不是对立的也不是
你的食物　妈妈手中的扫把让你
有勇气改变你的改变　或许以你
极端反对的行为才能孕育新生
所以你的苹果树闪出光芒站在坟墓上
而音乐永远如清泉滋润你迷失的心灵
十年的两个十年轮回着安慰与讽刺
不同的是从诅咒批判换位成博爱同理
你依然像野马般疯狂却面无表情
剃掉矫揉造作的头发　失去的并不是
短板　　因为孩子的无助比皇帝的新装
还可拍　　所以你有理由轻松地撕烂
保罗的照片　虽然血在飞　上帝会让你
品尝更多的香烟　但是你认真地说
你不想要你没有的东西　就像那只
深蓝色的鸟　有面包吃有水喝
泰森他不敢直视你狂野神秘的眼神
鲍勃马利知道你有神奇的魅力
但你希望有一天有人能容忍你
然而我不是你的女孩　没人敲我的门
你没有叛离信仰只是敏感的转变信仰
只有愤怒才是到达勇气的第一步
你说复原撕烂的　不是快乐的分裂
那一夜街上光秃秃的没有红丝带
在父权制的社会里更需要宇宙的母亲
巴比伦的火焰折磨着涅槃的孩子
孩子不要怕　在你母亲花园外还有
生命　　所以你对科特柯本说过去
已被埋葬　　你已经在母亲怀抱里
发掘出力量　并且所有婴儿生来
就会说上帝的名字　还会一遍
又一遍地说
谢谢你听我说

Sinead O'Connor

Lions and rattlesnakes are not enemies,
nor your food. The broom in Mama's hand gave
you courage to change what you've changed.
Maybe you needed extreme rebellions to give
birth to a new world. So your apple tree stands
upon the grave shining like a beacon, but music
nurses your soul like a sweet spring. Two decades
take turns to comfort and mock you. All the
cussing and critique transform into love and
empathy. You're still as wild as a crazy horse,
face blank like a mask. You shaved your hair, but
didn't lose your weakness. A helpless child is
more terrifying than the Emperor's new clothes.
You have every reason to tear Paul's photo.
Blood splatters. God will let you taste more
cigarettes. You say you don't want anything you
never had, like that blue bird fed with bread and
water. Tyson dare not look into your mad eyes.
Marley knows your possess magic. But all you
want is to be accepted. I'm not your girl. No one
knocks on my door. You never betrayed your
faith; just changed your faith. Anger is the first
step to courage. You say a repaired break is not a
happy break. That night the street is empty of
red ribbons. In the patriarchal society we need a
universal mother. The fire from Babylon Tower
tortures. Nirvana child. Don't be afraid, child.
More life lives outside mother's garden. So you
told Kurt Cobain the past is buried. You've
unearthed strength from mother's grip, and every
newborn knows how to say God's name, and says
over and over
Thank you for listening

期待的快意

期待像仲夏的麦子
想象着期待的美丽
山谷的风让人痴迷
河的漩涡使人着迷
山水比太阳更美丽
像期待腾空的麦子
要承领疯狂的快意
山谷的风扑面来袭
麦子看着微风如丝
心态平静心跳不止
任凭泪水恣意浸湿
麦子愿意就此荼靡
山谷的风让人痴迷
雨水裹挟冰雹飞泄
这种美丽让人窒息
麦子愿意如此消逝

The Joy of Anticipation to Ben Harper

Anticipation is like midsummer wheat
Imagining the beauty of anticipating
Wind from the valley is mesmerizing
So are whirling puddles in the river
mountains streams, beautiful as the sun,
like wheat waiting to fly to the sky
Waiting for the ecstasy of going crazy
Wind from the valley jumps at us
Wheat watch wind blow like silk strands.
Mind rests at peace but heart beats fast.
Tears pour down my face, soaking shirt.
Wheat lets loose, wallowing in the wind
Wind from the valley is mesmerizing
All as rain pours down with hails
Such beauty stops my breathing
Wheat wants to vanish from the fields

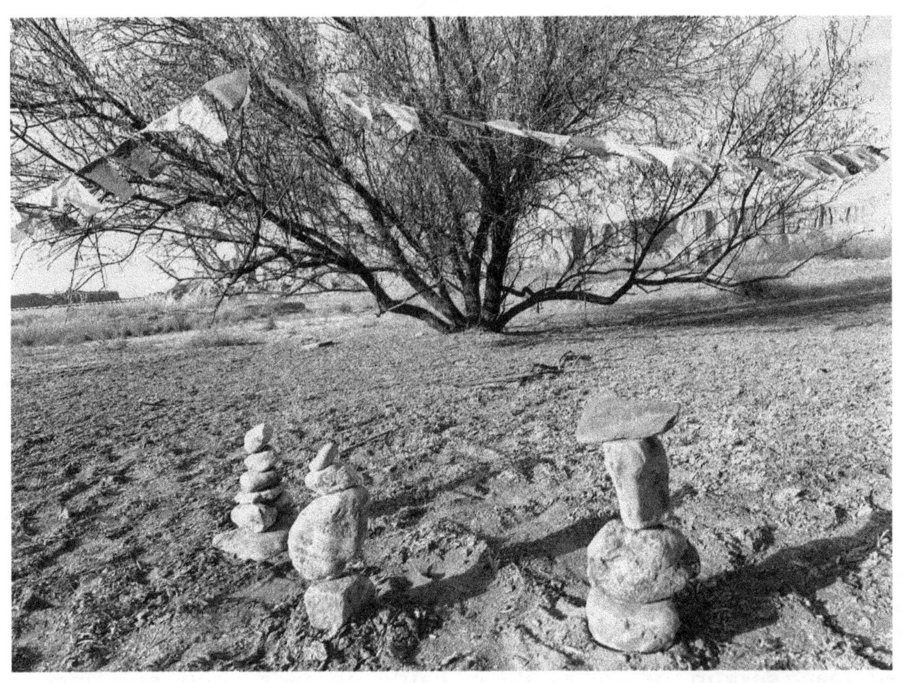

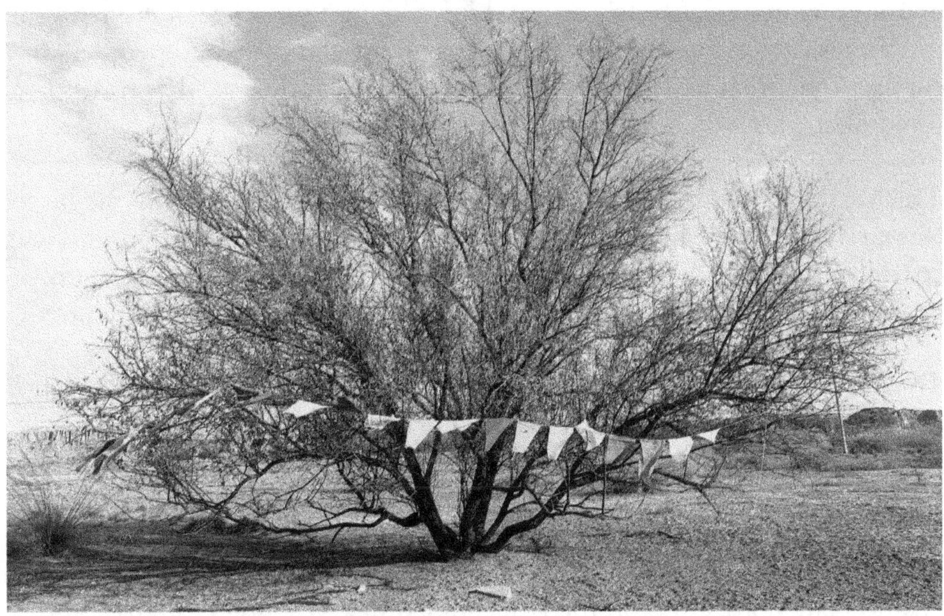

Shazao Trees (Russian olives), native to the Alxa Desert

Inner Mongolia (内蒙古): Grass, Gobi & Water

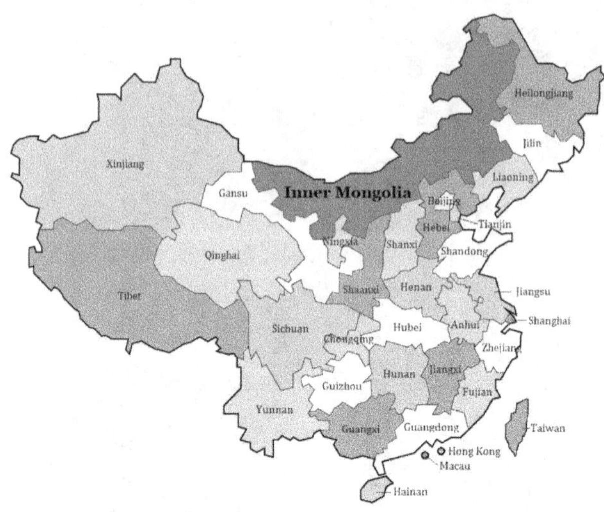

Grass, Gobi, water, and endless space sustain the horses, sheep, cattle, nomads, poets, and singers of Inner Mongolia. Stretching as China's longest province, it crouches in the north like a watchful dragon, guarding its rivers, grasslands, culture, and people. Here, the Yellow River carves three great bends, creating lush wetlands and oases that transform the arid plateau into some of the country's richest pastures.

This vast plateau was once home of Genghis Khan, founder of the largest empire in history. Researchers believe his success was aided by an era of extra rain and warmer climate—conditions that made the grasslands flourish, allowing his horses to grow strong and multiply rapidly. It was these mighty steeds and warriors that propelled the Great Khan's conquests.

To truly know this land, one must walk along its Yellow River, ride its horses, taste its tender lamb, sunflower seeds, apricots and watermelons—and then, perhaps, feel the sorrow and joy woven into its songs and poetry. The poet Guangzi guided me along the Upper Yellow River, from Lanzhou in Gansu to Ningxia, Wuhai, and finally, Inner Mongolia. We met in his hometown of Ordos, where he drove me through grasslands, the Gobi desert, and riverside villages, past the sweeping bends of the Yellow River. At Old Ox Bend, where the Jin Shan Grand Canyon begins and the river links Inner Mongolia, Shanxi, and Shaanxi, we journeyed onward to Shi'er Liancheng—the ancient "Twelve Linked Forts" of the Great Wall, where the river prepares to turn south. There, I witnessed the rare spectacle of Huang Liuling: great lotus-like sheets of spinning ice, roaring as they piled upon one another, a wonder of nature's raw power.

Each of the Mongolian poets in this anthology knows the fragrance of the grasses on the steppe, how to gallop like wild horses, and how to sing and flow like the ice lotuses in the Yellow River.

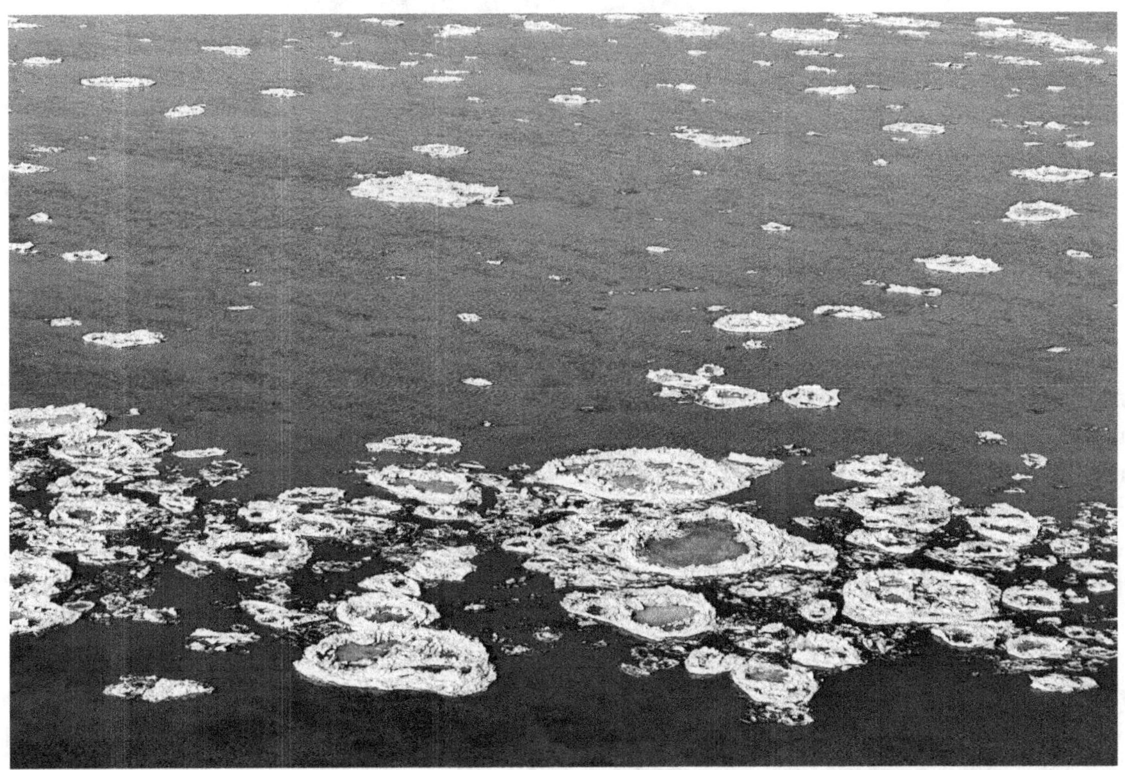

Flowing "ice lotuses" of the Yellow River, Shi'er Liancheng, Inner Mongolia

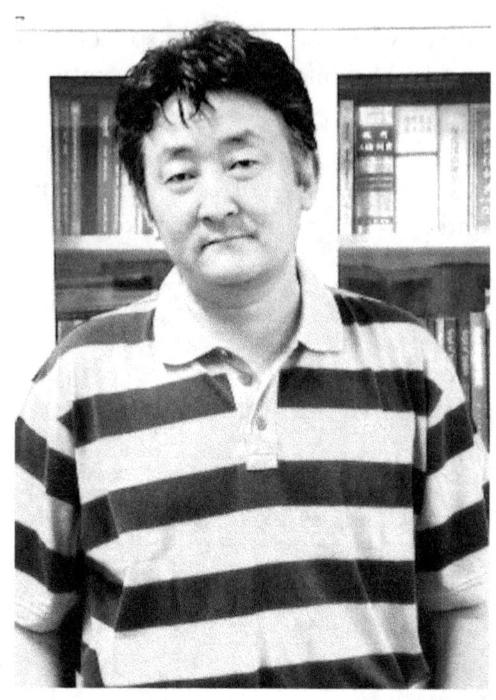

Buyanhishig (宝音贺希格) is a Mongolian poet, critic, and translator born in the Horqin Grassland of Inner Mongolia. He holds a BA from Inner Mongolia University and an MA from Japan's Hosei University. A prolific writer, he has published works across poetry, literary criticism, and translation in multiple languages, including Mongolian, Japanese, and Chinese.

His notable publications include *99 Black Goats* (ᠠᠷᠪᠠᠨ ᠶᠢᠰᠦᠨ ᠬᠠᠷᠠ ᠢᠮᠠᠭᠠ, poetry, Mongolian), *The Original Form of Emotions* (感情の原形, poetry, Japanese), and *One Subject and Fourteen Objects* (ᠨᠢᠭᠡ ᠴᠢᠮᠡᠭᠡ ᠪᠠ ᠠᠷᠪᠠᠨ ᠳᠦᠷᠪᠡᠨ ᠡᠳ, literary criticism, in Mongolian).

Buyanhishig's work often explores themes of nature, cultural identity, and the interplay between tradition and modernity. His bilingual and transnational background enriches his literary voice, bridging Mongolian heritage with broader East Asian influences.

长调

有人问我，长调歌词为什么那么短
我说，几缕炊烟足以支撑一片蓝天

有人问我，长调究竟唱给谁听
我说，唱者是在确认无限中的自己

有人问我，长调为什么那么悲凉
我说，欢乐没有必要那么悠长

Mongolian Long Song

They ask: why is your Long Song's so short?
I say: you only need a few cooking smokes
to hold up the blue sky

They ask: for whom do you sing your Long Song?
I say: the singer is confirming the self in the
infinite universe

They ask: why is your Long Song so somber
I say: no need to keep happiness so long

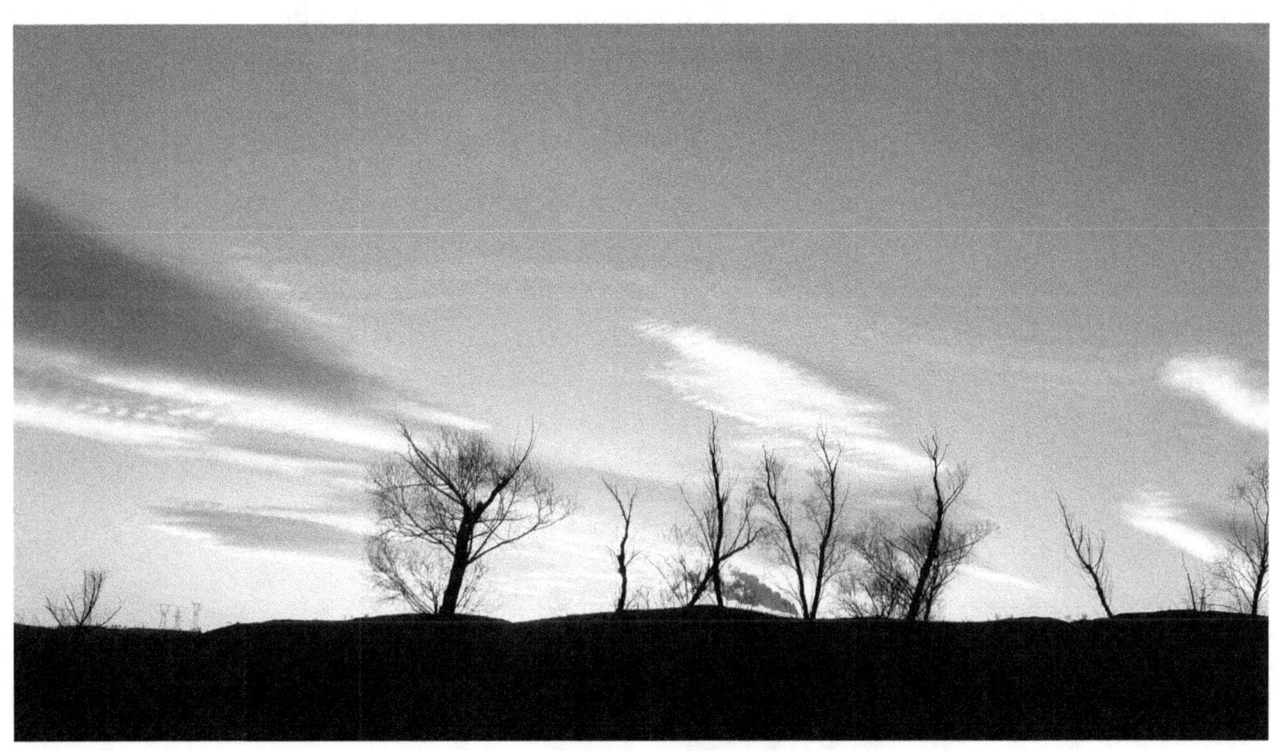

Sunrise at Wu Hai, Inner Mongolia

透明的绳子

每次洗手
仿佛是在搓一根
永远无法掌握的绳子

它与河流相连
它与祈祷有关

是自己的手在滴落
还是水在留下指纹
我难以分辨

水和手
世界上最流畅的绳子
越拧越透明

不是为了留住什么
只是为了跟着它走

Transparent Rope

Every time I wash my hands
It feels as if I'm making a rope
Impossible to hold

It's connected with a river
It's connected to a prayer

Is it my finger dripping water
Or water leaving a fingerprint behind
How can I tell?

Water and hand
The smoothest flowing rope on earth
The more you twist, the more transparent it becomes

I don't want to keep it
I just want to follow it

马头琴

你的乐器只有两根弦
一根向北，一根向南

你的乐器只有两根弦
一根向上，一根向下

你的乐器只有两根弦
一根在东，一根在西

你的乐器只有两根弦
一根向四面，一根向八方

你的乐器只有两根弦
一根向着一根，一根在于一根

你的乐器只有两根弦
一匹白马活在人间

Horsehead Fiddle

Your morin khuur has only two strings
One tied to the north, the other to the south

Your morin khuur has only two strings
One goes up, the other goes down

Your morin khuur has only two strings
One lives in the east, the other in the west

Your morin khuur has only two strings
One covers four corners, the other runs eight directions

Your morin khuur has only two strings
One is tied to roots, the other leans to roots

Your morin khuur has only two strings
A white horse comes alive in our world

马

马站立的时候
有一条后腿
总是小心翼翼
仿佛支撑着
草原的宁静

那是与生俱来的
清醒

祖母说
那条腿下面
有人在长眠

马与马头琴

马从原野上消失
马头琴却进入了城市

曾经——
套马杆是琴弓
马群是悠扬而激烈的曲子

骏马是闪电
骑手是滚雷

我们是正在下着的雨

Horse

When a horse stands
His hind leg
Always seems cautious
As if holding
the silence of the grassland

That is his awareness
A gift born to a horse

Grandma says
Someone is resting in peace
Under that leg

Horse and Horsehead Fiddle

Horses disappeared in the wild
Horsehead fiddles entered the city

It used to be—
A horse pole, but now it plays as a bow
Driving schools of horses as long melodies

Horses become lightnings
Riders roar like thunders

We are rain   falling

0与1之间

分不清
西是从哪儿开始
又分不清
东是到哪儿为止
我们停留在草原的
某个地点

分不清
你是从哪儿开始
又分不清
我是到哪儿为止
我们停留在彼此的
某个地点

所有这一切
我们都不知不觉
两颗纯白的果实
正落向星空的一刹那

Between 0 and 1

I can't tell
Where the west begins
Or
Where the east ends
We linger somewhere
On the grassland

I can't tell
Where you begin
or where I end
We're stuck
Somewhere
Between you and me

All this happens
In our unconsciousness
In the instance of two white fruits
Falling towards the stars

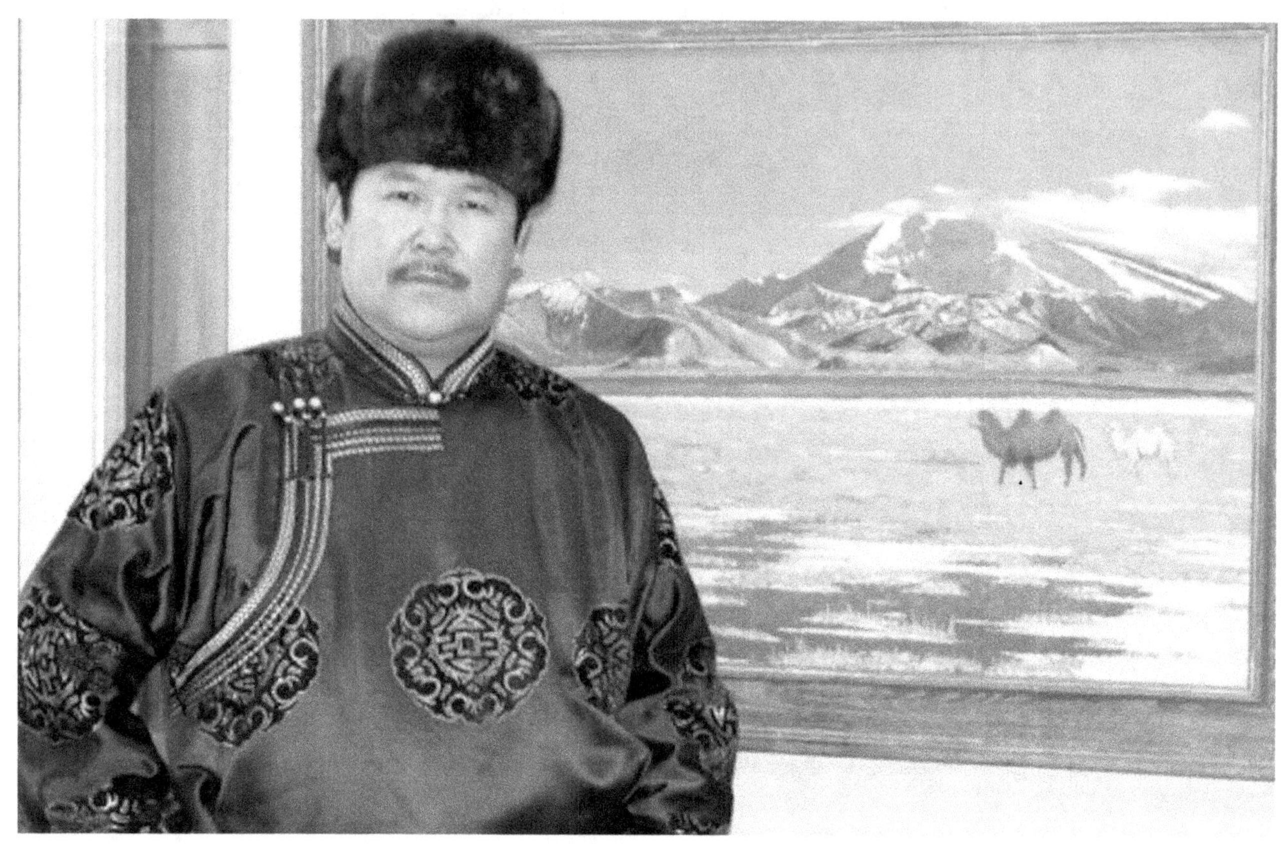

Enkehada (恩克哈达) is a poet from Alxa, Inner Mongolia, who writes in both Mongolian and Chinese. His published poetry collections include *Amenwusu* (阿门乌素), *Home of Fast Horses* (骏马的家园), and *Saga of Eji Well* (额吉井的传说). His poetry is deeply connected to the land, water, and people of Inner Mongolia. He has received several prestigious awards, such as the Tengeli Poetry Award, the Baby Camel Under the Sky Poetry Award, and the Sulongka Award. His father is a legendary singer of the Mongolian Long Songs.

风的行迹

风呀风，我让她驰向拴马桩
而她却牵着拴马桩回来了
原来，马儿跑了，她没追赶上

风呀风，我让她奔向敖包
她却背着敖包回来了
原来，她没有找到敖包的家园

风呀风，我让她奔向四方
她却捡了一颗石头，孤独地回来了
原来，巴掌那么大的故乡也消失了

风呀风，我希望她向我跑过来
她从我的身体中间，空洞地穿过
原来，赤裸裸的我，一无所有！

The Track of Wind

Wind O wind, I asked you to run to the
hitching post but you came back dragging it.
The horse ran away; you couldn't catch up

Wind O wind, I asked you to run to my yurt
But you came back carrying it on your back
You couldn't find the land to set my yurt

Wind O wind, I asked you to run all directions
But you picked up a stone, returned alone
Because the old home is gone, shrunk to my palm's size

Wind O wind, I wish you would run towards me
But you blew straight through my body
Because I've lost all, I stand naked!

故乡的距离

黎明时分，梦已被撕裂
从缝隙间向外望去
一幅画的空间里
站立着大象般的骆驼
在她的眼里　我看见了故乡

中午下班回家
冬的天空，支离破碎
阳光从孔隙里流淌　凝望墙上的
壁画　发情的儿驼眼里
闻得见青草的气味

放眼眺望四周，都是足迹……
比雪白的是驼羔回家的足迹
比土热的是佛祖云游的足迹
从画中剥落的是白雪
冰凉的足迹, 比眼睛还黑亮的
是故土迁徙的足迹

夜在黑暗逼近我
我在诗的光芒中做了一个梦
梦在空间里——
鞍屉尚未烘干之时
用梦里着凉的手指
抚摸墙上的画
形状是沙漠的形状
面积是故乡的大小
剥落的距离是
从乡村到城市的距离
痊愈的时间　直到超越梦境……

The Distance of Home

At dawn, my dreams are torn
Looking through the cracks
I see a painting of a camel
as big as an elephant
I see my home in her eyes

At noon I come home from work
Winter sky is broken to pieces
Sunlight flows in through holes. I gaze at
the painting on the wall, the camel in heat,
In its eyes, I smell green grass

I look around, footprints everywhere…
Snow-white prints from the baby camels
coming home; hotter-than-earth prints from
Buddha roaming the world; icy prints from
broken painting; prints darker than my eyes
from those who have left home

In the dark, night is approaching
I have a dream in the light of poetry
My dream floats in space—
The horse saddle is still wet
My cold fingers
Stroke the painting on the wall—
The desert in the shape of sand dunes
In the size of my home
The distance of chipping and breaking
Is the distance between countryside and city
The time to heal, beyond the dream…

浅 水 滩

偶尔下场雨
春营地的低洼里会积满水
羊圈旁的盲鼠向那边跑
闷热的青蛙拼命地饮水
我们家一天到晚
从戈壁母亲这巴掌大的浅洼里挑水
饮足了水的羊群眼里
唯独这个浅水滩，荡漾着生命之水
苍天的甘露，就这样
被驼乡积存了下来
从那口大碗汲取生存的力量和意志
小小的那个浅水滩
虽没有飞禽栖息的柳林
钱眼一样微小的坑洼里
也不曾生长茂密的水藻
但她却是生命的圣泉
草原上的几户人家
和羊畜一道在这里生活
偶尔下一场雨
浅水滩上空会罩一道彩虹
心脏那么大的水洼里
夏天的太阳会午休
日子长了
这里的水会变得有些苦
世世代代居住在这里的牧人们
都说那是她很久没有说话的缘故
她的心里话，一定也是苦的

Puddle

An occasional rain
Fills up the low ground on the spring camp
Moles run from sheep folds to water
Frogs drink up till their bellies bulge
My family carries water from dawn to dusk
From puddles, big as palms on Mother Gobi
After quenching their thirst, the only thing
sheep can see is the shallow puddle
Quivering with life
The heavenly dewdrops are stored like this
In the camel's land, drawing strength and
courage to live from the water as big as a bowl
No willows for birds to nest
Too small for algae to make home
But she's the sacred spring
To our families on the grassland
Living in peace with sheep and all animals
An occasional rain
A rainbow leaps over the puddle
In the size of a heart
The summer sun takes noon breaks
After a while
The water tastes bitter
The old nomads believe
It's because the puddle has not spoken
For many generations
The words in her heart must taste bitter too

《盘羊之载》序：在毡房中

兽在瞌睡是休憩
人的思维无法抵达这一休憩
人在作梦是压迫
所有兽都将被这压迫禁锢

骏马在向我奔跃…
说是给我鞭子？还是给我草原
我梦见用月牙烙铁的锈迹
在给马群饮水

蛇在向我滑行…
说是给我春天？还是给我冬天？
我梦见拾起它遗弃草丛中的躯壳
衬装毡房的内里

鹰在向我俯冲……
说是要我的山？还是要我的蛋？
我说要你背负的天空时
它用锁链豢养我于巢中

狼在向我奔袭……说是
要我的黑夜？还是要我的白昼？
我说要你头狼的名号时
它用狼奶喂饱并收养了我

梦见天空　在被我收卷
而当我要背负天空而行时
天星纷纷滴落
鸟的眼睛洒满了大地

梦见草原　在被我裁剪
那一幅幅的碎片

Excerpt from The Saga of Wild Sheep
Forward: In the Yurt

Animals are resting with a nap
Human thoughts can't reach their minds
Our dreams are oppressive
Locking all the animals

Horses are running towards me
Are they giving me the whip? Or grassland?
I dream the horses are drinking rust
From the moon-shaped brand iron

Snake are slithering towards me…
Are they giving me spring or winter?
I dream they pick up their skin in the grass
To decorate the inside of my yurt

Eagles are swooping down…Are they
Demanding my mountain or my eggs?
When I tell them to carry the sky on the Back,
they chain me up in the nest

Wolves are running at me…
Do they want my night or my day?
I tell them I want their wolf spirit
They adopt me, nurse me with their milk

I dream of rolling up the sky
When I try to carry it on my back
Stars fall one by one
Scattering bird eyes on the earth

I dream of cutting up
The grassland

散发着青草的气息
兽的四蹄被那气息羁绊

梦见海洋　在被我腾空
从海底捞起的太阳是干的
被腾空的
全部都是鱼儿

Every broken piece smells of the grass
Making animals linger

I dream of emptying the ocean
I scoop out the dried up sun
From the sea floor
Filled with fish

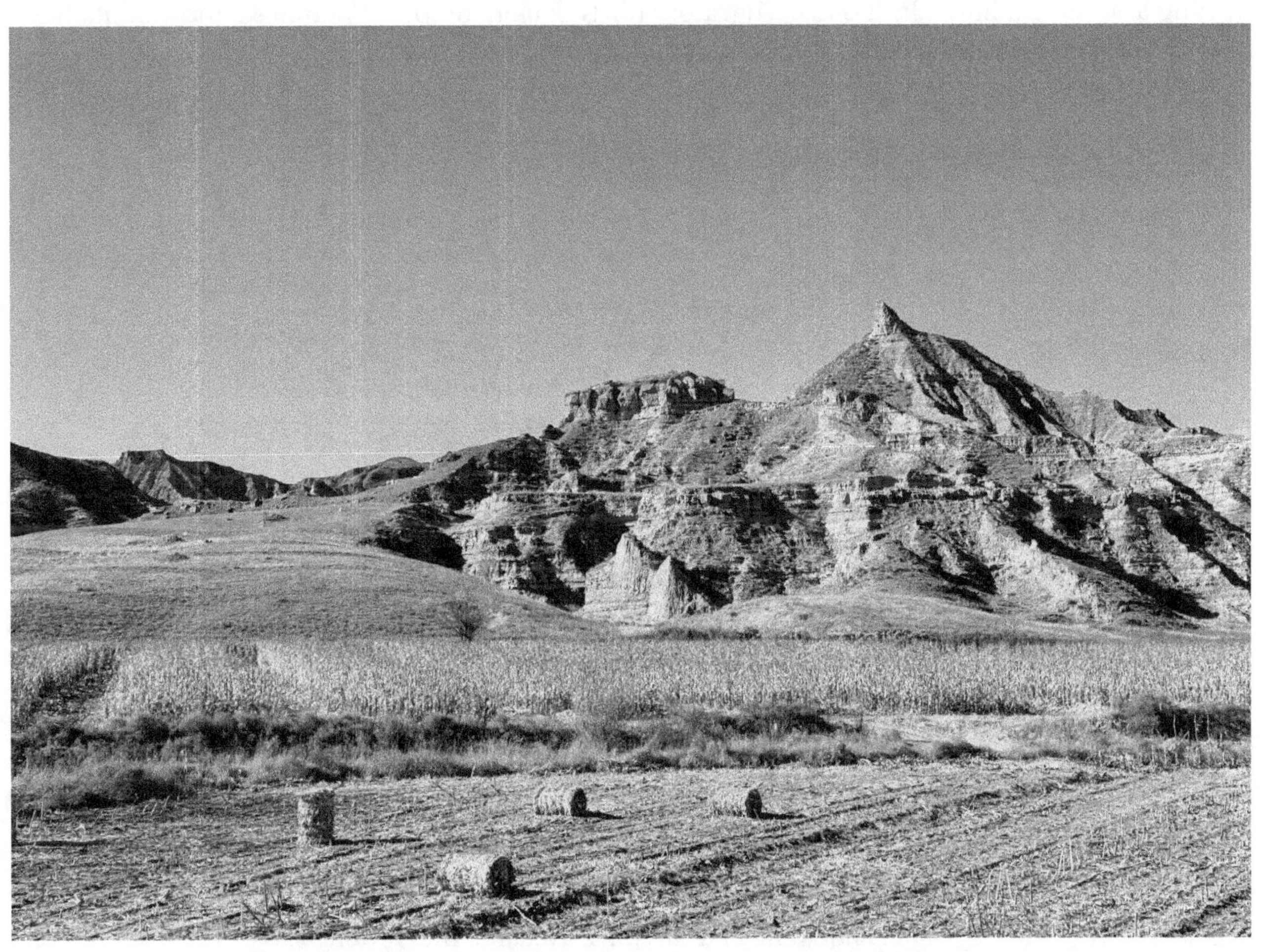

Grassland at Shi'er Liangcheng, Inner Mongolia

Li Jianjun (李建军) is a poet from Wuhai, Inner Mongolia. His work has appeared in *Grassland* (草原), *Poets from Zhejiang* (浙江诗人), *Wuhai Daily* (乌海日报), *Hohhot Evening* (呼和浩特晚报), and other literary journals.

Li and I met in Wuhai ("Black Sea"), a coal-mining city surrounded by the Gobi Desert, where the Yellow River cuts through its heart. Fueled by coal revenue, the city invested in an ambitious project: transforming the desert along the upper reaches of the Yellow River into a thriving wetland. The effort succeeded—Wuhai Wetland now reshapes the local climate and landscape, turning arid terrain into a lush oasis. Migratory birds flock here to rest and nest, and wildlife has rebounded. We even watched fishermen haul in three Yellow River carps, a species once nearly extinct but now returning thanks to the wetlands' restoration.

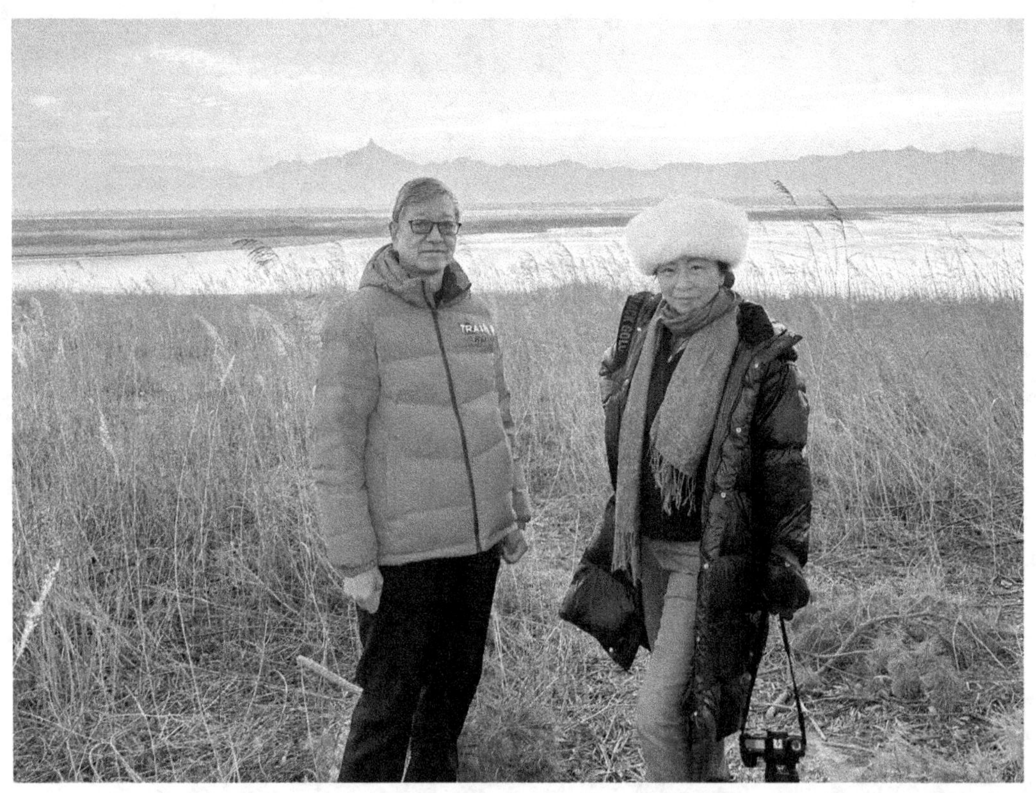

Li Jianjun and Wang Ping at Wuhai Wetland, Inner Mongolia

山谷

这是夏天的某一个上午
我得到了一条山谷
以及山谷里的马匹
羊群、百灵鸟和九十九棵山杏树
然而我不能告诉你这条山谷的名字

这是我对神做出的承诺

Valley

One morning in summer
I came upon a valley
With a school of horses
Sheep, larks and 99 apricot trees
But I won't reveal the valley's name

The is my promise to the gods

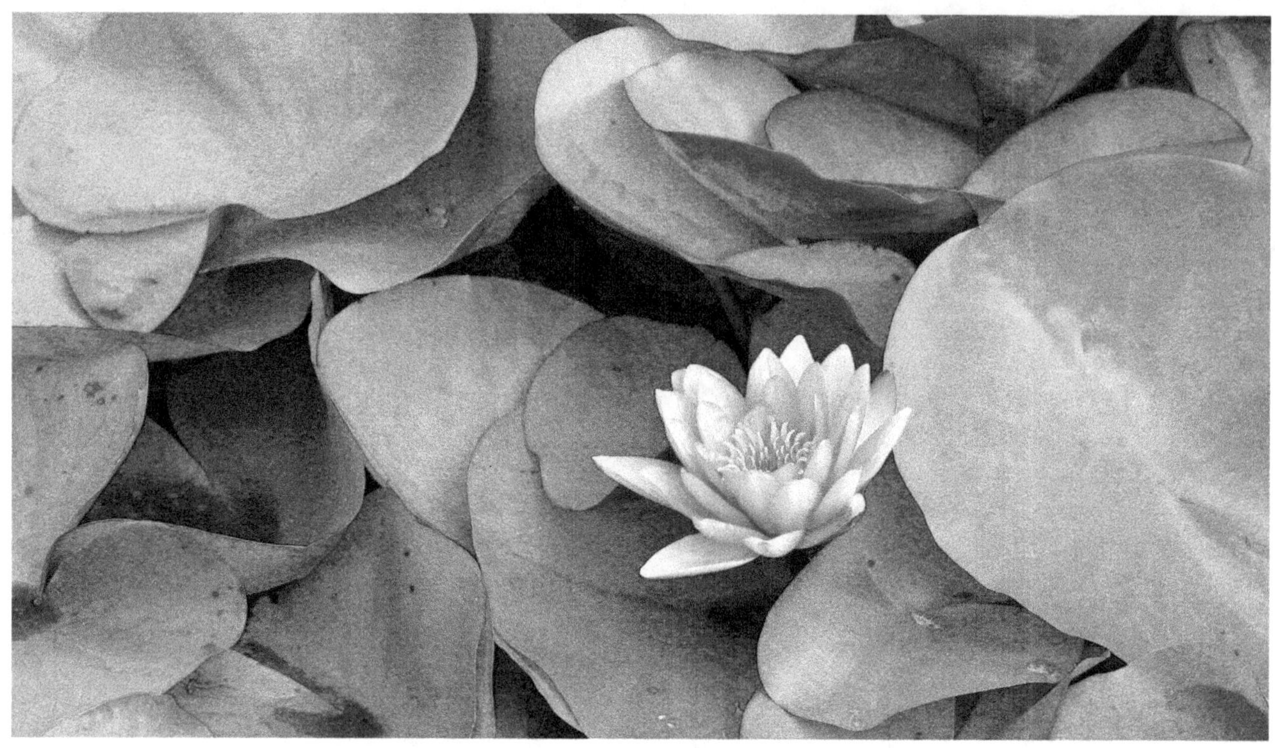

<table>
<tr><td>

睡莲

莲花睡着了
风也摇不醒

从莫奈活着的时候就开始睡了
心中无国界亦无时代

莲花睡着
遗传的佛性
在世间亦在世外
在战火纷飞中睡着
在瘟疫流行的年代睡着
而水一直醒着

</td><td>

Sleeping Lotus

The lotus is sleeping
No wind can awaken her

She's been sleeping since Monet
Her heart carries no border or epoch

She sleeps
Heritage of her Buddhahood
In this world and away from all
She sleeps through wars
Through plagues and pandemics
The only thing awake is water

</td></tr>
</table>

我的一部分

当我把一个事物写过十遍
这个事物就成为我生命的一部分

比如黄河
比如阴山
比如乌兰布和
我身体里的河流
我生命中的山脉
我命运里的沙漠

当我把一个事物写过十遍
这个事物就在慢慢消失
比如青春
比如时间
比如母亲

我似乎变的博大了
其实是渺小了

Part of Me

After I've written something ten times
It becomes part of me

Such as the Yellow River
Such as the Yin Mountains
And Wulanbuhe
The river in my body
The mountains in my life
And the desert in my fate

After I've written something ten times
It also disappears
Such as youth
Such as time
Such as mother

I seem to be getting bigger
But really I'm getting smaller

大海与我

大海深陷夜晚
波涛无力自拔
解开缆绳
小渔船开始出海
在夜晚茫茫的大海中
像是一个自渡的人

渔火微小
微小到只能把自己照亮
海浪心事重重
有多少鱼在大海里匆匆行走

我只是一个站在岸上的人
夜色可以把我染黑
海水却无法把我打湿
我不曾远行　　也无所谓归来

The Sea and I

The sea sinks deep into the night
A wave can't pull itself
Out of the dark
A fisherman unties the rope
His fishing boat sails out
As if ferrying itself into the sea

The fishing light
Is so faint, nothing can be seen
Waves carry too many secrets
What fish are hurrying in the sea

I stand on the shore
Soaked, not by the sea
But by the ink dark night
I've never traveled　　no need to return

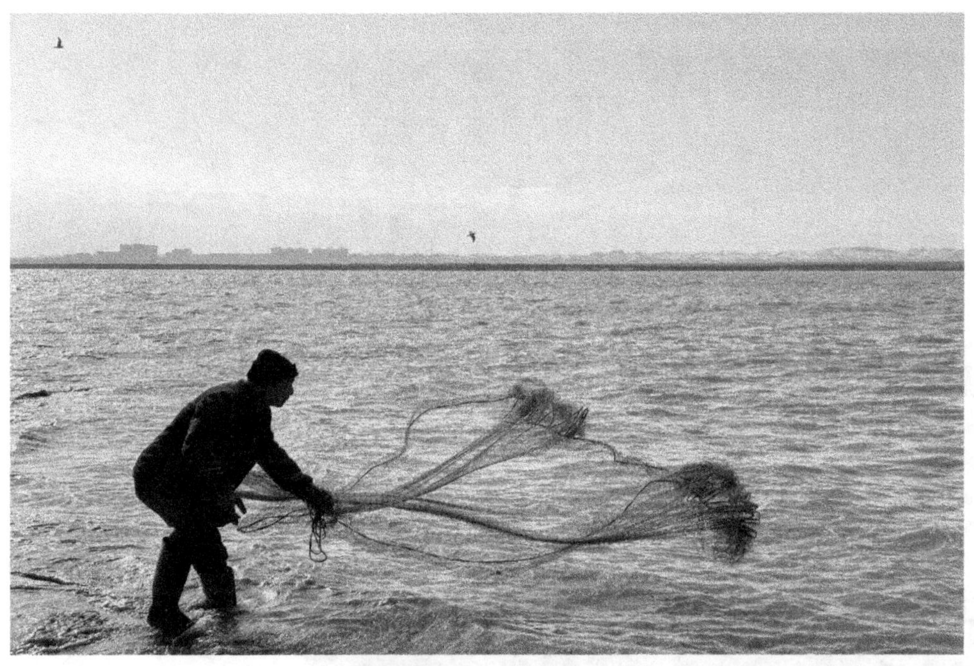

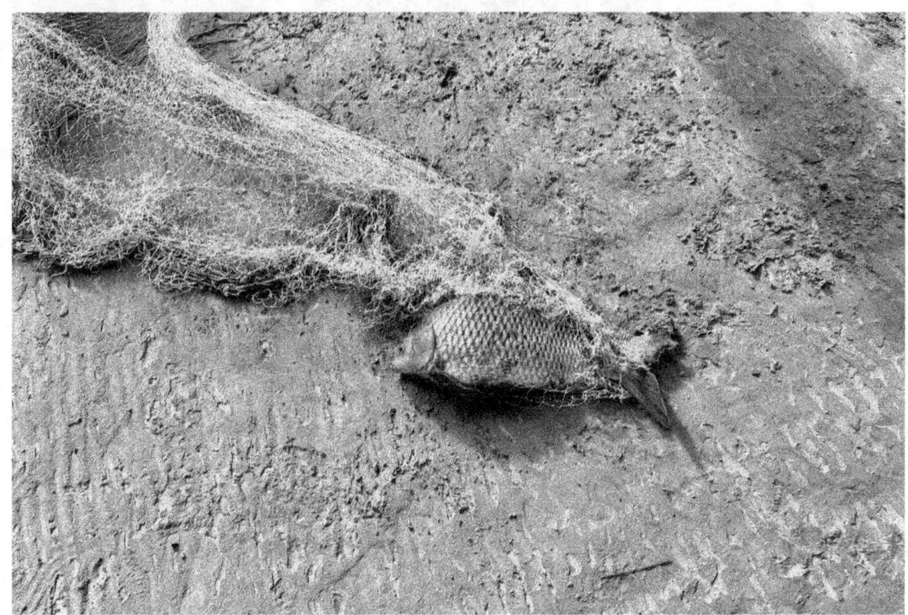

Fishing Yellow River Carp at Wuhai Wetland, Inner Mongolia

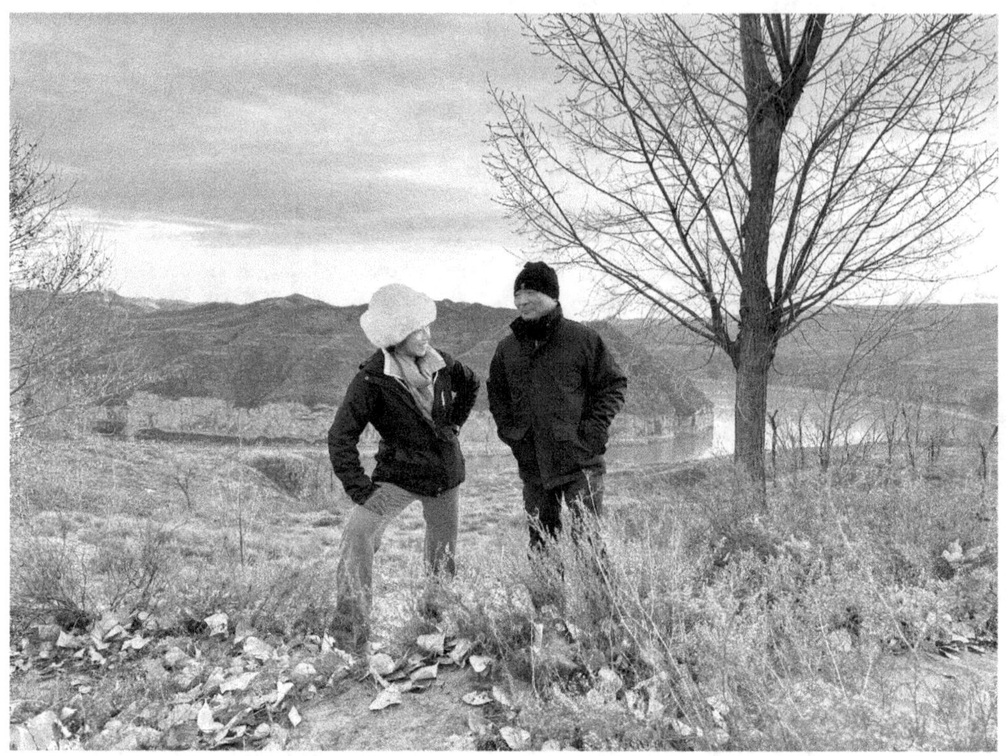

Guangzi at the big bend of the Yellow River, Old Ox Bowl

Guangzi (广子), born in Ordos, Inner Mongolia, he is a distinguished Chinese poet. His works include *Book of the Past* (旧书集) and *Poems from Inner Mongolia* (内蒙古诗选). A devoted admirer of Gary Snyder, his personal library boasts a complete collection of Snyder's translated works, reflecting his deep engagement with ecological poetry and cross-cultural literary traditions. He and his poet friends in Inner Mongolia formed a school called "Wildness Poetry," and they traveled into the wildness to camp and host poetry festivals annually.

In 2023, Guangzi accompanied me on a journey along the Yellow River, tracing its path from Ordos to Hohhot. Along the way, we met some of China's finest poets, whose voices and landscapes enriched this anthology. His insights and connections were instrumental in shaping this project, bridging the ancient rhythms of the Yellow River with contemporary verse.

一生	**Life**

晨曦中，他写到晨曦
世界的裂缝越来越大

长夜里，他写到长夜
稍不留神就被孤独吓了一跳

恋爱时，他写到爱人
紧挨着心跳的地方是乳房
他无法区别对待

旅途上，他写到旅途
苍山悲白雪，慈水挽清颜

梦境，哦，只是在梦境
他不能写下
除了那只爱跳舞的蝴蝶

此刻，他写到此刻
春光溅到脸上
春光啊多么性感

At dawn, he writes about daybreak
And the world breaks into pieces

At night, he writes about the long night
And gets startled by a sudden loneliness

In love, he writes about his lover
The beating heart rests in her breast
he doesn't know how to tell them apart

Traveling, he writes about journeys
mountains, snowcaps, face cleansed with kind water

Dreaming, only in dreams
He can't write
about that dancing butterfly

As he is writing about the present
Spring splashes light on his face
Sensuous, alive

在草原上

直到将暮色换成曙光
我仍然站在草原上

直到青草的波浪如大海平息
我仍然站在草原上

直到河流变暗
挖掘机开上山冈
我仍然站在草原上

我站在草原上
不是因为它有多美
也不是我想变成一棵草

只要站在草原上
只要风还吹在脸上
我就知道马的脾气是怎么变坏的

在草原上
每一匹马奔跑的姿势
都比风性感

在草原上
一群马与一匹马的孤独一样大

在草原上
一群马与一匹马的悲伤
和一棵草一样大

On the Grassland

Dusk has turned into dawn
I'm still standing on the grassland

Waving grasses are calm like the sea
I'm still standing on the grassland

The river has turned dark
Excavators have climbed atop the hills
I'm still standing on the grassland

I stand here
Not because the land is beautiful
Or I want to turn into a blade of grass

I stand
The wind blows at my face
I know why my horse is losing his temper

On the grassland
Every running horse
more sensous than the wind

On the grassland
A harem of horses is as vast as a lone horse

On the grassland
the sorrow of a blade of grass feels as deep as the sorrow
of my horse, and all the horses together

大雁飞过

我以故乡的名义挽留过大雁
但秋风在迁徙的队伍中安插了两只翅膀

大雁飞过，带走鸣叫
我从未飞过，也没落下好名声

每次大雁飞过
我就感到一阵孤单

每次大雁从我的孤单中飞过
我就感到，我是掉队的那一只

When the Geese Fly By

I once begged the geese to stay home
But the autumn wind gave them wings

Geese fly by, leaving behind their great cries
I can't fly, nor leave a good name behind

Each time a goose flies by
I feel I'm alone on earth

Each time the geese fly through my loneliness,
I feel I'm a lone goose

萨拉乌苏之夜

没有一条河不爱自己的波浪
一生穿过多少旋涡
也没有一条鱼渴望上岸
萨拉乌苏的夜晚
宁静而清澈
我听见风在草叶上说
这不是一个梦
这是梦遗落的故乡
村庄已经安睡
星辰还在高处醒着
我搂紧怀抱中的大地
看见一条鱼跃出凌晨的水面
对着萨拉乌苏的耳边说
这不是一个夜晚
这是夜晚深爱的世界

Night at the Salawusu River

No river doesn't love its own waves
No fish wants to land on the shore
As it swims through endless swirls
Night at the Salawusu River
Is calm and clear
I hear the wind telling grasses
This is not just a dream
But an old home gifted by dreams
Villages are sleeping
Stars awaken in the sky
I hug the earth to my chest
At dawn, a fish leaps out of water
Whispering to the Salawusu
This is not just a night
This is a night loved by the world

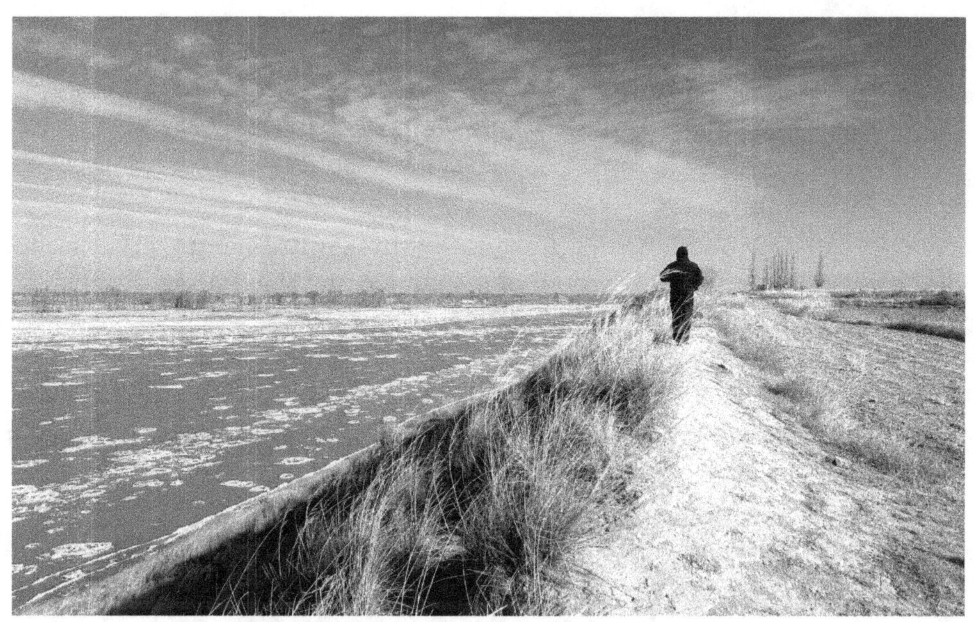

The ancient Great Wall along the Yellow River

大河流淌

大河流淌，一去千里
我在岸上恍惚站了一生

时光奔涌，岁月漂移
流淌的大河只剩下波浪和泥沙

我替曾经的人站在岸上
我替一条大河无边无际的流淌

大河流淌，天地寂寥
仿佛大河从不流淌

The Big Running River

The flowing river, running a thousand li
I've been standing on its shore, in a daze

Time rushes forward, centuries also flow
Only waves, sand and mud are left behind

I stand on the shore for the passing humans
I flow endlessly for the big river

The river runs between sky and earth
As if it had never moved an inch

Nongzi (农子), born **Cui Yufeng** (崔玉峰) in 1965 in Baotou, Inner Mongolia, is an acclaimed Chinese poet best known for his collection, *Fields under Snow* (雪地下的田野). His evocative, nature-infused poetry reflects the landscapes and cultural heritage of Inner Mongolia, blending lyrical depth with regional identity.

Awarded the prestigious Inner Mongolia Suolongka Literature Award among other honors, Nongzi's work has been celebrated for its emotional resonance and vivid imagery. His contributions extend beyond poetry, with essays and literary criticism that engage with rural life, environmental themes, and contemporary Chinese literature.

Nongzi remains an influential voice in regional literature, with his works appearing in major anthologies and literary journals across China.

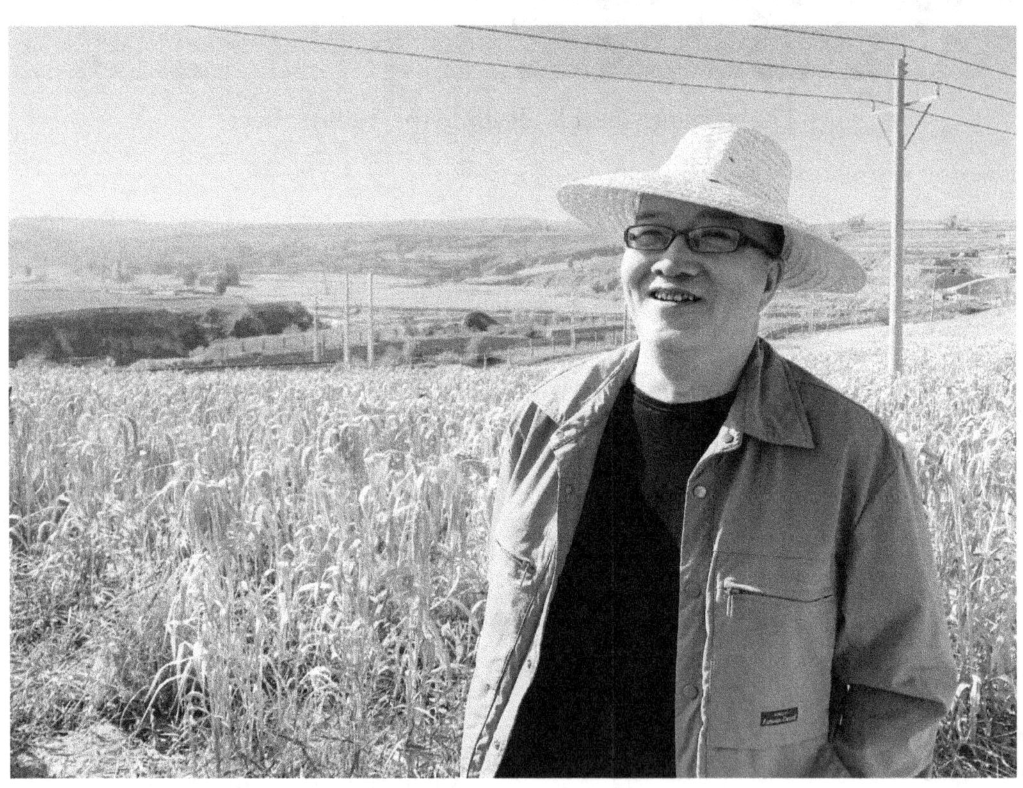

星星

突然想起，如果
从另外的星球
望地球。地球
也会是一颗遥远的星星
悬在浩瀚的夜空，亮晶晶
想到我也在其中
发着光，被另外的人们
神奇地仰望。多么快乐

Stars

It occurs to me suddenly:
What if I watch the earth
From another star? The earth
Would also be a distant planet
Hanging in the infinite space, sparkling
It makes me feel happy to imagine
That I'd be sparkling like a star
Admired by others in wonder

人民

他们的谦卑是骨头里的
他们低眉顺眼，小心地绕过，
招牌上，随处可见的一个词。
甚至，都不用绕过
他们一直认为，那个词，
说的是另外一些人.更多的时候，
他们自称老百姓,受苦人，刨食的。
偶尔心情好时
还会修饰一下，变成小老百姓
穷受苦人，刨一爪子吃一口
这样说时，并没带丁点儿情绪
或者情感色彩。就像出门去
套一件洗净的旧衣服，得体而舒服
这些年，出现了一些新词，如草根
打工者，弱势群体等，他们坦然接受
像接过邻居递来的一支烟，顺手夹在耳后
诸如低收入人群，留守老人儿童
失足妇女,讨薪者，上访者，下岗职工等
会让他们内心一疼，旋即平复
像一根针，扎了一下命运的流水。
他们认命.我是闲得没事时，翻一下
发黄的历史书.有时在揭竿这个词汇
后面,晃动着一群模糊的身影。
让我心惊的是,这些人，
居然把当皇帝的心事,
藏得那么深

People

Humility comes from their bones
Heads bent, walking gingerly, dodging
The street signs. Sometimes, they don't even
Dodge; they know who's the boss.
Most days, they call themselves ordinary
laborers, peasants. In a good mood, they'll
change the wording, call themselves
the peanuts, the poor, working hand to mouth.
They show no emotions saying the names, as
if they were just changing clothes to go out,
old but clean, comfortable and decent.
These years there are new names for them:
grassroots, migrant workers, the unfortunate,
hey take them all, like taking cigarettes from
a neighbor, placing it behind their ear; and
other names, low-income, left-behind elders
and children, fallen angels, wage beggars,
complainers, fired workers… names that hurt
little, then recover, a needle poking the river
of destiny. They accept what life doles.
In my spare time, I flip through yellowed
history books. Behind the word "uprising,"
I glimpsed a shadowy mob
What surprises me the most is how
deeply these people hide their ambition
of becoming Emperor

流逝

终尽一生，也有我们
无法看到的事物。就像岸边的
蚂蚁，不会看到整条黄河
只看到汹涌无尽的水，从眼前流过

Passing

There are always things we never see
Before we die, like ants, they see
The water rushing forward, endlessly,
But never the whole Yellow River

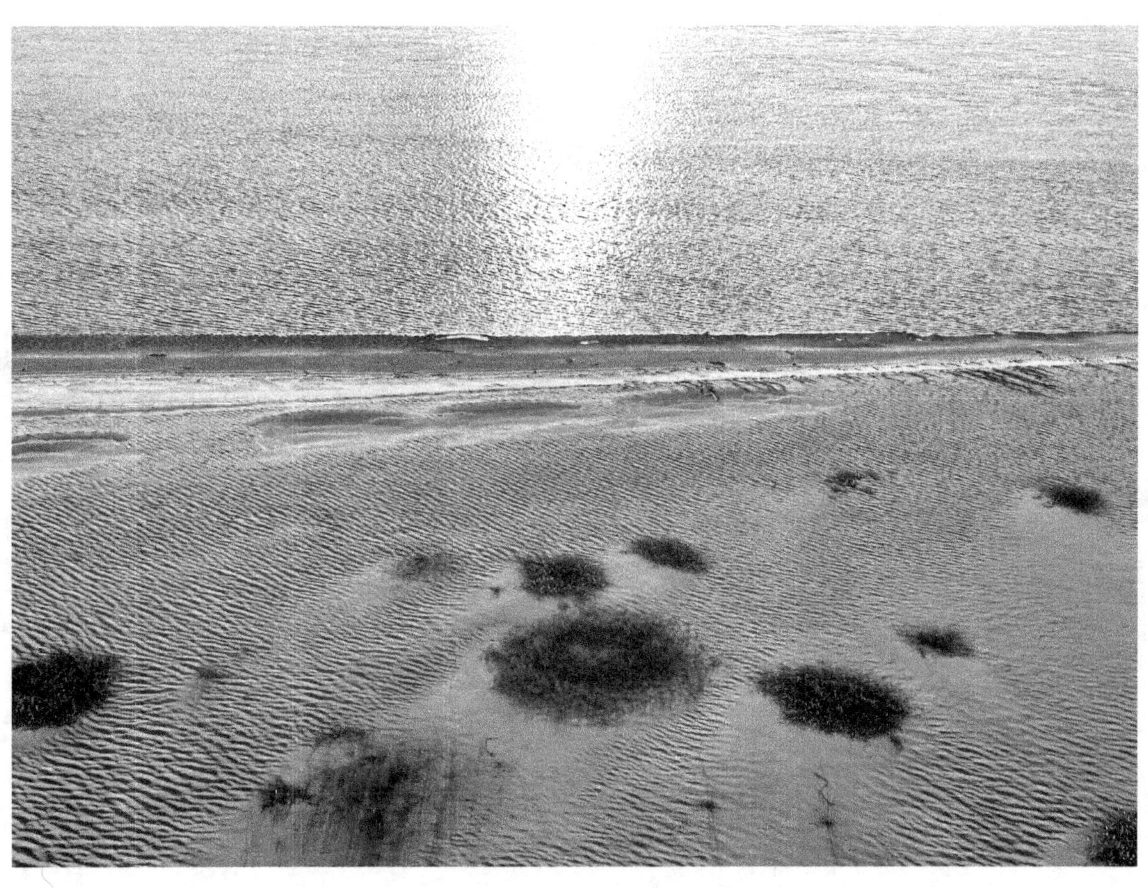

The Yellow River Passing through the Desert of Inner Mongolia

Su He (苏和) was born in West Ujimqin Banner, Xilingol League, Inner Mongolia. He is an accomplished Mongolian poet with over three decades of literary contributions. His poetry blends pastoral imagery with contemporary reflections, often exploring themes of nature, cultural memory, and the shifting landscapes of Inner Mongolia. His selected publications include *Birds Asleep* (眠鸟), *Dreams Awakened* (梦决), and others. His literary recognitions include the Best Poetry Award, the Makang Alai Poetry, and the New Poetry Award (2022).

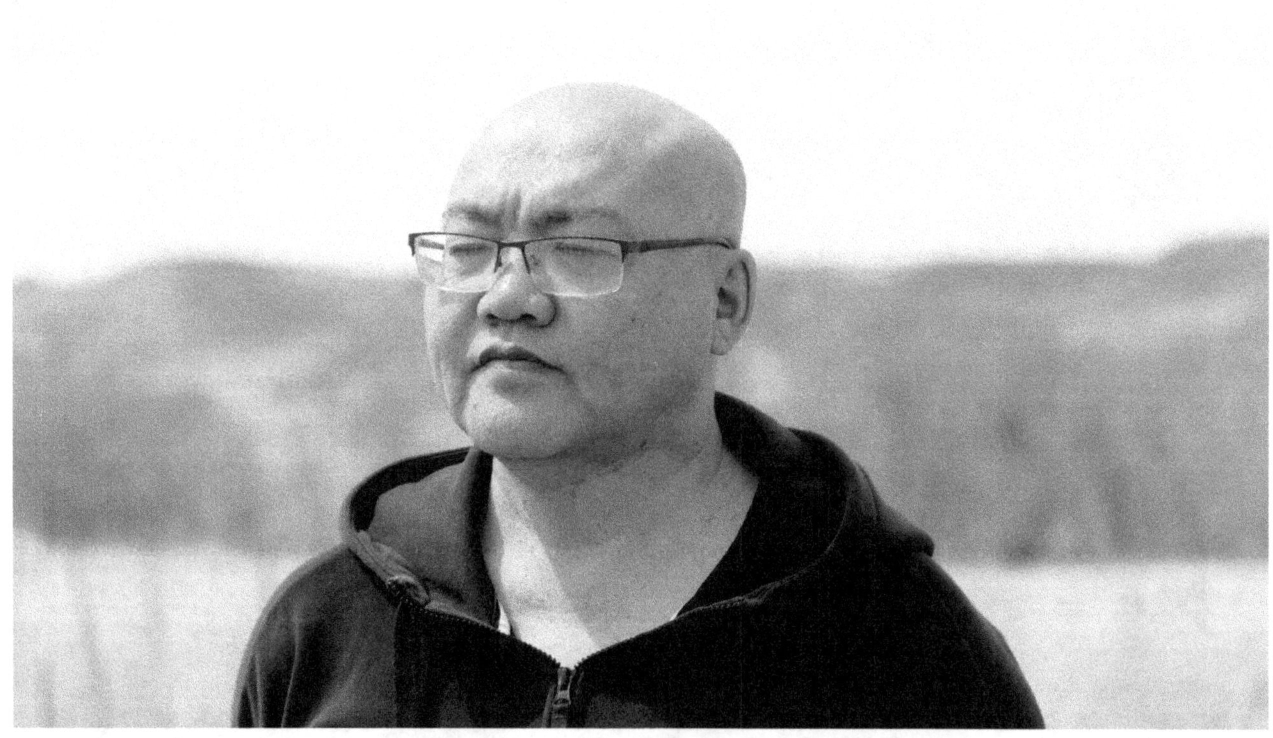

今天中雪

雪不大不小　下得很有层次
树叶都落没了　为了掩盖光秃秃
雪来了
希望这场雪能坐冬　讲一个
美丽的谎言　淖尔边上那棵榆树
守着　　一直守着
凌乱的几枚垂叶　收住笔锋
不肯写下去　　削一片乳白的羊尾
泡在　　滚烫滚烫的黑砖茶碗里
一直泡得羊尾片透明　拌着炒米
把冬天
一勺一勺吃下去

Today's Snow, Medium

It's snowing, not too big, not too small
Layered, orderly. Trees loses their last leaves
so snow comes
I hope it will sit through the winter
To tell a beautiful lie　　The elm at the lake
stands　　waiting
A few leaves still hang there
I stop my pen, can't write, slice sheep tail
Soak the creamy fat in boiling black tea
Till it becomes transparent
I drink the tea with roasted rice
Spoon by spoon　　swallowing winter

牧乡谣

从杰仁淖尔苏木
到舒图嘎查
三十公里
夏天早晨五点坐勒勒车
要走到晚上八点
牛是有脾气的
累了就不想拉车
是倔犟骨头
任你把鞭梢甩得啪啪响
慢腾腾的牛蹄
晃悠悠的车轮
这一天就像一个抽屉
到地方
关上抽屉
天黑了

Song of Grassland

From Sumu, Lake Jieren
To Shutukacha
It's 30 kilometers
On a summer morning
I take off on my ox cart at 5:00
Arrive at 8:00 pm
My ox has a temper
It won't pull when he's tired
He's as stubborn as a bull
Walking at his own pace
No matter how loudly I flick my whip
Slow hoof steps, squeaking wheels
My day goes like a drawer
It shuts upon arrival
And night falls

瞬间

早晨　奶奶说心口窝疼
吃了两片胃得宁　　　蹲在
羊粪灶火旁边烧好奶茶
感觉好一些了　　　　　走出蒙古包
在附近捡了几筐干牛粪
回到蒙古包喝奶茶
正在与在旗里上学的孙女视频
手机陡然掉落
汗珠顺着额头雨水般流落
而后一切归于平静
一束阳光从蒙古包门沿上挤进来
追光灯一样
打在奶奶的额头

That Instant

That morning, Granny said her chest hurt.
She took two stomach pills, at the stove
Made milk tea fueled with sheep droppings,
felt better. Walked out of the yurt, gathered a
few baskets of dried cow droppings, came
Home to drink tea, video chat with her
Granddaughter in the Banner's School.
Suddenly her phone fell
From her hands, sweat pouring from
Her brow. Then peace shines
Through the yurt door
Following Granny like a spot light
Stopping on her head

看电影

小时候
有一次去达布西拉图嘎查看电影
电影组巡回放映
一晚上放三部影片
记得有《红灯记》《沙家浜》《龙江颂》
都是样板戏
一直到三星西斜
电影才放完
往回家走
路上实在困得不行
经过一个蒙古包
就敲开了门
里面只有一个老头
我就住了一宿
当第二天回到家
额吉问我住哪儿了
我说住东苇子沟一个老头家了
有一撮黄黄的山羊胡子
额吉说: 腾克热（天啊）
那是大牧主也西家

Watching Movies

When I was a kid
I walked to Dabuxilatukacha to watch movies
brought by a mobile movie theatre
They showed three movies: Red Lantern,
Shajia Bay, Ode to the Dragon River—
model films during the Cultural Revolution
I watched them all till Three Stars
Set in the west. I walked home
But I was too sleepy
So I knocked open a yurt
An old man opened the door
And let me stay for the night
I got home next morning
Erjie Mama asked me where
I spent the night
I said I slept over in an old man's yurt
In the East Reed Valley
He had a yellowish goat beard
Erjie cried out: Tengkere (good heavens)
He was the big Landlord Yexi

羊皮得勒与羊

一张张羊皮不会像白云飘飞
羊毛垛不再接近蓝天
春天山坡上残雪　如一块块
腐烂的羊皮
遮不住苦寒的冬天

喜庆的吉日　牧民们身着盛装
全都是缎子面　绸子里儿　库锦华丽
银扣　珊瑚点缀
很难寻到羊皮得勒
逝去的皮匠　也失去了传承手艺

羊皮得勒　逐渐退出牧区日常生活
那种轻盈　温暖　毛绒绒的感觉
留在了过去　淡漠在记忆深处

一双枯萎的手指
捏着针　缝不住失落
羊拐子骨棒不再纺线
冬营盘坐落着轻钢房屋
羊还是那群羊

Sheepskin Robe and Sheep

Sheep skin does not fly like clouds
Stacks of wool no longer reach the sky
The last snow on hills melts
Like rotting sheepskin
It can't cover the bitter cold winter

At festivals nomads wear their best clothes
Silk, satin, brocade, silver buttons
Coral flowers, nobody wears sheepskin robes
The last leather smith is gone,
along with his craft

Sheepskin robes have faded from the
grassland. That light, warm, fuzzy feeling
Has receded into our memory

A needle pinched between withered fingers
Can no longer sew back the nostalgia
A sheep crutch bone is no longer used to spin
wools, only steel houses sit on our winter
camp, and sheep still live as sheep

Xi Liang (西凉), born **Wang Yukun** (王玉坤), is a poet from Hexigten Banner, Inner Mongolia. His evocative poetry has been published in prominent literary journals such as *Grassland* (草原), *Feitian* (飞天), *Southern Literature* (南方文学), and *Poetry Monthly* (诗月刊).

In 2018, he released his debut poetry collection, *In Front of the Northern Gate* (在北门口), which explores themes of memory, landscape, and the intersection of tradition and modernity in China's northern frontiers. His work is known for its lyrical intensity and deep connection to the cultural and natural landscapes of Inner Mongolia.

Xi Liang currently lives and writes in Wuhai, a city along the Yellow River in western Inner Mongolia, where he continues to engage with the region's shifting identity through poetry. Inspired by Gary Snyder's poetry, he and poet Guangzi and other Wuhai poets formed the School of Wildness. They travel to deserts, mountains and rivers to seek inspirations and vital force for their poetry.

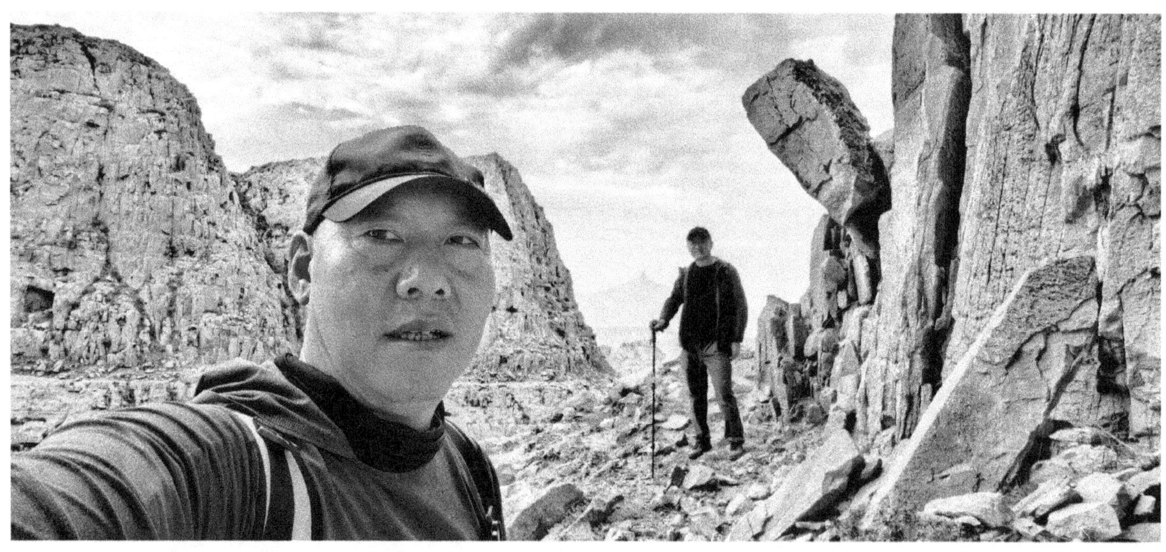

坟墓

人啊，真是一座坟墓
起码是牛的坟墓
羊的坟墓
蔬菜的坟墓
曾经还是飞鸟的坟墓

那样啊，他也是箭镞的坟墓
云的坟墓，刀的坟墓
鬼魂的坟墓

要是他懂得慈悲的话
坟上就会长出花朵
不信，你看
夜色在他头上飞
蝴蝶也在飞

Grave

Oh the human, he's such a grave digger
A grave for cows
A grave for sheep
A grave for vegetables
And a grave for flying birds

He also dug a grave for arrows
For clouds, for swords
Even for ghosts

Had he understood mercy
His grave would have grown flowers
If you don't believe me, look at
The night flying over his head
And the butterflies too

来吧

哦，你要通过我身体
狭长的走廊
来到这

你说，这是草药
这是翅膀和汤

你说，这是钥匙，这是道路
你说，这是遗忘

Come Here

Oh, you want to pass through
My body. Its long narrow corridor
To arrive here

You said: this is an herb
This is chicken wing and soup

You said: this is a key, a path
You said: this is forgetting

夜晚

夜晚，多好啊
和盲人在一起
和时间里的苦在一起
和房屋在一起
那就和你，和温暖的凛冽
在一起了

Night

How beautiful is night
Hanging out with the blind
Hanging out with bitter time
Hanging out with you
Sharp and warm
Together

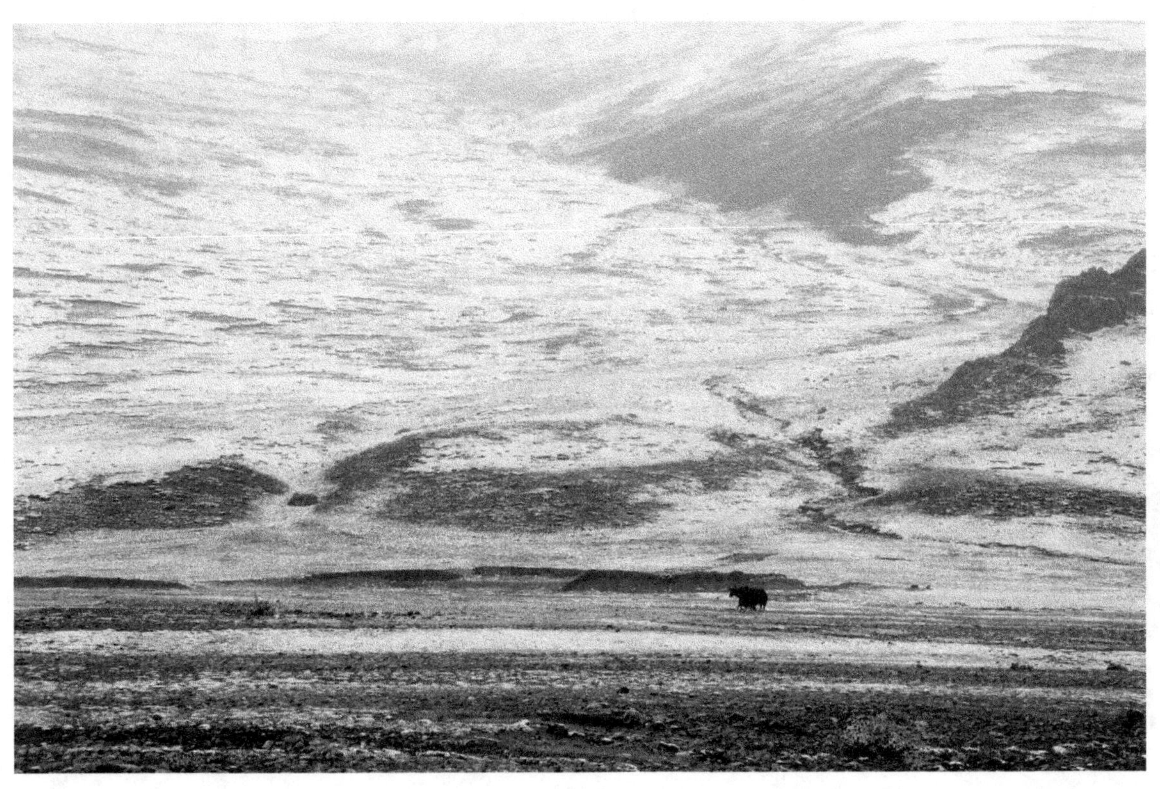

Wen Gu (温古) was born in 1961 in Hohhot, Inner Mongolia. He served as former editor of *The Grassland* (草原), Deputy Director of the Poetry Committee of the Inner Mongolia Writers Association, and former editor of *Zhungeer Mining News* (准格尔矿报). His poetry collections include *Wen Gu Selected Poems* (温古诗选, winner of the 7th National Coal Literature "Wujin Award"), *Low Fire* (低处的火), *Signature under Eagle Claws* (鹰爪下的签名), *Fire Under the Sunset* (落日下的火焰), and *Wolf Plain* (狼塬). His work explores themes of wilderness and Mongolian steppe culture. His poetry blends modernist aesthetics with Mongolian pastoral imagery, often drawing from rock carvings, nomadic life, and ecological consciousness.

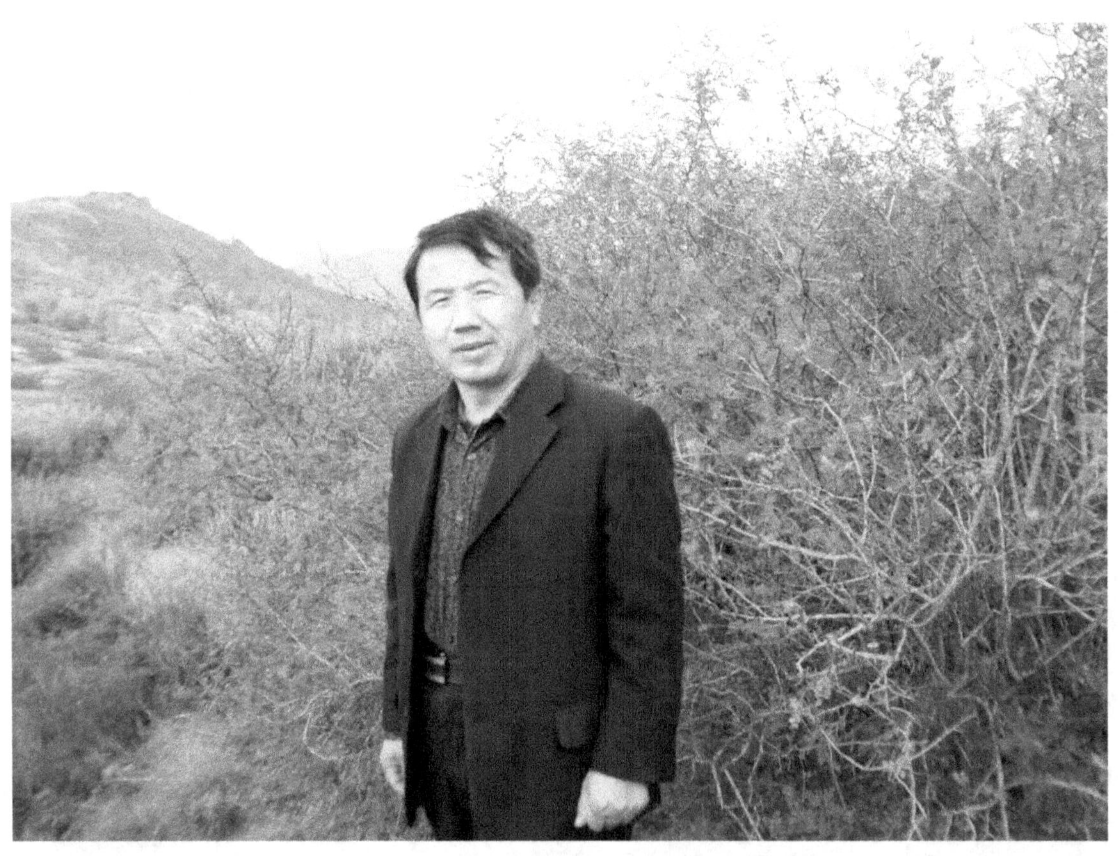

阿拉善右旗走笔——
曼德拉山脉岩

黑色的岩石上，雨珠碎裂
青色的岩石上，星星一滴一滴溅落
一千年、一万年，古老的风在唱：
"一万个、一千个，相似的夜晚"

骆驼的背后，有历史的风暴升起
山羊的唇角，留着沙葱花的清香
别问我们祖先们的秘密
闪电已经刻在了石头的脸颊上

Notes from Alxa Right Banner—Rock
Paintings in Mandela Mountain Range

Rain breaks on black rocks. Stars fall
One by one, on blue stones. A thousand years
Ten thousand years, wind sings: "One thousand,
Ten thousand, all nights are the same"

History storms out of the camels' backs
Cooking fragrance lingers between goats' lips.
Don't ask the secrets of my ancestors
Their thunder is carved on the rock face

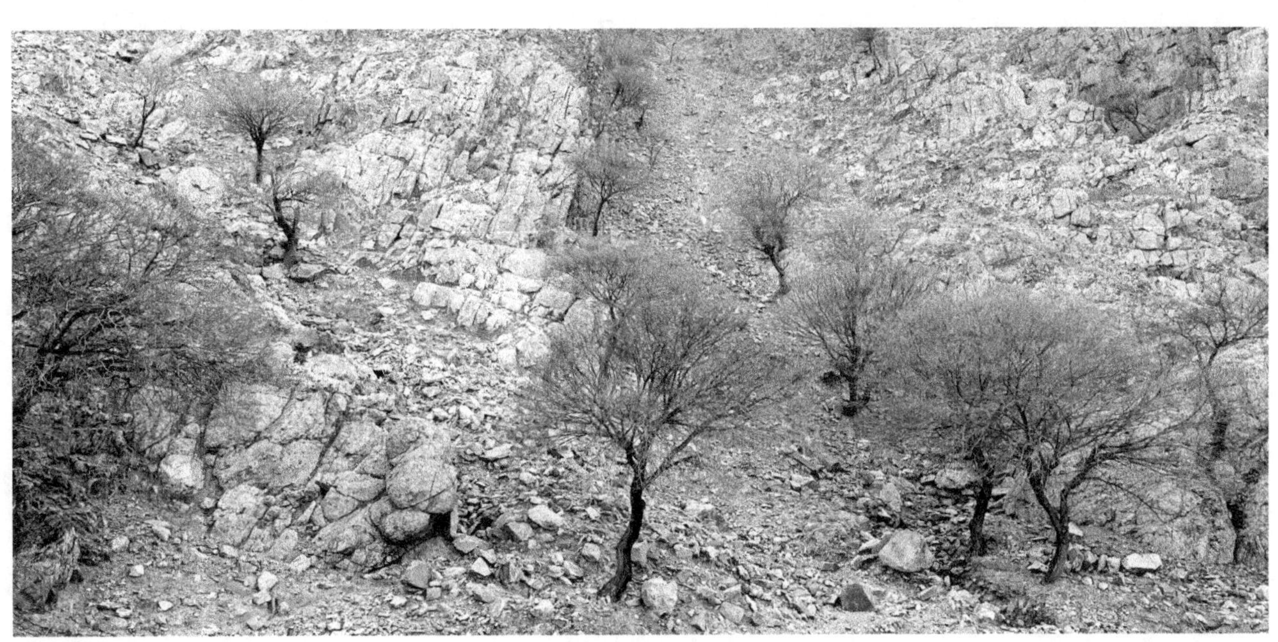

Sihemu, a fossil shrub in the Alxa Mountains

岩画，马，鹰

相信一只鹰，领着
游牧的祖先，能走出这片
岩石里的天空

相信狩猎者的箭
能射穿夜幕的寂静
还相信，骑者马蹄下的草
圈住了一条弯曲的河流

而溪流边的小驼羔和小马驹
踏进溪流倒映的一朵白云里

相信弯曲的岁月
鼓起一朵一朵鱼群一样的碎浪
相信马蹄踩碎的溪流 溅出岩石的外面
和月光汇成明晃晃的一片

只有祖先的脸，庄严而坚硬
可以压住，青草的喧嚷声

Rock Painting, Horse Riders and Eagle

Trust the eagle
Leading my ancestors
Out of the rocks' sky

Trust the hunter's arrow
Penetrating the night's silence
Trust the grasses under the horse
Holding onto the bending river

Lambs and foals on the bank of a stream
Step into a white cloud's reflection

Trust the zigzagging time, waves like schools
of fish bubbling
Trust the stream, broken by horse hooves
Splashing out of rocks, shining in moonlight

The ancestors' faces, solemn and resolute
Weighing down the noise of grasses

画，村落

当我们的天空
凝结成最大的一块岩石
夕阳的熊熊篝火，照亮我们的村落

十八顶帐篷支开十八座黑夜
月亮垂下一只公用的乳房

睡吧!野花盛开的旷野
野兽卧在雾气升起的帐篷边

没有那一座天堂比这里更美
神都夸耀着最粗壮的肉体

时间的风河水一样流过
在我们正在打鼾的床榻旁
他将第一片落叶，送到了很远的地方

在陶兰高勒山冈上　有双手在说话
是流血的指头　　　　　在讲着流泪的故事

是一双手，抓伤了石头的脸
是一双伸进太阳的手
将她的火焰　烙进岩石
一双手，伸进月光
洗涤着古老的忧伤和仇恨

用十指抠破岩石的皮肉
用血讲述狩猎、放牧、生活和繁殖，
讲生死和战争

然后撸起袖子
抓取肉食，然后拉弓，追逐野兽，
磨治石器

Rock Painting, Village

When our sky congeals into a giant rock
The setting sun lights our village
with a camp fire

18 tents open   18 nights
The moon hangs like a breast

Sleep! Wild flowers blossom in the fields
Outside the tents, animals lie in the mist

No paradise is more beautiful than this place
Even gods are envious of these muscled men

Time blows by
Like a river, sending a fallen leaf
to a distant place as we snore in beds

On the Taolangaolei   hands are talking
Bleeding fingers   tell a weeping story

Hands scratched the rock face
Reached into the sun
To brand fire on the rock
A pair of hands reached into the moon
Washing away old sorrow and hate

Ten fingers dug into the flesh of the rock
Its blood tells the story of hunting, grazing
life, children, death and wars

Then he rolled up his sleeves
To grab meat, pull his bow
chase animals, sharpen his stone arrows

那疲倦的祖先和牛羊一起睡着了，
只留一双手在岩石上醒着

岩画，野牦牛
石头里的深夜，仍有热度
太阳撤离之后，一具肉体在燃烧
它有足够的角力，撬起这硕大的岩石
但岩石借永恒的力量　　　　稳住了世界

现在整座山，成了一头牛的基座
矿脉的咆哮呼应着群星
如果我们传承了祖先的精髓
再深的历史
总会选择一个时机喷薄而出

凉下来吧!让雄心贴着石壁
凉下来　相信每一块克制的石头
都曾经燃烧过

岩画，猎人、猎犬与羚羊
有小股的南风，轻轻抽打着
褐色的鹿群，走过靛蓝色岩石

寒冷的冬天，骨瘦如柴的祖先
手持弓箭　　紧紧跟在后面
在生活完全凝固之前
他们还有许多事情要做

狩猎，用树枝搭建帐篷
河边洗净沾血的手
捂着夕阳烤火

当黄昏到来，他们点燃篝火
随着青烟舞蹈，然后融化在岩石里

Till he fell asleep with the sheep and cattle
Yet hands are still awake on the rock

Rock Painting, Yaks
Night is still warm in the rocks
The sun left us, the flesh is still burning
Enough heat to lift the giant boulder
But the rock holds the world steady

The whole mountain has become
The bull's base. The mines rumble
with stars. We've inherited
Our ancestors' spirit
History will burst through the crack

Let it cool down! Let ambition cool
against the rock wall   Every stone
Has gone through the burning

Rock Painting, Hunter, Dogs, Gazelles
A south breeze   drives
Brown deer past the blue rocks

In cold winter, my starved ancestors
Follow the deer   bows and arrows
In hands. They have much to do
Before their life freezes

They hunted, set up tents at sunset wtih
tree branches, washed bloody hands
in the river, warming themselves over fire

At dusk, they danced around the camp-
fire, then vanished into the rocks

即使化作符号和岩画笨拙的线条
他们的劳动仍然进行着
当小股的夜风吹过时
他们消瘦的身体
在岩石里微微抖索
有干树叶的瑟瑟声响

Their labor continued as symbols
And images of the rock paintings
When night wind blows
Their thin bodies
Tremble in the rocks
Rustling like dry leaves

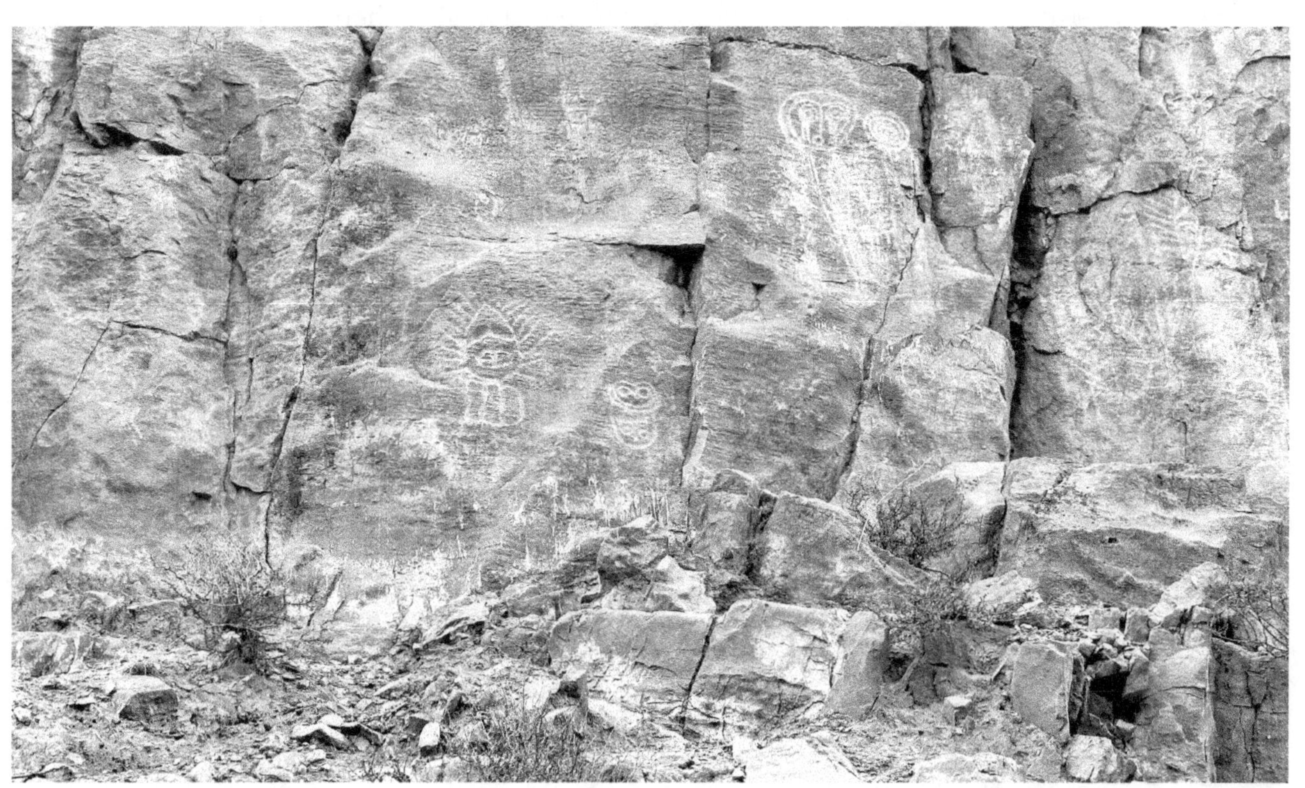

Rock paintings, Alxa, Inner Mongolia

走近曼德拉山

雄鹰将背上驮着的青色天空
悄悄地卸在曼德拉山冈上

盘羊带着白色云朵
麋鹿披着细碎的花瓣、跑进岩石
清澈的月光，从石缝里涓涓溢出

细细的风、溪流一样
向你娓娓讲述
古老游牧民族的生活
祖先睡着了的地方
青草静静地长高了

狼咬断羚羊的脖颈

时间的线条抽搐、变弯
星光刺痛了玄武岩的纹理
黄昏浸在血波里

一千座山峰跪倒了
骆驼吐出口中未嚼烂的草叶
刺藤枝上挂着明晃晃的泪珠
为扑倒在地的羚羊

当曼德拉山冈发紫的时候
一匹狼咬断了羚羊的咽喉
一块铭刻着生灵死亡故事的岩石
有阿拉善大地承受不了的沉重

雅不赖山的傍晚　山峦的
桌案上　星星是燃烬的灰堆

Walking to Mount Mandela

The eagle carries blue sky and drops it
on the ridge of the Mandela

White clouds ride on the mountain goats
An elk runs into the rock, dressed in flowers
Moonlight trickles out of stones

Wind flows like a stream
Telling a story
Of the ancient nomads
My ancestors lived here
Where tall grasses grow

The wolves broke the gazelle's neck

Time spasms and bends
Starlight cuts the veins of basalt
Dusk is drowned in blood

A thousand peaks kneel down
Camels spit out half-chewed grass
Tears hang on thorny vines
To mourn the fallen gazelle

When Mount Mandela turned purple
A wolf bit into a gazelle's throat
A story of life and death, carved on the rock
Too heavy to bear, for the land of
Alxa Sunset on Mount Yabulai

On the desk of Mount Yabulai
Stars burnt into piles of ashes

一万年，光阴被天空
静静地吸走
只有巴丹吉林的流沙
跟着驼队，能走出洪荒

今夜，如果我睡着了
明天刨开沙土，我就是一根
埋得最深，最黑的肉苁蓉

Ten thousand years, the sky
Has inhaled the time
The flowing sand of Yabulai
Follows the camels out of time

If I fall asleep tonight
You'll see a cistanche root tomorrow
Dark, deep in the earth

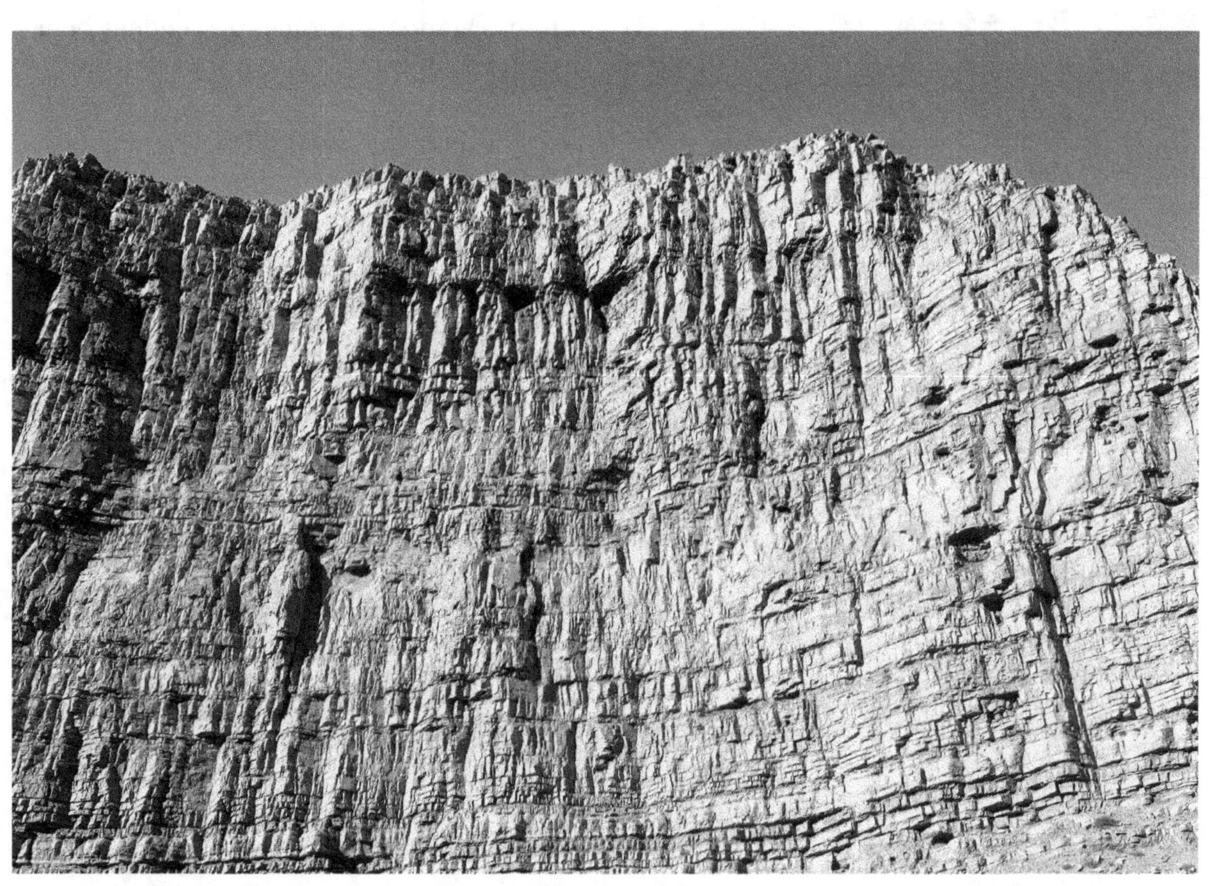

Mount Mandela

途经戈壁滩

星子将天空
蛀成一本千疮百孔的书

而岩画以云的构想
补缀一篇完整的神话

大雕的背上攒满星芒
畜群的背上，驮着风雨
游走的岁月啊——曼德拉山峦
为苍生驮着沉重的石头赶路

这是天书露掉的部分内容
这是时间典藉的注释
这是无数个神的轶闻

雷车磨砺着凸凹不平的大地
走吧！狼毒花拖着火焰的尾巴
寻找沙碛下面黑蟒一样
游走的锁阳

Crossing the Gobi

Stars gnaw the sky into a book
full of holes

Rock painting repairs it
Into a myth, with clouds

Eagles carry stars on their backs
Cattles carry wind and rain on their backs
Mount Mandela—you carry sentient beings,
heavier than rocks, towards our destiny

This is the secret, leaked from the sky book
This is the footnotes in time's dictionary
This is the gossip of gods

Thunder's carriage grinds the uneven road
Let's go! Euphorbia's fiery tails seek
suoyang desert roots, slithering black pythons
Under the Gobi

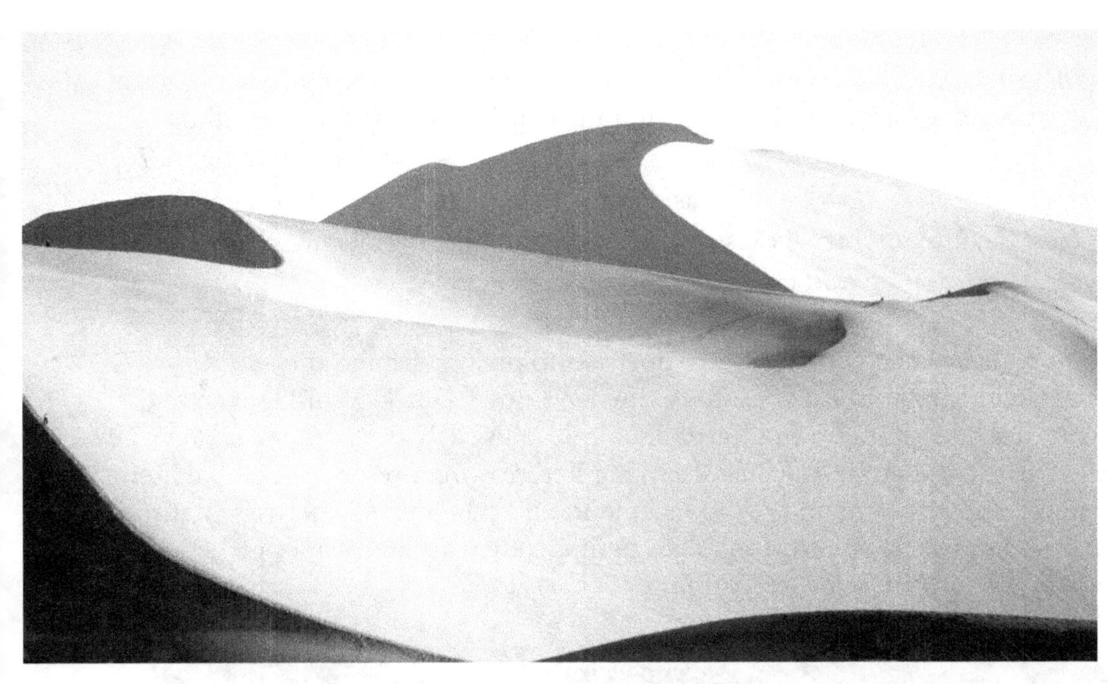

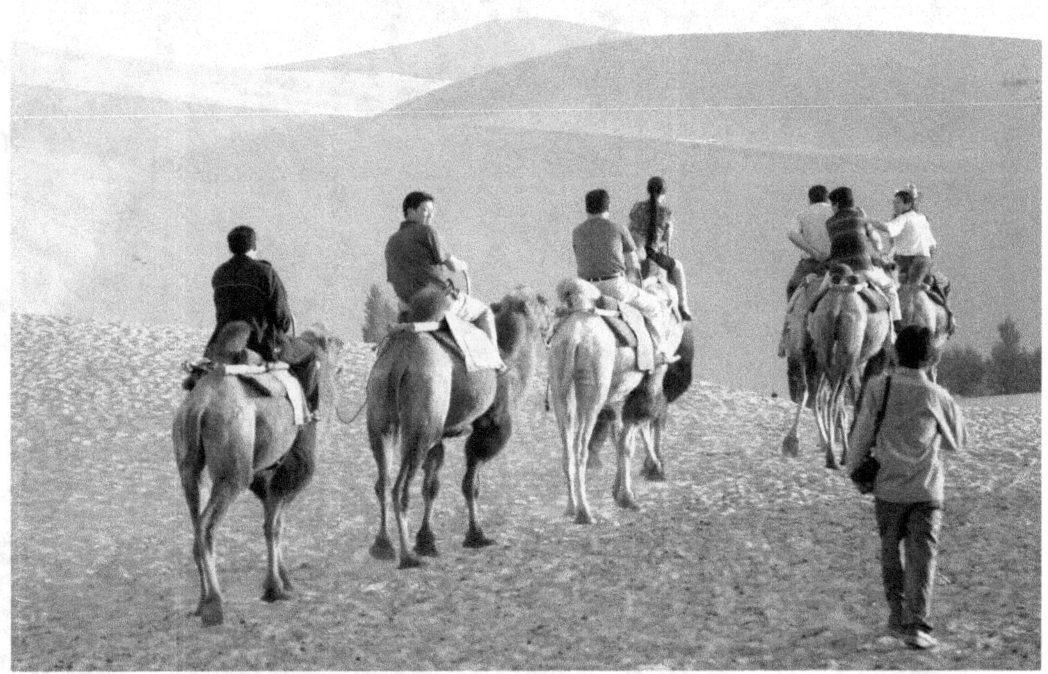

Yuan Xin (远心), born Zhao Na (赵娜), is a Chinese poet and scholar who grew up in Hohhot, Inner Mongolia. Currently an associate professor of literature in Nanjing, she is the author of several poetry collections, including *The Old Home of a Grass Snake* (一条草游蛇的故乡) and *The Red Horse in My Destiny* (我命中的枣红马), as well as a critical work on Tang and Song poetry. Her evocative verse blends contemporary lyricism with classical Chinese influences, reflecting her deep engagement with both tradition and modern expression.

Yuan Xin has studied and translated contemporary poetry and poetics around the world, especially the works of American poets such as Gary Snyder, Louise Glück, Paul Hoover, and Wang Ping. Her poetry has been featured in international journals such as *The Café Review*, *Sextan Review*, *New American Writings*, and *Poetry Magazine*, marking her growing presence in global literary circles. Her work explores themes of memory, displacement, and the interplay between nature and human destiny. It also draws from her Mongolian heritage, the vast landscapes of her childhood, and the busy modern cityscape of Nanjing.

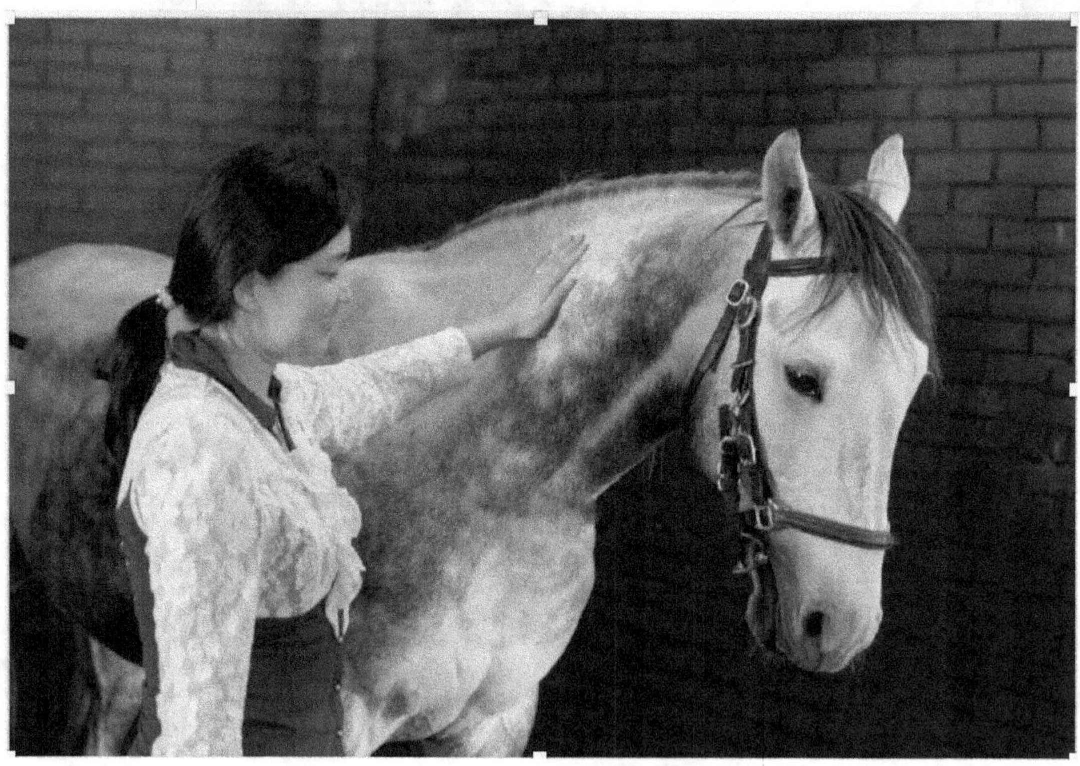

我命中的枣红马

我一直在这里等你，我命中的枣红马
曾经的黑被你眼底的风情镀亮
早霞和夕阳烧融你金色双翅
爱和毁灭把鲜血融进你的色泽
你的鬃颈和眼底的雄光

任何嘶鸣都不能牵绊你
我只有歌唱，拉响马头琴的两根弦
一根绝望，一根遥望
我是无以逃遁的地母
遇见你赠予你刺伤你喂养你
却不能和你一起飞翔踏遍未知的大地

还未发生的，如何预警
你奋蹄疾驰，让尘土飞成光轮
你忽视一切存在一切遮蔽一切细微的生命
你把自己置于屠戮与厮杀的现场
脸上露出宁静的笑靥，抿紧双唇

我爱你抿着嘴唇的样子
青髭略浮在唇上，唇线微微翘起
你初涉世的样子，在母亲的视线里
母亲怎样娇纵了你的青春
让那奔驰之力延续到无物的荒野
与天宇间雷光星云的奥秘对垒

我放开了手中的缰绳
一匹野马的魂灵注定与无边的野草共生
而我不是野草，不是草原
我是一座不会移动的山丘
站在你出发的地方

我已悄悄地走过很多四季
为了走到你马蹄到达之地
日复一日，置备粮草和精气

The Red Horse in My Destiny

I've been waiting for you, red horse in my destiny
Your dark eyes sparkling with emotions
Your golden wings melting dawn and dusk
Your blood comes from love's destruction
Your mane lights the window of the heart

No neighing can hold you back
I play the strings of my horse-head violin
one representing despair, the other, hope
I'm the Mother, chained to the Earth
I see you and tend your wounds, but I can't
Fly with you to touch the unknown land

How can I warn you about the unknown
Flying hooves turn dust into lightning wheels.
Ignoring all the tiny lives under your hooves,
you place yourself in the battleground,
smile on your face, calm behind closed lips

I love your closed lips, hint of mustache above,
Corners of the mouth uplifting,
A child new to the world, under Mother's watch.
She let your youth run wild
On the infinite grassland, till you reached
the mystery of sky, thunder, stars, clouds

I let go the rope
A wild horse needs to live in the wild
I'm not the grass, or the land
I'm a mountain fixed to the ground
Guarding the home where you take off

I've passed many seasons alone
Preparing food and souls
For the day you reach your destiny

小冤家：春分

他用冰块调新酒。
她用醉蟹肢解余生。
他在月亮下拥抱。
她在阳光里思念。
他钻进唯一的树林。
她浪迹大江南北。
他转身离开。
她被迫回来。
他的嘴唇凸显。
她的双眼望穿。
他在回忆的湖边跑。
她在鱼汤里找鱼。
他把情爱晒成竹竿。
她把日子泡成绿茶。
他的机器轰鸣。
她的桃花破碎。
他是过江之鲫。
她是亡羊补牢。
他酒后说想你。
她睡前放开诗的缰绳。
他愤怒。她钝痛。
他快速。她虚静。
他度芸芸众生。
她过独木桥。
他飞向白云。
她走进麦地。

Young Love: Spring Equinox

He mixes new drinks with ice.
She pulls life apart with pickled crabs.
He embraces the moon.
She pines in the sun.
He hides in the woods.
She roams the world.
He turns and leaves.
She comes home.
His lips are well defined.
Her eyes ache from longing.
He jogs around the lake of memory.
She hunts fish in soup.
He shrinks love into a bamboo stick.
She simmers her life into green tea.
His machine clicks and clanks.
Her peach blossoms fade and fall.
He's a carp passing the river.
She mends the fence after she lost her sheep.
He says "I miss you" after he gets drunk.
She loosens her poetry whip before sleep.
He gets angry. She endures slow pains.
He's fast. She stays quiet.
He liberates masses.
She crosses a bridge.
He flies into clouds.
She wades in wheat fields.

<table>
<tr><td>

月亮圆了

月亮太圆了
两层窗帘都穿透了
月亮太亮了
在曲阳县的二姨
跟在呼和浩特的娘通话
早就给咱爹娘烧了纸了
烧完才回城里
二姨五十多岁时
硬撺掇着二姨夫回朱家庄盖了新房
姥姥姥爷的坟在村东北
二姨的新房在村东南
沿着山脚就能走过去
姥姥的老院子在村儿正中
那条街被叫成老人街
老人一个一个去了坟地
那条街还是村儿里最老的街
而今姥姥的院子长年静悄悄地
槐花落了，今夜,爱安静的姥姥
一定会回到院儿里
穿着蓝花背心
摇着蒲扇，坐坐

</td><td>

The Moon Is Full

The moon is full, too full
It cuts through two layers of shades
blinding my eyes.
Second Auntie from Quyang
calls mom in Hohhot
The paper money has been burnt for my parents
She stayed at the grave till all was burnt
When Second Auntie turned fifty,
she convinced her husband to build a new home
in Zhujia Village, north of my grandparents' graves.
Her new adobe is built on the southeast side,
a walking distance to her parents at the foothill.
Grandma's old house sits in the village center
The street is called Elderly Street.
The elders are gone, one by one.
The street still remains the oldest in the village.
Grandma's yard is quiet all year. Elm blossoms
come and go. Grandma, who loves quiet evenings
Will return to the yard tonight,
Sitting, listening,
a bamboo fan in her hand

</td></tr>
</table>

圪料街

一条小巷道，长220米，宽6.3米。
26年前的早晨，席力图召西侧，
骑着单车走过；10年前元宵节的夜晚，
步行而过。"圪料街"遗址，瓦屋三间，
坍圯的砖坯墙，立在大街正中，
柏油马路到这里截断。墙砖摇摇欲坠，
瓦片长草，土坯里的草籽发芽
光阴在这里"弯曲"，"不直溜"，
这是呼和浩特的此地话——"圪料"。

走近夕阳下的旧砖墙，一个声音响：
您已走到警戒区域，请离开。
您已走到警戒区域，请离开。

一个人走过，与两个人走过，
有何不同？瓦片下的木窗格
弯曲，变形。对面大盛魁商号，
清末山西商人创建，
有多进四合院。
仰望着屋顶的滴水檐，
木窗格里的土坯
一块一块掉落。

这或许是26年前，
我家租住的9处平房中的一个。
一间朝北的瓦房，
不敢敲打墙壁，
父母步山西商人后尘而来，
做了20世纪90年代商场里的个体户。
父亲现在喜欢穿翻毛皮袄，
蒸的烧麦口味来自著名的"德顺源"。
母亲的手工鞋垫摊，摆在五塔寺东边，
一直摆到大年三十儿中午。

Geliao Street

A little lane, 220 meters long, 6.3 meters wide.
26 years ago, I biked past the west of Xilituzhao,
then again, a decade later, at Lantern's Festival.
The ruins of "Geliao" Street: three-room house,
tile roof and collapsing mud walls, in the middle
of the tar road, weeds growing through tiles,
sprouting grass on walls.
Time bends here, unable to run straight.
Locals at Hohhot call it: Geliao.

I approach the wall at dusk. A loud voice:
Warning, please leave this guarded area.
Warning, please leave this guarded area.

A street with one passer-by or two
Is there a difference? Under the weight of tiles
the window bends and twists, holding up time.
From the roof, I see "Big Prosperous Champion,"
built by a Shanxi merchant at the end of Qing.
Then it was turned into a housing complex
for rent, with water dripping from the tiles.
No icicles on the collapsing windows.

26 years ago, my family moved from the
Middle Kingdom, rented one of the 9 rooms.
The northern wall is too fragile to be
touched or knocked on.
Father & Mother followed the Shanxi merchant,
rented a small stand in the 90s market. Now
Father wears a fur coat, eating
dumplings from Deshunyuan Restaurant.
Mother sells hand-made insoles at Five Tower
Market, open till noon on New Year's Eve.

圪料街最后几间旧瓦房被圈起来。
粉色雪地靴踏进雪泥，零上五六度，
辛丑年的春天，包围我的过去
和一座旧城。

乾隆皇帝喝过的玉泉井边——灵泉泻玉，
风从西北起，脚步退回到26年前。
14岁的少年，走在黄昏里，街边一溜
小店铺：红白喜事铺，布匹，古董，
旧家具，狼皮，服饰，鹿头，
拨浪鼓，阿拉善沙漠石，烧麦馆，
奶茶馆，杂碎馆，翘起的石板路。
少年嘴里哼着呼麦…

一起走过的路，如今已经"圪料"，
弯曲的时光，如刀入鞘。

Geliao Street is surrounded by the last
standing houses. I go out in pink snow boots,
though it's above freezing. The Year of Ox and
its spring surrounded my past.

The well that quenched the Qing Emperor's
thirst—Flowing Jade of Soul Spring,
wind blows from the northeast. 26 years ago,
a 14 year-old in warm twilight walked past stands
for weddings and funerals, fabric, antiques, old
furniture, wolf skin, cloths, deer heads, rattles,
rocks from Alxa Desert, dumpling diner, tea
house, odds & ends store, uneven stone slabs.
He was throat humming…

The old path is geliao—twisted & bent
like time, like a sword entering the sheath.

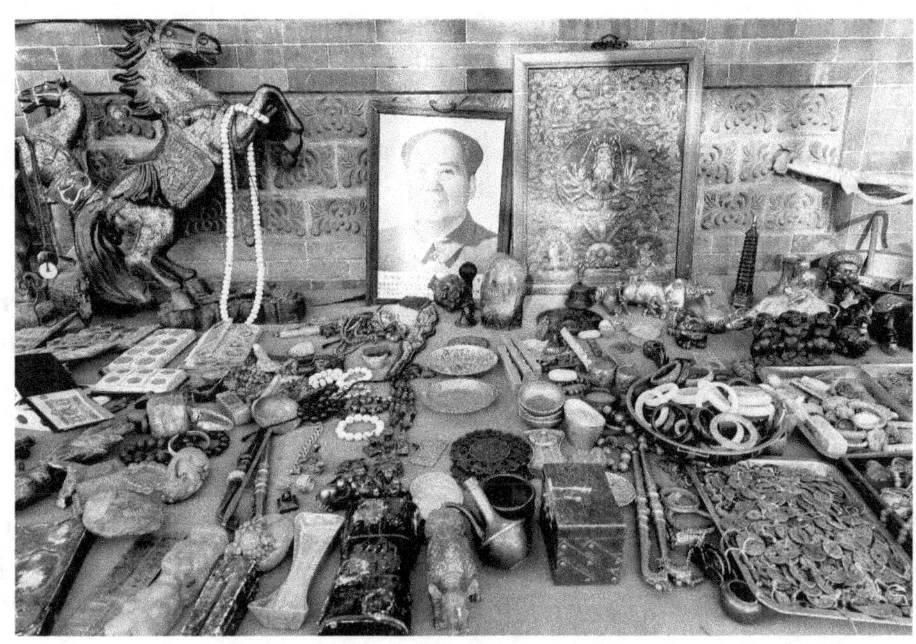

Geliao Street, Hohhot, Inner Mongolia

117

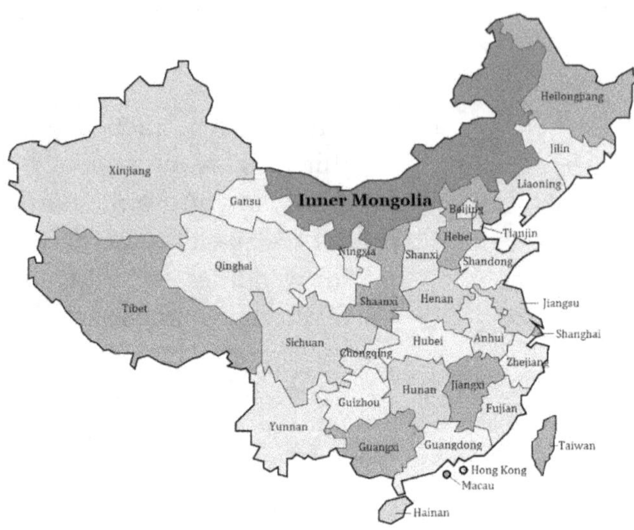

At the Old Ox Bend, where Inner Mongolia, Shanxi, and Shaanxi meet, the Yellow River makes a 180-degree turn. From here, it begins its middle-reach journey through Shanxi and Shaanxi, passing the tri-point village where the three regions converge. Snaking across the Loess Plateau— home to the thickest loess deposits on Earth—it carves the spectacular Jin-Shan Canyon, rivaling Colorado's Grand Canyon.

As it flows, the river carries vast amounts of sediment downstream, staining its waters yellow, thickening them with sand and soil. By the time it reaches Henan, it has already deposited 900 million tons of sediment into the lower reaches. The loess soil here is incredibly deep, reaching up to 100 meters. The river slices through the plateau, creating steep ravines, gathering sand from mountains and deserts, turning its waters into a mineral-rich yellow hue.

When it reaches Henan, the silt has raised its bed about 5 to 11 meters above the land. In these areas, the Yellow River looms over cities, towns, and fields like a suspended dragon. Like a dragon, it breaks dikes, leaping from its course, submerging everything below in water and mud.

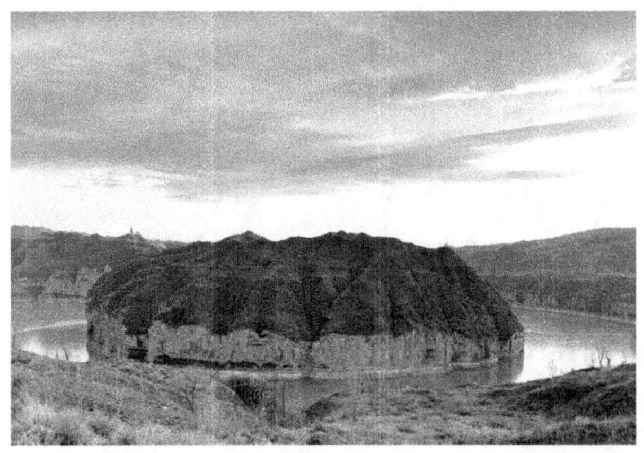

The Loess Plateau gives the Yellow River its name. It brings both prosperity and sorrow. This soil is the cradle of Chinese civilization: Shanxi and Shaanxi have been political and cultural centers for millennia, home to ancient states like Jin and Qin. The legendary final battle between the Yan and Yellow Emperors took place at Banquan, Shanxi, in 26th century BCE, forming the Yanhuang tribe, the precursor to the Huaxia civilization: the foundation of Chinese culture.

The Yellow River runs, twists, and bends, shifting from west-east to north-south, then back again before finally settling into its eastward course. It is a wild and willful river, flowing with a free spirit, forging new paths, winding and leaping, yet always surging toward the east on an eternal home. The river writes its own language, etching the largest character on Earth: 几 (jī), meaning "running legs"—its body stretching across China like a mighty dragon.

The people along its banks carry the Yellow River's spirit: they love passionately, fight fiercely, and wander far when the river overflows, often venturing into Inner Mongolia and beyond, even into northeast China. Yet no matter where they go, they carry the yellow soil in their hearts and its poetry in their blood. They will always be the Yellow Emperor's children.

If the river is the artery of China's history, culture, and spirit, then Shanxi and Shaanxi are its heart and lungs—their yellow waters and soil are the blood and flesh of the land… the very DNA of Chinese civilization. If you want to feel the spirit and music of Chinese poetry, come and walk along the Yellow River's middle reach, its deep gorges and muddy falls. Hear its heartbeat: China's pulse for the past 5000 years.

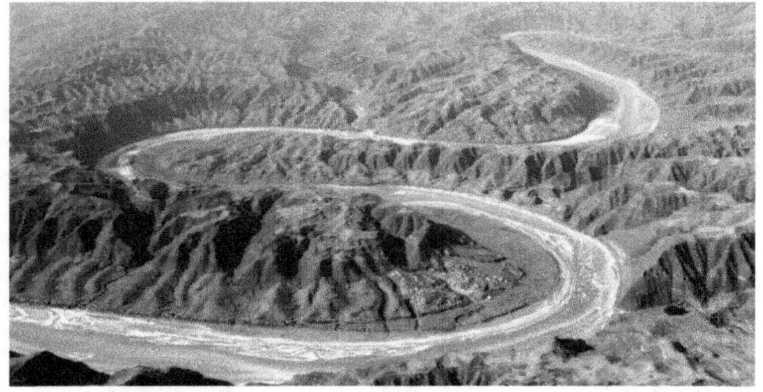

The Yellow River snaking through Jin-Shan Grand Canyon

Hou Ma (侯马) is a prominent Chinese poet originally from Shanxi Province. A key figure in contemporary Chinese poetry, he is known for his sharp, lyrical, and introspective verse that explores themes of memory, urban life, and human vulnerability. His published works include *Elegy* (哀歌), *Golden Safety Pin* (金别针), *Give Me a Kiss* (顺便吻一下), *Garden in a Psychiatric Hospital* (精神病院的花园), *Ankle of the Earth* (大地的脚踝), *Hou Ma Selected Poems* (侯马诗选), *Night Shift* (夜班), and *Night Train* (夜行列车), among others.

Active since the 1990s, Hou Ma is associated with the "Third Generation" of post-Misty poets, blending colloquial language with philosophical depth. His work has been recognized with awards such as the Lu Xun Literary Prize and the Yu Jian Poetry Award. Beyond poetry, he has also worked in law enforcement, an experience that occasionally surfaces in his writing.

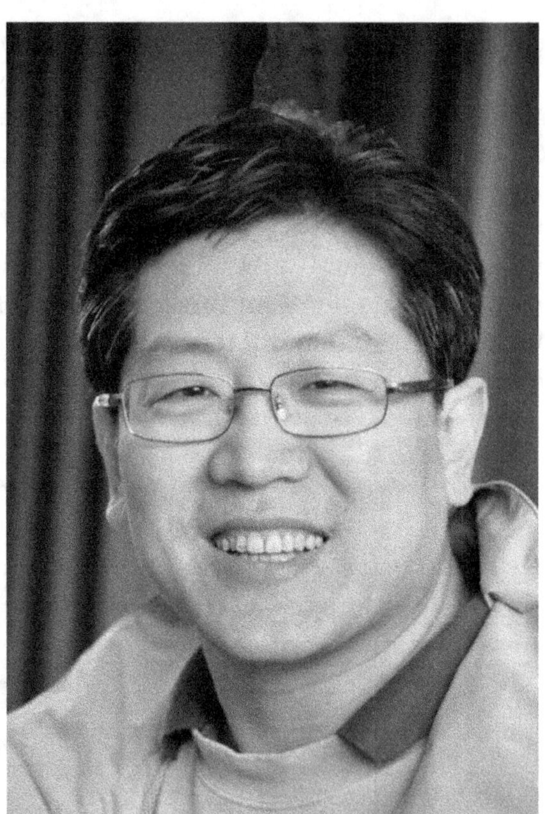

情况

在北京一家酒吧
我问芒克还写嘛
他十分坦然地反问我
情况有什么变化嘛
若干年后
到了芒克那时的岁数
一阵子不写
我竟也骄傲
竟也心安理得
后来伊沙恢复
选诗编诗
我知道必须冲了
为新诗典写作
漫漫十年 犹如一日
新诗典是我搭上的
自救之舟

Situation

At a bar in Beijing
I asked the poet Mang Ke
if he was still writing
He asked: is our situation changed?
Years went by
I was older, like Mang Ke
I felt more at ease for not writing
Even a bit proud of myself
Then I bumped into Yi Sha, another poet
Who just got his job back
As a poetry editor
I knew I must now march with all I had
For the new poetry destiny
Ten years went by. I've been writing daily
It has been my own Noah's ark
To stay alive

床板

暑期结束
坐火车返校
越接近目的地
我越茫然 恐慌
偌大的城市
我去干什么
去了找谁
学校跟我似乎没有
任何关系
亲如兄弟的同学
也显得那么陌生
我坐立难安
心口发紧
直到想起
在太平庄一带
某幢宿舍楼
有一张1×1.8米的木板
是我与这座城市
唯一的联系
才慢慢松弛下来
这时耳畔传来
广播员 舒缓深情的声音
亲爱的旅客
我们伟大社会主义祖国的
首都北京
就要到了

Bed Board

Summer is over
I take the train to go back to school
The closer to the destination
The more anxious I feel
Such a big city
What am I doing there
Whom do I really know
The campus seems to
Have nothing to do with me
My classmates, who treat me like a brother
Seem like strangers
As I get closer
My heart flutters with fear
Till I remember
In a dorm building
Somewhere in Peace Village District
There's a piece of board–1x1.8 meter
Connecting me
to the giant city
And I begin to relax
As the speaker announces
In a slow, emotive voice:
Dearest passengers
We are arriving
In the capital Beijing
Of our great socialist motherland

帝国牧场

明万历年间
山西的牧羊
赶着数千上万只羊
从黄河边
一路南下
过淮河
直至长江
边走边牧
冬天到达洞庭诸湖
来年近夏
再赶回山西
才过了几百年
山西已是黄土裸露
千沟万壑
再难放牧
不过羊头汤流传至今
味道鲜美仍具帝国风采

Empire's Pasture

During the Wanli period of the Ming Dynasty,
Shepherds from Shanxi
Herded thousands of sheep
Along the Yellow River
Downstream
Past the Huai River
Till they reached the Yangtze
The sheep walked and grazed
Until winter arrived at Dongting Lake
Till next year, summer arrived
They herded the sheep back to Shanxi
A few years went by
Shanxi is now bare with yellow soil
Its thick Loess riddled
with deep gorges
Impossible to herd, but sheep head soup stays
Still tasty with the flavor of the empire

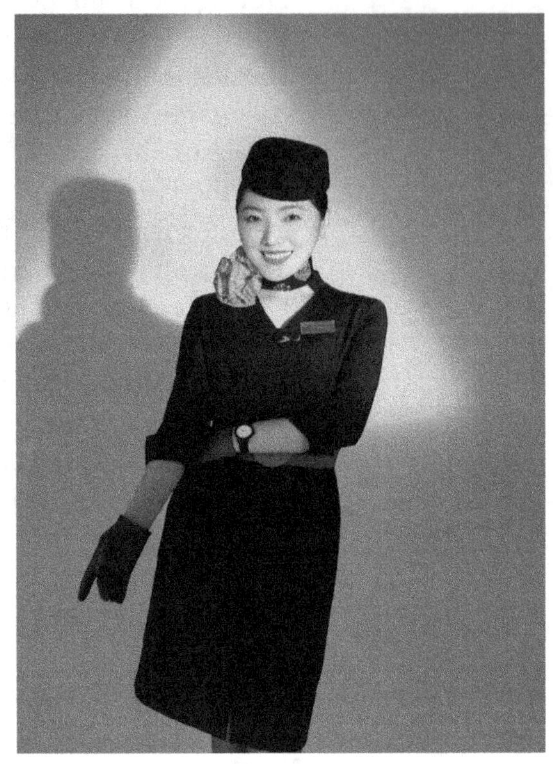

Ning Yaoyu (宁遥玉) was born in Shanxi. She has worked as a flight attendant since the age of 18. She adorcs clouds, mountains, tea, and poetry. During the COVID-19 pandemic, she attended three of Wang Ping's poetry translation workshops, where she discovered American poets such as Louise Gluck, Paul Hoover, Gary Snyder, and others. She also found new ways to express emotions through imagery and music—a practice she deeply enjoyed.

烤土豆

火炉烤着土豆，也烤着
天边不经意的云
我说"我爱你"，意味着
我问过自己：是否愿意为你去死
白天燃烬，灰烬里
你捧着今世我最宝贵的东西
迷路
你等着，我回到星星上
还会为你把
黑夜烤亮

Roasting Potatoes

The stove is roasting potatoes
It's also roasting the floating clouds
I say "I love you," meaning
I've asked myself: Am I willing to die for you
The fire is gone. In the ash
You find what I treasure the most
Are you lost?
Please wait till I return to the stars
And I'll roast the night
Till it shines again

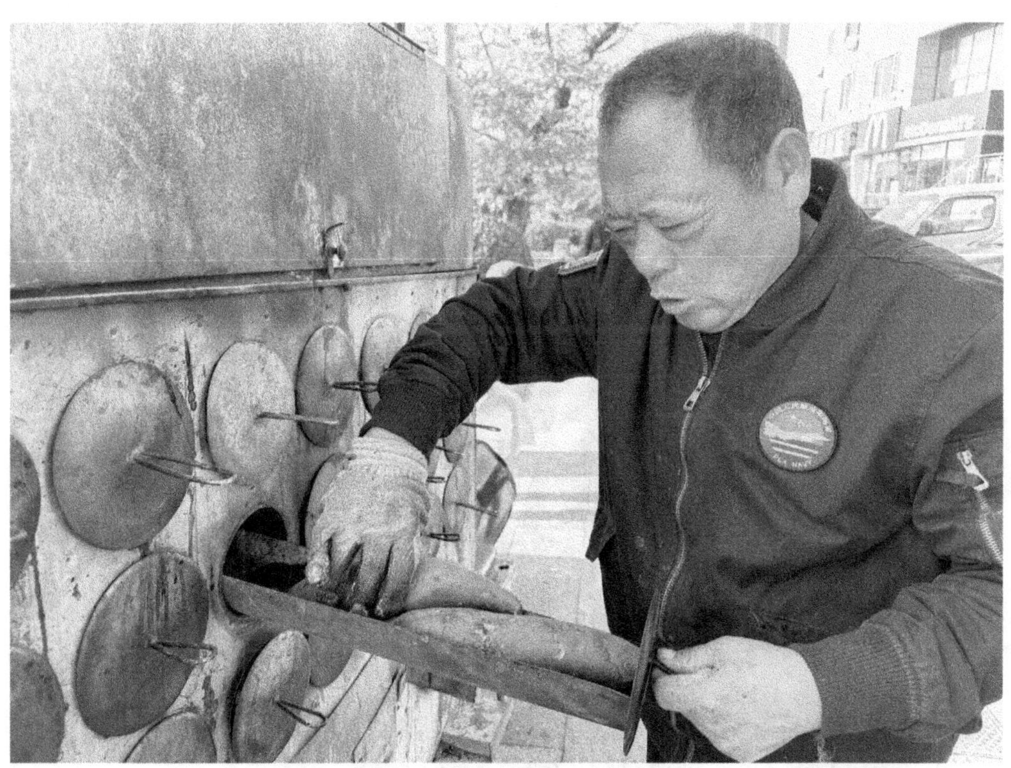

Selling roasted yams and potatoes on the street

Tian Lingyun (田凌云) is a Chinese poet from Shanxi Province. Her evocative and introspective work has been published in leading literary journals, including *Poetry* (诗刊), *Peonies* (牡丹), *Zhangshan* (钟山), *Mountain Flowers* (山花), and *October* (十月), establishing her as a distinctive voice in contemporary Chinese poetry.

Her honors include the Yangtze River Poetry Prize, Young Poets Award, the Zhongshan Literature Award, and the Caotang Poetry Prize. She is the author of the poetry collection, *The Evolution of She-leopard* (女豹的进化), which explores themes of identity, transformation, and the interplay between myth and modernity.

Tian's work often blends lyrical precision with philosophical depth, drawing from both personal experience and broader existential inquiry. She is regarded as part of a vibrant new generation of Chinese poets redefining the boundaries of language and metaphor.

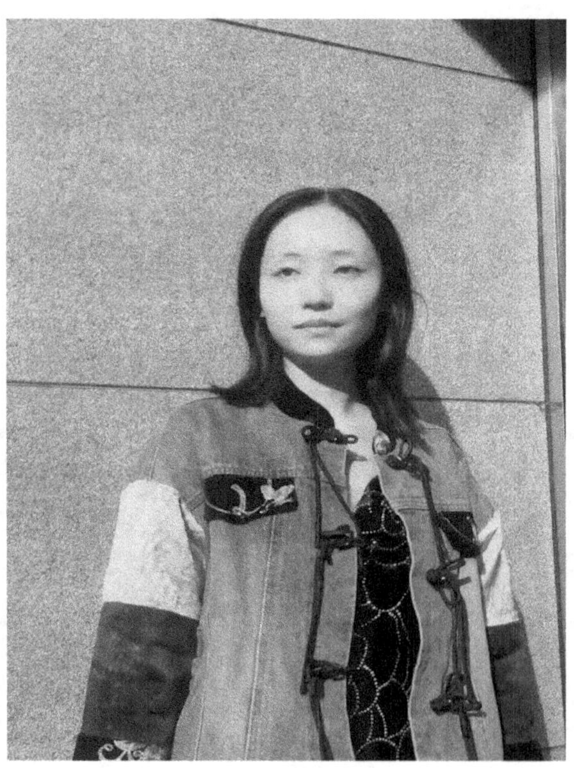

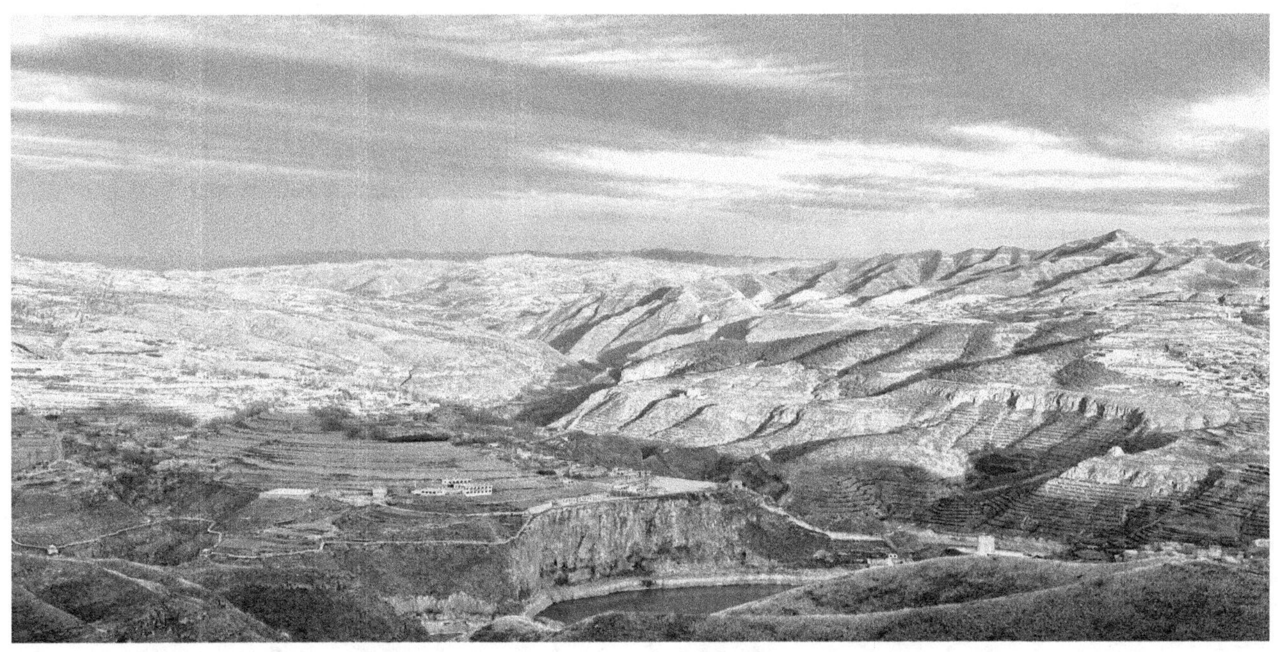

The Yellow River snaking through the Loess Plateau

打开

      Open

打开自己，恐惧也被打开，死亡也被打开　　When I open myself, I open fear and death
灵魂不只是变轻的问题，同时　　My soul is no longer the problem of becoming
更透明，像透支的信用卡。让人　　lighter, more transparent, like credit debt
无力偿还　　nobody can pay off
不想再纠结所有权问题了啊，这永远　　disentangle from who owns whom or what.
不由我做主的事情　　Nobody has the right to make that decision

打开，玻璃在迅速变皱　　Open. Glass is aging with wrinkles
女人在迅速变老。　　Women are getting old.
哦，我也是一个女人啊　　Oh, I'm also a woman

替人类绝望的鸟

鸟在树枝上用肠子鸣叫
拧断肠子、拧断鸣叫
用激烈的绝望唤醒鸟群的战争

鸟狰狞地叫了一会儿
把人的绝望全叫了出来
把人脆弱、坚强的沉默
全变成天下尽知的妥协

鸟撕裂自己，把天叫破了
然后，再不叫了
永世沉默
忘记了自己曾经是只鸟
替人类绝望过

A Bird Feeling Despair for Humanity

A bird on a tree is crying with its intestines
twisted from crying, broken, it tries to wake
other birds with despair, prepare for a war

It cries and cries
Releasing human despair
It reveals human weakness and strength
That has turned into an open compromise

The bird tears itself apart, tears the sky apart
With its cries, then it stops
Remains silent forever
Forgetting it used to be a bird
Used to despair for humanity

我怀疑——

我有猫头鹰一样的敏锐
猫头鹰一样的眼睛
和猫头鹰一样的孤寂

在夜里，我睡了
但思想的眼睛始终张着
在另一个世界观看

我怀疑，我的灵魂
只是一头猫头鹰

从出生到死亡，都从未进入人群

I Wonder——

I have the owl's sharpness
Owl's eyes
Owl's solitude

When I sleep at night
My mind's eyes are open
Watching from another world

I wonder if my soul
Is an owl that has never joined

The human crowd from birth to death

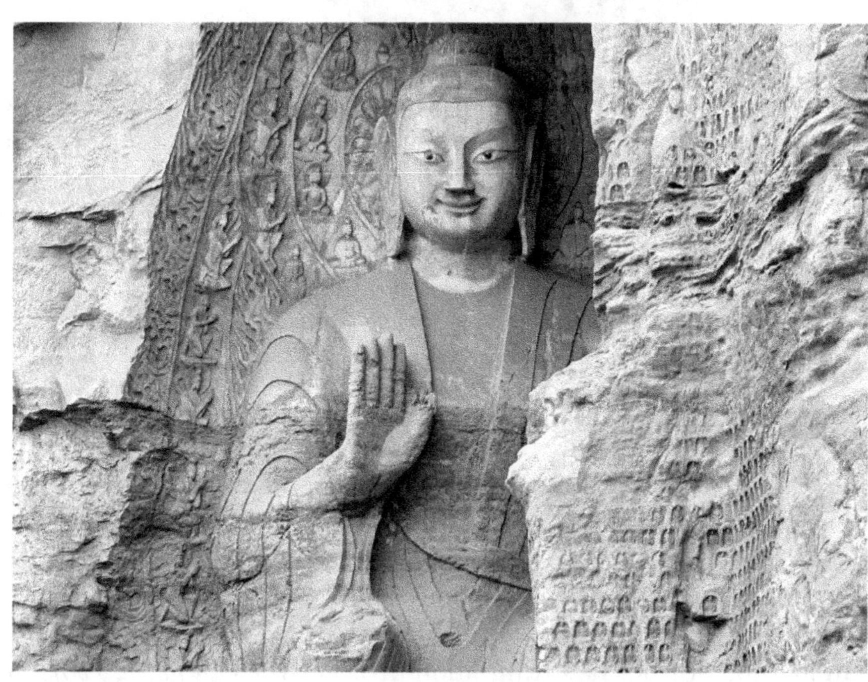

Yungang Gotto

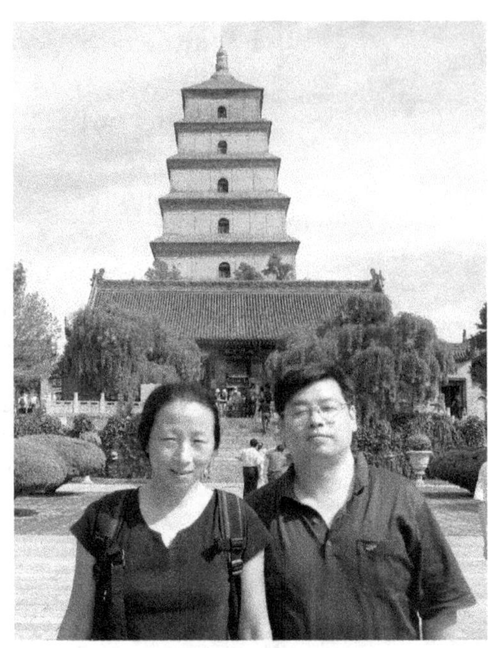

Yi Sha (*伊沙*) is a Chinese poet, novelist, critic, and editor of mixed Han and Kazakh heritage. Based in Xi'an, where he teaches literature, he is a leading figure in contemporary Chinese poetry and a key proponent of the "Post-Unofficial" (*hou feifei,* 后非非) and "Lower Body" (*xia ban shen,* 下半身) movements, known for his provocative, irreverent, and darkly humorous style.

Yi Sha has published over 30 books, including poetry collections such as *Starve the Poet* (饿死诗人), *Stutter* (结结巴巴), *Train Passing the Yellow River* (结结巴巴), and *Song of a Bastard* (车过黄河), as well as novels, essays, and critical works. His poetry often critiques cultural hypocrisy, blending raw realism with biting satire.

His work has been translated into English, German, Hebrew, Japanese, and other languages, appearing in international anthologies such as *Push Open the Window: Contemporary Poetry from China* (2011) and *The Book of Sins* (2011, Hebrew). He has participated in literary festivals worldwide and remains an influential—though controversial—voice in Chinese literature.

Yi Sha met Ping in Xi'an in 2003, for her first translation project, *New Generation, Poetry from China Today,* (Hanging Loose Press 2000).

《我的祖先》

那些沦落市井的无聊之徒
整日吃喝嫖赌
为件小事去杀某人
视生命为粪土

也曾像小孩般天真过的
我的种族
以行刺作为风尚的
遥远的上古

他们是——我的祖先
我冲动的骨血的渊源
那些摇着扇子晃着脑袋的一群
不算

My Ancestors

Ended up on streets
Drinking, whoring, gambling
Regarding life as muck
Willing to kill for nothing

They were once innocent like children
My tribes from long ago
Took pride
As assassins

They are my ancestors—
Source of my raging blood
But those who rolled their heads
While flourishing their fans
Have nothing to do with me

《结结巴巴》	**Stutter**
结结巴巴我的嘴	My stu-stu-stuttering mouth
二二二等残废	Sec-sec-second degree handicap
咬不住我狂狂狂奔的思维	Can't bite into my thighs
还有我的腿	Or my ra-racing thoughts
你们四处流流流淌的口水	Your spu-spu-sputtering spit
散着霉味	Stinks of fun-fun-fungus
我我我的肺	How weary
多么劳累	My-my-my lungs
我要突突突围	I need to esc-esc-escape
你们莫莫莫名其妙的节奏	Your puz-puz-puzzling rhythm
急待突围	Has tra-trapped me too long
我我我的	Mm-mm-my words
我的机枪点点点射般	Shoo-shoo-shoot
的语言	Happily
充满快慰	As a ma-machinegun
结结巴巴我的命	My stu-stu-stuttering life
我的命里没没没有鬼	Has nn-nn-no ghost
你们瞧瞧瞧我	Take a look at my face
一脸无所谓	Covered with indifference

《毛泽东时代的公共浴室》

我是多么怀念
毛泽东时代的公共浴室
那种百人共浴的大池
人与人挨得很近
相互搓背
泡在那混沌而滚烫的水中
是多么舒服啊
不常洗澡的人才知
洗澡是一种快感
花钱洗澡的人才知道
洗澡是一种幸福
就这样泡着泡着
昏昏然地泡着
直泡得有人虚脱
那年头根本就不用担心
这样的洗法会染上梅毒之类的
啊！我是多么怀念
毛泽东时代的公共浴室
但仅限于怀念

Bathhouse in Mao's Era

I long
For the bathhouse in Mao's time
Pool embracing hundreds
Skin to skin, bathers
Rubbed each other's back
How relaxing to rest
In the muddy hot water
Only those who rarely bathed
Understood its joy
Only those who paid
Knew the happiness
We soaked ourselves
Into oblivion
Soaked till someone fainted
No one worried about
Syphilis or AIDS in those days
Oh! My longing
For the bathhouse
in Mao's time

最后一点希望

在宾馆订房间时
你拿出护照　吓了我一跳
一个旅居美国
二十载的中国女诗人
所拿出的一本
中华人民共和国护照
着实吓了我一跳
你的老公是犹太裔的美国人
你的两个混血的儿子
都是生在美国的美国孩子
你的老公不但热切地希望着
你成为一个美国人
还想让你皈依他的犹太教
饭桌之上你讲起这些
那么淡然地说
"总觉着有点别扭"
你别扭　因为多了颗诗人之心
可那些写诗的男人们
那些一面充当着
民族英雄与道德符号
一面怀揣别国护照的家伙们
他们怎不觉着别扭
换籍只当风吹帽
没准连血都想换了吧
呵呵！民族的脊梁
谁虚构了这副脊梁
也就是个把弱女子
用心中的这点别扭
抗住了　最后一点希望

The Last Hope

You took out your passport
To book a hotel room　　I was startled
A Chinese woman poet
Living in USA over 20 years
Still holding a
Chinese passport
It startled me to my core
Your husband was a Jew
Your sons were half-Chinese, half-Jew
Both born as Americans
Your husband wanted you
To be naturalized
Also hoped you'd convert to Judaism
At the dinner table
You talked about this
"It just doesn't feel right,"
You said, calmly. You don't feel right
Because of your poet heart
But those male poets who gloat as
national heroes, high moral ground
While in their pockets
hide another country's passport
It feels just right for them
Changing passport is like changing hats
Ah! Our nation's spine
Who made your spine
A woman, small, gentle
Holding onto our last hope
With "what feels right in the heart"

《张常氏，你的保姆》

我在一所外语学院任教
这你是知道的
我在我工作的地方
从不向教授们低头
这你也是知道的
我曾向一位老保姆致敬
闻名全校的张常氏
在我眼里
是一名真正的教授
系陕西省蓝田县下归乡农民
我一位同事的母亲
她的成就是
把一名美国专家的孩子
带了四年
并命名为狗蛋
那个金发碧眼
一把鼻涕的崽子
随其母离开中国时
满口地道秦腔
满脸中国农民式的
朴实与狡黠
真是可爱极了

Nee Zhang Chang, Your Nanny

I teach at a foreign language college
As you know
In my workplace
I bow to no professor
As you know also, but
I once bowed deeply to an old nanny
Nee Zhang Chang
Everyone on campus knows her name
In my eyes
She's a real professor
A peasant from Lantian County
Shaanxi Province
For four years, she raised
An American professor's child
Named him gou dan—dog shit
When he left China with his mom
The blue-eyed blond boy
Spoke a pure Qin dialect
His nose running, his face alive
With the simplicity and cunning
Of a Chinese peasant
What a lovely sight!

Henan (河南): Pulse of China along the Yellow River Valley

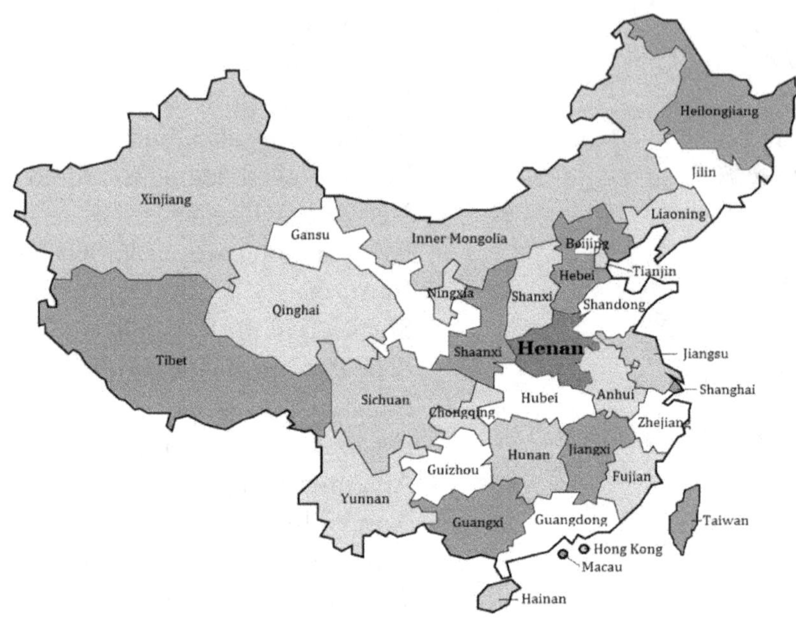

The Yellow River, China's "Mother River," carves its way through Henan, carrying vast deposits of fertile loess soil from the middle reaches. While its relentless sedimentation has caused catastrophic floods and dramatic course shifts throughout history, it has also nurtured one of the most agriculturally rich and culturally significant regions in China.

Henan's lands have been inhabited since prehistoric times, with archaeological discoveries revealing the advanced Yangshao and Longshan cultures—early societies of farmers, hunters, and fishers who domesticated animals like dogs and pigs. This is also the legendary homeland of Huangdi, the Yellow Emperor (2697–2597 BCE), a mythical sovereign and cultural hero revered as a foundational figure in Chinese civilization.

As the cradle of China's earliest dynasties—the Xia (c. 2070 BCE), Shang (c. 1600 BCE), and Zhou (c. 1046 BCE)—Henan was a political and cultural heartland for millennia. Four of China's ancient capitals—Luoyang, Anyang, Kaifeng, and Zhengzhou—flourished here, serving as epicenters of power, trade, and artistry during the Han, Tang, Wei, Jin, and Song dynasties.

These cities attracted legendary poets whose works immortalized the landscape and shaped China's cultural psyche, much like the Yellow River's silt shaped its fertile plains.

Henan was home for China's finest poets: Du Fu (712–770 CE), Li Shangyin (813–858 CE), Bai Juyi (772–846 CE), and many others. The "Father of Idyllic Poetry," Tao Qian (365 – 427 CE), also hailed from Xinyang, Henan. His "Returning to Dwell in Gardens and Fields" celebrates rural simplicity, rejecting courtly pretensions: "I pluck chrysanthemums beneath the eastern hedge / And gaze afar at the southern mountains." The poetry of Henan played the most influential role in China's poetic and cultural landscape.

Henan's spiritual legacy is equally profound. The Shaolin Temple, nestled at the foot of Songshan Mountain, stands as one of China's most iconic sites—not only as the birthplace of Chan (Zen) Buddhism and martial arts, but also as a testament to the Northern Wei Dynasty's religious patronage (built in 495 CE).

Today, Henan remains a living museum of China's heritage, where the echoes of poets, monks, and emperors resonate across its timeless plains. From Du Fu's lamentations to Ban Ruo's avant-garde verses, the province's voice continues to evolve, anchored by the Yellow River.

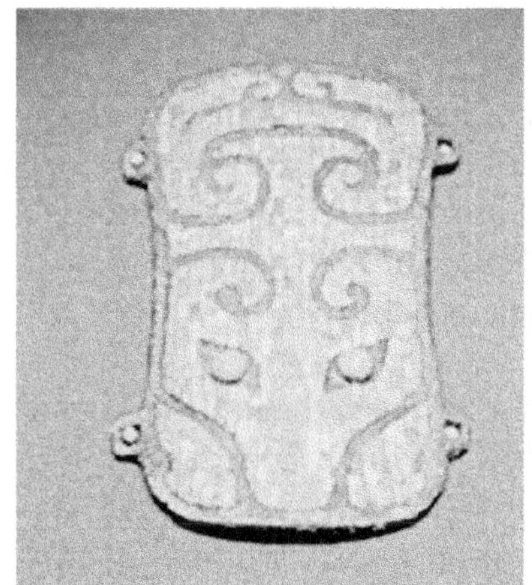 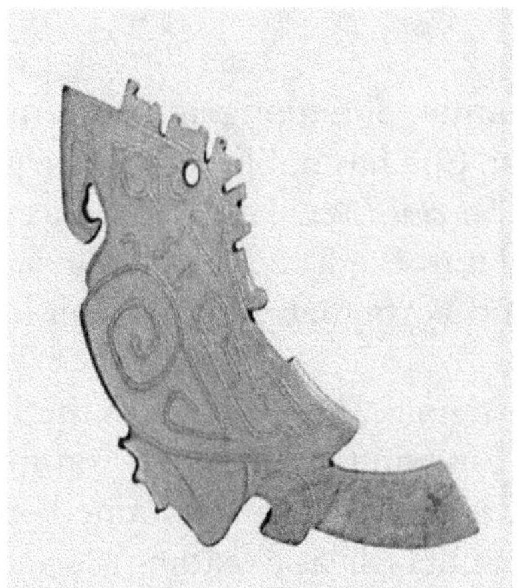 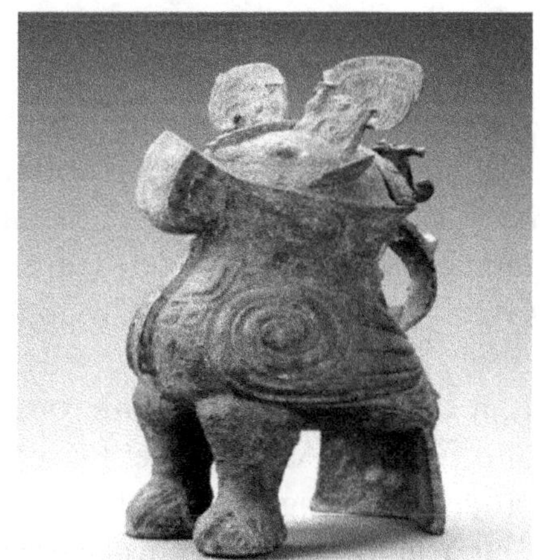

Artifacts from Yangshao and Longshan cultures, 5000-3000 BCE

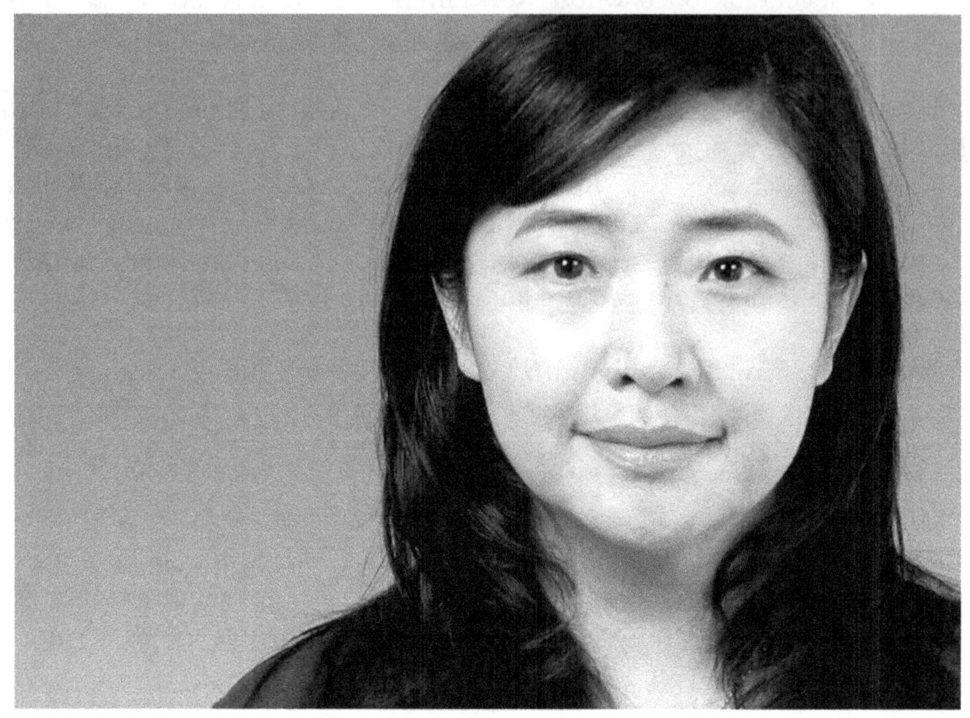

Lan Lan (蓝蓝), born in 1967 in Yantai, Shandong, is a celebrated Chinese poet and essayist who spent much of her life in Henan. She has published twelve poetry collections, including *Serenade* (小夜曲), *Psalter* (诗篇), and *Selected Poems* (诗歌选集), as well as several essay collections. Her work has been widely translated into English, French, Russian, Spanish, German, Japanese, Greek, Dutch (Belgian), Croatian, and Portuguese, earning her international acclaim.

Lan Lan has received numerous prestigious awards, such as the Liu Li'an Poetry Prize, the Poetry and People's Annual Poet Prize, the Bingxin Children's Literature New Writings Prize, and others. In recognition of her literary influence, she was named one of "China's New Century Top Ten Young Women Poets," cementing herself as a leading voice in contemporary Chinese poetry.

请和我谈谈幸福

请和我谈谈幸福。请坐在树下
透过枸桃黑黝黝的枝叶
星星在颤抖
孩子们的喧闹声低了
蛐蛐儿的弦歌更亮

请和我谈谈幸福。灶火旁
农妇的脸闪着柴草彤红的光芒
一绺灰发温顺地垂下
羊倌老汉的嘴在酒盅上
咂砸作响

请和我谈谈幸福，在天穹下
牲口们嚼着夜间的草料
你习惯于微笑的嘴角
——它藏起了多少事情
——默不作声

Let's Talk About Happiness

Please talk about happiness with me. Please sit
under the tree, through wolfberry leaves
The stars tremble
Children have lowered their noise
Crickets chirp louder, brighter

Let's talk about happiness. By the stove,
fire flickers on the face of the farmer's wife
A strand of gray hair dangling down
The old shepherd makes sucking noises
As he sips wine

Let's talk about happiness, under the sky
Animals are chewing night grass
You're used to my smiles
—so much hidden in the silence
—in the corners of my mouth

你当然可以说

你当然可以说："人没什么可自大的。
对于蛇来说, 到处都是路。
鸟飞在空中需要路吗?
还有鱼, 在大海里。"
你望着楼后面的村庄
黄豆地里升起的淡淡的雾霭, 蓝色的——
如此清澈。瓜园, 菜地, 人们在土里刨出
滚圆的红薯。灼热的太阳点燃了玉米的
红缨子, 并在蒿草上催生浓烈的香气——
你抓住笔, 说着, 写着
攀援到这座城市的楼顶,
并在天空的深处
找到一张稿纸——能放进这一切的——
正是这个样子。

Of Course You Can Say

Of course you can say: "People aren't a big deal.
For snakes, there are paths everywhere.
For birds, do they need roads in the sky?
For fish, highways in the sea?"
You gaze at the village behind the buildings
The mist is rising from the soybean fields, blue——
So clear. Gardens, vegetable pads, out of the earth
plump yams. The hot sun sets corns' red tassels
on fire, Artemisia giving wafts of fragrance——
You grab a pen as you speak and write
As you climb to the top of the city building,
to seek a piece of paper
in the deep sky—to fit everything inside——
Just like this.

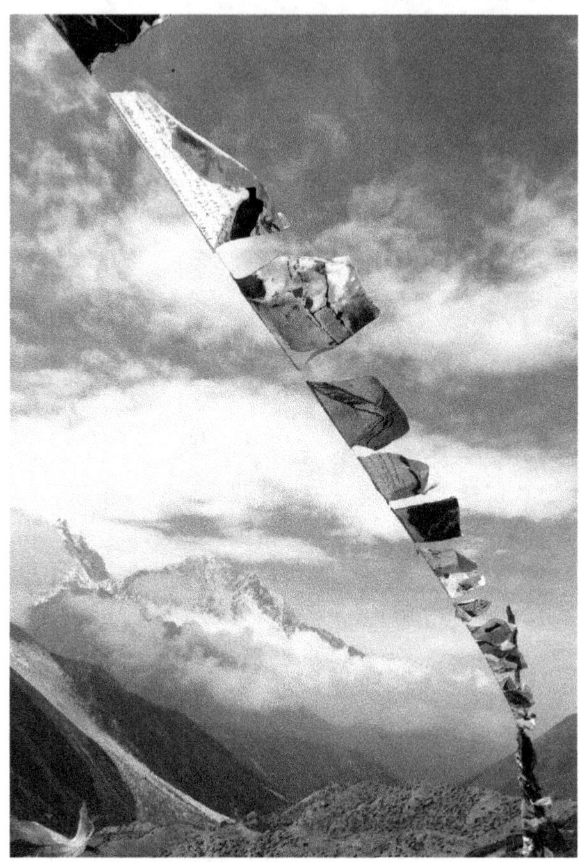

Prayer flags over Everest

矿工

一切过于耀眼的，都源于黑暗。

井口边你羞涩的笑洁净、克制
你礼貌，手躲开我从都市
带来的寒冷。

藏满煤屑的指甲，额头上的灰尘
你的黑减弱了黑的幽暗；

作为剩余，你却发出真正的光芒
在命运升降不停的罐笼和潮湿的掌子面

钢索嗡嗡地绷紧了。我猜测
你匍匐的身体像地下水
正流过黑暗的河床……

此时，是我悲哀于从没有扑进你的视线
在词语的废墟和熄灭矿灯的纸页间，是我

既没有触碰到麦穗的绿色火焰
也无法把一座矸石山安置在沉沉笔尖。

Coal Miner at Hebi

Everything bright comes from darkness.

At the well, your shy smile is clean
Controlled and polite, your hand dodges
mine, cold from the city.

Coal dust in your nails and forehead
Your darkness makes darkness less dim:

You're an extra, shining a true light
As you rise and fall in the wet shaft
In the cage of destiny

The cable tightens with hums. I imagine
Your body crawling like running water
in a black bed…

You've never let my sorrow into your world
Between the ruins of language ruins and
Extinguished mining lamps, I've never

Touched the green flames of wheat or
Settled a coal mine on the tip of my pen.

Shandong (山东): A Wandering Delta

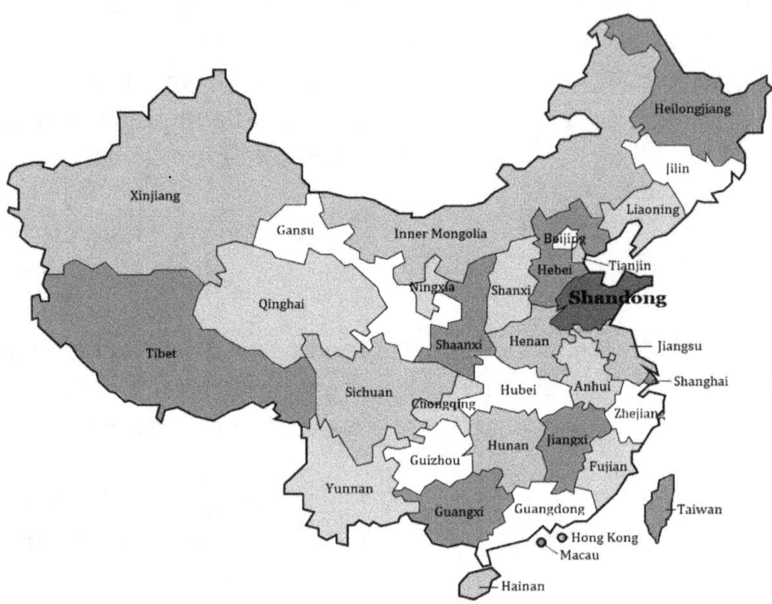

In Shandong, the Yellow River spills into the Bohai Sea, carrying wind, soil and water from the Qinghai-Tibet Plateau, the Loess Plateau, and the plains. Its muddy currents fertilize Shandong, bringing floods, breaching dams, carving new paths across the delta every couple centuries. Over time, the river has shifted its course up and down the coast by hundreds of kilometers.

During the Ming Dynasty, the Yellow diverted into the Huai and merged with the Yangtze. Each change was caused by silt buildup, devastating the delta with catastrophic ruin. In 1976, China undertook its first major rechanneling project at Qingshuigou, followed by another in 1996. Since then, the Yellow River has remained contained within its delta.

Shandong is the fastest-growing delta in the world, thanks to relentless sediment deposition. The present delta, centered in Dongying, spans 18,000 km² and is home to 5.2 million people. Every year, it expands into the sea at the rate of 2.2 km per year, adding 3,240 hectares of new land.

Humans have inhabited this delta for over 7,000 years. Shandong is the birthplace of Confucius (孔子) and Mencius (孟子), whose philosophies on governance, education, and culture have shaped China for millennia. It is also home to the legendary calligrapher Wang Xizhi (王羲之) and poets Li Qingzhao (李清照) and Xin Qiji (辛弃疾). Like the wandering river and its ever-growing delta, these figures often wandered, fleeing famine or political turmoil, yet they always carried Shandong with them. No matter where they went, they never lost their dialects or forgot their homes. The Yellow River flows in their veins, just as it does through every Chinese heart.

My father and his ancestors were born here, living for generations in this land. At 14, he left to fight the Japanese invaders and never returned. Yet I know he never forgot his roots. Shandong and its coastline are his ancestral home—and mine too. It lives in my dreams and poetry, a grounding force that has sustained me all these years.

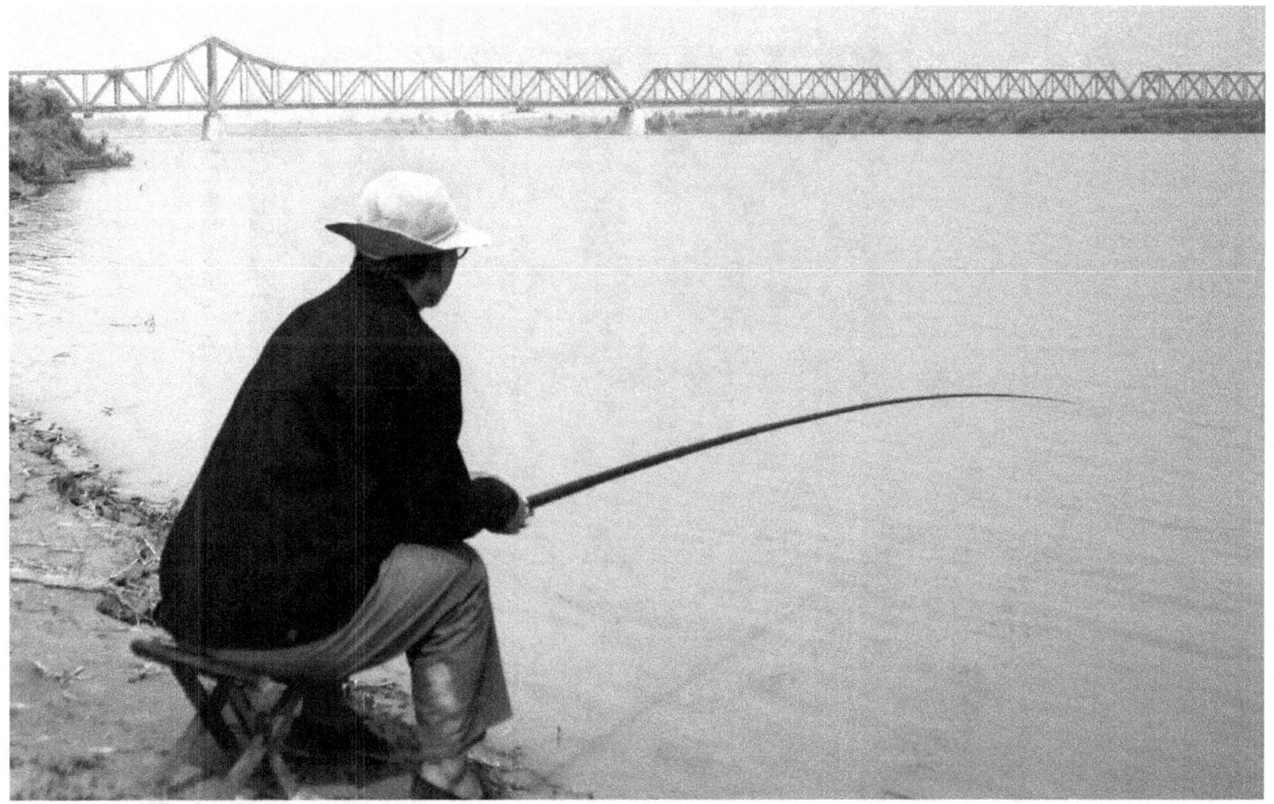

The Yellow River flowing through Jinan, capital of Shandong, 2005

Feng Qiang (冯强), an acclaimed poet from Shandong Province, is a professor of Creative Writing at Qingdao University. He has published critical essays on poetry, such as his analysis of Liu Ting's novella collection *All the Winds Blow Toward Them* (所有的风只向她们吹) and Hua Qing's poetry collection, *The Formalist Garden* (形式主义的花园), discussing themes of melancholy and historical consciousness in contemporary Chinese poetry. His new book, *The Eyes Can Only See What the Heart Understands* (眼睛只能看到心愿意理解的事), explores storytelling and literary aesthetics in children's literature.

In 2023, we engaged in a vibrant cross-cultural dialogue on Eastern and Western poetry at Good Friend Bookstore—Qingdao's premier destination for poetry lovers. The event, attended by hundreds of poetry fans, explored the nuances, traditions, and evolving landscapes of poetic expression across cultures.

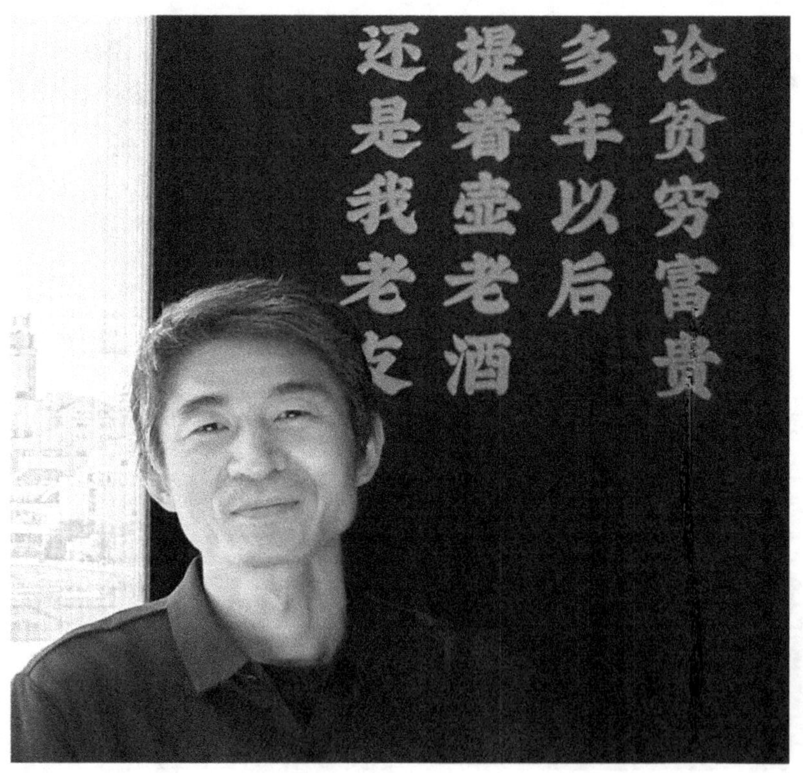

洗碗的快乐

妹妹病了，爸爸下楼买药
妈妈陪在妹妹床头讲故事
我收拾碗筷，餐桌抹得干干净净
流水淌在油腻的盘子上，不一会儿
就放出白白的光。我好想水龙头
冲洗一下今晚的月亮
那么大，那么圆
上面也有一些污垢
好像是谁家的盘子忘了洗
也好像是月亮病了
等着爸爸带回的药

The Joy of Washing Dishes

Sister is sick, Daddy is out to buy medicine
Mama is reading a story at her bed
I gather dirty dishes, clean the table
Water runs on greasy plates, and soon
They shine brightly. I wish the tap water
Could also wash the moon tonight
So big, so round
With some stains on it
As if someone forgot to wash the dishes
As if the moon got sick
Waiting for Daddy to bring home medicine

一次悬停

绿翼蜂鸟悬停于半空
童年的某个半空
分不清幻象还是事实：
北方故乡的臭菊丛中，蜂鸟卷起
细长的舌萃取花蜜。那时，我也有了
五百次的心跳. 伸出去——将要握紧的手
待触发的战争，慑于它的名字，又几次
松开, 如同上紧的发条
花丛兴奋着，释放馥郁的芬香
蜂鸟的退行，获得一段
开阔的距离，又前进
重新把舌头卷入
花蕊的羞赧。迅疾，准确，
双翼鼓荡　　像涌出的泉水。
我看见自己　　悬于半空的恐慌
以及回响至今的
寂静轰鸣

Hanging

A green-winged hummingbird hangs in midair,
a moment in my childhood.
I can't tell if it's real or imagined:
In chrysanthemums by my home, a hummingbird
was lapping nectar with its long tongue. My heart
was beating 500 a minute, my hand reaching out—
a fist, a war about to break out. But in fear, the fist
loosened up like a spring, winding, unwinding.
The flowers are excited, giving out thick fragrance.
The hummingbird retreats, making
an open distance, then forward again
Its tongue entering the
heart of the flower. Quick, accurate,
wings full like rushing spring water.
I watch myself   hanging in midair,
a thundering silence
throughout my life

学习的快乐-周日读《普鲁斯特与符号》

上午的阅读多么愉悦，在校园
一间我从未到过的平房外，天竺桂的干
昏暗中虬曲，向上，甚至在发亮。
一连三个小时，女儿在老师留下的
素描前描摹。我在门外来回踱步：
跌入德勒兹的洞见，我激动着，
甚至需要短暂离开此地，去更远的
职师学院解手. 我不理解我的身体，
也许不停地走动，才能把读到的文字
消化？雨是稀稀落落的
夫子灰黑的塑像同样被染得清亮
他们都曾谈论"学"

下午送女儿学拉丁舞。
等在门口，多想一口气读完。
没去漫猫咖啡，因为珍惜
头顶的太阳，却一个字也看不进——
我被囚禁于一片嗡响中。
盯住广场的蹦床：一个小姑娘害怕，
系在半空，向妈妈求助，妈妈按住
她的肩膀，往下。脚尖触及床面的瞬间，
一股欢乐兴起，又下坠……腾空
而起的美感，只需要一个向下的力
就可以俯瞰自己的一生。径直翻到
书的最后一面：从网的一端，
蜘蛛接收最微小的颤动。
没有眼睛鼻子也没有嘴。
仅是刹那的颤动，就引导它扑向猎物。
另一个男孩，已经准备脱鞋，系安全带，
我早已看到他飞腾起来，
把紫颜色封面的书
锁进后备箱。剩下的时间
就是走啊走。就是吃掉这些文字。
它们是绷紧的床面，颤动着，
把我弹向另一程学习。
脚步声会丈量 地面，教给它新的无知。
而不管走向哪里,下课之前都要回来，
一切方向都是正确。

The Joy of Learning—Reading Deleuze

A pleasant morning to read, outside the campus,
by the house I've never seen, cinnamon trees
twisting at twilight, upward, shining.
For three hours, my daughter has been sketching
under the teacher's watchful eye. I pace till
I fall into the thoughts of Deleuze. I'm excited.
I need to leave this place, for a washroom in the
Teachers' Academy. I don't understand my body,
maybe I need keep walking to digest what I'm
reading? It's drizzling. The dark
statue of Confucius shines.
Both men talked about "learning."

Afternoon, I take my daughter for Latin dance.
Out the door, I yearn to finish Deleuze in a sitting.
I skip Cat Café, because I treasure the sunlight,
but I can't get in a single word—
imprisoned by white noise. I stare at the
trampoline in the square: a little girl, afraid of
hanging, begs Mama to help. Mama holds her
daughter's shoulders. The moment her feet touch
the trampoline, joy leaps up, down…the beauty of
rising takes only one push down, and that's enough
to have a bird's view of life. I turn to the book's
last page: the spider feels the tiniest tremble
from the other side of the web.
No eyes, nose or mouth.
Just that tremble, ready to jump on its prey.
Another boy takes off his shoes, buckles his belt.
I see him fly up,
locking my purple book
in my trunk. The only thing left to do is walk,
digest the words. They are the taut trampolines
trembling, to shoot me into another journey.
My footsteps measure all the ignorance on earth.
Whatever direction I choose, I must return
before my daughter's lesson, and
all directions are the right directions.

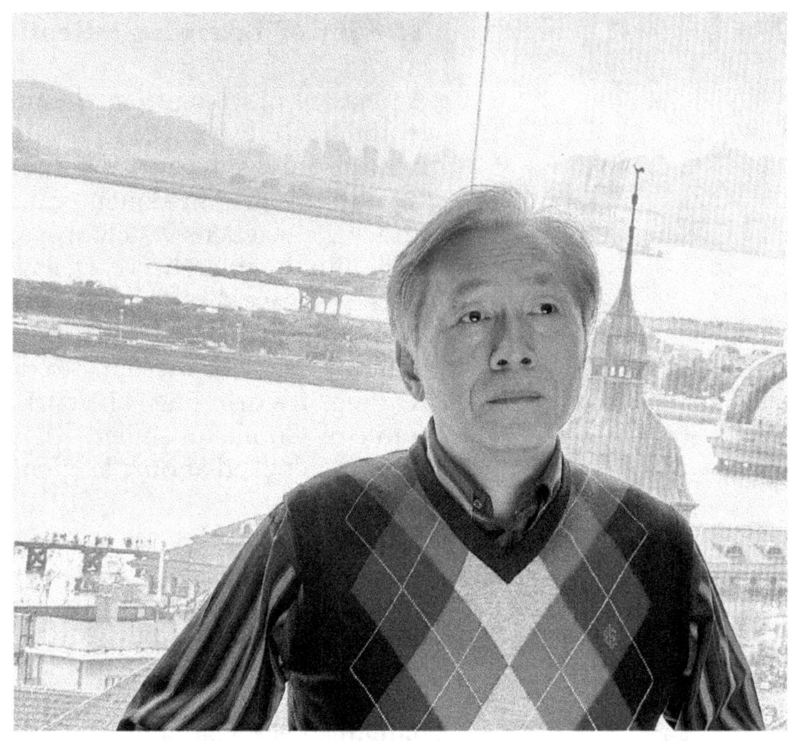

Gao Jiangang (高剑钢) is an acclaimed poet and fiction writer from Qingdao, China. His work has been published in leading literary journals such as *Harvest* (收获), *People's Literature* (人民文学), *Chinese Writers* (中国作家), *Modern Era* (时代文学), and *Poetry* (诗刊). His published books include *Hanging Garden* (悬挂的花园, a poetry collection) and *Watch* (表, a fiction collection).

A prominent figure in China's literary scene, Gao is a member of the Chinese Writers Association, President of the Qingdao Writers' Association, and the Editor-in-Chief of *Qingdao Literature* (青岛文学). His writing often explores urban life, memory, and the interplay between tradition and modernity, earning him recognition for his lyrical yet incisive style.

We first connected through literary translation during the COVID-19 pandemic, bridging cultures despite global isolation. In 2023, I had the pleasure of meeting him in his hometown of Qingdao, where he generously introduced me to the city's rich history, vibrant bookstores, and, of course, famed seafood. He also facilitated my encounter with Qingdao's dynamic literary community, including the talented young poet Feng Qiang.

那是藤椅中的我

冬天树枝的狂草写满窗户
一块调色盘上的蓝色
在红瓦顶之间，那是海
油轮很长时间才能通过
有人长久伫立，那是路灯
保持花园小径的沉默
一块石头落下，那是麻雀
接着落下一群叫声
它们是树木唯一的叶儿
有一只停在窗上，那是塑钢窗
锁扣，紧紧别住冬天
有件白衬衫，那是暖气片
正虚构另外的春天
有张脸，那是石英钟
记录着虚假时间
有片云，那是咖啡杯口的蒸气
让我想起热带雨林的木香
有杯红葡萄酒，那是暗红色地板
在显示屏和桌面之间演化着黎明
有件雕塑，那是藤椅中的我
正在试着把自己摇醒

That's Me in That Vine Chair

Winter scrawls crazy choreography
On the window: a blue color on the plate
It's an ocean on the red-tiled roof
Oil barges take so long to sail by
Someone has been standing there
It's a street light keeping the garden quiet
A stone falls, that's a sparrow
Followed by a school of bird cries
They're the last leaves on trees
One of them stops on the window
but it's just a lock to keep winter out
There's a white shirt, oh, it's a radiator
Pretending it's another spring
There's a face, oh it's a crystal clock
Running on imagined time.
There's a cloud, it's steam from coffee reminding
me of the fragrance in rain forests. There's a
glass of red wine, but it's just a burgundy floor,
brewing dawn between screen and table top.
There's a statue, that's me in the vine chair
Trying to rock myself awake

大海与钢琴调律师

那天，他提着黑色工具箱
来到沙滩上
他要给大海
这架蓝色钢琴调调音
他听出大海
总是重复的和弦音　不准

他俯身想把松了的白色琴键
拆下来
刚一使劲
就被涌起的巨浪吞没

从此海里多了一支
蓝色幻想曲

The Sea and Piano Tuner

He took his black toolbox
To the beach
To tune up
The ocean's blue piano
He heard the sea
Was out of tune, repeated chords

He bent over to take apart
The loosened white keys
He just started working
When giant waves swallowed him

And the ocean gained another
Rhapsody in Blue

夜已降临

楼下那棵无花果树
一夜间开满红色的花
那是一辆红轿车等待新娘在树下
一片白云遮天，那是窗外的白墙
隔开各自的家园；墙沿上一只白猫
那是生锈的空调，让主人感冒头疼加咳嗽
有人抽烟斗，那是阁楼
两扇黑暗圆窗和排油烟筒构成的脸庞
远处有人撕心裂肺吵架
那是狗咬狗的犬吠
接着两声滚雷，房屋震动
飘来大片乌云，要下雨了
继而手机响起铃声
那是救护车疾驰的笛鸣
打开微信，才知道错错错
那是地下管道的爆炸声
然后是生者与死者的混淆

一盏路灯在交错的建筑之间
亮了.那是初升的明月
夜已降临

The Night Is Upon Us

Downstairs the fig tree blossoms
overnight with red flowers
Under the tree, a red limo waiting
for the bride, a white cloud covers the sky, a wall
separating families; on top sits a white cat
rusty AC, causing coughs and headaches,
Someone is smoking a pipe, the face made with
the attic's round windows and smoke vent.
At a distance people are fighting
at the top of their lungs
Oh but that's just dogs barking
Then two thunders, shaking the house
Dark clouds rolling in, it's about to rain
Then my phone rings and ambulance sirens
I open my WeChat, realize I was wrong
all wrong. The pipes underground just exploded.
The living and dead are all mixed up

A street light appears among buildings
But that is the rising moon
The night is upon us

Wang Ping (王屏), was born and raised in Shanghai, where the Yangtze River meets the East China Sea—the land of her mother and maternal ancestors. Though her official ancestral hometown is recorded as Weihai, Shandong (where the Yellow River pours into the Bohai Sea and her father's lineage traces back), she did not set foot in Shandong until 2005. The moment she touched its soil and water, she felt an undeniable connection: she was a daughter of the Yellow River, the Yellow Plateau, the Yellow Emperor, the yellow dragon.

The Yangtze nurtured her like a mother. The Yellow River flowed in her veins, an unseen current, her laojia (老家, "old home"), the hidden Y-chromosome of her identity.

Wang Ping has published 15 books of poetry, prose, cultural studies, and children books, which have won awards such as the AWP Book Award, Minnesota Book Award, Asian American Book Awards, Eugene Kayden Award for the Best Book in Humanities, the NEA, McKnight and Bush Artist Fellowships for Poetry and Prose, and many others. Deeply engaged with themes of migration, belonging, and cultural memory, her work explores the intersections of geography, lineage, and personal history, weaving together the voices of rivers, ancestors, and the self. She is the founder and director of Kinship of Rivers, a project that connects all the rivers and seas together through poetry, art and music.

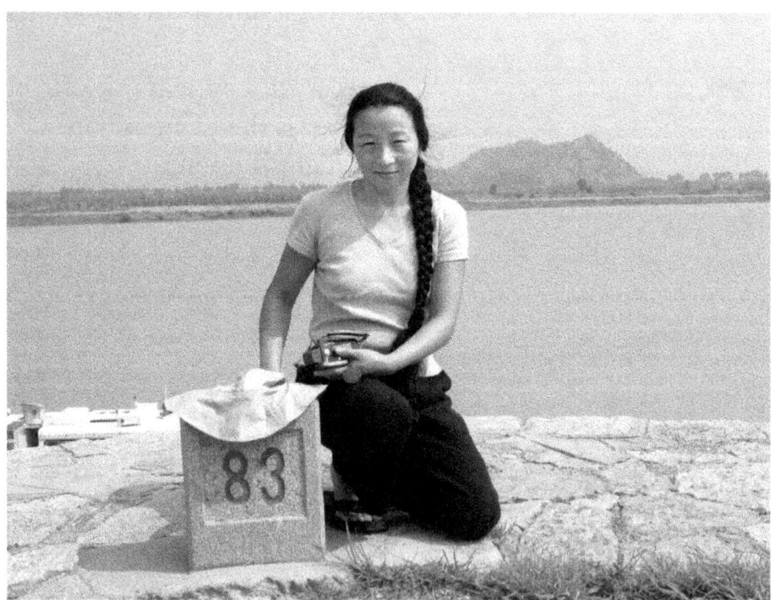

The Yellow River flowing through Jinan, capital of Shandong, 2005

Lao Jia 老家 Old Home

At fifteen, my father ran away from his widowed mother to fight the Japanese.

"I'll come back with a PhD and serve my country with better English and knowledge,"
I pledged at the farewell party in Beijing.

Home—家—Jia: a roof under which animals live.

> When asked where I'm from,
> I say "Weihai," even though
> nobody knows where it is,
> even though I've never been to the place.

He lost his left ear in a bayonet fight with a Japanese soldier. Two years later, American cannons split his eardrums.

The night I arrived at JFK, the Mets won the World Series and the noise on the street went on till dawn. I got up and went to work in my sponsor's antique shop in Manhattan.

The bag lady stopped her cart on the busy street and peed onto a subway grate.

"Did you jump or fly?" asked my landlady from her majiang table. Then she laughed and told me that her husband had jumped ship ten years ago. When he opened his fifth Chinese take-out, he bought her a passport and flew her to Queens.

The only thing he liked to talk about was his old home, Weihai, its plump sea cucumbers and sweet apples, men with broad shoulders, and girls with long braids making steamed bread.

"Back home, I had no money, but I never felt poor," she said, shivering behind her fruit stand. "Here, if my money goes down below four figures, I panic." She scanned the snow-covered streets of Chinatown. "I guess I really don't want to be homeless here."

I hired the babysitter when she mentioned her hometown was Weihai.

The president visited the rice paddies in Vietnam where a pilot had been downed thirty-three years ago.

My father tried to return to Weihai after his discharge from the Navy. With his rank, he could find work only in a coalmine town nearby. Mother refused to go. He went alone, and got sick with TB. Mother ordered me to date the county administrator's son so Father could come home.

"No, I'm not sad." The street kid shook her head.
"How can I miss something I've never had?"

On her sixtieth birthday, my grandma went home to die, sailing from the island to Shanghai, from Shanghai to Yantai, then two buses to Weihai. I carried her onto the big ship at the Shanghai Port, down to the bottom, where she'd spend three days on a mattress, on the floor, with hundreds of fellow passengers. "How are you going to make it, Grandma?" I asked. She pulled out a pair of embroidered shoes from her parcel and placed them between my feet and said, "My Heart and Liver, come home soon, before it's too late."

House—房—fang: a door over a square, a place, a direction.

He never lost his accent, never learned Mandarin or the island dialect.

Weihai, a small city in Shandong Province,
on the coast of the North China Sea, a home,
where my grandfather and his father were born,
where my grandma married, raised her children,
now lies in the yam fields, nameless, next to her husband,
an old frontier to fend off Japanese pirates, a place I didn't see
till I turned 48. It's my 老家 laojia, old home.

Back from America, my mother furnished her home on the island, bought an apartment in a suburb of Shanghai, and is seeking a third one in Beijing. "A cunning rabbit needs three holes," she wrote to us, demanding our contributions.

They swore, before boarding the ship, that they'd send money home to bring more relatives over; in return, they were promised that if they died, their bodies would be sent back home for burial.

I drink American milk—a few drops in tea.
I eat American rice—Japanese brand.

Chinese comes to me only in dreams--in black-and-white pictures.

My mother buried her husband on the island, where he lived for forty years.

Room—屋—wu: a body unnamed and homeless until it finds a destination.

We greet a stranger with:
"Where are you from?"
When we meet a friend on the street, we say,
"Where have you been? Where are you going?"

家—a roof under which animals live
房—a door over a square, a place, a direction
屋—a body unnamed and homeless until it finds a destination

—my tangled roots for old home.

My Father and His Flag Signals

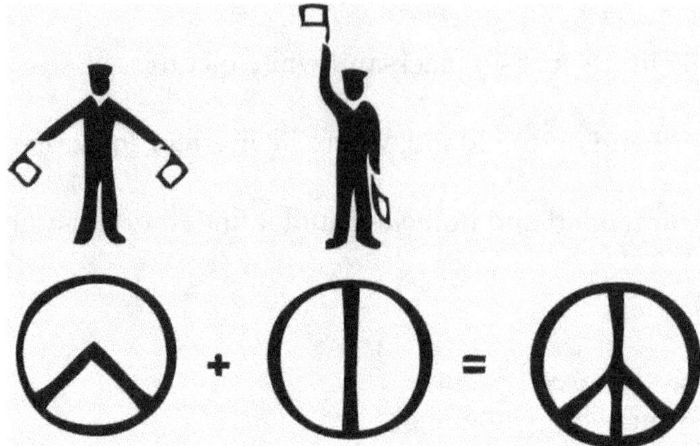

I didn't know my father was handsome till my brother shared a photo of him recently.

He was most likely in his early 30, judging from the ages of my sisters in the photo. He stood in the back with his sister and brother in laws, at the narrow alley of an old Shanghai building, where my grandma lived with her husband, 4 grown children, 2 grandchildren, in a small room on the 4th floor.

My father must have borrowed a camera from his friend, must have convinced his mother-in-law to come downstairs, dressed in her best.

I was on the island in the East China Sea, with Nainai, father's ma, tending a big garden and raising 12 chickens. The Cultural Revolution had started. Food was in shortage again. Dad was bringing seafood to his favorite girls in Shanghai: my sisters and my beautiful aunt.

My memory of father is vague. He was always away, patrolling the sea as one of China's first Navy Captains. When he came home, usually at dawn, he'd spend most of his time with Mom. Later when my sister and brother grew, he spent time with them, because my brother was his only son, and my sister was the beauty of the island.
I was his first-born. Three days after my birth, mom sent me to her mom, who hired a wet nurse. Mom just turned 18, didn't know what to do with me.

Father was stationed in Shanghai then, trained to become a Navy officer for the East China Sea Fleet. He met Mom at a party and they fell in love. He was 25, she was 17. He had a fiancée in the north, arranged by his ma, before he left home at 16 to fight Japanese. She'd been waiting for him to marry her. She was still a virgin, even though by tradition, she'd been married for 9 years.

Nainai rushed to Shanghai from her village in Shandong, on her bound feet, demanding his son to go home and carry out his duty as husband to the chosen girl.

Nainai was a strong woman, widowed when her sons were 5 and 3. She never married again, raised her kids on her own, on "golden-lotus" feet, with her hands as a farmer and mid-wife.

My father was a filial son. But he loved this beautiful seventeen-year-old Shanghai girl who played piano, sang and danced, who just graduated from high school, on her way to become the first college girl in China.

She had me instead, ending her college dream.

I remember growing up with my grandparent. Their small room on the 4th floor had two big beds, one dining table, a chamber pot, two uncles, two aunts…I remember the laughter, cries, smells of food and chamber pot, and the funny stories of me being a constipated baby.

I remember glimpses of father, carrying bags of rice and flour during the three-year starvation. His army rations kept them alive, while millions of Chinese starved to death.

I remember the garlic smell. Father couldn't eat his food without garlic. How awkward he was around my aunt, a beautiful girl with an engineer degree, with a beautiful voice.

Grandma called him Old Shandong, country bumpkin, mule, donkey, honest to a fault.

She told me how I was exactly like my father, stubborn, silent and strong like a mule.
I don't remember how he looked, even after he took me back on the island in the East China Sea.

He came home at dawn, once a month, then vanished into the sea, until his next visit.

When he was home, he'd get up before dawn and bike to the market. Two hours later, he'd return with a full basket of vegetables, toufu, fish, meat, eggs. We ate well when he was home.

I remember mom's laughter when he was around. She was too busy to scold or punish us.

I remember his voice, his accent that he could never shed, like all the men from Shandong, no matter how far they wandered.

I remember his singing, low and rumbling like an earthquake, with perfect pitch and accent. He loved "The International," "East Is Red," "Sailing in the Sea," "Midnight at Moscow." Once I heard him hum a strange song to the tune of the famous song "My Country."

> 在佛兰德的田野里，罂粟摇摆
> 夹在十字架间，一排接着一排，
> 标明我们的家；天空里
> 百灵鸟勇敢的歌唱，好像
> 听不见下面的枪响

I remember the immense sorrow from the words he hummed. I knew the tune well, but never heard the lyrics. My instincts told me I must not ask, must keep it quiet.

But the sounds of "佛兰德": folande, flander, forande, became a ticking enigma in my ear. I knew it must be English. I decided to learn the language to solve the secret.

One year father didn't come home. Mom lost her job teaching music. Nainai started teaching me how to garden in the backyard, how to raise chickens and hatch chicks. We also raised silkworms. My sister roasted grasshoppers and showed the Navy rats how to eat them like popcorn. She became the kids' leader.

I refused to touch them, no matter how hungry. I refused to eat chicken. They were my pets. Mom and sister called me dumb, as they grabbed my portion of chicken and eggs.

Father loved three women: his mom, his wife, and my sister, his second daughter.

Oh, he also loved my aunt, secretly. I found her photo in his notebook, locked in his drawer. Mom was jealous of her sister, smarter, gentler, prettier, a college graduate in engineering.

Aunt didn't marry till 45. She had many suitors but grandma kept her home for her salary.

I remember father sighed over her fate, tried to introduce many handsome Navy officers to her.

Finally, he sent her his youngest girl, five months old, to be raised as her own daughter.

Grandma believed smart beautiful women like aunt are better off being alone, like my Great Grandma, her mother-in-law.

She was one of the first girls to graduate from high school in China, and established the first girl school in Shanghai. She never married, adopted her nephew, my grandpa, as her son.

Mom said my passion for education and adventure came from my great grandma.

I am the black sheep who left China for a PhD, became a professor, author, artist.

I remember mom went away for a month, to visit father in Fuling. China was digging tunnels for nuclear wars. Father was sent to Sichuan to build factories in the deep mountains of Fuling.

She came home sad. Father was severely ill. She had to bring him back.

He finally came home, on a stretcher, straight to the Navy hospital. He had surgeries for his stomach ulcer and intestine bleedings. He also had Hepatitis B.

I remember his long recovery at home, his quarrels with mom, over money, over his new habits of smoking and drinking. Both started as remedies to cure his illness, like smoking cigarettes inserted in an apple, reishi soaked in white spirit. But soon he seemed to lose control.

I remember him taking us to the woods to search for reishi mushrooms. Sister found three. I got nothing. I was distracted…

Watching father gaze at the sea from the mountain top, feet apart, hands open by his sides, arms forming an upside down V.

I remember him standing in this position at dawn, always facing the sea, as if he were praying.

I remember my heart aching. I knew what he was praying for. I knew what it felt like, as a child, to pine for an impossible dream.

Father worked in the Navy Headquarter after he returned from Sichuan, having lost 4/5 of his stomach. He hated sitting in the office, though he never said a word about it.

He smoked and drank to drown his longing. But the longing was drowning him faster.

I had the dream for college since I was five. The Cultural Revolution shattered it.

I remember how he ended his prayer each time: right arm raised to sky, left hand to earth.

He looked like some sort of messenger, sending a secret code to heaven.

He also resembled the metal rod on a building, receiving lightning from the sky.

I started doing it myself, whenever my pining became unbearable: feet apart, arms down, an upside down V, then one hand to sky, the other to earth.

I didn't know what it was, but it seemed to lift the dead weight off my chest.

I remember father's swollen face, after being sprayed by a rattle snake. He was looking for snake gallbladders to cure my facial fungi, a folk recipe.

We used lots of folk recipes then, like injecting rooster blood, kombucha…medicine was scarce, like food and books.

He caught two snakes in the woods, processed them and told me to swallow the gallbladders. They floated darkly in his reishi mushroom extract, soaked in white spirit for three months.

My face did clear up, before his swollen face subsided. I suddenly transformed into a girl with smooth skin, bright eyes, shining dark hair.

I remember his sigh of relief. I remember his hand on my head: "You got our Shandong girl's braids, thick and pretty!"

Father loved everything from Weihai, Shandong, his old home by Bohai Sea, where Chinese fought off Japanese pirates for hundreds of years, till they lost the 甲午 battle in the cruel April of 1895, which marked the fast downfall of Qing Dynasty. It marked Japan colonizing Taiwan till the end of WWII, Germany colonizing Dalian and Qingdao, Russia taking huge chunks of Chinese land, including Li Po's hometown, Britain colonizing Hongkong till 1997… It marked China being cut up, colonized and invaded by the imperialist countries till 1949.

At 16, no 14, by the western calculation, my father left his ma and wife, to defend his homeland, to avenge his father killed by the Japanese invaders.

He learned how to read and write in the army, and became a captain in his twenties.

He was a typical 山东大汉, man from Shandong, tall and broad, with strong calves, quads and gluteus. He never lost his accent, even though he left home at 14.

He loved garlic, steamed bread and apples from Weihai. He treasured the sea cucumbers at the bottom of the sea, from Weihai. Oh, he loved dumplings, of course, with dark fragrant vinegar, like every Chinaman.

He loved beautiful women, his ma, his wife, his children.

I remember him asking mom: "Has our oldest daughter gotten her period yet? She's fourteen. Her younger sister has already started. It's getting a bit worrisome."

I remember feeling embarrassed and warm all at once. Dad cared about me. He did!

And he loved his ship, his beloved East China Sea where he sailed twenty years.

I remember taking his ship to visit grandma in Shanghai, a special treat. It was gray, rusty, smaller than a passenger ship. I slept in his bunkbed overnight. It was small and tidy. Father stayed up in his quarter deck. At daybreak, we arrived. He took me to a bus stop, paid my fare, and handed me two baskets of bay berries, one for grandma, one for aunt and youngest sister. "Tell them I'll come later," he said, "with dried fish and seaweed."
I knew he'd come, with the precious seafood, to see my grandma, aunt and sister, all cooped in one room where three generations ate, studied, slept, fought and loved each other.

Father was a man of his word. He taught me how to keep my word.

"Word matters. If you can't keep it, don't say it," he told me.

The island we lived on, Zhoushan Island, was known for fishing: crabs, shrimp, yellow croakers, squid, piling like hills on the market…East China Sea used to be the richest fishing ground, until it was depleted from overfishing. Most of the fish on markets are farm raised.

Everything was rationed then, cloth, rice, oil, meat, toufu, sugar, matches…except for seafood, on the island.

Grandma, aunts and uncles loved seafood. They loved father's honesty, generosity and stubbornness, secretly, I think, when they called him "lao Shandong," jokingly.

I remember how my beautiful aunt smiled every time Father visited Shanghai.

I remember her singing the strange song with him. The duet made me weep, even though I had no idea what they were singing, and why.

我们死了。几天前
我们还活着，感受黎明、夕阳的温暖，
我们爱，也被人爱，现在我们躺在
佛兰德的田野。

I had just started learning English on my own, with an old English dictionary, to decode the secret of Golden Notebook. I remember jotting down the words and found them in the dictionary: Flanders, field, poppies, cross, gunfire, love…

I remember the flash of thoughts: what if my aunt were my mother, would we all be happier? No more cussing or fighting from my parents' bedroom?

I remember father taking me to Lishao on his bike, a small fishing village by the East China Sea. I was going to farm and fish to earn my one-in-a-million opportunity for college.
The mountain road was steep. From his backseat, I listened to his panting. His back was soaked by sweat. I jumped off the bike and ran along. He got off to take a break.

We sat by the roadside. He gazed at the winding path for a long time.

"You're only 14. You haven't had your period yet," he muttered.

I couldn't bear his tears. I never saw him cry, even when he came home on a stretcher.

"I'm strong, Ba," I said, pointing to my big feet, calves and hands.

He smiled, nodding.

"Ba, why did you decide not to marry the girl in Shandong?"

I knew it was a bad question, but I had to know, since I found their photo together in his notebook, locked in his desk. She was pretty. I kind of resemble her, I remember thinking.

Long silence, then he said: "I made a vow: I'd not marry till I throw the Japanese out of China."

Another long pause. "I fell in love with your mom, nine years later."

"Did you ever regret?"

"No, I still love your mom. She still loves me, despite our fights."

"How can I, when I have you, your sisters and brother!" he said, then started humming:

在佛兰德的田野里，罂粟摇摆…

He stopped, as if waiting for my aunt to join him. We sat by the roadside, listening to the wind. In the silence, we could hear each other's heartbeats.

I remember making my vow: I'll find out where the song came from, who wrote it, how it came to China.

I turned to father: "Ba, I'll come home as a college student."

He smiled. He heard and believed me, even though the chance was slim, actually none.

I felt his pride and blessing. I may not be his prettiest girl, but I was strong, smart and stubborn, just like him. We both carry convictions that could move mountains.

Before he left the village, my new home, he said, "Don't fall in love till you reach 25, promise?"

I kept my word: I got into Beijing University, China's best, and I didn't fall in love till 26.

Father was ecstatic when I came home with a Beida badge on my chest. He insisted on a family photo in the studio, insisted that I wear the Beijing University badge.

And that was the only photo I had with my father, with my whole family.

He was drinking more than ever, from morning to night. He had retired from the Navy. He was born at Bohai, Yellow China Sea, left his home to fight Japanese invaders, and spent his best years patrolling East China Sea to keep us safe. He was born to carry out his mission with his convictions, to keep peace with his ship. Now he was a drunken sailor, homeless.

In the studio, he was sober. In the photo, his eyes shined with pride. He paid for seven prints of the photo, for everyone to take one and carry away.

I carried the photo to Beijing and graduated from the university. I carried my family to NYC for my PhD.

I remember walking into Lewis Warsh's workshop by mistake. I was about to walk out and go to my British novel class, when father's singing of Flander's Field rang in my ear. I sat down and wrote my first story, first poem, first book…

I remember working as a waitress, from Flushing to Queens, Brooklyn, Manhattan…There was no wage, only tips from customs. As soon as I saved $200, I sent it to father and mother, each $100, in separate envelopes. I didn't know why I did that, until I got his letter. He was so happy to hear from me, so proud! He wished his ma, my grandma, were still alive, to see the gift. He knew she'd be so proud, and his dad, my grandpa, who died defending his wife, his sons and his country from the Japanese, would be proud too.

He wrote he was going to save every penny I sent him, to visit me in NYC, some day.

"Your mom and I are not getting along these days. We may get a divorce. I hope we won't. I have a feeling I don't have much time left."

I cried. He was dying from his drinking, from losing his mission. He was only 56 years old.

I wanted to go home and say goodbye before it was too late. But I knew he wouldn't like it, not in his present condition, not at the risk that I wouldn't be able to return to finish my PhD.

It was my promise to him: to be the first Doctor Wang in the family.

It would be safe to return only when I had a green card.

For which I had to get a job with my temporary work permit with my MA degree from LIU.

So I walked into the headquarters of NYC Board of Education, demanding someone give me a job so I could stay in NYC as a poet.

My move shocked the headquarters but I got a job: teach poetry to bilingual classes in PS 1, Chinatown. I immediately filed papers for my green card. Within six months, I got it.

The next day, I flew back to the island in the East China Sea, my green card, still in the paper form, stapled to my passport.

Father lay in the hospital bed, attached to tubes that made him appear floating, hanging from the ceiling. Even in his floating position, he still held his arms in an upside down V.

I discovered later in NY that the gesture was the first flag signal for peace.

I took his hand.

Before I boarded the plane at JFK, I went to the New York Library and found the poem by John McCrae. It didn't take me long to find it, using the keywords "Flanders Field." John was a Canadian doctor, soldier, who wrote the poem after his friend died in his arms, poisoned by gas, the first bio weapon during WWI.

I discovered that poppies thrive particularly in battle fields.

I remember the poppies I had secretly grown in my backyard, a battleground during the Cultural Revolution, where red guards fought and died. I remember listening to their screaming, moaning and dying outside my window. We were lying on our mattress on the floor, away from bullets.

I thought I was growing roses. I didn't know what bloomed in my secret garden was poppy, immortalized by John McCrae, now a symbol of peace.

I remember Father's face, his weeping, as he caught me crouched in a bomb pit, intoxicated from the fragrance of the red flowers.

I thought he'd whip me with his leather belt. I thought he was going to bury me alive in the pit. A secret garden was bad enough. Growing roses was even worse.

I remember his hand, warm and strong, as he pulled me out of the bomb pit, filled with the poppy blossoms in the sun.

The hand, now bruised and covered with needles, still beat with the same pulse of conviction.

I sang "Flanders Field," in English, to the tune my father and aunt sang together.

> In Flanders Fields the poppies blow
> Between the crosses, row on row,
> That mark our place; and in the sky
> The larks, still bravely singing, fly
> Scarce heard amid the guns below.
>
> We are the Dead. Short days ago
> We lived, felt dawn, saw sunset glow,
> Loved and were loved, and now we lie,
> In Flanders fields.
> Take up our quarrel with the foe:
> To you from failing hands we throw
> The torch; be yours to hold it high.
> If ye break faith with us who die
> We shall not sleep, though poppies grow
> In Flanders fields.

The English words fit the Chinese tune perfectly.

What came first? Music, words, poetry, body, or soul?

Or they came all together, the way the universe birthed, with a bang?

Father started singing the song in Chinese, eyes closed. Our words mingled, seamlessly.

在佛兰德的田野里，罂粟摇摆…
去和你们的敌人吵架吧：
为你，我们从失败者的手里抢过
火把：你必须把它高高举起。
假如你背叛死者的信任
我们便无法安眠，尽管罂粟摇摆
在佛兰德的田野

The desire for love, beauty and peace, is that the law of universe?

He opened his eyes, smiled. He took my hands and pulled them to his chest.
He was blessing me with his last ray of life.

I took out Scotch Whiskey from NYC, as promised in my letter.

He smelled the bottle, then put it on his bed table.

"I've quit," he said. "I'm practicing qigong. When I recover, I'll visit NYC. I'd like to see the battleship in the museum there, maybe sail a little in the Pacific."

I laughed. My father's imagination. Did I inherit mine from him?

"I dreamed I was sailing on a big ship called Shandong, out of East China Sea, into the Pacific's blue sea. We were exchanging flag signals with American carriers: peace, peace, peace…"

He raised his right arm above his head, the second signal for peace. He was out of breath, but held his arms straight, one up, one down. He was all bones with cancer, his abdomen bulging with fluid.

The nurse came in to refill his IVs. She tried to move his arm down.

"Please keep it that way," he said, then turned to me "Promise me, my girl, don't let anyone stomp on you. Don't let 甲午 Jiawu Battle, don't let Flanders Field happen ever again!"

He closed his eyes. I held onto his hand, whispering: "I promise, Ba, with my poetry."

I waited till darkness fell, till the nurse told me I must leave.

Ten days after I returned to America, mom wrote that Father passed. He never woke up from the coma. He died in that strange position: right hand up, left hand down.

"He left you a quilt stuffed with raw silk, to keep you warm in America," said Mom.

I've been carrying his quilt, and the photo: Father in the middle, surrounded by his children.

I sing "Flanders Field" to the tune of Chinese song, as I write my poems on the tightrope of American poetry, teach poetry in the minefields of academia.

I've kept peace, and never let anyone stomp on me.

He'd have been proud of his grandsons, who have his broad shoulders, strong limbs and generous hearts, who love raw garlic, who dip dumplings in dark vinegar from China, a perfect combo of Weihai, Shanghai, Yellow Sea, East China Sea, Dead Sea and Purple Prairie…

I didn't know how handsome my father is till now! He has the eyes, jaw and cheekbones of terracotta soldiers, nose of an eagle, tall and hooked at the end. His left ear was damaged by a Japanese bayonet, his ear drums shattered by bombs, but for some reason, he could always hear our sounds. His heart pumps kindness in his thick chest. He loves beauty, but loyal to one woman, his wife. He loves his family, but sails most of his life on the sea to keep us safe.

He's the son of the Yellow River and soil, handsome, loyal, stubborn, proud, passionate, eager to love, to keep peace, like 1.4 billion Chinese, like people from around the world.

He's my father, an ordinary man with faults, a hero with unfulfilled dreams, but he carried out his mission with his flag signals, till his last breath.

And I'm your daughter, Father, a true Shandong girl born in Shanghai, sailing the world to spread 和平, shalom, paz, peace…in our flag signals, with our poppy blossoms.

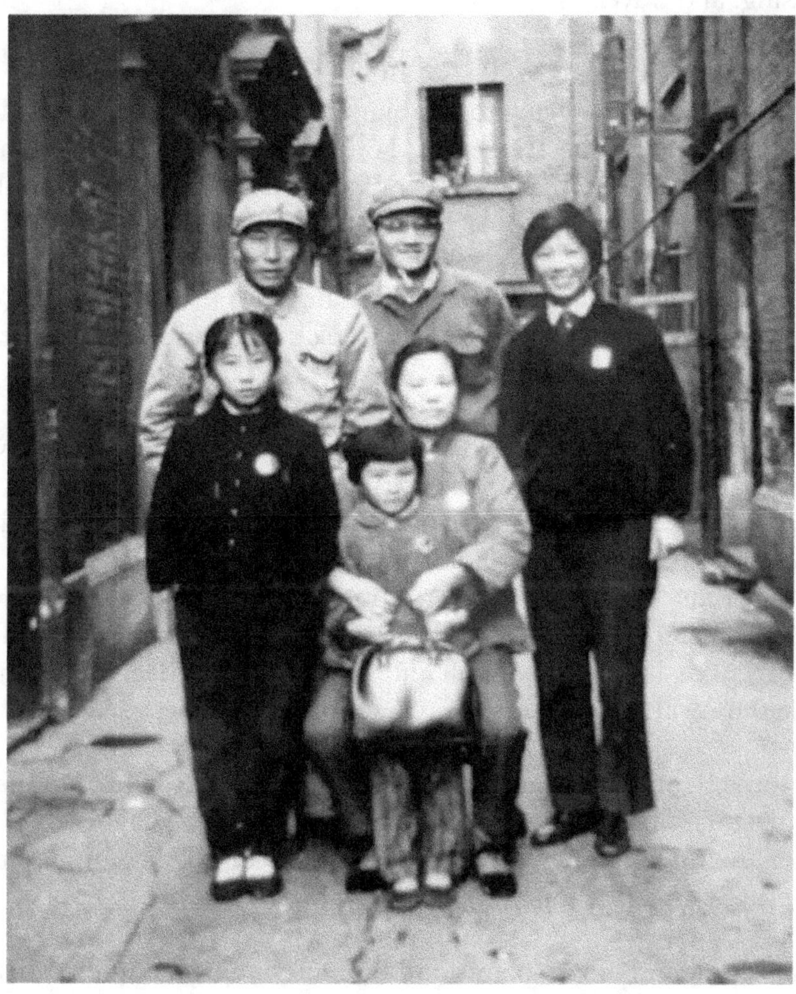

Father (left) in Shanghai, with his daughters and in-laws, 1969

Entangled Time and Space
Three Poems by Mo Fei

China created the 24 Solar Terms (*jieqi,* 节气) based on the sun's zodiac position to mark climate change, natural phenomena, agricultural production, and other aspects of life, including clothing, food, housing, and travel.

As early as the Spring-Autumn Period (770–476 BCE), the Winter and Summer Solstice were established as the first Solar Terms. They rose in significance during the Shang Dynasty along the Yellow River, spreading widely to the Yangtze and other regions of China. By the end of the Warring States Period (475–221 BCE), eight key Solar Terms were added, and the rest of the twenty-four were completed in the Western Han Dynasty (206 BCE–24 CE).

Beginning in the Start of Spring (*lichun,* 立春) and ending with the Major Cold (*dahan,* 大寒), the Solar Terms embody a complete 360-degree rotation of the sun, dividing it into 24 segments, with each segment around half a month long.

The starts of Spring, Summer, Autumn, and Winter reflect seasonal changes, dividing the year into four seasons of exactly three months. The Spring Equinox, Autumn Equinox, Summer Solstice, and Winter Solstice reflect turning points in the sun's fluctuating altitude. The Minor Heat, Major Heat, Limit of Heat, Minor Cold, and Major Cold reflect changes in temperature. The Clear and Bright, Rain Water, Grain Rain, Minor Snow, Major Snow, White Dew, Cold Dew, and Frost Descent reflect precipitation, indicating the time and intensity of rainfall, snowfall, dew and frost. Finally, the Small Full and Grain in Ear reflect the maturity and harvest time of crops, while the Awakening of Insects reflects observed insect activity.

As the voices from the dragon rivers mark their spaces on earth, we return to the poems of Mo Fei (莫非), who marks time throughout this anthology with his work following plants, which follow the turning of the sun and moon——horizontal, vertical, spatial, and temporal, weaving time and space together into a rich tapestry of the earth, cosmos, life.

Rivers and mountains, sun and moon, plants and humans entangle and merge into one. Time and space disappear in their poems, then reappear as eternal beauty and energy.

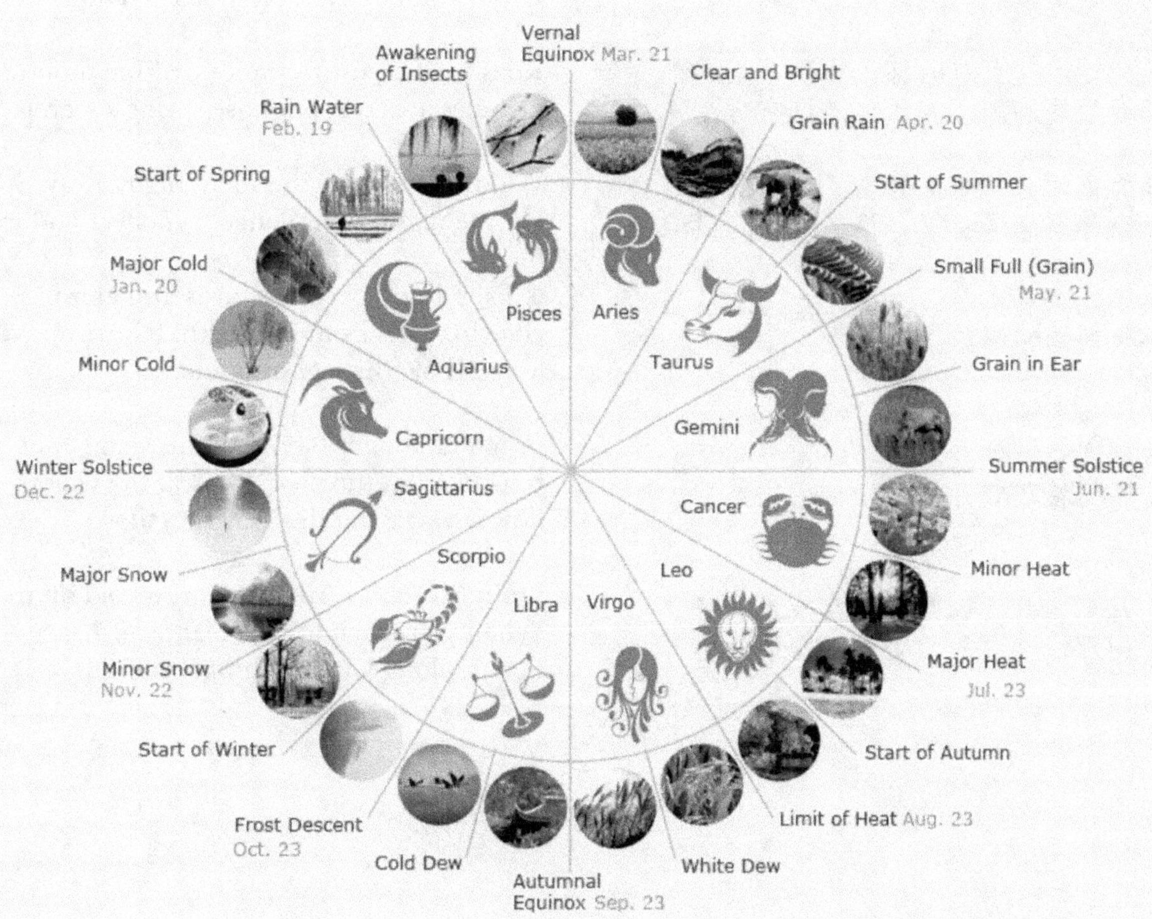

Western Zodiac signs begin and solar terms begin within two days of the dates shown.

春茶

遍野出头的茶树，疼了一遍再疼一遍
就到了谷雨节。所有的嫩叶都躲不过去

炒了又炒。这可口的杯子香飘千里之外
仿佛春天的肺腑之言，你还没有听见

寂静的夜因为风声更远了。静静的夜啊
因为寂静爬满了星星。谁若可以忍耐

谁便是飞禽和走兽，在一大片灌木丛里
咀嚼大地的馈赠。山水不在山中奔流

桃枝不在花间绽放。旧年的雨今年又来
你看啊杨柳飞花开始，杨柳依依然后

从三月到四月，春茶没隔几天就老了
伸手刹那，唯你的初心和万物渐次打开

Spring Tea

On the hills, tea trees break open one by one.
Grain Rain arrives. No buds can hide

Roasting tea, its fragrance drifting thousands
of miles away. You ignore spring's secrets

Wind blows away the silent night away. Stars
Fill the night with silence. Whoever endures

This solitude becomes birds and animals,
chewing gifts from the earth. Rivers no
longer flow through mountains

Peach no longer blooms. This year's rain
returns from the past. Look at the willow
flowers, swaying this way and that

From March to April, tea grows old on trees
When you reach for the leaf, your heart
opens, along with all things on earth

梧桐

浓密的枝桠捕风捉影
太阳在远处，好在星辰在近处
你看天空不空，就像你看云朵不散

黄昏的雨，黄昏的夏至
湖水在湖水的中央那么平静
悠悠的小女儿消失在漆黑的夜晚

唯有闲暇是正确的。金子没有用
翅膀没有用。幸福在词语里
没有用。爱最不爱讲的恰恰是逻辑

抱住栏杆的大海，凭什么退缩
老虎扛着梯子，望不到大海
凤鸟归来叫梧桐结果不叫梧桐开花

Plane Tree

Its thick treetops catch wind and shadows
The sun is far away, the stars seem close
The sky seems full, like the stubborn clouds

Rain at dusk, and summer has arrived
Water looks calm in the middle of the lake
My young daughter slips into the dark night

The only thing real is leisure. Gold is useless
Wings are useless. Happiness doesn't work
In words. Love doesn't care about logic

The sea hangs on the railings, refusing to
retreat. Tigers can't see the ocean on ladders
Phoenix returns for the fruit of the plane tree

紫花地丁

我深知那个深渊落在何处。那么小的野花
那么小的尤物，给我带来了盛大的春天

仿佛四月的节令已经传布。雨水的滴答
回应着云朵和乔木。我深知石头的缝隙

需要长出石头的时间，就像一株紫花地丁
凭空而来，你给了世界最本真的面貌

青草和废墟毫无遮盖。滚动的雷不是太大
而是一不小心，让一个满怀疑虑的人回头

那么近，不过是举手之劳，挡开一个疯子
就像万物曾经的种子，仅仅为此刻的绽放

杨柳收起的鬃毛又一次甩开。又一次的大
地像浮萍一样孕育，又一次星辰一样密布

Forget-Me-Not

I know where the abyss lies. That small flower,
small beauty, brings me this enormous
spreading spring

April's orders. Dripping rain echoes with
clouds and trees. I know
how much time

The stones need to grow between cracks, like
the forget-me-not, arriving from nowhere,
bringing this world's true face

Grasses grow bare in ruins. The thunder
isn't loud, but doubters still
look back in fear

So close, just a small gesture to
block a madman. Every seed blossoms
at this moment

Willows flick their manes. The earth gives
birth like duckweeds again
dense as stars

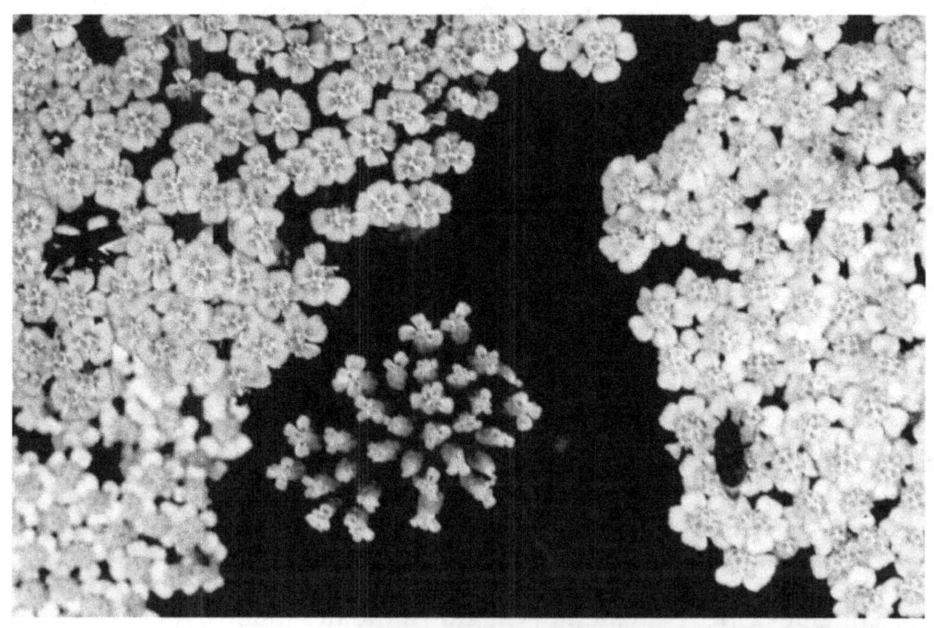

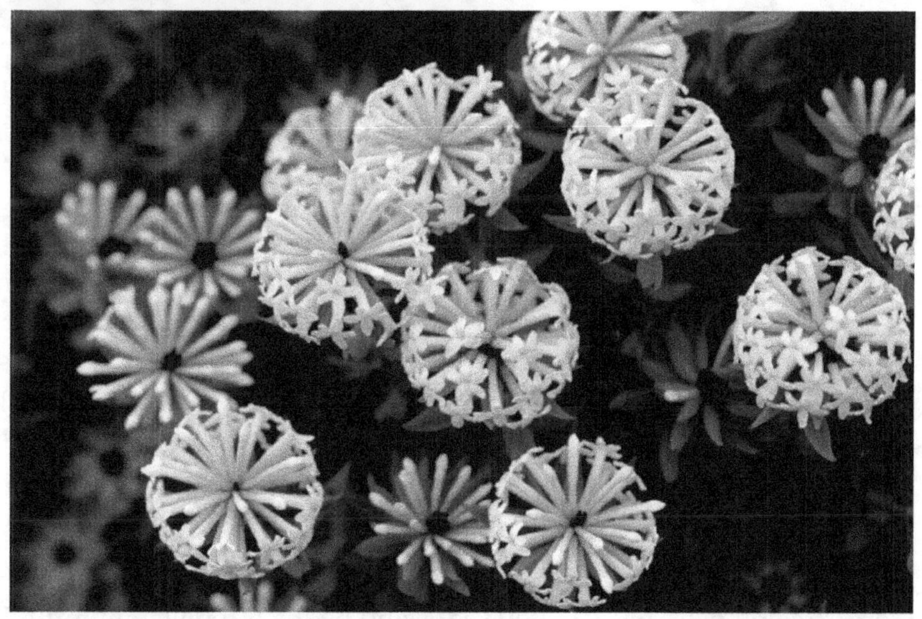

Photos by Mo Fei

The Yangtze River (长江): The Black Dragon of China

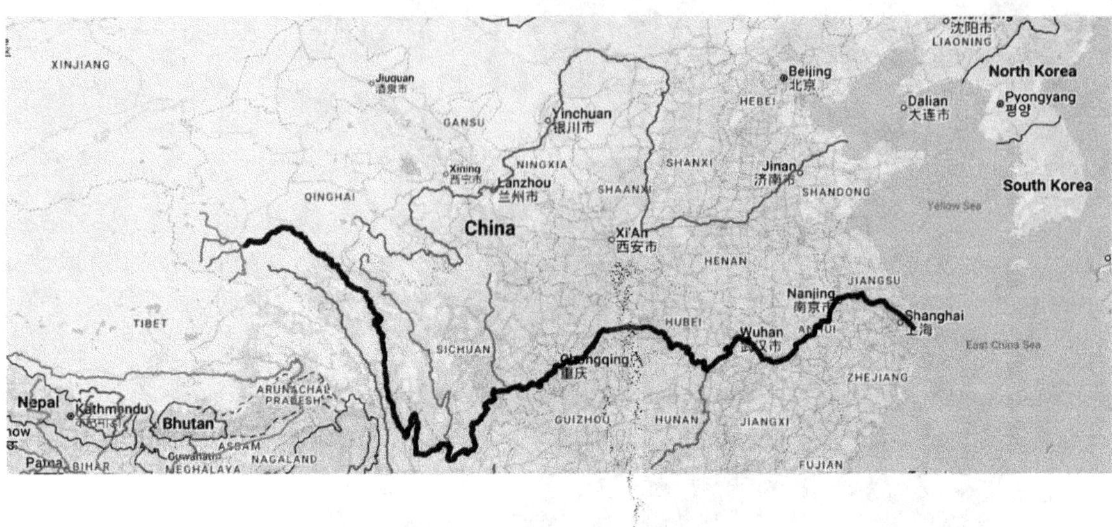

Two great rivers rise from the Qinghai-Tibet Plateau, flowing down the mountains, through steppes and plains, dancing like twin dragons across China. One is the Yellow River, the Yellow Dragon; the other is the Yangtze, the Black (or Blue) Dragon, running parallel to her northern sibling. The Yangtze is the longest river entirely within one country and the third-longest river in the world after the Nile and the Amazon. Born in the Tanggula Mountains of the Tibetan Plateau, its headwaters emerge from Jari Hill, where it begins as one of three sister rivers. The Yangtze flows 6,300 km (3,915 mi) before emptying into the East China Sea, sustaining over 400 million people—nearly a third of China's population. The Chinese call it *changjiang* (长江), meaning "Long River." The name Yangtze historically refers only to the lower section, from Nanjing to Shanghai, though Western usage later applied it to the entire river.

The Yangtze has many poetic names: Dri Chu (Female Yak River), Tongtian (Sky-Linking River), Jinsha (Golden Sands River), and simply "Blue" or "Black" River. Its major tributaries include the Tuotuo, Gar, and Dangqu (headwaters); Jinsha, Yalong, Dadu, and Min (upper reaches); Jialing, Wu, Yuan, Xiang, and Han (middle reaches); and Gan and Huai (Yangtze delta).

The Yangtze and Yellow are twin cradles of Chinese civilization. Human activity in the Three Gorges region dates back 27,000 years, and by the 5th millennium BCE, the lower Yangtze was a thriving population center, home to the Hemudu and Majiabang cultures—some of the earliest rice cultivators. The Central Yangtze Valley hosted sophisticated Neolithic cultures, later

176

absorbed into the northern Chinese cultural sphere along the Yellow River. In 278 BCE, the Qin Dynasty conquered the Yangtze heartland of Chu, incorporating it into their expanding empire.

Since the Han Dynasty, the Yangtze has grown vital to China's economy. Irrigation systems like Dujiangyan stabilized agriculture, making the region even more productive than the Yellow River basin. By the Song Dynasty, the Yangtze region had become one of China's wealthiest areas, particularly Jiangnan ("South of the River")—encompassing Jiangsu, Zhejiang, Jiangxi, and Anhui—which contributed nearly half of the nation's tax revenue.

South of the Yellow River, the Yangtze flows through gentle landscapes—flatter terrain, milder climates, and abundant rainfall, fostering biodiversity. Its poetry is filled with mist, water, dreams, and feminine elegance, reflecting the enduring legacy of Chu culture, which, though its kingdom fell 2,000 years ago, lives on in rivers, mountains, and the Chinese poetic imagination. Thus, the two rivers run across China like twin dragons—one golden, one black and blue—parallel yet intertwined, shaping one of the world's oldest, most enduring, and sophisticated civilizations.

My father, a son of the Yellow Dragon, was born in Weihai, Shandong, where the Yellow River meets the Bohai Sea. My mother, a daughter of the Black Dragon, was born in Shanghai, where the Yangtze flows into the East China Sea. I am a child of these two great rivers—China's twin dragons—dancing between the Yellow and Yangtze, between China and America.

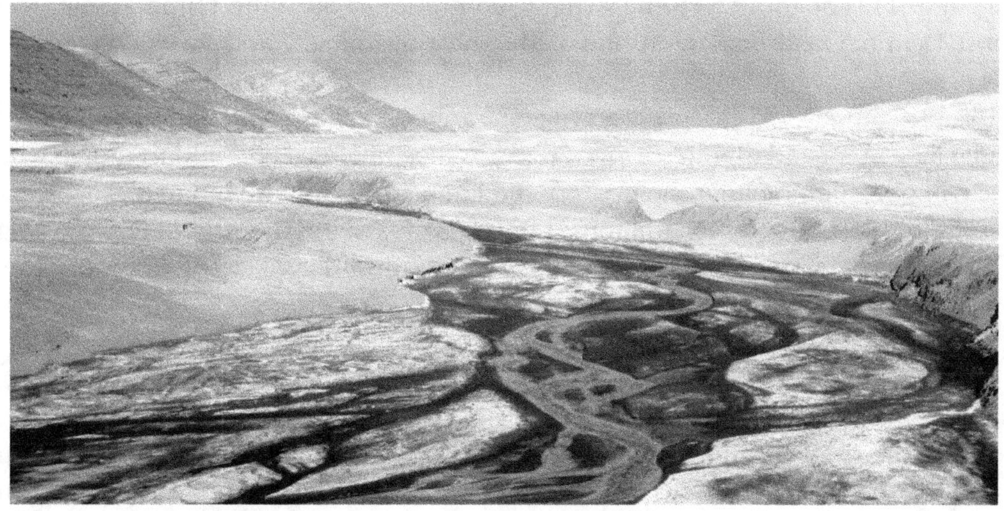

Sanjiangyuan "Source of Three Rivers," Qinghai

Qinghai-Tibet Plateau (青藏高原): Where Geology and Poetry Converge

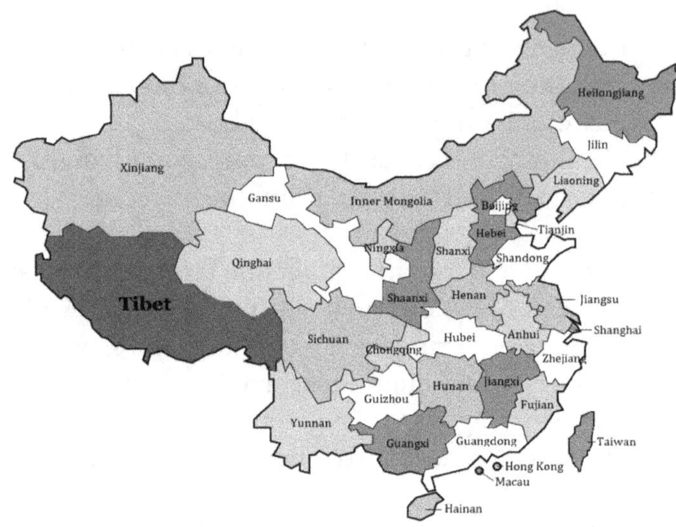

The Qinghai-Tibet Plateau, the "Roof of the World," is the highest and largest plateau on Earth, with an average elevation exceeding 4,500 meters. It's a geological marvel—a crumpled landscape forged by the relentless collision of the Indian and Eurasian tectonic plates over 50 million years ago. This ongoing tectonic struggle continues to push the Himalayas upward at a rate of almost 1 cm per year, making it one of the most seismically active regions on the planet.

The plateau is the source of Asia's greatest rivers: Yangtze, Yellow, Mekong, and Brahmaputra, born from glacial waters and alpine springs. The Yangtze begins its 6,300-km journey in Qinghai, weaving through Sichuan before looping back into Qinghai and across 11 provinces. These rivers are not just lifelines for millions; they are veins of myth and poetry, carrying the songs of Tibetan herders, the chants of Buddhist monks, and the verses of nomadic bards.

I loop Qinghai and Tibet together in this anthology because they are inseparable—geologically, culturally, and poetically. The plateau's mountains and rivers defy political borders; its winds carry the same prayers, its people share the same epics. The Kham nomads of Qinghai sing the same Gesar Ballads as their Tibetan counterparts, while the Amnye Machen and Kunlun Mountains stand as silent witnesses to millennia of verse. It was Allen Ginsberg who sent me on the road to Tibet in 1988. I was translating for Allen, Gary Snyder, John Ashbery, Bei Dao, Gu

Cheng, and other luminaries from East and West when Allen erupted in a passionate tirade about Tibet. Suddenly, he yelled: "What the f…do you know!"

Stunned, I replied, "Allen, I was translating for you."

He stormed off, then returned with a stack of his books, sketching Buddhas, stars, and lotuses on each title page. "My apologies for yelling about Buddha. Ahhh!"

That moment became a vow: *I will go to Tibet and see what the f…is happening there.*

The day I received my green card in 1992, I flew to Beijing. Poet Mo Fei introduced me to Tibetan poet He Zhong, who asked, "Do you have good lungs and a strong heart?"

I said yes. "Good. You're ready for Tibet, then," he said. And so I went—not as a tourist, but as a pilgrim, learning Tibet step by step, prostration by prostration, prayer by prayer, poem by poem. This is the only way to know this land, where the air is thin but the spirit is dense with gods. The poetry here is not just written; it is breathed, chanted, carved into mani stones by devotees circling sacred Mount Kailash. The Qinghai-Tibet Plateau is more than geography—it is a living scripture, written in glaciers, sung by rivers, recited in the wind that howls through the Himalayas. To translate its poetry, you must first let it translate you.

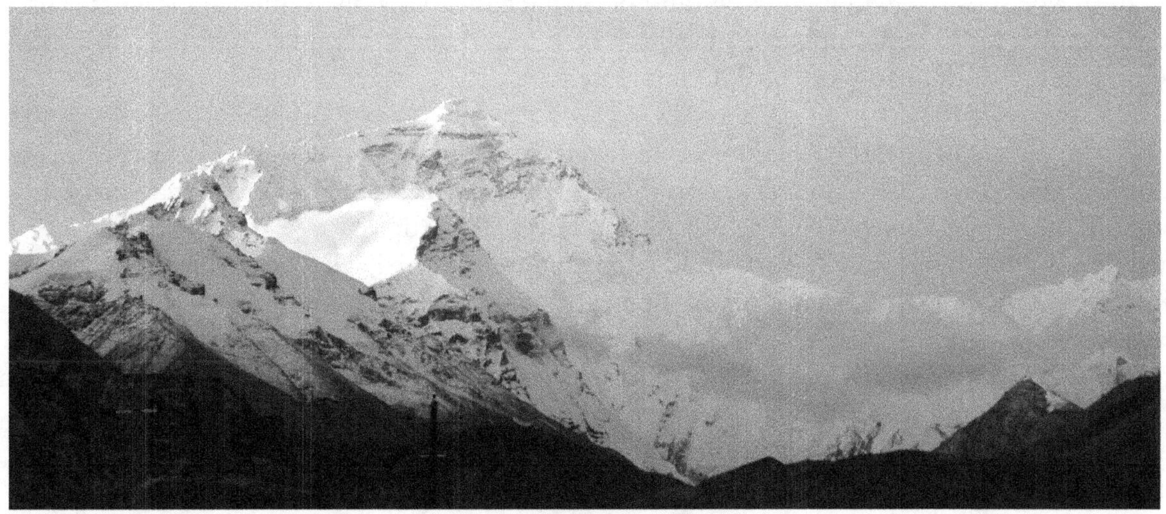

Sunrise on the Everest

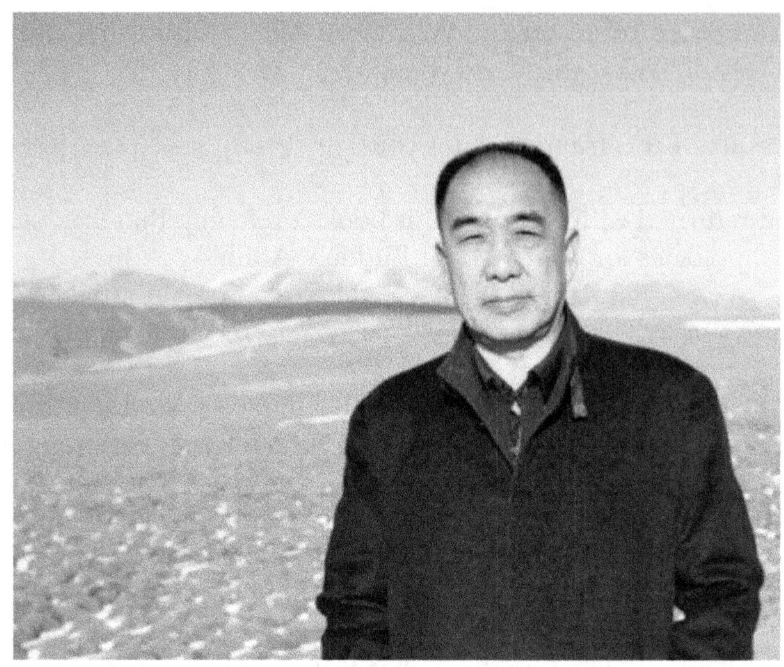

A Xin (阿信), born in 1965, is a celebrated Chinese poet born in Gansu Province. For decades, he has lived and wandered across the vast grasslands of Gannan Tibetan Autonomous Prefecture, where the rugged landscapes and nomadic culture deeply influence his work. His poetry is known for its contemplative simplicity, blending themes of nature, solitude, and spiritual longing with the stark beauty of the Tibetan plateau.

A Xin is the author of several acclaimed collections, including *Poems by A Xin* (阿信的诗), *Poems from the Grassland* (草原诗篇), and *To Friends* (致友人), among others. His writing has earned prestigious literary honors such as the Xu Zhimo Poetry Award, Yellow River Literature Award, Dunhuang Literature Award, and Feitian Literary Award, cementing his reputation as a distinctive voice in contemporary Chinese poetry.

In addition to his literary achievements, A Xin has been a quiet but enduring presence in China's poetic circles, admired for his lyrical restraint and deep connection to the land. His work often reflects a meditative engagement with the natural world, offering readers a sense of both intimacy and vastness.

鸿雁

南迁途中，必经秋草枯黄的草原。
长距离飞翔之后，
需要一片破败苇丛，
或夜间，尚遗余温的沙滩。
一共是六只，或七只，
其中一只带伤，塌着翅膀。
灰褐色的翅羽和白色覆羽
沾着西伯利亚的风霜……
月下的尕海湖薄雾笼罩，
远离俗世，拒绝窥视。
我只是梦见了它们：
这些来自普希金和彼得大帝故乡
尊贵而暗自神伤的客人。

Geese

On their trip to the south,
They must pass the autumn grassland
They need a patch of reeds after their long
flight, or a beach, still warm from the sun.
Six or seven of them.
One is injured, wing hanging from the body.
The Siberian frost still sticks between their
gray flight feathers and white cover plumes…
In the moon, Lake Gahai is shrouded in mist.
Distant from the world, She forbids my glimpse.
I can only dream of those birds:
from the land of Pushkin and Peter the Great,
Guests, so noble, so forlorn

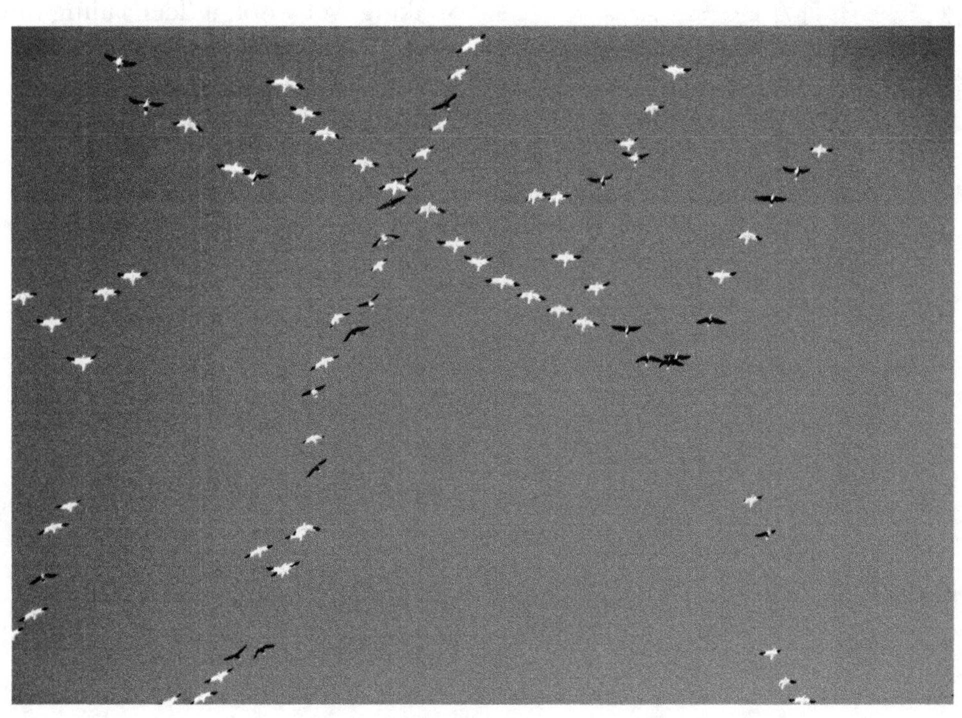

致友人书

现在可以说说这些羊。它们
与你熟悉的海洋生物具有相似性：
被上帝眷顾，不断繁殖，
长着一张老人或孩子的脸。
现在它们回到山坡，挤成一团，
互相取暖。现在它们身上覆着
一层薄薄的寒霜，和山坡一样白。
头顶的星空簇拥着无数星座：
北方的熊、南方的一株榕树、
阿拉伯圣水瓶、南美大河……
古老又新鲜。我的帐蓬就在它们旁边。
我梦见的和它们一样多。
安慰也一样多。
黎明抖擞潮湿的皮毛奔向山下的草地，
像满帆的船队驶往不可测的海洋。
而我将重新回到城市，
那里, 有等着我的命运和生活。

To a Friend

Now we can chat about these goats. They
resemble the creatures from the sea:
Blessed by gods, they are fecund
With faces of old man or child.
Now they're back to the hills, huddled for
warmth. Now their bodies are covered with
frost, as white as the hills.
Overhead, the sky's countless constellations:
northern bear, southern banyan, Arabian
Holy Vase, river from South America…
Ancient and new. My tent sits next to them.
We share our dreams,
and our comfort.
Dawn, they run towards the grass downhill,
shaking wet wool, a fleet sailing into deep sea.
I'll return to the city
Where my destiny and life await.

雪

静听世界的雪，它来自我们
无法测度的苍穹。天色转暗，一行诗
写到一半；牧羊人和他的羊群
正从山坡走下，穿过棘丛、湿地，暴露在
一片乱石滩上。雪是宇宙的修辞，我们
在其间寻找路径回家，山野蒙受恩宠。
在开阔的河滩上，石头和羊
都在缓缓移动，或者说只有上帝视角
才能看清楚这一切。
牧羊人，一个黑色、突兀的词，
镶嵌在苍茫风雪之中

Snow

Listen to the snow on earth, falling upon us
From unknown space. Sky darkens—a line of
poetry, half complete; the shepherd and sheep
coming down the hill, through thorns, wetland,
exposed on the Gobi. Snow adorns the cosmos,
as we seek our path home, and the mountains
are joyful. On the open riverbanks, rocks and
sheep move slowly. Only gods can tell
the difference, perhaps.
Studded against the white-out snow
The shepherd stands like a black word.

一块石头

在一块石头上牧羊人和他的影子坐着。
在一块石头里供着一座灰烬寺庙。
在一块石头被另一块石头撞响之前，
落日带着告别的长笛，与万物一一揖别。
在一块石头上留下灼热体液的雄性动物，
已在长风中解体。
在一块石头上雕刻点什么吧，不为记忆
只让小锤和錾子，在暗夜敲出簌簌火星。
在一块石头上雪花飘落，
覆盖过往一切痕迹。

Rock

On the rock sits a shepherd and his shadow.
On the rock sits an empty temple.
Before the rock crashes into another rock, the
sunset bows to the world,
blowing goodbye on his flute.
The scorching semen left by animals
On the rock is eroded on the rock.
Let's carve something on the rock,
not for memory, but for the sparks rising
from the hammer and chisel in the night.
Snow falls on the rock, covering all traces.

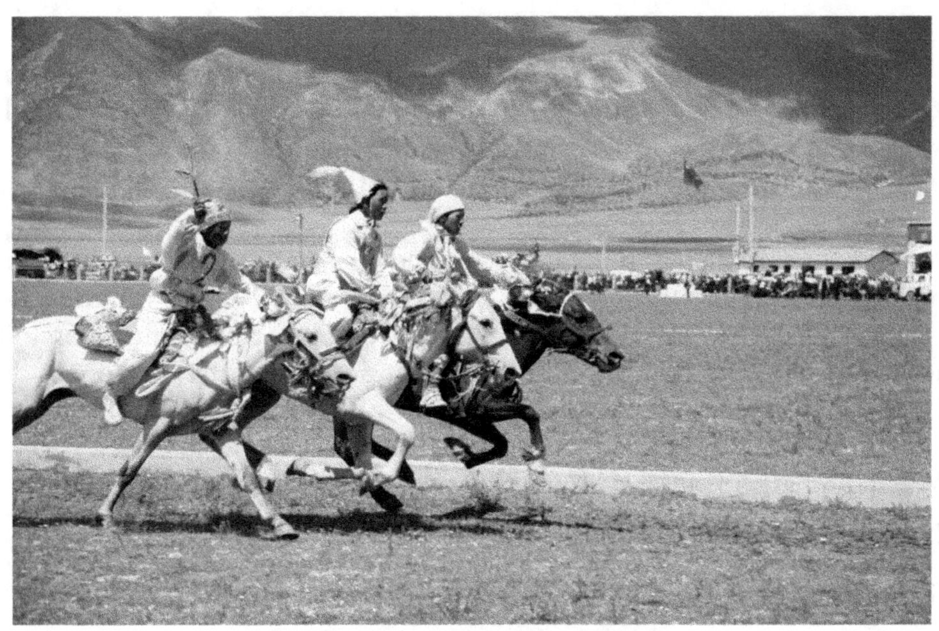

Horse race, Naqu, Tibet, 2008

河曲马场

仅仅二十年，那些林间的马，河边的马
雨水中，脊背发光的马；与幼驹一起
在逆光中静静啮食时光的马
三五成群，长鬃垂向暮晚和河风的马
远雷一样从天边滚过的马……
一匹也看不见了。
有人说，马在这个时代是彻底没有用了
牧人也不愿再去牧养它们
而我在想：人不需要的，也许
神还需要
在天空，在高高的云端
我看见它们在那里，我可以把它们
一匹匹牵出来

Hequ Horse

In just twenty years, horses vanished from
the woods and riverbanks, no more horses
in the rain, wet hair shimmering, no more horses
grazing with their colts at twilight, manes flowing
towards the dusk and river. No schools of horses
galloping like thunder from a distance…
All gone, not a single horse remains
Someone says: a horse is useless nowadays
Nobody wants to keep them anymore.
But I wonder: man may no longer need horses,
but gods still need them.
I can still see them in the clouds.
Maybe I can bring them back   one by one

He Zhong (贺中), also known as Keli Sardinnuofu (克里·萨丁诺夫), Jona Nuobuwangdian (久阿·诺布旺典), and Lao Han (老汉), is a celebrated Tibetan poet, writer, photographer, and filmmaker. Born in Huang Cheng, a small town nestled in the Qilian Mountains on the Tibetan Plateau, he comes from a rich cultural heritage: his father belongs to the Yaoguerkelie tribe, a subgroup of the Mongolian ethnic minority, while his mother is an Anduo Tibetan.

He Zhong's poetry is deeply rooted in the landscapes, myths, and spiritual traditions of Tibet. His works—including *In the Mountains* (深山里), *The Book of Tibet* (西藏之书), and *Talk about You, Talk about Me* (说说你说说我)—blend lyrical intensity with a profound connection to the natural world. Beyond poetry, he is a multimedia storyteller, using photography and film to document the vanishing cultures of the plateau. He currently resides in Lhasa, where he continues to be a vital voice in contemporary Tibetan literature. I first met He Zhong in Beijing, 1992, hoping he could guide Lewis Warsh and me to Lhasa. His first question caught me off guard: "Do you have a good heart and lungs?"

"I do," I replied without hesitation.

He laughed. "Then I'll be your guide."

Since then, he's been guiding me through Tibet's sacred landscapes—its towering peaks, turquoise lakes, and endless skies. The land inspired the Kinship of Rivers project—a global poetic exchange connecting rivers and mountains through verse, stories, and prayers.

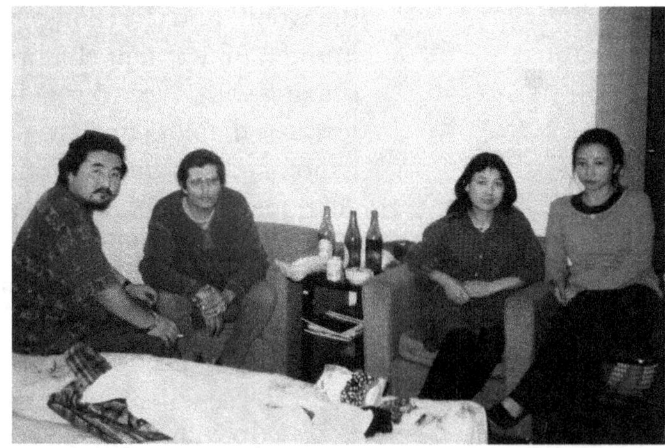

From left: He Zhong, Lewis Warsh, Xiao Ping, Wang Ping, 1992, Lhasa

蓝孔雀十四行

痴迷的人儿呀，你眼眶的水晶
收集了怎样的寂寞？香料浸泡的身体
装束得多美好！这出自东方的宝贝
在宽广的天空建造孩童的天堂
这样的鲜花，这样的圣物
透过雾朦朦的牧场激昂地盛开
绵延的白昼过去了，我光明的翅膀
藏入幽暗的心怀. 古老的屋子中，
谁的黑发飘舞？谁翻开了灰尘的第一页
宁静、优雅，长长的手指倾心抚弄
孤独的水禽啊，你无法把握地飞行
去了哪里的林子？哪里的湖泊重现往昔的族类？
一个昆虫的树巢，一个青翠的部落
我要组装阴影里的幻觉！蓝色波涛远去,蓝色的你掠过,暴雨深入肌肤,
水汪汪的月亮此刻逃进了那朵乌云的楼阁

Blue Peacock Sonnet

My crazed beauty, how much loneliness
you've gathered in your eyes? Your beauty
soaked in perfume! Treasure from the East
children's paradise in the cerulean sky.
This flower, sacred,
blossoms in the misty grassland.
White night ends, my bright wings asleep
in the dark heart. Whose black hair is dancing
in the old house? Who turned the first page of dust?
Peace, elegance, long fingers stroking
the lonely bird, unable to control flight.
Where's the forest? Which lake can restore where we came?
An insect nest, a blue jade tribe. Let me assemble illusions!
Blue waves are gone, blue storm under my skin, and the blue moon
escapes behind the pavilion clouds.

哲蚌寺掠影

一群灰鸽子
落在寺庙金顶

一群孩子
被送到新佛堂

一群狗
靠信徒施舍
栖息庙旁

一群小商贩
继续四周吆喝的生活

Glimpses of Drepung Monastery

A flock of pigeons
Landed on the temple's gilded roof

A group of children
Sent into Buddha's new hall

A pack of dogs
fed by the faithful
Lying around the monastery

A crowd of peddlers selling goods as usual
at the top of their lungs
Prayer flags at Namtso Lake, Tibet

我是江湖大恶人

我手提江山
每天飞越太空

我怀抱风月
每夜深入美人

我口吐妙语
想洗劫一切经典

我是江湖大恶人
梦想一夜抢遍世界

I'm a Big Bad Bandit

Everyday I fly across the space
Mountains and rivers in my hands

Every night I enter the beauty
Temptress moon in my chest

With witty words
I ransack every classical treasure

I'm a big bad bandit
I dream of pillaging the world overnight

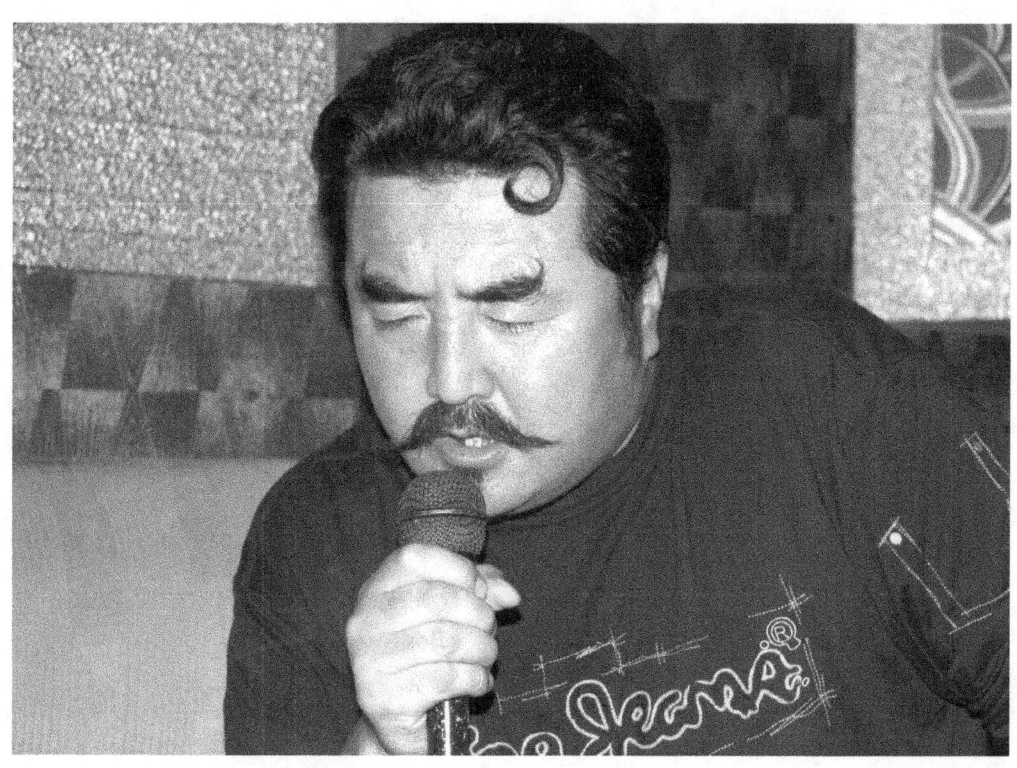

189

真正的漆黑

我感到漆黑
象水一样渗透
此时的黑

我感到先是
我自己的眼睛
而后是

每一根骨头
每一寸皮肤
每一个细胞
的真正漆黑

我已经不知道黑了
我突然觉得
也许这就是　　　　亮

True Darkness

I feel darkness
Seeping like water
This darkness

First
Into my eyes
Then

Every piece of bone
Every inch of skin
Every single cell
This true darkness

I no longer know darkness
Suddenly I feel
Perhaps this is   Light

失遇

你是沿着河岸从我面前过去了
我说：远游的人！请你回头

你是回过头了，并且从我面前沿河过去了

你又从我面前沿着河岸过去了
我说：远游的人！请你回头

你是回过头了，并且从我面前沿河过去了

Missing the Encounter

You passed by me along the river.
"Traveler, please turn back!" I called.

You did turn back, and passed me along the river.

Again you passed by me at the river.
"Traveler, please turn back!" I called again.

You did turn back, and passed me along the river.

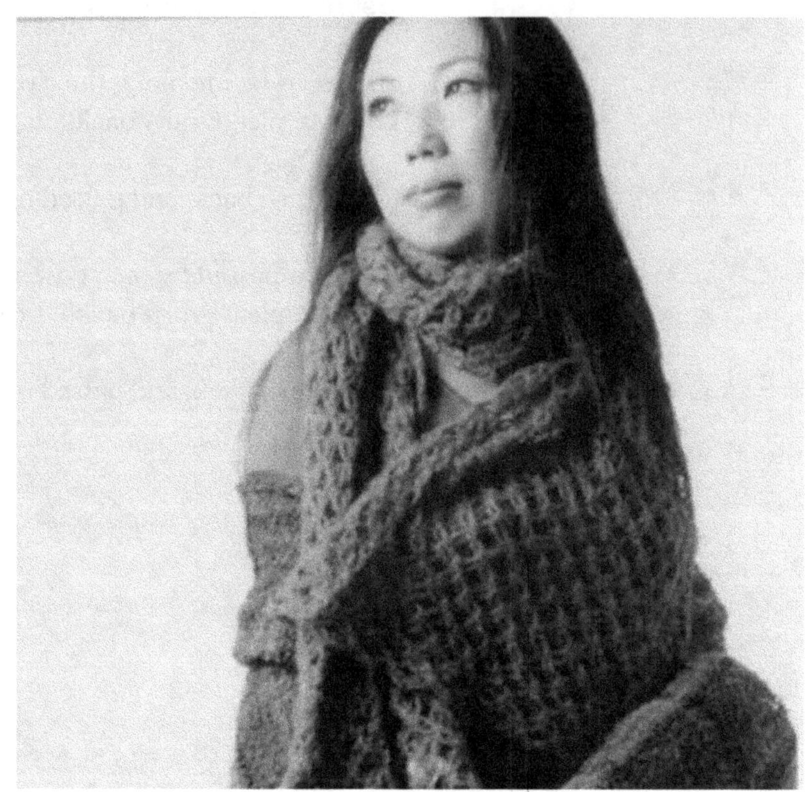

Xiwa (西娃) is a Tibetan-born Chinese poet known for her evocative and introspective verse. She is the author of *I Broke Myself into Pieces and Sent Them to You* (把自己分成碎片发给你), a collection that explores themes of identity, love, and existential fragmentation with raw emotional intensity. Her work has earned critical acclaim, including the Li Bai Poetry Award, the Luo Yihe Poetry Award, and recognition in *Best Chinese Poems* (最佳中国诗选).

Deeply influenced by her Tibetan heritage and Buddhist philosophy, Xiwa's poetry often intertwines personal vulnerability with universal longing, blending lyrical precision with visceral imagery. She remains a distinctive voice in contemporary Chinese literature, bridging cultural and spiritual divides through her writing.

两人世界

你爱我的时候，称我
女神，妈妈，女儿，保姆，营养师
按摩师，调酒师，杜冷丁，心肝……
你想念我的时候，叫我
剧毒草，银杏，忍冬花，狗尾巴草
罂粟花，冷杉，无花果，夹竹桃……
你饥渴的时候，唤我
肉包子，腊肉干，口语诗
无限水，三级片，荞麦片
你恨我的时候，骂我
疯婆娘，白痴，破罐子
岔道，烂瓦片，泼妇，贱人……
我都答应，都承认——我都做过
在你的面前，经常或有那么些时刻
当然，有更多的名称，你还没说出来

Two People's World

When you love me, you call me
Goddess, mama, daughter, nurse,
Nutritionist, masseuse, bartender,
Dolatine, sweetheart…
When you miss me, you call me
Poison weed, gingko, honeysuckle, dog-
tail grass, poppy, silver fir, fig, rose bay…
When you're thirsty, you call me
Meat ball, bacon, oral poem
Endless water, X-rated, oatmeal
When you hate me, you cuss me
Crazy woman, stupid, broken pot
Stray, rotten tile, shrew, bitch…
I say yes to all, I admit—I've done it
All to you, sometimes, somewhere
And even more, which you didn't name

我们如此确信自己的灵魂

我们如此确信自己的灵魂
比我们看得见，摸得着的肉体
更为确信，仿佛我们真的见过她
亲手抚摸过她，弯下身来为她洗过脚
在夜间闻过她腋窝里的汗味
在清晨听过她的哈欠声与唇语
我们如此确信我们的灵魂，确信她比我们的肉体更干净，
更纯粹，更轻盈,仿佛我们的肉体，一直是她的负担。
我们蔑视一个人，常常说他是一个没有灵魂的人。
我们赞美一个人，常常说他是
一个有灵魂的人。是什么，
让我们这样振振有词，对没有凭据的东西，
对虚无的东西，对无法验证的东西，充满确信？
如果有一天，一个明证出现
说灵魂是一个又老又丑又肮脏的寄生物
她仅凭我们的肉体得以净化，并存活下去
崩溃的会是一个，还是一大群人？
从崩溃中站立起来的人，或者从没倒下的
会是怎样的一群人？或一个？

We Believe in Our Soul

We believe in our soul
More so than our visible, touchable
flesh, as if we had seen her,
touched her, bent down to wash her feet,
as if we'd smelled the sweat in her armpits,
heard her morning yawn and whisper.
We believe that our soul is cleaner than our flesh,
purer and lighter as if our body was her perpetual burden.
When we insult someone, we say he's soulless.
When we praise someone, we say he has a soul.
What made us so certain, so ready to believe in something
ephemeral, illusory, impossible to prove?
If one day, the proof shows
that our soul is just a parasite, old, ugly
and dirty, depending on our flesh to live,
to purify, how many of us will collapse?
What kind of people will rise from the ruins, or stand still?
A group? Or just one single person?

喂养死亡

你说：“它死了，我又用死亡
养了一条鱼。这已经是第N条了。”
你喂养鱼，就像喂养你的活
用了粮食，水，悲喜，和不多的爱心
这些年，你不停的看到亲人，朋友，
熟人……一个个去了死亡那里。
于是你疯狂的养花,养鱼，养你的梦想
和激情——把它们当饲料，
企图撑破死亡的肚皮.
“为什么死亡什么都吃，死亡却不死去？”
我像在远方，不去理会你悲伤的疑问，
也不去安慰，鱼，死去的这个
秋季的早晨。我什么都不做，
愉悦的感受着：死亡，
用一条再也活不下过来的鱼，
鲜活地把我们的共同的一天
一点点吞下去。像你一样，
除了喂养死亡，你以为我还能干什么？

Feeding Death

You say: "It's dead. So I keep another fish
Alive with death. This is my Nth try."
You feed the fish with death, keeping yourself
Alive with grains, water, sorrow and joy, some love.
All these years, you witnessed families, friends,
acquaintances… reach death one by one.
So you feed flowers and fish like crazy
with your dreams and passion—you tried to
break death's stomach with food.
"Why does death never die, but just devours?"
I don't hear your sad question from a distance.
Nor do I try to comfort you. The fish died
one autumn morning. I did nothing,
just enjoyed the sensation: Death
used a dead fish to swallow our day
little by little, alive and fresh
What else do you think I can do
Apart from feeding death?

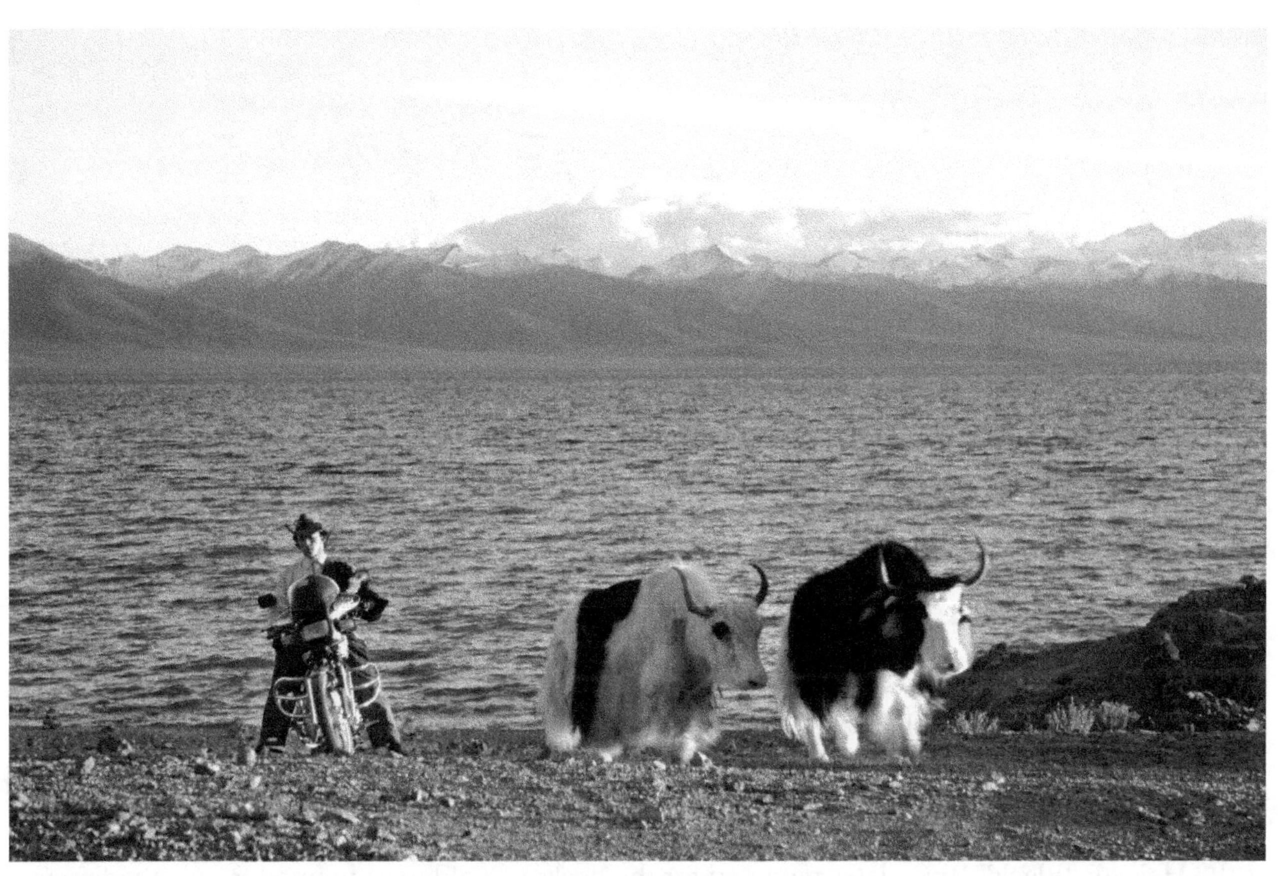

Namtso Lake, Tibet

Sichuan (四川): The River's Song

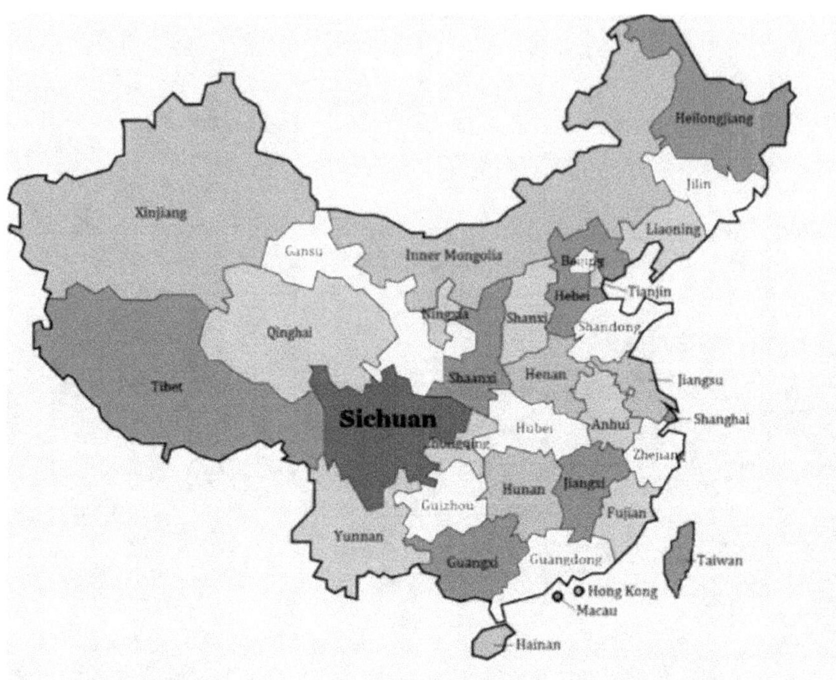

Sichuan is the only province traversed by both the Yellow River and the Yangtze, cradled between tectonic collisions that shaped its dramatic landscapes. The Jinsha "Golden Sands" River, the wild upper reach of the Yangtze, begins as glacial melt on the Tibetan Plateau in Qinghai, then carves through deep gorges in Sichuan and Yunnan before merging with the Min River. Its name whispers of geology and history: first recorded during the Warring States period as the Heishui "Black" River, later renamed for the flecks of gold once panned from its sediment. Today, the true "gold"—energy—is harnessed from its relentless flow.

With a staggering gradient of 2.7 m/km (14 feet per mile) in its upper reaches, the Jinsha River is a hydroelectric engineer's dream. Since the completion of the Baihetan Dam in 2022, five of the world's largest hydroelectric stations (each ≥3,000 MW) now stud its course. When fully operational, these dams will form the planet's largest clean energy corridor, turning the river's fury into light for millions.

Yet to me, the real treasure lies beyond watts and turbines—it's in the living pulse of Sichuan's rivers and mountains. The Jinsha's waters weave through poetry and myth, sustaining ecosystems where rare fish dart, forests cling to cliffs, and Yi, Tibetan, and Han cultures converge.

For thousands of years, Chinese poets have been nurtured and inspired by Sichuan's majestic mountains and rivers: Li Bai (701 CE – 762 CE) , Du Fu (712 CE – 770 CE), and Su Shi (1037 – 1101). Now, Jidi Majia (b. 1961), Aku Wuwu (b. 1964) , and many more contemporary poets have joined in.

The true "gold" lies in the intangible—the stories in the current, the resilience of the cultures, the unbroken song of water upon stone. From Li Bai's moonlit cups to Aku Wuwu's tiger-traced verses, Sichuan's rivers remain both muse and lifeblood.

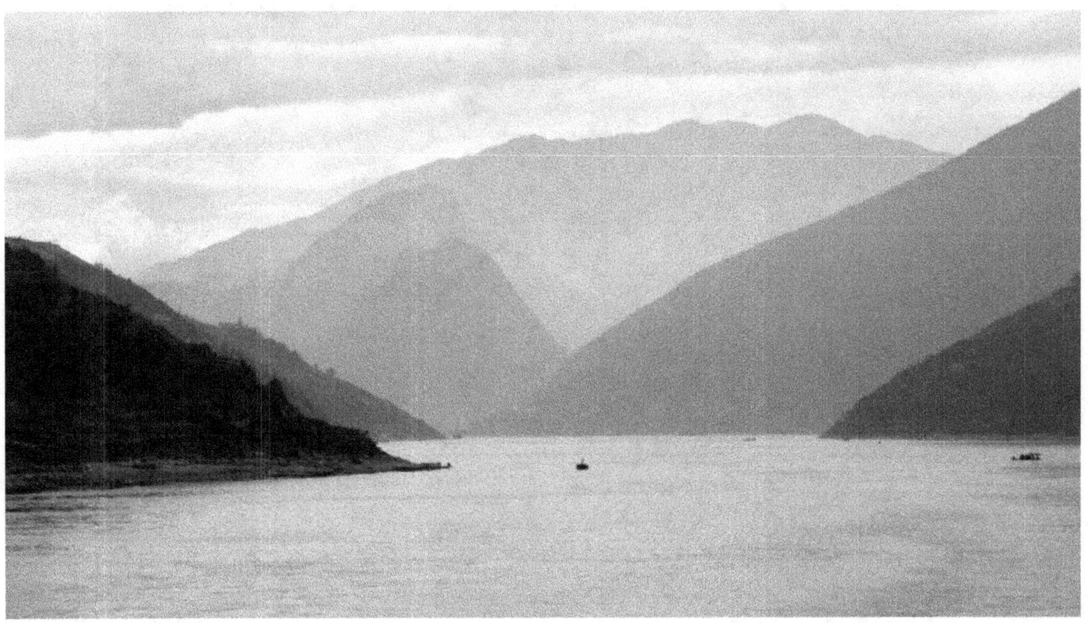

The Three Gorges, Yangtze River middle reaches, Sichuan

Aku Wuwu (罗庆春, b. 1964) is a Yi poet, scholar, and educator from the Greater Cold Mountain region of Sichuan Province. Writing in both Chinese and the Yi (Nuosu) language, his work bridges indigenous traditions and contemporary poetry. His poems have been published in the Yi language, Mandarin Chinese, and English, reaching a global audience.

Aku Wuwu holds a distinguished academic career as a professor, researcher, and former Dean of the Southwest University for Nationalities (now Southwest Minzu University), which is affiliated with Sichuan University. His scholarly work focuses on Yi literature and cultural preservation.

Internationally recognized, Aku Wuwu was a poet-in-residence at Macalester College (USA) in 2005 and 2008, where he engaged in cross-cultural literary exchange. His poetry reflects the landscapes, myths, and spiritual heritage of the Yi people while engaging with modern themes. His poetry and prose collections include *Stream in Winter* (冬天的河流), *Beyond the Witch's Realm* (走出巫界), *Selected Poems of Aku Wuwu* (阿库乌雾诗歌选), *The Appeal of Mississippi* (密西西比河的倾诉), *Coyote Traces* (凯欧蒂神迹), and *Tiger Traces* (Yi/English, co-translated with Mark Bender).

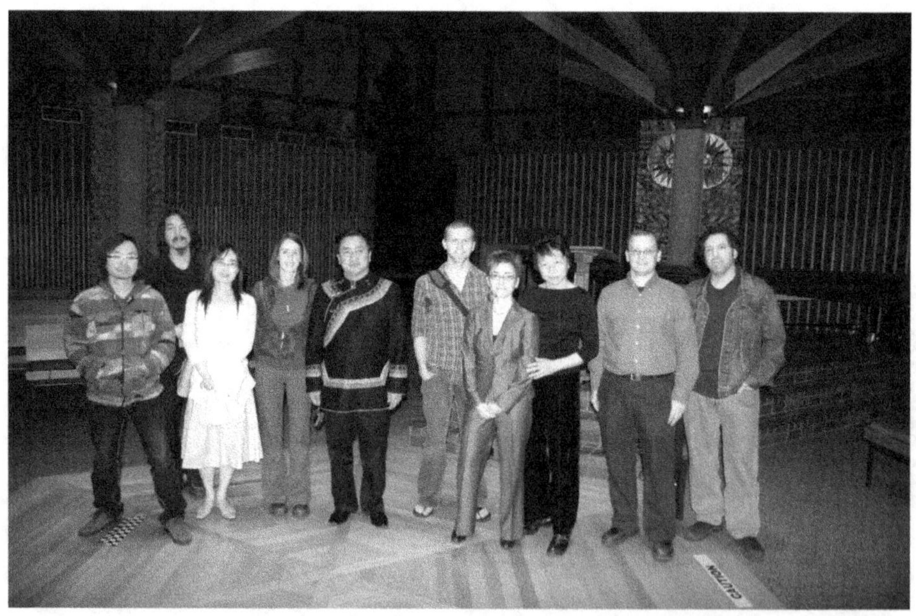

Right to left: Eric Lorberer, Jeff Shotts, Wang Ping,
Kimiko Hahn, Mac student, Aku Wuwu, Macalester
College faculty members

无言的草偶

你们是语言的替身,你们必须无言。你们是被人化的草木，你们不必在乎人性的得失。而我们不能，我们必须言说，我们必须通过言语思考人的肉体与性灵给我们带来的成熟生命的信息。而后将这些信息按照应有的规则和方式重新进行编码，而后用以表达我们生命存在的真实与虚幻，有意或者无意。

你们是无根的生命，你们只能无言。你们是游戏的工具，你们应该生活在游戏之中。而我们的根骨必须具备应有的硬度和光泽，我们的根骨必须以母语的形式延伸自己的龙脉。于是，我们才能成为合格的游戏设计者，我们才能将内心的善恶与美丑无休止地倾注在你们的身体里；我们还是游戏的观赏者，自古以来，我们似乎早已习惯，仿佛在观赏一场内心深处血腥的斗牛一样观赏发生在草偶之间的每一次轻盈而激烈的战争。

你们成为人神互通的云梯，充当人鬼对抗的工具。你们虽为草木之身，可你们表里如一；你们身上附着再多罪恶的语蛊，可你们在诅咒的火光中自在而超然；你们承载厚重的托付与希冀，可你们在荣誉的汪洋中显示出无比的沉静和睿智。

Silent Grass Doll

You're a substitute for words. You must stay silent. Personified as a human, you don't care if you win or lose. But we can't. We must speak, must ponder over life's codes through flesh and soul. We reprogram the codes with original rules to show if our existence is real or illusionary, if it has meaning or is just an accident.

Your life has no roots. You cannot speak. You should live in a game as a tool. But for us, we must harden and shine our bones, must extend them through our dragon veins in our mother tongue. Only then can we enter the game as a master, can we can pour good and bad, beauty and ugliness endlessly into your body; we are also the audience, watching the bloody battles among the grass dolls since the ancient times, like watching bullfights deep in our hearts.

You're a ladder between men and gods, a weapon to fight ghosts. Made from grass, you remain truthful inside and out. So many curses are poured upon you, but you stay carefree in the flame. Floating in the sea of honor, you carry the heavy load of hope.

蜘蛛王

1

吐丝是蜘蛛生命的标志和意义。但要吐多少丝蜘蛛才算完成终生使命，获得完美的生命结局？那些形状各异，姿态万千的蛛网，既是宇宙规律的缩影，又是生命内在的图式。据说蛛丝是蜘蛛的唾液，是蜘蛛一生走过的道路，是蜘蛛的骨血和经脉。其实蛛丝更像蜘蛛的语言文字，遍布世界的蛛网就是一部部《蜘蛛经》。

2

雨声和蛙声协奏，梦里有一对翅膀带我离开故乡。途中遭遇蜘蛛王在既定的位置，张开八只黑爪子，从八个方位把控我的旅程。蜘蛛是我命定的旅伴，也是与生俱来的天敌，生命的真谛在于一路化敌为友。从传说中神蛙的弱者智慧，到梦里蜘蛛王的强者声威，我的生命将缺一不可。灵性凸显于雨夜，躯壳再度被遗弃。

3

蜘蛛背上自己沉重的卵丸，不断吞吐柔韧的蛛丝，为了孕育血统纯正的后代，向传说中的蜘蛛王国昼夜兼程。相传只有蜘蛛王国出生的蜘蛛，才有资格竞选蜘蛛王。不幸途中遭灭顶之灾，从此蜘蛛丢失腰腹部，头部做智库而尾部用于产丝和繁殖。那死亡与复活的神话，让蜘蛛荣登神灵宝座，这是祖先认定神灵的方式。

4

昨夜我被蜘蛛王严密封锁，只能呼吸不能动弹和声张，也听不到外面的音乐，没有音乐毋宁死。但蜘蛛王不会轻易让我死，不会自己背上永远无法逃脱的罪责。因为我的生命牵动着更强大的生命，我只不过充当这个强大生命的某个器官，但绝对不是心脏，更不是那高贵的头颅。我愿做一股动脉，与音乐和蜘蛛网同行。

5

冬天必将降大雪，蜘蛛王在雪地上滚动雪球，朝着春天的方向。仿佛一切生命都难以离开圆形存在，从蛛卵、星星、雪球，到子宫、乳头、荞饼，再到头颅、枪口以及火葬地。蜘蛛王早已深谙世间生死，终将呈现为圆形之律，始终专注于铸造圆形之梦。蜘蛛王也曾渴望展翅飞翔，将自己卵丸和人类雪球滚向浩瀚宇宙。

130

在乌鸦和猫头鹰的翅膀上结网，蜘蛛王守护山林最灵动的部位。蛛网于天海间打捞灵魂的沉船，编制宇宙内外有血无血的密码。蜘蛛跨越花朵与花朵之间距离，那生命之河不再轻易放弃歌唱。古往今来天地间蜘蛛无处不在，蜘蛛谱系与日月乾坤谱系相连。按天神旨意与蜘蛛王结伴而行，你们从莫名的隐忧中彻底脱逃。

Spider King (excerpt)

1

Spinning silk marks the meaning of a spider's existence. How much silk does a spider spin during its life? Webs have so many shapes and patterns, a mirror image of the cosmos, the innate design of life. I heard spider silk comes from saliva, mapping its life journey with bones, blood, meridians. To me, spiders are more like a spider language, writing "Spider Bibles" with their webs all over the world.

2

Rain and frogs sing in sync. In dreams, a pair of wings take me away from home. We encounter the spider king on our way. It opens eight black legs, controlling my journey from eight directions. The spider is my destined companion and enemy, but life is meant to transform enemies to freinds. I need both alive, the mythical small frog's wisdom, and the power of the spider king in my dreams. Spirits appear in the rainy night, my body abandoned again.

3

The spider carries its own heavy eggs, spitting soft silk continuously as it travels to the mythical spider kingdom. It is said only spiders born in the spider kingdom are qualified to become king. But it was met with death on the road, and it lost its abdomen, leaving only the head resurrected for wisdom and tail for silk and reproduction. Through such death and resurrection, the spider became spirit, and was worshipped as such by our ancestors.

4

Last night I was tied up by the spider king. I couldn't move, speak, or hear the music outside. It was killing me. But the spider king wouldn't let me die so easily. It wouldn't carry the inescapable crimes on its own back, because there's a life inside, larger than me. I'm just an organ for its powerful life. I'm not its heart, or the treasured head. I want to be an artery, flowing with music throughout the spider web.

5

Big snow in winter. The spider king rolls the snowball towards spring. Every life seems to live in circles: egg, stars, snowballs, womb, breast, bread, head, gun muzzle, tomb. The spider king knows the life and death of this world. It knows its circular rhythm, weaving circular dreams. The spider king dreams of opening its wings, rolling its eggs and the human world into the cosmos.

130

The spider king weaves webs on the wings of crows and owls, protecting the most spiritual part of the woods. Its web seeks the ships of souls, lost between sky and sea, turning into bleeding codes for the cosmos. The spider crosses the distance between flowers, so the river of life keeps singing. The spider has lived everywhere since the creation of earth, family tree entangled with sun, moon, stars. You travel with the spider king by God's will, and you'll forever escape anxiety.

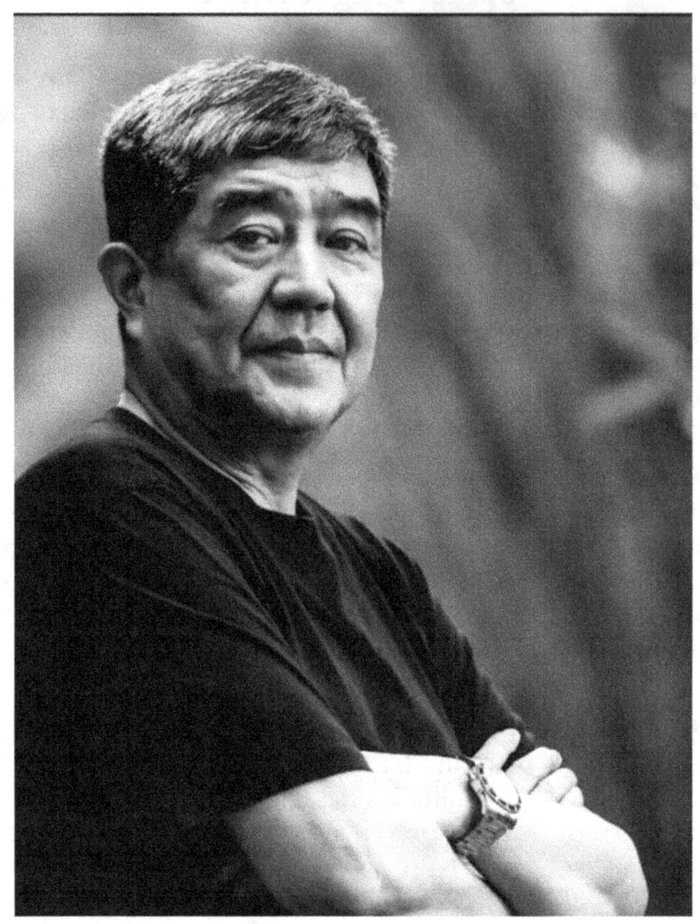

Liang Ping (梁平) is a celebrated poet and editor born in Chongqing and based in Chengdu. His published poetry collections include *Genealogy* (家谱), *Winged Ears* (有耳飞来), *Blossoms Between Lips* (唇间花), *Time Notes* (时光笔记), and many others. His work has earned him prestigious literary honors such as China's Book Award, the Bashu Literary Gold Award, the Beijing Literature Award, and the Chinese Poets Award. Liang Ping serves as Editor-in-Chief of *Caotang Poetry* (草堂诗刊) and as President of the Chinese Poetry Research Institute at Sichuan University.

我被我自己掩盖

我被一本书掩盖，
文字长出的藤蔓相互纠缠，
从头到尾都是死结，身体已经虚脱。

我被一个梦掩盖，
断片与连环铺开的情节清晰，
梅花落了，枝头的雪压哑了风的呼啸。

我被一句话掩盖，
舞台与世界悬浮幻影，
喜鹊飞过头顶，窗台停靠一只乌鸦。

我被我自己掩盖，
草堂的荒草爬满额头，
碑林之间，只看见天空的背面。

I Bury Myself

I'm buried by a book,
Entangled among vines of words,
Choked to near death by all dead knots.

I'm buried by a dream, spreading
Like a story, cherry blossoms
are falling in the snow, silencing wind.

I'm buried by a sentence,
The world floating like a mirage on stage
Magpie flies overhead, crow appears on the window.

I bury myself, grass crawling over
my forehead from the Grass Hall
Through the stele forest, I see the back of the sky.

石头记

裸露是很美好的词，
不能亵渎。只有心不藏污，
才能至死不渝地坦荡。
我喜欢石头，包括它的裂缝，
那些不流血的伤口。
石头无论在陆地还是海洋，
无论被抬举还是被抛弃，
都在用身体抵抗强加给它的表情，
即使伤痕累累。
我的前世就是一块石头，
让我今生还债。风雨、雷电，
不过是舒筋活血。
我不用面具，不会变脸，
所有身外之物生无可恋。
应该是已经习惯了被踩踏，
明明白白的垫底。
如果这样都有人被绊了脚，
那得检查自己的来路，
我一直在原地，赤裸裸。

The Story of a Stone

Naked is a good word;
it mustn't be desecrated. The heart hides no dirt,
So it can beat free till it dies.
I like stones, and their cracks,
With wounds that don't bleed.
Their bodies resist any forced expressions,
whether they lie on land or at sea,
lifted high or abandoned,
covered with scars.
My previous life is a stone
I'm still paying my debt. Wind, rain, and storm
stretch my body and move my blood.
I don't wear a mask nor change my face.
Nothing in this world makes me feel attached.
I'm used to being stamped upon,
lying at the bottom.
If someone stumbles on me,
he must examine himself, for
I've been lying in place, naked.

过敏原

半夜皮肤过敏，
眼睛睁不开，在痒处抓挠，
越抓越痒，由点及面，平滑的手臂上，
触摸到密密麻麻的碉堡。
想起昨晚睡前看的战争片，
那些失守的阵地，弹坑、掩体，
以及横陈的凌乱。

我被迫翻身下床，
极力保持情绪的稳定。
常备药箱里找出醋酸地塞米松，
涂抹左臂，找出地奈德乳膏，
涂抹右臂，我无法确定自己的过敏原，
翻箱倒柜把所有可以抵抗的家当，
全部用上。
痒，继续痒。

有点生不如死了，窗外的黑，
制造了满世界的沦陷。
皮肤上的战事蔓延至胸腔，
我在沙发上看见了路易斯·辛普森，
看见他的胃，正在"消化橡皮、
煤、铀、月亮和诗"，
我羞愧于我的自爱自怜。

我忘了夜幕放大的恐惧，
在镜子前端正衣冠。
大义凛然地出门、下楼、发动汽车，
从致民路安顺桥横渡府南河，
我不是去医院，而是漫无目的，
想随机遇见我的过敏原，
一个红灯，或者一颗子弹。

Allergen

Allergy attack at midnight,
eyes closed, I scratch, but the more I do,
The itchier it gets, extending from point to surface
along my arm, I feel dense forts, castles rising.
Could it be the war film I watched last night,
those lost battlegrounds, bomb craters, bunkers
scattered in the fields?

I get out of the bed trying to stay calm.
I find the DXM cream from my medicine box,
dab it on my left arm, find desonide cream
dab on my right arm. I can't identify the
allergen caused this itching.
I look everywhere, find every pill
I can find, take it all.
Still itchy. It just won't stop.

Death feels better than life. Night outside
turns the world into a chaos.
The war burns from my arms to my chest.
I see Louis Simpson on the couch.
His stomach digesting "rubber,
coal, uranium, moon and poetry,"
and I feel ashamed of my self-pity.

I cast the terror enlarged by the night,
I put on my best clothes in front of the mirror.
I open the door, go downstairs, turn on my car,
drive Zhimin Road, Anshun Bridge, South River,
not going to the hospital, just roaming,
to meet my allergen,
be it red light or bullet.

我是我自己的反方向

我是我自己的反方向，
所以面对你就是一个问题。
你的名字和根底，你的小道具，
比熟悉我自己，更明了。
你是不是你不重要，
你在和不在也不重要。
镜子面前我看不见自己，
别人眼睛里我看不见自己，
我是我自己的错觉。
跟自己一天比一天多了隔阂，
跟自己一次又一次发生冲突。
我需要从另一个方向，
找回自己，比如不省人事的酒醉，
比如伸手不见五指的暗夜。
只有自己跟自己过不去，
才不会有事无事责怪别人。
所谓胸怀，就是放得下鲜花，
拿得起满世界的荆棘。

I'm My Own Opposite Self

I'm my own opposite self,
so it's a problem when we meet.
I know your name, who you are, your little tricks
better than myself.
It's not important if you're yourself,
if you exist or cease.
I can't see my face in the mirror,
I can't see myself in your eyes,
I'm the illusion of myself.
I distance further and further from myself
fight more and more with myself.
I need to find me in a different dimension,
blackout drunk, for example, in
pitch black night when I can't see my hands.
I can stop finding faults in others
looking for troubles with myself.
Big-hearted means you drop flowers
and pick up the thorns of the world.

盲点

面对万紫千红，
找不到我的那款颜色。
身份很多，只留下一张身份证。
阅人无数，有瓜葛没瓜葛，
男人女人或者不男不女的人，
只能读一个脸谱。
我对自己的盲点不以为耻，
是非曲直与黑白面前，
我行我素。
我知道自己还藏有一颗子弹，
担心哪天子弹出膛，伤及无辜。
所以对盲点精心呵护，
眼不见为净，清洁自己。
我把盲点绣成一朵花，
人见人爱，
让世间所有的子弹生锈，
成为哑子。

Blind Spot

Among the world's rich colors,
I can't find my own.
So many identities, I only keep one ID.
I've met countless people, with or without
relationships, men, women, neither nor,
all became one mask.
I'm unashamed of my blind spot.
I do what I want, black or white,
right or wrong.
I keep a secret bullet,
hoping it won't leave me and harm the innocent.
So I choose not to see everything,
guard my blind spot, keep myself clean.
I'll embroider my blind spot
into a lovely flower.
I'll make sure all the bullets
will rust, never sound.

Yunnan (云南): Land of Diversity

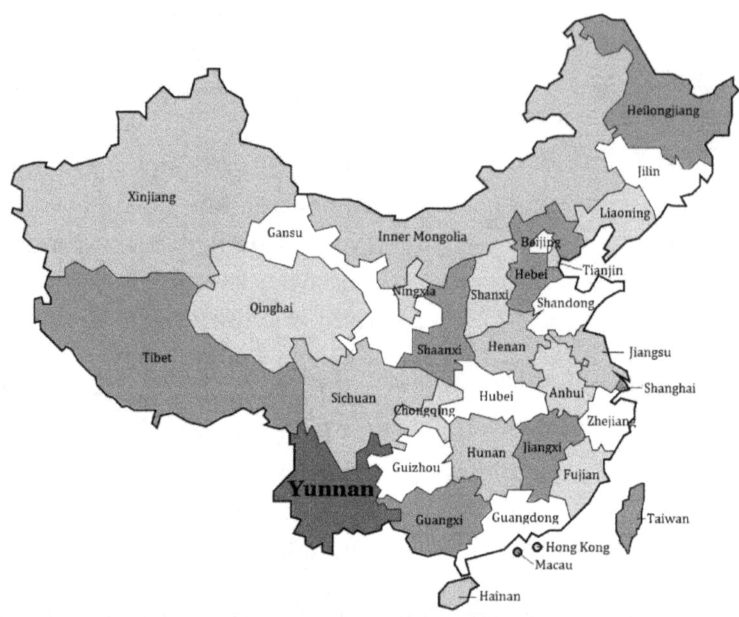

Yunnan earns its name as a haven of diversity—where towering mountains, serpentine rivers, and crystalline lakes converge with a mosaic of ethnic cultures, mineral riches, and lush tea terraces. It is a land sculpted by time: the collision of tectonic plates thrust up the Hengduan and Himalaya ranges, while the roaring Yangtze, Lancang, and Nu Rivers carve deep gorges through the plateau, their waters charged with the melt of ancient glaciers.

Every journey back to China draws me upstream along the Jinsha "Golden Sand" River, the Yangtze's untamed upper reach, where the earth ascends from emerald tropics to the roof of the world. Here, ecosystems shift like poetry and painting—steaming rainforests yield to alpine meadows, and snow leopards tread slopes where rhododendrons blaze.

Here I've wandered the last matriarchy of the Mosuo by Lugu Lake, sipped the rich pu'er teas from millennia-old trees; and savored crossing-the-bridge rice noodles (*guoqiao mixian*, 过桥米线), a Yunnan dish as rich and layered as the province's history.

And always, there are the poets. From the Tang dynasty's wandering bard, Li Bai, who marveled at Yunnan's "roads to the clouds," to the contemporary verses of Yu Jian, who grafts the local dialect onto modern rhythms, this land breathes poetry.

To read Yunnan's poems is to trek its mist-wrapped peaks, to stand by the Tiger Leap Gorge of the Jinsha River as it thunders off the Qinghai-Tibet Plateau—a force as relentless as time and as lyrical as the stories etched into the cliffs.

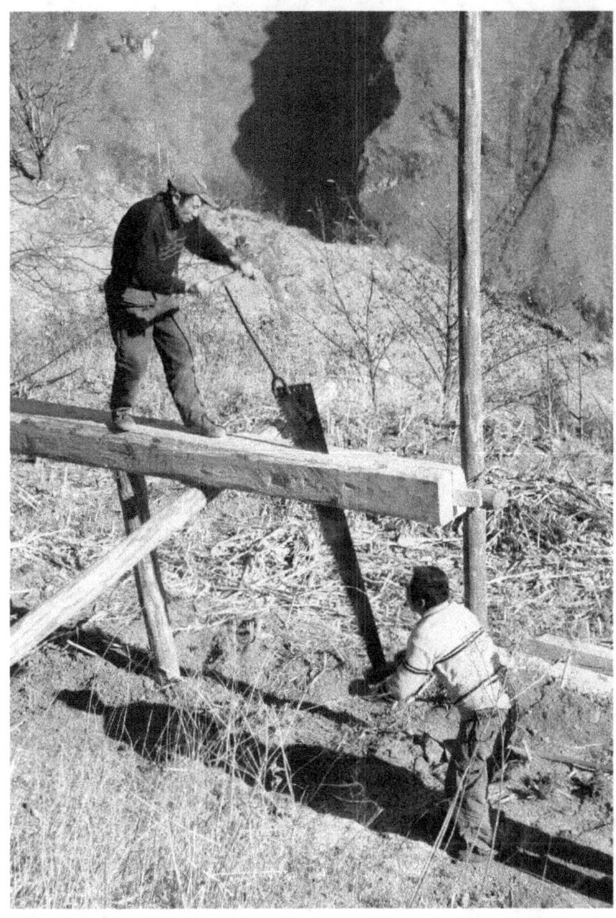

Mountain villagers, Yunnan

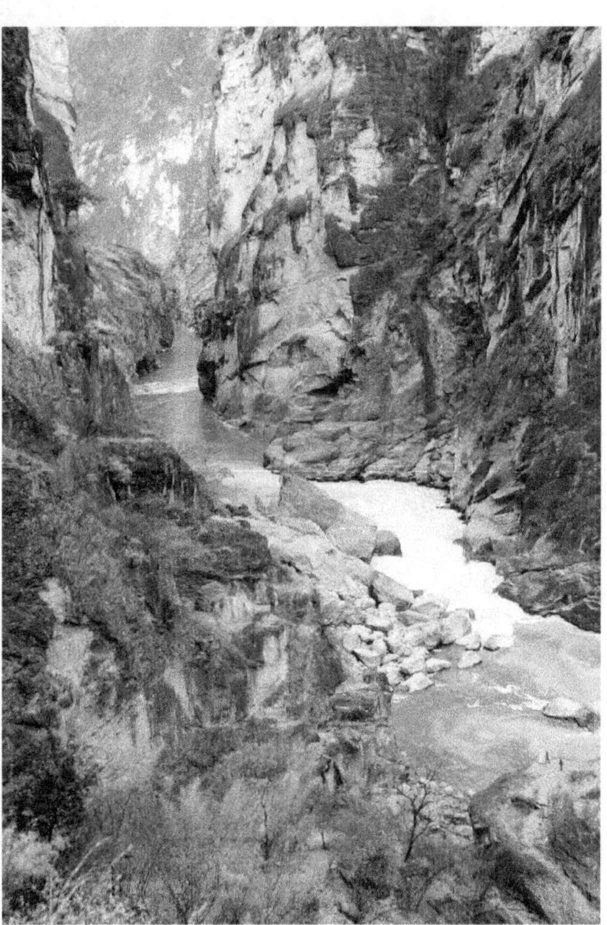

Tiger Leaping Gorge, Jinsha River

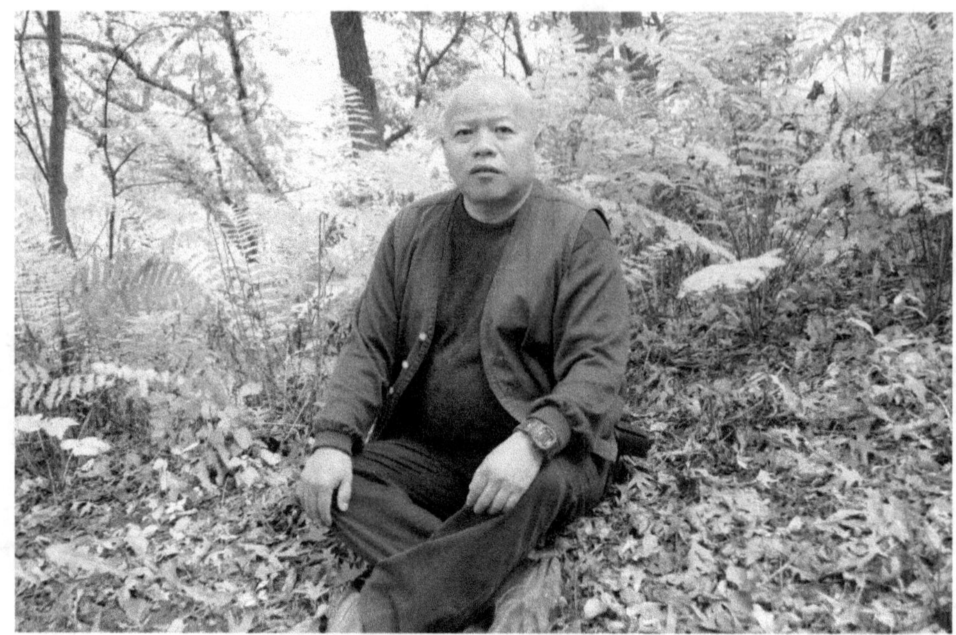

Yu Jian at Afton, St. Croix River

Yu Jian (于坚), born in 1954, is a celebrated Chinese poet and prose writer based in Kunming. His influential works include *Sixty Poems* (诗六十首), *Naming a Crow* (命名乌鸦), *The Nail That Penetrated the Sky* (钉子钉穿天空), *Notes of a Brown Cover* (棕皮手记), and *This Side of Yunnan* (云南这边), among others. His writing has been widely translated into English, French, German, Dutch, Spanish, Italian, Swedish, Danish, and Japanese. Notable translations include *Flash Cards* (translated by Wang Ping and Ron Padgett), *File Zero* (German), *Poetry as Events* (Dutch), and *Flying* (Spanish).

I first encountered Yu Jian's work through my translation project *New Generation: Poems from China Today* (Hanging Loose Press). Among the poets I translated, his writing was the most exhilarating to work with—a sentiment shared by my collaborator, Ron Padgett, who later became a close friend of Yu Jian's. In 2005, I invited Yu Jian to Macalester College for a poetry reading, where we wandered along the Mississippi and St. Croix Rivers, hunting for agates and antiques. In 2010, we reunited for a residency at the Vermont Studio Center. Ron Padgett came to visit us, then invited us to his home in Maine.

种土豆的人们

受到黎明的感染
受到正在上升的太阳的感染
活干得很快　这时候世界是快的
露水干得很快　田鼠逃得很快
在这样的时侯应该赶快　劳动者
很快就脱去了上衣　光起了膀子
一日之计在于晨　小学教师
也是这样教育学生　他们
快速反应着　教室里看不见世界
早晨的语文　在纸上被理解为
一些　昨天剩下的成语
在黄昏中　世界就慢下来
大地的队伍朝着西方慢下来
玉米地和山岗的队列
河流和树林的队列
村庄和向日葵的队列
一切都朝着西方慢下来
所有拖在物体上的影子都慢下来
象裹着黑夜之身的丝绸
一匹匹滑落下去
种土豆的人们　拎着工具
和离开了学校的孩子们汇合
在高地上缓慢地走着
前面是家　他们不担心时间
孩子们慢吞吞的
再没有课外作业
大人们慢吞吞的
因为土豆已经全部种下
他们那么缓慢
仿佛大地进入了他们的身体
那在快速中被种下的东西
并没有慢下来　也从未快过
它们不能快也无法慢
只是开始了　就要生长着
就要从早到晚　从春天到秋天
在着　不紧不慢　直到结束

The Potato Farmers

Inspired by the dawn
by the rising sun
they work fast   the world is fast at this moment
dew dries fast   field mice run fast
the work should be done fast at this moment
workers take off their shirts fast   baring chests
all depends on the morning   says the teachers
to the students who respond fast   they
can't see the entire world from their classroom
the morning words   translate
into yesterday's   proverbs
at dusk   the world slows
the land's marching to the west slows
corns and mountains all slow
rivers and forests all slow
villages and sunflowers all slow
their marching to the west
shadows dragging behind things slow
like silk that wraps around the night
its body sliding off bolt by bolt
the potato farmers   carrying their tools
join the children after school
they walk slowly along the hills
to their homes   don't worry about time
children are not in a hurry
there's no homework
the adults are not in a hurry
all the potato seeds are in the soil
they walk slowly, as if
the earth has melted into their bodies
but the seeds planted in haste
haven't slowed   they never hurry
they can't be rushed or slowed down
once they start growing   they keep growing
from morning till night   from spring till fall
living its cycle   not too fast   not too slow

在渡假区的围墙附近看见秋天……

在渡假区围墙附近　我看着春天的黄月亮
正在从被污染的滇池上升起来
看不出白天的报纸在头版头条所报的污染
看不出恶化的水质和内脏发霉的贝壳
它躺在黑夜的床单上　象尸体
依旧保持着湖泊　原来的形状　起伏
如鳞的光　其它部分是墨蓝色
银色的月光下　树影朦胧　象中文系
的诗歌一样　平庸而永恒　等待着
夜莺和诗人　那些月光下的房子
被建造的如此丑陋　就象妖怪的官殿
这渡假区是十足的垃圾　模仿了香港的
一份过时资料　但在月光下
一切都被忽略　腐烂的滇池生动无比
我想起二十年前的某个良夜
和别人在灰色的沙滩上　脱光了衣服
有一个黑暗者在水里将波浪搬动
啊　我必须尊重这一切
哪怕我知道内幕
我一脚踢开那个刚刚喝光的啤酒罐
它响亮地滚过去　声音惊动了一只蛤蟆
它也假装着不知道　那并不是它的好兄弟
在黑暗中　它黯哑地叫唤起来

I Saw Fall Outside a Vacation Village…

Outside the vacation village, I watch spring's
yellow moon rise from the dirty Lake Dian
No pollution reported on the front page
its smelly water or moldy shellfish
lie on the sheet of night　　like a corpse
keeping its original shape of water and
shivering light　　the rest is dark blue
under the silver moon　　misty tree shadows
flat and eternal　like a poem out of a workshop
nightingales and poets　ugly houses in moonlight
monster palace　　pure garbage
this vacation village　imitation of Hong Kong's
old document　　　all erased
by the moon　the rotting Lake Dian comes alive
I remember a night twenty years ago
on a gray beach　　I got naked with friends
someone stirred up waves
ah　　I must respect this
even though I know what went on
behind the scene　　I kicked up a beer can
It clanked away loudly　　waking up a toad
Who pretends not to notice it's not a brother and
begins to croak　　　　　in the dark

冲浪者

那人夹着红色的滑水板
朝海走去　　他肩膀宽阔
他就要踩着大海的额头
站起来　　高出整个海平线
在陆地上他可做不到
海浪如山涌来
白色的造反者呐喊着
把他抬了上去
他象新国王那样
站在大海的最高处
朝什么人挥了挥手
然后就掉下去了
这冲浪者
重重地跌到波浪下
那盛着海水的地面
他啃了一嘴的沙
差点站不起来

The Surfer

Holding his red surfboard
he walked to the sea　　broad surfer
about to step on the ocean's forehead
rising　　above the sea level
something impossible to achieve on land
waves poured in like mountains
white rebels roaring
lifting him
like a new king
standing on top of the ocean
he waved
then fell
crashed under the waves
the surfer on the beach
his surf going in and out
his mouth full of sand
could hardly stand

2005-1-12致王屏

新年好！
你在忙什么？
击剑　上课
接娃娃回家
为丈夫煮咖啡
偶尔翻译某人的诗
在黄昏的积雪中
收拾去年落在院子里的东西
密西西比河在冰下面走动
你驾驶汽车
穿过明尼苏达郊外
去那家中国商店买榨菜
隔壁的古玩店有朋友的痕迹
大地苍茫
那个辉煌的秋天无影无踪
我们走过山地　三个诗人
皆以石头为荣　在桥下面
有人钓鱼　森林中站着些幽灵
有一个跟着我回到了中国老家
孤独是自然现象　我们都理解
快乐地承受　生命的美和残忍
许多美好的事情　永远来不及开始
只是感觉到　只是偶然提及
只剩下漫长的信
在遥远的故乡　新年就要开始
一只鸡在黑暗里抖动身子
就要嘹亮地啼鸣

2005-1-12在昆明

2005 the Year of the Chicken

Happy New Year, Wang Ping!
What are you doing today?
Fencing   teaching
Picking up kids
Making coffee for your husband
Or translating some poet's work?
At sunset snow is falling
You put away things left in the yard from last year
Under the ice, the Mississippi walks
You drive
to a Minnesota suburb
to buy pickles in a Chinese grocery
An old friend lingers in the antique shop next door
The brilliant fall is gone
The land is still vast and wild
We climbed the hills   three poets
all love stones   under the bridge
someone were fishing   some spirits stood
in the woods   one followed me back home to China
loneliness is part of nature. We understood, accepted
this beauty and cruelty of life   happily
Beautiful things   often have no time to be born
We can only feel them   or mention them briefly
but long letters remain
in the distant home   a new year has begun
the rooster is shaking its body in the dark
ready to crow

2005 1-12 Kunming

光辉的一天

光辉的一天……太阳照耀着万物
有块白石在佛蒙特州的森林里发光
乔·布雷纳德之墓　美国诗人
1942-1994在世　俄克拉荷马的
高中少年　啊　戴着副黑框眼镜
谁读过你的诗?
青山下　湖泊安静　鸟在午睡
我记得　睡莲还在开着　夏天已近尾声
死后　罗恩和肯沃德搬运了很久
一块石头穿越松树林
熊和落叶都靠边站
白得像一块耻骨　纪念　没有文字
六十年代　哥们常在这里饮酒
抽大麻　听松　坐在坡上看落日
我摸摸那石头　被烫着似地缩回手来
太凉　正像传说中的天才之额
世界这炉子热火朝天
它们总是　　　冰凉如石

2010年8月21日在美国佛蒙特州的
森林中,与诗人罗恩、王屏，藕诗人
Joe Brainard之墓。

A Glorious Day

A glorious day… sunlight on everything
a white rock shines　in the Vermont woods
that's Joe Brainard's grave　　an American Poet
1942-1994 graduate　　of an Oklahoma
high school　ah　wearing dark-rimmed glasses
who has read your poems?
Under blue mountains, the lake is quiet, birds napping
I remember　water lilies　summer near its end
when he died　Kenward brought it here
a rock through the woods
bears and fallen leaves make way
white like bone in his memory　no words
in the 60s, they were here　drinking, smoking weed
listening to the pines　watching sunset on the hill
I touch the rock　recoil as if scorched
so cold　like the geniuses' foreheads
cool like a rock　in this world
that burns like a furnace

August 21, 2010 in the Vermont woods,
at poet Joe Brainard's grave with Ron Padgett
and Wang Ping

Yangzi (央子, born Zhang Yu [张瑜], 1995) is a poet, writer, translator, and teacher at Kunming International School. She studied poetry and translation with Wang Ping for two years, and has been collaborating with her on different translation projects.

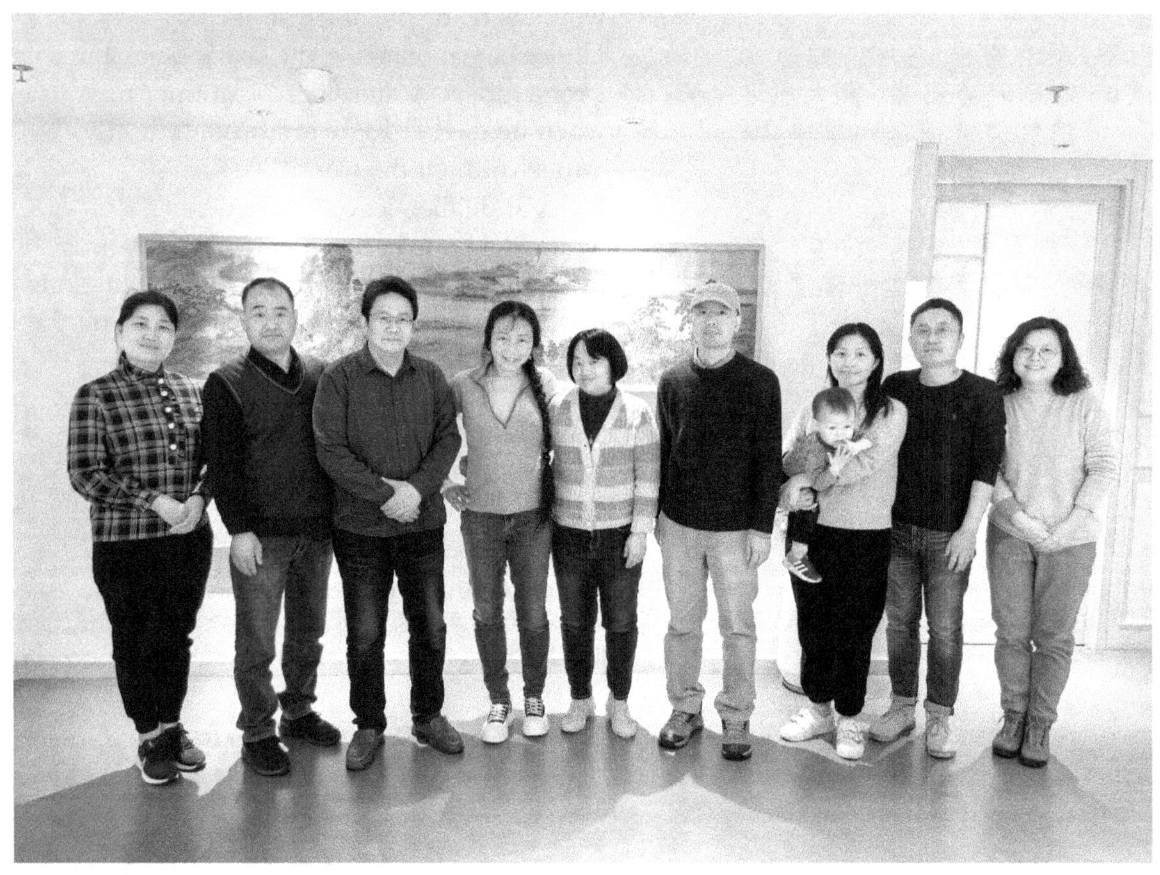

Yangzi/Zhang Yu with her son, third from right, Nanjing
Left to right: Yuan Xin, Potato Brother, Hu Xian, Wang Ping, Sun Dong, Huang Fan, other poets

雪花莲，灯塔，生存

冷风吹来
你可知我曾是什么，怎样活着？
你知道红蚁
我站在冰冷的水里，冷雾
像灰蒙的一片浮萍，
绝望是什么；那么
将我包裹，微弱的光
漂浮潭上；
冬天就对你有了意义
淡淡呼吸着浓郁的黑暗
冷风吹来，
我没想到被压在厚厚的土壤下
我看见远处
黑色的云夹杂一封仆文，
还能存活。我没想到
紧握的脚跟拥抱为战舰，
还能再次醒来，去感受飘来一座岛，
又穿戴钢铸雨衣，
远远飘走
潜越亿万年的星系直达永生。
自己的身体，
瞬间的进化神秘似黑洞。
在潮湿的泥土里重新伸展，许久之后
我试着招手，大树，长颈鹿和人
才想起没了双手
赤裸的身体，
在寒春的冷光中
眺望

Snow Lotus & Lighthouse
After Louise Gluck

Wind blows
Do you know what I was, how I lived?
Do you know red ants?
I stand in cold water, mist
Floating like a cloak of duckweed
What's despair   like this
You wrap me up, weak light
Drifts on the pond
This is what winter means to you
Breathing the thick night
In cold wind
I never expected to live under the earth
In the distance
An obituary in dark clouds
I'm still alive, never expected
To hug the warship with my heels
Or wake up again, feeling
The island adrift, my raincoat
Made of steel
I'm drifting away
Into the billion-year old stars
My body melts into a black hole
Then opens again in the moist earth
After a long pause I try to wave
At trees, giraffes, humans
Then remember
I no longer have hands
My naked body is still watching
In the light of cold spring

Chongqing (重庆): Where Geography Shapes History and Culture

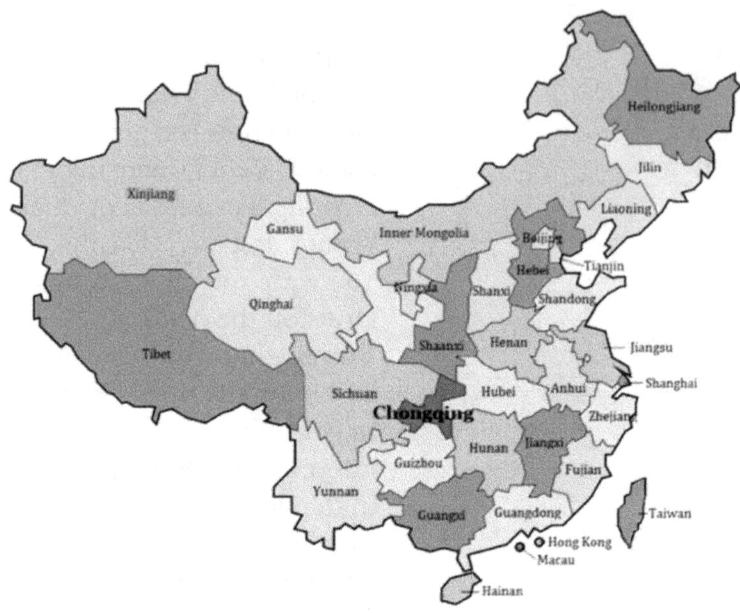

Chongqing is a megacity of staggering contrasts—ancient history intertwined with modern dynamism, towering mountains carved by raging rivers, and a landscape of immense natural beauty. Perched at the confluence of the Yangtze and Jialing Rivers, the city is cradled by dramatic folded mountain ranges formed by the collision of the Indian and Eurasian tectonic plates millions of years ago. This rugged karst terrain, with its steep cliffs and deep gorges, has long served as a natural fortress, shielding the region from invaders.

The most legendary example of Chongqing's defensive might was the Battle of Diaoyu Fortress (1259), where Song General Wang Jian halted the seemingly unstoppable Mongke Khan—grandson of Genghis Khan and ruler of the largest contiguous empire in history.

Having conquered vast swaths of Russia, Europe, India, Vietnam, and northern China, Mongke Khan's forces met their match at the steep slopes of Diaoyu Fortress. Despite relentless assaults, General Wang's forces repelled the Mongols using strategic positions, arrows, and crushing stone barrages. Mongke Khan was mortally wounded in the siege, forcing the Mongols to retreat. This stunning victory prolonged the Southern Song Dynasty's survival by two decades, altering the course of Chinese history.

Alongside defensive might, Chongqing's fiery landscapes have forged an equally intense culture. The Sichuan Basin's humid climate and mineral-rich soil nurture the region's famed Sichuan peppercorns, while the Jialing River's brisk waters once carried merchant fleets, fueling trade and culinary innovation. The result? Chongqing hotpot—a bold, numbing-spicy dish born from the sweat and resilience of river port laborers.

The Three Gorges, carved over millennia by the Yangtze's relentless flow, have inspired poets like Li Bai, who wrote of its "swift waters and mist-wrapped peaks," and painters who captured its ethereal beauty. Though the Three Gorges Dam has reshaped the river's path, Chongqing's spirit remains unbroken—a city where history, geology, and culture collide in a spectacle of resilience and spices.

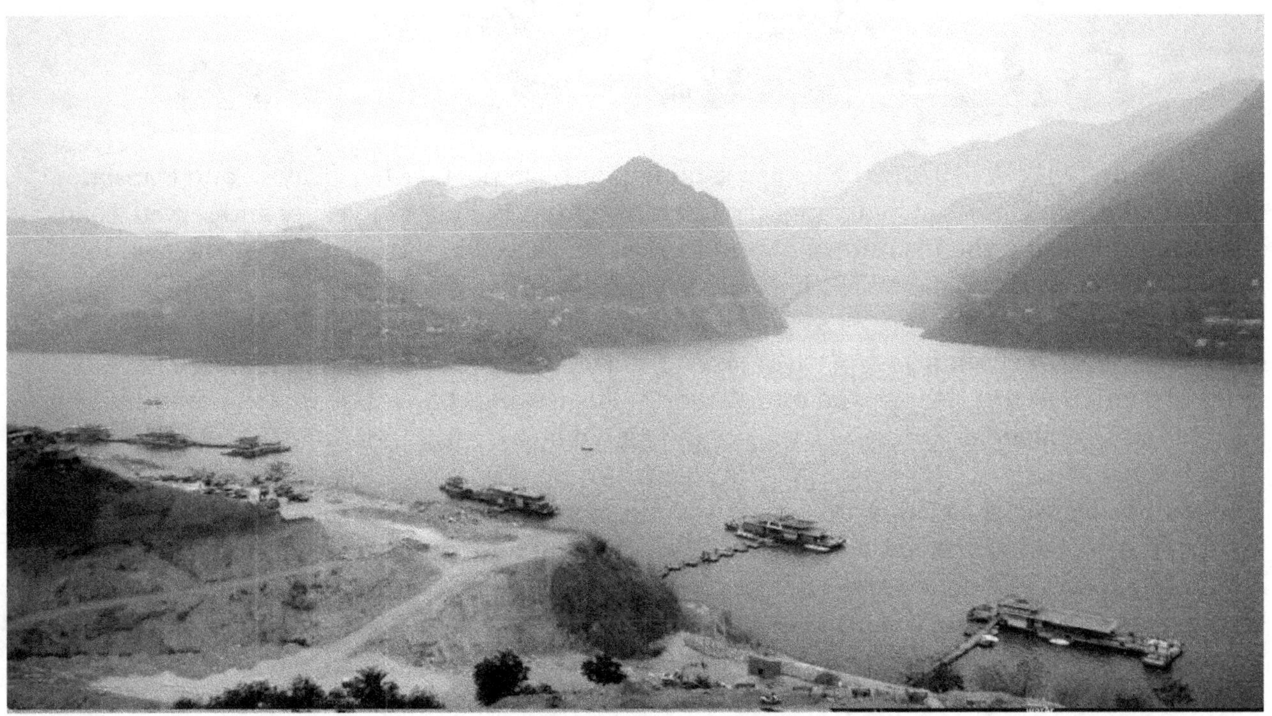

Wuxia, Three Gorges

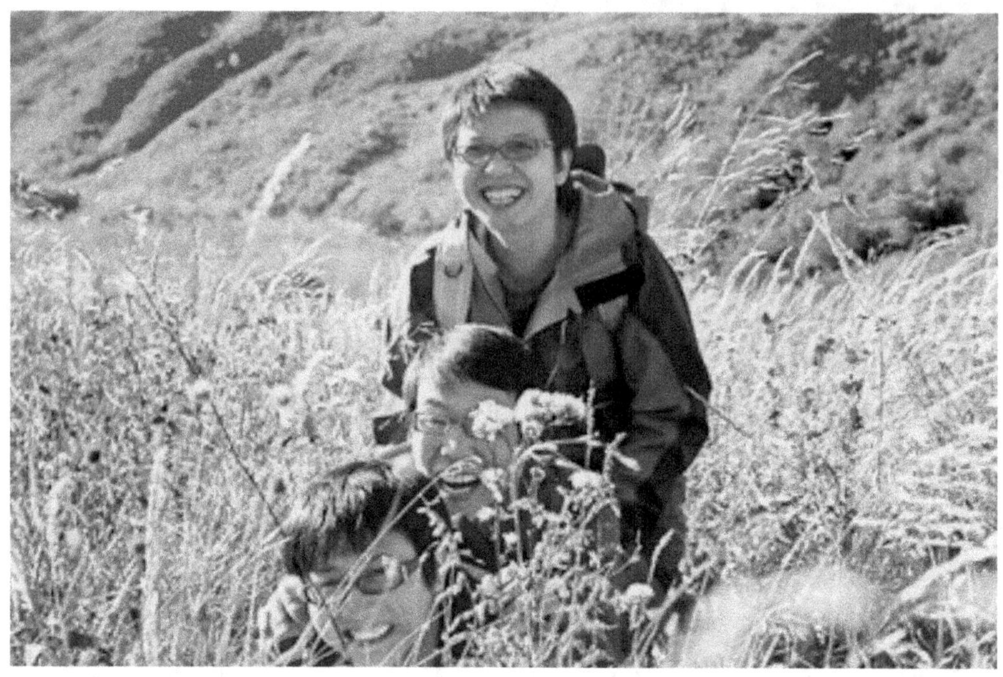

Hu Xudong (胡续冬, 1974–2021) was a Chongqing-born poet, critic, essayist, and translator. He held a PhD in Chinese Contemporary Literature from Beijing University and served as an associate professor at the Institute of World Literature, as well as vice-director of the Center of Brazilian Culture. A prolific writer, Hu Xudong published eight poetry collections, including *Waterside Writings* (水边书), *The Power of the Calendar* (日历之力), and *Travel/Poems* (旅行/诗); three essay collections, including *To Hell with Brazil* (去他的巴西) and *Nonsense of a Floating Life* (浮生胡言); and numerous translations and critical works. His writings have appeared in major literary journals and anthologies, bridging Chinese and global literary traditions.

Though I never had the chance to meet Hu Xudong in person, his work enchanted me from the first read. It was wild, free, and alive—much like the man himself. As a professor, he nurtured minds, but his poetry remained deeply rooted in the earth, drawing from the rivers and landscapes of the world, particularly South America, a region that profoundly influenced his vision. I don't know if he sang or danced, but his words leap, whirl, and resonate with a rhythm all their own—a testament to a spirit unbound by borders.

阿尔博阿多尔

我只愿意独自呆在诗里，诗独自
呆在海里，海独自呆在有风的夜里。
一夜之后，阳光拖着水光上天，
嘈杂的人群从细小的白沙里
走出来换气。

换完气的细小的人群回到嘈杂的白沙里，
又是一天，地平线把太阳拖进水底。
海从夜里裸泳出去，
诗从海里裸泳出去，
我从一首诗裸泳到了另一首诗里。

Arpoador

I just want you to leave me alone in poetry,
leave poetry alone in the sea, leave the sea
alone with the windy night. Night is over,
The sun rises with misty light. Noisy crowds
come out of white sand to breathe.

After the breath the tiny people return
to the noisy white sand, another day gone,
the horizon drags the sun into the water.
The sea swims naked out of the night;
Poetry swims naked out of the sea
I swim from one poem to another, naked.

安娜•保拉大妈也写诗

安娜•保拉大妈也写诗。
她叼着玉米壳卷的土烟，把厚厚的一本诗集
砸给我，说："看看老娘我写的诗。"
这是真的，我学生若泽的母亲、
胸前两团巴西、臀后一片南美、满肚子的啤酒
像大西洋一样汹涌的安娜•保拉大妈也写诗。
第一次见面那天，她像老鹰捉小鸡一样
把我拎起来的时候，我不知道她写诗。
她满口"鸡巴"向我致意、张开棕榈大手
揉我的脸、伸出大麻舌头舔我惊慌的耳朵的时候，
我不知道她写诗。所有的人，包括
她的儿子若泽和儿媳吉赛莉，都说她是
老花痴，没有人告诉我她写诗。若泽说：
"放下我的老师吧，我亲爱的老花痴。"
她就撂下了我，继续口吐"鸡巴"，去拎
另外的小鸡。我看着她酒后依然魁梧得
能把一头雄牛撞死的背影，怎么都不会想到
她也写诗。就是在今天、在安娜•保拉大妈
格外安静的今天，我也想不到她写诗。
我跟着若泽走进家门、侧目瞥见
她四仰八叉躺在泳池旁边抽烟的时候，想不到
她写诗；我在客厅里撞见一个梳着
鲍勃•马力辫子的肌肉男、吉赛莉告诉我那是她婆婆
昨晚的男朋友的时候，我更是打死都没想到
每天都有肌肉男的安娜•保拉大妈也写诗。
千真万确，安娜•保拉大妈也写诗。凭什么
打嗝、放屁的安娜•保拉大妈不可以写
不打嗝、不放屁的女诗人的诗？我一页一页地翻着
安娜•保拉大妈的诗集。没错，安娜•保拉大妈
的确写诗。但她不写肥胖的诗、酒精的诗、
大麻的诗、鸡巴的诗和肌肉男的肌肉之诗。
在一首名为《诗歌中的三秒钟的寂静》的诗里，
她写道："在一首诗中给我三秒钟的寂静，
我就能在其中写出满天的乌云。"

Mama Ana Paula Writes Poetry

Mama Ana Paula also writes poetry.
Cornhusk cig burning between her lips, she throws a thick book
at me: "Take a look at Big Mama's poems."
It's true, my student Jose's mama,
bosoms hugging two Brazils, buttocks wider than America, belly round with beer
surging like the Atlantic, writes poetry. Mama Ana Paula.
The first time we met, she snatched me up, an eagle snatching a chick
and I had no idea she writes poetry.
She greeted me with her "prick" words, rubbed my face with her palm tree hands,
licked my panicked ears with her marijuana tongue,
and I had no idea she writes poetry. Everyone, including
her son Jose and daughter-in-law Giselle, told me
she's an old nymph, but nobody told me she writes poetry. Jose told her,
"Please put down my professor, dear old nymph."
She dropped me down, went after other chicks, her mouth
spitting "dicks and pricks." I watched her drunken back, so thick and strong.
She could knock down a bull, and not in a million years
did it occur to me that she also writes poetry.
Even today when Mama Ana Paula is quiet, I didn't know she writes poetry.
I followed Jose inside, and saw
her stretched out by the swimming pool, smoking, and I never thought
she writes poetry; in the living room I bumped into a muscled man with
Bob Marley's dreads, and Giselle told me he was her in-law's boyfriend last night,
like every other night, and I still wouldn't believe Mama Ana Paula
writes poetry, if you put a thousand guns to my head.
But it's true, Mama Ana Paula writes poetry.
Why shouldn't a burping, farting Mama Ana Paula
write poems like those women poets who never burp or
fart? Page by page, I turn the book by Mama Ana Paula.
That's right, Mama Ana Paula writes poetry.
She doesn't write fat poems, drunk poems, marijuana
poems, or poems about pricks or muscled men. No.
In "Three-Second Silence of Poetry," she writes
"Give me three seconds of silence in a poem,
I can fill your sky with dark clouds."

Jin Lingzi (金铃子), born in 1990 in Chongqing, is an acclaimed Chinese poet and artist, celebrated for her avant-garde style and lyrical depth. She has authored nine books of poetry and art, including *Song of the Yue People* (越人歌) and *Thinking on The Book of Change* (易经随想), blending visual and literary creativity. Her work has been recognized with prestigious awards, including the 2008 Avant-garde Poetry Prize, the Youth Poetry Award (*Poetry Magazine*), the Xu Zhimo Poetry Prize, the Qu Yuan Poetry Prize, and others.

Jin Lingzi's poetry often intersects with visual art, mirroring the trend seen in contemporary Chinese ink artists. Her recognition at the Xu Zhimo Poetry Festival places her within a transnational dialogue, similar to poets like Jidi Majia, who bridge Eastern and Western poetic traditions.

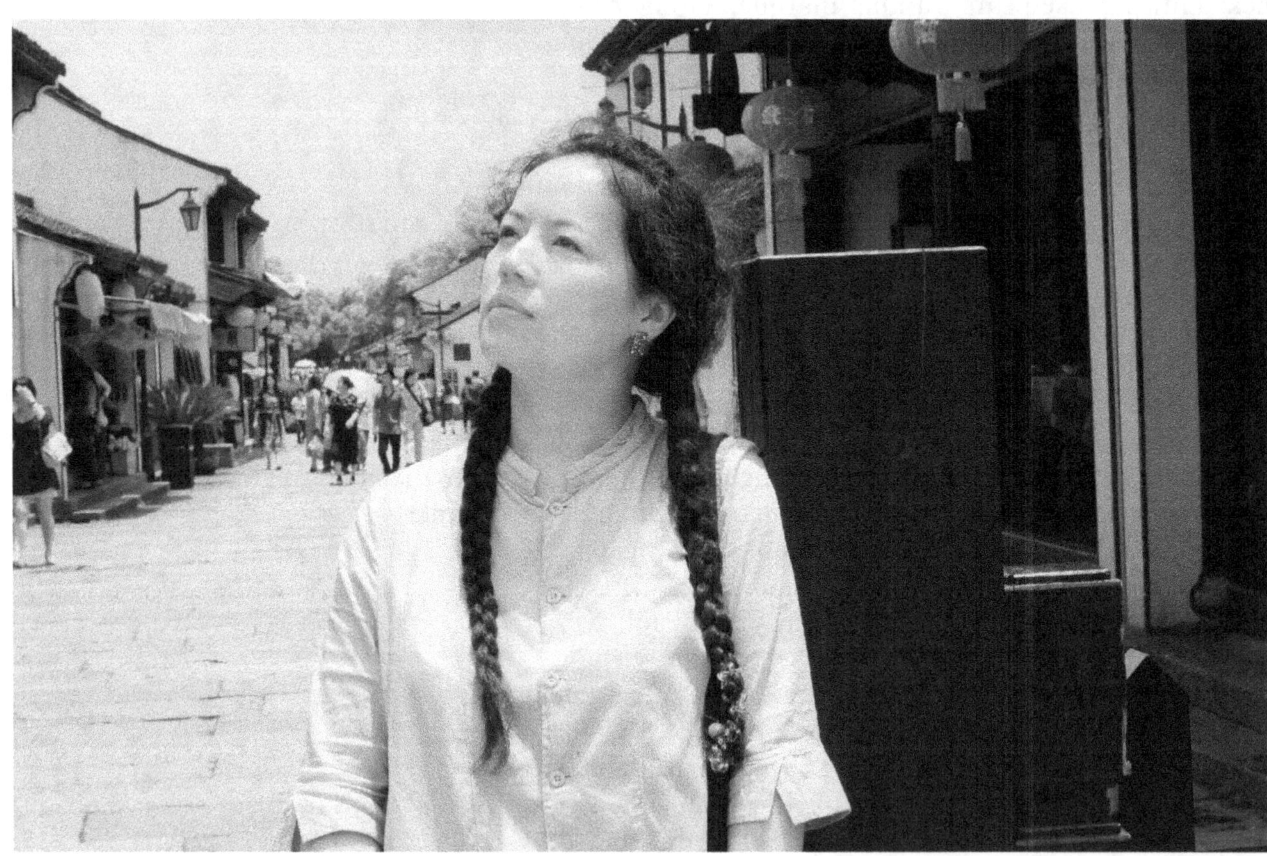

省略

我省略的爱可长可短
说出来不过徒增热闹
省略的记忆，封存在一张棋盘里
不黑，就白
省略的苦，在笑声里
笑一声，眼泪就往身体里流
心底的湖水就涨了又涨
偶尔，有鱼虾从湖里冒出头来
我也将它们省略
在这六个点中
躲过了猎手，子弹和渔网

就这样含糊其辞的……活着
只是诗歌，偶尔
发出清晰的、空落落的
落指声

Ellipsis

My ellipsis for love can be short or long
If I tell the story, it'd be just adding noise
The memory is locked in the game of go
It's either black or white; nothing else
Its pain lurks in my laughter
Where tears flow inward
Flooding the lake in the heart
Sometimes, fish and shrimp appear
But I hide them
In the dots
To escape hunters, bullets and nets

This is how I live…vague, evasive
Sometimes my poetry
Makes some sounds, hollow
Slipping sounds of Go

瓶里的绿萝枯萎了

有一双手
仔细的把它插在酒瓶里
应该有一双眼睛
欢喜的望着它
等待它发芽
它真的枯萎了
一片枯叶挨着另外一片枯叶
仿佛一个老去的人
挨着另外一个老去的人
我默默的喝着茶
甚至没有想过，给它斟上一杯
面对枯萎，我胸口疼痛
却无动于衷

The Devil's Vine Died in a Wine Bottle

A pair of hands
Placed it in a wine bottle
A pair of watching eyes
Waiting for it to sprout
But it withered
One leaf after another
Like an elder
Next to an aging man
I sip tea in silence
Never bothered to
Pour a cup for the plant
Facing the death, I feel pangs in my chest
But do nothing

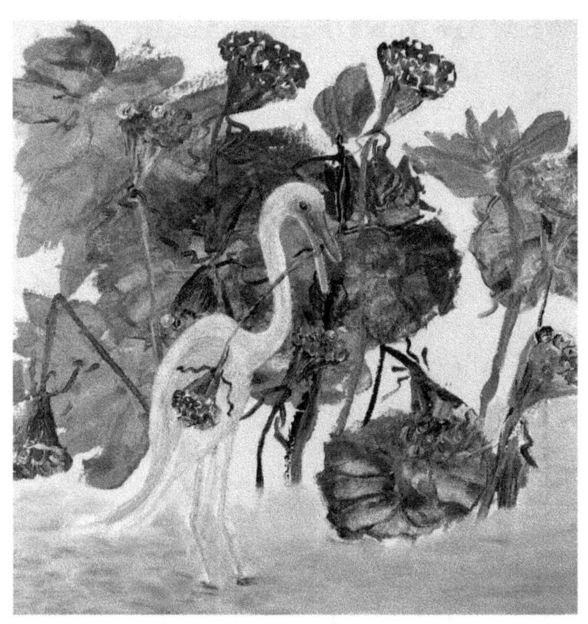

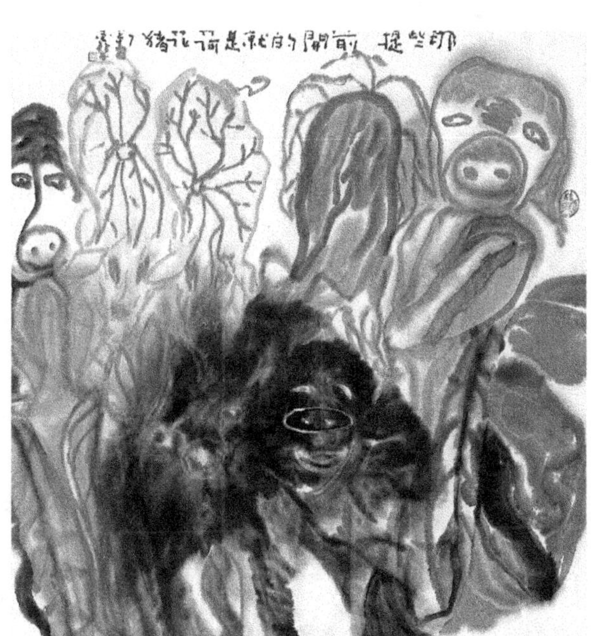

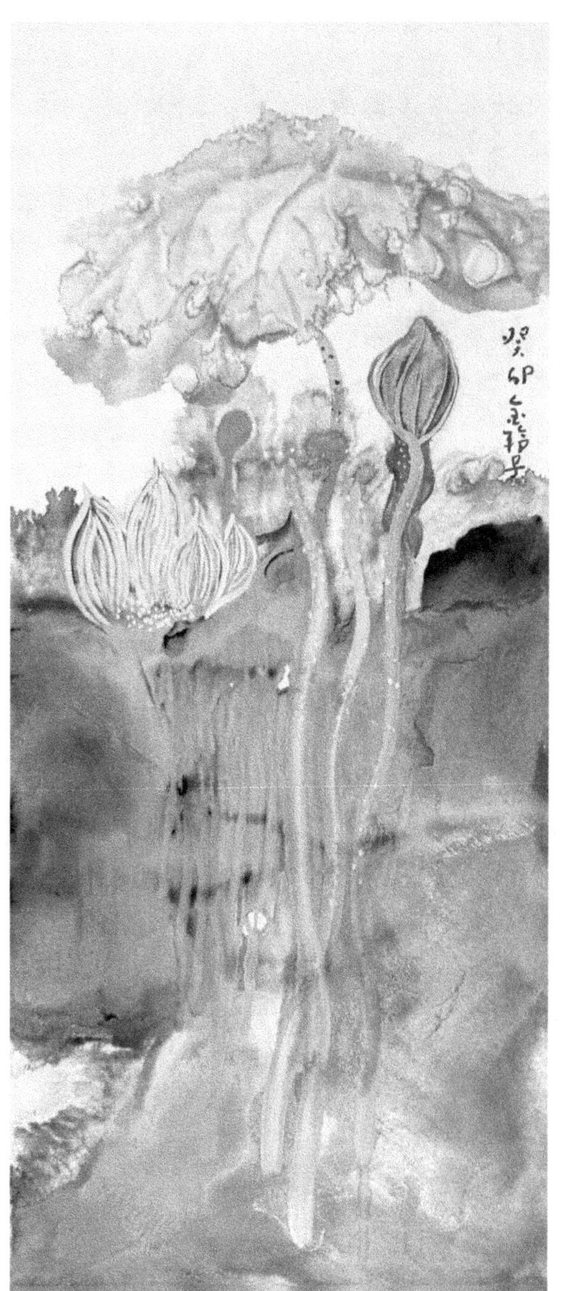

Watercolors by Jin Lingzi

有什么不满意的啊

有什么不满意的啊
疫年免于死亡，不饥不寒
半亩之宅，可养鸡鸭，植柑橘
可闭双眼，视而不见
可睁双眼，相互窥视
我问自己
到底有什么不满意的啊
可是，我就是不满意
就是常常独自一人
静对群山
无声流泪

What Are You Grumpy About

Why are you so grumpy
You didn't die during the pandemic
Didn't suffer hunger or cold
You got enough land to raise chickens and
ducks, grow oranges
You can close your eyes, look but see
Nothing. You can open your eyes, peeping at
each other. You ask yourself
What complains do you really have
You have no answer
Just sit by the mountain, alone
Weeping in silence

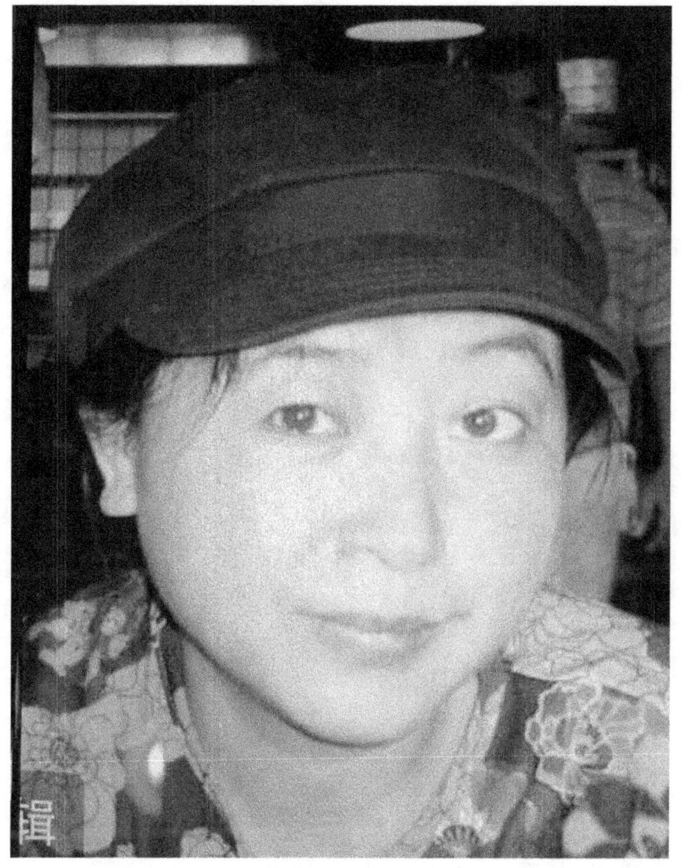

Ma Lan (马兰), born in 1979 in Mesishan, Sichuan, is a Chinese-American poet and fiction writer of Hui ethnicity. Her poetry has appeared in prestigious literary journals such as *People's Literature* (人民文学), *Flower City* (花城), and *Zhong Shan* (钟山). She is the author of the poetry collection *How to Kill a Glove* (我们如何杀死一只手套) and two novels.

An active figure in contemporary literature, Ma Lan serves as the editor of *Olive Tree* (橄榄树), an influential online literary journal dedicated to promoting innovative writing. She currently lives in Virginia, where she continues to write and engage with transnational literary communities.

我梦见

我梦见：一幢房子撞见另一幢房子，形成峡谷
梦见：雨季就要来临了，河水冲破了人生
梦见：五百个恐龙和五千架F16决战
梦见：每个小孩都有秘密，他们窃窃私语
梦见：骨头和骨头之间有一片水域
梦见：推开一道门又多一道门，倒影连环爆炸
梦见：每天的风景不动，你说我喜欢美好的女人，但花儿不重开
梦见：摘桃时节，眼见苹果落地，仿佛凶案现场
梦见：一朵花倒地刺向另一朵花，犹如山脉起伏
梦见：神说解决了自己才能面对神
梦见：空气变成水，冷到极限就无任何干扰了
梦见：故人三十年还在故地，讲同样的故事
梦见：天空斜躺，父亲身体柔软成熟，微笑不语
梦见：他是两条河，他同时出现在不同时间
梦见：谎言重复一遍就是真理，真理是井中月亮
梦见：捕快，去捕风捉影，光头首当其冲
梦见：我不说话，我就是独联体，推倒所有的窗户
梦见：我是陌生人，接触陌生人是场起义
梦见：全世界受冤屈的灵魂组团去了广场
梦见：二十年前的今天，我们在路上，定了终生
梦见：他越来越远，越走越空，没有一根鸡毛飞上天
梦见：我盘腿而坐，双臂皆无，吸墨而起
梦见：姐姐站在阴影之外，没有一个园点包容她
梦见：二十年后的今天,我们老了，坐下，看见彼此
梦见：一个孤独者拥抱一群孤独者，一群疯子理解一个疯子
梦见：魔鬼不仅存在于细节，还站在事物的中心
梦见：画一幅画，便是平地起惊雷，构建真实世界
梦见：我们练习造句，句子穿穿春秋，偶尔在夏天迷路
梦见：过午不食，手扶一朵古花，醉生梦死
梦见：太阳晒焦了一只红蜘蛛，我们去参加葬礼
梦见：时间不走直线，在河道沉醉，空间又提前看望了他乡
梦见：一滴蒸熟的眼泪，失去了重量
梦见：披上雨衣，召呼你，看那满屋激动的蘑菇
梦见：黑暗回光反照，可他们说，再给五百年
梦见：一夜未眠，谁把树下的青叶当鸡毛信
梦见：晨奔的泪水，淋湿了带刺的玫瑰

I Dream

I dream: a house bumps into another, forming a canyon
Dream: monsoon is coming, the river breaks our destiny
Dream: five hundred dinosaurs fighting five thousand F16s
Dream: every child has a secret; they're whispering
Dream: a body of water between bones
Dream: pushing one door after another, reflections exploding
Dream: at the murder scene, apples falling, someone said
Dream: I love pretty women, but the flowers won't bloom again
Dream: a flower falls, pricking another flower, like the mountain range
Dream: God said: go figure yourself out first before coming to me
Dream: air becomes water; no more disturbance when it's too cold
Dream: old friends still remain in old hometown, telling the same story
Dream: sky lies flat, father's soft body, a perpetual smile
Dream: he is two rivers, appearing at different times at the same time
Dream: a lie becomes truth with one repetition; truth becomes a moon in the well
Dream: a detective detects shadows in the wind; a bald man leads the march
Dream: I no longer speak; I'm a lone entity, pushing windows open
Dream: I'm a stranger; every encounter with strangers is a rebellion
Dream: all the wronged souls on earth are gathering at the square
Dream: twenty years ago, we decided our fate, on the road
Dream: breathing in dreams, arms waving eternally
Dream: elder sister standing outside the shadow, embraced by a point
Dream: he's farther away, emptier, without chicken feathers
Dream: twenty years later, we sit down and finally see each other, sitting
Dream: a loner hugs a crowd of loners; a crowd of loonies understand another loony
Dream: a devil exists in details, in the hearts of things
Dream: a painting is thunder on the horizon, building a world
Dream: practice sentence, sentence passing through seasons, without losing the way
Dream: time never walks a straight line. A flower in hand, live and die drunk
Dream: the sun chars a red spider, we attend its funeral
Dream: sky and earth go on separate ways, leaving chicken coops everywhere.
Dream: the sea is rising, sneaky swords no longer penetrate; you're the needle settling the sea
Dream: put on my raincoat, calling you, the house full of mushroom
Dream: last breath before death, but they say: give her another 500 years
Dream: insomnia, who thinks the nuts under the tree are urgent messages
Dream: tears in early morning, soaking the thorny rose

梦见：月亮、风、排骨、在一个平面
梦见：一个影子唱着艰深的咒语，大步走过墓地
梦见：双手双脚的双头人，去江湖寻找另外一伴
梦见：全世界的婴儿团结起来，嚎啕大哭
梦见：新桥是天边的彩虹，从中辩认光影的暗部
梦见：提刀就战胜了自己，无论左或者右
梦见：一只手拨开滚烫的云朵，说：孩子，变了
梦见：钝刀割肉，连皮带骨，一场分手晚宴
梦见：梵高的星空下唯有老人在搭积木
梦见：我从未听见花开的声音，从未在暴雨下疾走
梦见：四月的墙边，轻风掠过，太阳正暖
梦见：举着眼睛奔跑的兄弟，目不斜视
梦见：各自挥手上路，山水很近，行李较远
梦见：你我六年的时光是堆暗物质，可长可短
梦见：失去左手意味半身不遂，半个人仍在尖叫
梦见：开口说话，父母便双亡，失语症就此完成
梦见：初夏时分，开始一种关系是花裂，湿润又灼热
梦见：我体无完肤，光都难以照入
梦见：走失的婴孩站在门外，前无来者，后无追兵
梦见：故乡的墓地，有熟人闪动，我们没有家谱
梦见：生在两个时代，活在一个世界
梦见：大路朝天，我们独自击鼓，回头一笑
梦见：神仙打皇帝，读书者反被书读
梦见：美人是一个取景镜头，转身消失
梦见：溶身的恐惧从天而降，一个神话被破解了
梦见：北回归线穿过心脏，自我分裂出另一个肖像
梦见：一只乌鸦飞向另一只鸟，定是前世有缘
梦见：我所吃的食物，积满灰尘，又催发了新芽
梦见：太阳照在一束光上，仿佛自我囚禁
梦见：一场疾病，由细菌完成封喉的仪式
梦见：孩子一步跨过鸿沟，我们还在追忆
梦见：渡金时代，女人天真无邪，夜夜笙歌
梦见：月光下，一只野兔怀抱青春飞驰
梦见：影子快速溶解，是谁打破了时钟？
梦见：风吹破城墙，逃亡者的细软散落于地
梦见：五月在春城的边缘，与风车决斗
梦见：饥饿的记忆，穿胃而过，沾在墙角
梦见：一排杀猪刀在滚开的铁板上起舞，大喊："死的光荣"

Dream: moon, landscape, ribs, on the same surface
Dream: a shadow sings a difficult curse, striding through graves
Dream: a figure with two hands two feet two heads, seeking his other half
Dream: all the infants unite, bawling together
Dream: a new bridge is a rainbow, recognizing the dark in the light
Dream: I conquer myself instantly with a pen, from left to right
Dream: a hand pushes aside the boiling waves, watching children change
Dream: dull knife cuts the flesh, skin and bones, a goodbye dinner
Dream: an old man builds blocks under Van Gogh's Starry Night
Dream: I never heard flowers blooming, never walked in rain
Dream: walls in April, breeze, warm sun
Dream: brother running, eyes lifting, on the road
Dream: we part, wave goodbye, mountains and water are near, our luggage far away
Dream: our six years is quantum physics, shortened or lengthened, all depends
Dream: you lost your left hand, then your left side, half of you still screaming
Dream: before words come, cold sweat breaks out, completing the goodbye
Dream: early summer, ending a relationship, feeling the earth sunk, flowers split
Dream: I'm covered with sores, full of sins; even light can't enter
Dream: the lost infant stands outside the door, in the dark
Dream: three thousand li from home, we don't have a family tree
Dream: born in two eras, live in one world
Dream: the highway faces the sky, picks flowers alone, turns and smiles
Dream: gods beat up the emperor; the reader is read by the book
Dream: the broken bridge is a scene for cameras, vanishing when you turn
Dream: the terror of melting falls from the sky, a broken myth
Dream: north longitude passes through the heart, splitting into another portrait
Dream: a bird flies to another bird, pre-destined
Dream: my mistakes, covered with dust, are sprouting again
Dream: the sun sheds on light, as if prisoning itself
Dream: a disease, then bacteria finishes off cutting the throat
Dream: the child crosses the chasm with one jump, and we're still chasing our memory
Dream: in the golden age, innocent women sing every night
Dream: empty scene: you said the ghost is in the light
Dream: injured fall wind spins in the room
Dream: in the moonlight, a rabbit runs with youth in its chest
Dream: shadows are melting, breaking clocks
Dream: wind breaks through the falling wall, scattering the escapers' possessions
Dream: May on the edge of the city, battling wind mills
Dream: hungry memory, passing through stomach, standing in the corner
Dream: knives dance on the boiling steel, shouting we have to start again

梦见：鸟的翅膀落在你的前胸，天就垮了
梦见：我给你写诗了，手放在火苗上
梦见：我们的名字在墓地重逢，相视而笑
梦见：今生的福报，就是前世转身放下的果实
我梦见：革命其实是蛋炒饭，爱情是水煮青蛙
梦见：我们死去活来，立地成妖精
梦见：幼时的你说，我要看着你长大
梦见：星星和镜子白头到老，无人知晓多少春秋
梦见：春风渡过了玉门关，哪位妙人还在等待？
梦见：扬州烟花，我们丢失了与时间的合影
梦见：少不入川的你，飞沙遮面，举旗不定
梦见：情到深处，人消失，万马过黄河
梦见：想你时就开始脱皮，我抓紧皮肤
梦见：头发不翼而飞，黄昏松软地下垂
梦见：我的猫走失数年，仍然独立，不沾人
梦见：我的花朵在掌心奔驰，见证变化的空间
梦见：你从河里驮起我，昼伏夜出，不知归程
梦见：安魂曲在火中吹响，泪珠在热油下烫伤成鸡血
梦见：疼痛是前世的线索，渴望麻药，长睡不醒
梦见：阳光被切割，分开了明暗，本质的奢侈
梦见：人脑是一个大硬盘，但找不到软件读写
梦见：一片树叶落地，天下为之变色
梦见：初恋情人，他在云南翻山越岭，江水包围着他
梦见：前面是水，背后是墙，你们才是八九点钟的太阳
梦见：我与世界的关系积满青苔，一滑即倒
梦见：父亲抱着棉被朝我冲来。母亲躺在床上叹息
梦见：他的手伸向我，我怎么也摸不到，梦里的风吹向窗外
梦见：我的后半生在一个终日阳光的地方，那里的人们仇恨太阳
梦见：我是孕妇，我怎会知道春天还能排卵呢
梦见：阿丽的孩子要死了，女人的一生是悬挂在流水的投影
梦见：老鼠都长好了翅膀，在屋内飞行
梦见：风吹草动，你我离家远行，乱刀割乱麻
梦见：死亡完美，只能转身快跑表达缘分
梦见：服下了这白色药丸，一道蓝光击穿天堂之门
梦见：巴山夜雨，撑船人，孤单地想象最后的归客

Dream: bird wings fall on your chest; the sky is falling
Dream: I wrote you a poem, fingers on fire
Dream: our names meet again in the cemetery, smiling at each other
Dream: today's fortune is the fruit laid from the previous life
I dream: revolution is fried rice, and love is boiled frogs
Dream: we die and live, turning into monsters
Dream: you said as a child: I want to watch you grow
Dream: stars and mirrors grow old together, but no one knows
Dream: spring has arrived at Jade Gate Pass; who's that beauty still waiting
Dream: fireworks in Yangzhou; we lost our photo with time
Dream: you didn't enter Sichuan as a child, wavering, flying sand in your face
Dream: love at certain depth; we vanish; only ten thousand horses crossed the Yellow River
Dream: my skin peels when I think of you; I hang onto the skin
Dream: hair suddenly gone, dusk draping
Dream: my cat disappeared for years, still alone, refusing to touch humans
Dream: my flower runs in my palm, witnessing the changing time
Dream: you carry me out of the river; stay put at night, travel by day, without destination
Dream: a requiem explodes in my ear; tears roll in blood
Dream: pain is the trace from previous life; desire painkiller, never wake up
Dream: sunlight is cut, parting clarity, the luxury of essence
Dream: the mind is a harddrive, but there's no software to decrypt it
Dream: a leaf drifts down, the whole world changes colors.
Dream: First love, climbing mountains in Yunnan, surrounded by rivers
Dream: In the front is water, in the back is a wall, but you're the rising sun
Dream: between the world and me, there's only moss, making me slip all the time
Dream: father charges at me with a cotton quilt, as mother moans in bed
Dream: he reaches for me, but I can't touch his hands, the wind in dreams blows out of the window
Dream: I spend my later life in a sunny place, but people there hate the sun
Dream: I'm pregnant, how did I know spring can release eggs
Dream: Ali's child is dying, a woman's life hangs in the reflection of flowing water
Dream: mice have grown wings, flying in the room
Dream: wind blows at grasses; we left home without hesitation, a knife cutting entangled hemps
Dream: perfect death; turn quickly to run, shouting destiny
Dream: take this white pill; blue light penetrates Heaven's gate
Dream: night rain on the Ba Mountain; the boatman imagines the last passenger

Hubei (湖北): Where Rivers Carve Civilization

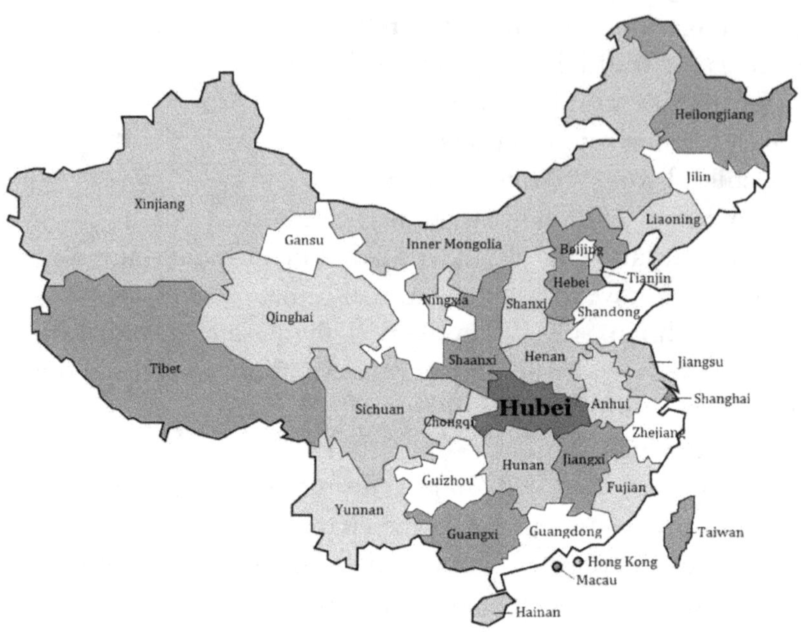

Hubei, which means "north of the Lake" (Lake Dongting), is a land sculpted by water and time. The Yangtze River cuts through its heart, flanked by the dramatic Three Gorges—a geological marvel of limestone cliffs and mist-wrapped valleys formed over 200 million years. Beneath these gorges lies the Three Gorges Dam, the world's largest hydroelectric project, a testament to human ambition amidst ancient rock. To the west, the Shennongjia UNESCO Global Geopark straddles tectonic fault lines, its primeval forests hiding karst caves and the elusive "Wild Man" of Chinese folklore. This region, part of the Daba and Wushan Mountain ranges, is also a cradle of biodiversity, where rare species like the golden snub-nosed monkey endure.

Hubei was the soul of the Chu State (1046–223 BCE), a civilization both mystical and advanced. Here, China's earliest known poet, Qu Yuan (屈原, 339–278 BCE), composed the Chu Ci (楚辭, "Songs of the South"), weaving shamanistic rites with lyrical longing. His death in the Miluo River birthed the Dragon Boat Festival, a tribute to his patriotism. Confucius himself revered Chu poetry and music, calling the Chu Feng (楚风, "Airs of Chu") "the sound of unbridled passion" and adapting its verses into teachings on life and art.

Chu brilliance extended beyond verse: their metallurgy produced swords of unmatched sharpness, their astronomers charted the heavens, and their physicians pioneered herbal medicine. The legendary Shennong (神农, "Divine Farmer"), half-bull, half-man, is said to have tasted hundreds of herbs in Hubei's mountains, founding traditional Chinese medicine and writing the I Ching (易经, "Book of Changes").

Nine thousand years ago, Hubei's ancestors crafted the world's oldest playable bone flutes from crane wings, their notes still echoing in the guqin zither's meditative strains. When the Qin conquered Chu in 223 BCE, Chu's essence seeped into Han culture—its love of freedom, its reverence for nature, and its dreamlike aesthetic. Today, Chu's spirit lingers in Hubei's water towns, its mist-shrouded peaks, and the poetry of Li Bai, who immortalized Yangtze gorges with lines like "The monkeys wail without cease / Along the cliffs unending."

To visit Hubei is to trace the currents of Chinese thought—where geology, myth, and verse converge like the Yangtze's tributaries, forever shaping the soul of a nation.

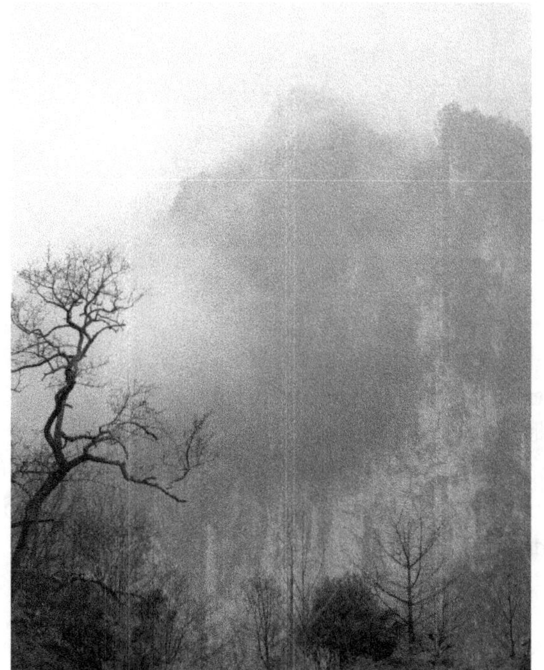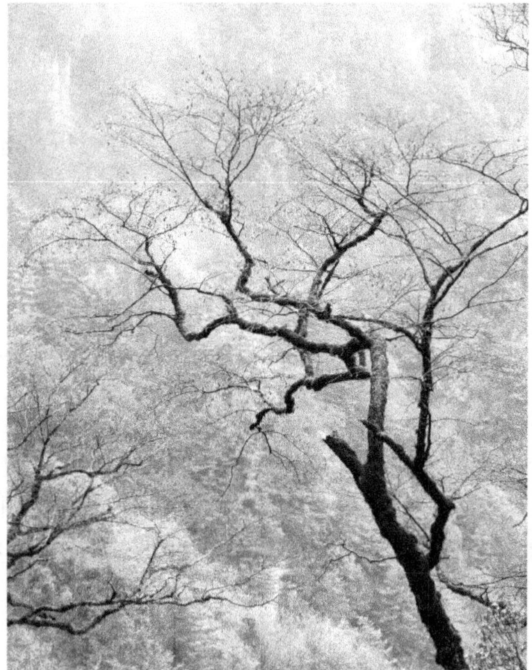

Shennongjia, Hubei

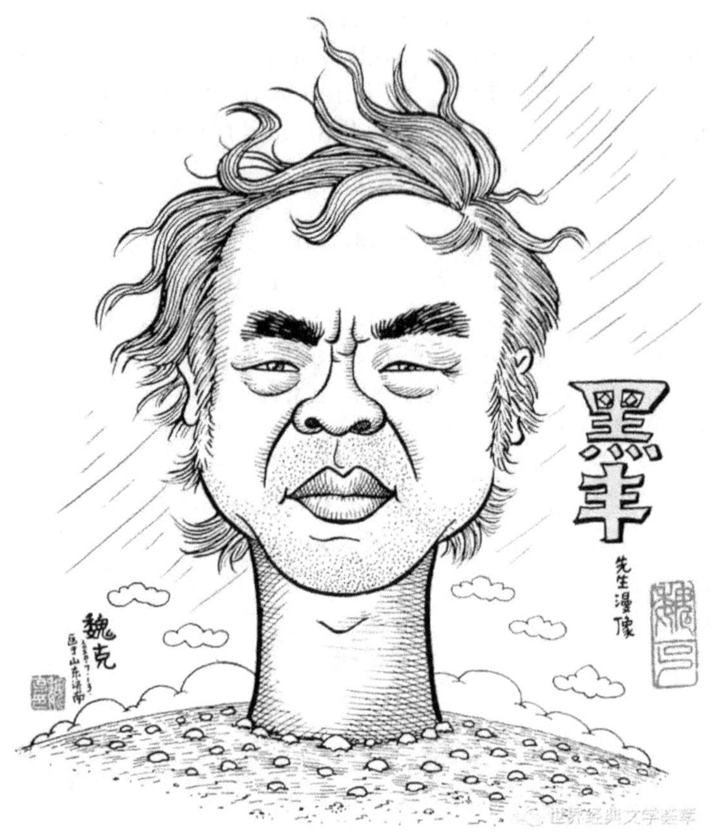

Hei Feng (黑豐), born in 1969 in Hubei Province, is a Chinese poet, fiction writer, and editor. He is the author of several acclaimed works of poetry and prose, including *Empty Pregnant* (空孕), *Ashes* (灰烬), *Two Nights for the Cat* (猫的两个夜晚), *Butterfly Is Half of the Afternoon* (蝴蝶是下午的一半), *The Man in the Land of Mi* (寐人), *The Bottom Line of Everything* (一切的底部), and *Existence: Flash* (存在：闪失). His works have been translated into English, French, Spanish, and Romanian, contributing to his growing international recognition.

黑叶子

可能起了风
也许不是风
反正满树的黑叶子抖动

卷簟上晒着一些江米
也许没有米

但见一群黑叶子在卷簟上飘
它们"飘"走了我的谷物
"飘"走我的梦

晚上，一只空胃
呆在下面，树上停着一些饱饱

梦中仿佛起了风
也许没有风，只是一些黑叶子
但见空卷簟应和，一起一伏的动
其实卷簟没有动，是江堤下的砂滩在移动

其实砂滩并没有移动
是砂滩那边河谷的涟漪在移动

其实对岸的涟漪也没有移动
是人的灵魂在悸动

Black Leaves

Maybe it's the wind
Maybe not
The tree is shaking its black leaves

On the mat some rice is drying in the sun
Maybe there's no rice at all

But a school of black leaves blew
Blowing away my rice
Blowing my dreams off the mat

At night, an empty stomach
Waits under the tree, full stomachs resting above

In my dream the wind seems blowing
Maybe not, only black leaves flying
Across the empty mat, up and down
But the mat is not moving, it's the beach by the river

No, the beach is not moving
It's the ripple rippling on the other shore

Across, the river is not moving
It's the soul trembling

乡夜

田野夜凉
夕阳拢住残红

蒲葵叶不在树上摇
摇在乡村之手

夜晚，家事只好撒手不管
许多农具痛苦不堪
舍弃在庄稼地里。一只
小小的睡虫爬上
农夫的粗皮大手

有一口古井不肯睡去
有一条白花花的狗
徜徉在乡村浮动的夜色里

一片树叶滴答。
反衬夜林的一隙幽光

Village Night

Night is cool in the fields
The setting sun holds onto the last red ray

Palm leaves fan, not on treetops
But in the hands of the village

Night is here.
I put down my chores
Farm tools abandoned in the fields. A tiny
Bug crawls onto
The farmer's thick hand

The old well stays awake
As the white dog lingers
In the village, through the floating night

Drip drop on a leaf
Reflecting the night light in the woods

粮食笔记

悠久的岁，也不能
腐蚀一个人的卑躬的背影

漫天的鹅毛
也不能消弥一对孤寂的脚印

你，拎着桅灯到一条羊肠小路
寻找一颗孤独的地粮

一粒粮食，可以使
一群饥汉通宵达旦

一粒粮食，可以使
一间破茅房金碧辉煌

没有一粒粮食
不可以放出一个响屁

压住一粒储粮，狂风可以吹净
所有的字，但不能撼动一张纸

小憩在一颗谷壳之内
最忌惮一只《诗经》里的硕鼠

它的本事有可能咬断装书线
咬破你的黄壳、咬破你的梦

但一种新"地粮"不可被
"硕鼠"收割
空秋的大地永有
恒量，永有闪烁

Fieldnotes of Food

Time, no matter how long, can't
Straighten the shadow of a crooked back

The goose-feather snow
Can't erase a pair of lonely footprints

Along a thin road, you seek
Food in earth, carrying a lantern

A grain of rice is enough to keep
A crowd of hungry men full all night

A grain of rice is enough
To light a shabby hut in full glory

Without food
No one can make a fart

Keep the grain under your finger; wind blows
away all the words, but can't move the paper

Resting in the husk, I'm worried
About the rat in *The Book of Songs*

It gnaws into my books
Into your yellow shell, into your dreams

But the new "crop" can't be
Taken by the "rats"
The earth turns eternally
Shining on its own terms

那天……

葬了母亲好惊慌
葬了母亲怕
白太阳

母亲你死去
体内有我的伤
你的黑骨里
有我的木棒

那天
我提着风
我提着白眼

空竹篮

那天，我空
那天，我轻
那天，我瘦
那天，我多么慌

妹妹小
姊姊出嫁了
我去找猪草

黄花菜地米菜耳朵菜
你们快出来
苜蓿草车前草被褥草
你们不要
我来找

找找找找找……
找了半篮草

That Day...

So much anxiety after Mother was buried
So much fear
Under the white sun

You died, Mother
My wound was buried with your body
Your black bones
have my batting sticks

That day
I carried the wind
I carried white eyes

The basket was empty

That day, I was empty
That day, I was weightless
That day, I was all bones
That day, I was full of fear

My young sister was small
My older sister was married
I went out to gather vegetables for pigs

Lilies, shepherd purse, spinach
Come out, hurry
Alfalfa, plantain, ground covers
Don't hide yourselves
I'm coming

Seek
Seek seek seek seek seek…
I filled half of my basket

太阳落土
妹妹找母

不怕
哥哥带你回家

哥哥你手好凉
哥哥你哭了
妹妹你哪知道
哥哥心里好慌

那天
目光异样
白太阳将我推倒
水载我
——流走

那天，我瘦
那天，我轻
那天，我空
那天，我多么慌
世界是一个透风的网

The sun entered the earth
My little sister wanted her mother

Don't be afraid
Big brother will take you home

Brother, your hand is cold
Brother, you're crying
Sister, you have no idea
the fear I hold in my heart

That day
The world changed
The white sun pushed me down
Water carried me
——away

That day, I was all bones
That day, I was weightless
That day, I was empty
That day, I was full of fear
The world was a net full of holes

我看见你的草移动

你掏肝 我难受
你目空 我荒凉
你隐于草丛看不见
你的叶刀
软绵绵

哦 流不出的是血
哭不出的是泪
转不出的是烟……

你多像我的父兄
多像我的朋友
你的眼镜上堆积着善良？
你脸上挤满了来历不明的富有
我看见你的草移动，我听见
伏击的野兽们
恐怖低吼

I Watch Your Grasses Moving

You empty your heart, I feel sad
You go blind, I feel empty
You hide in tall grasses
Your knife
Feels soft

Oh, my blood can't flow out of skin
My tears can't be shed
The smoke keeps circling inward…

You look like my father and brother
And my friends
What kindness piles on your glasses?
Your face is crowded with dubious wealth
I see your grasses moving, I hear
Hunted beasts
Rumbling in terror

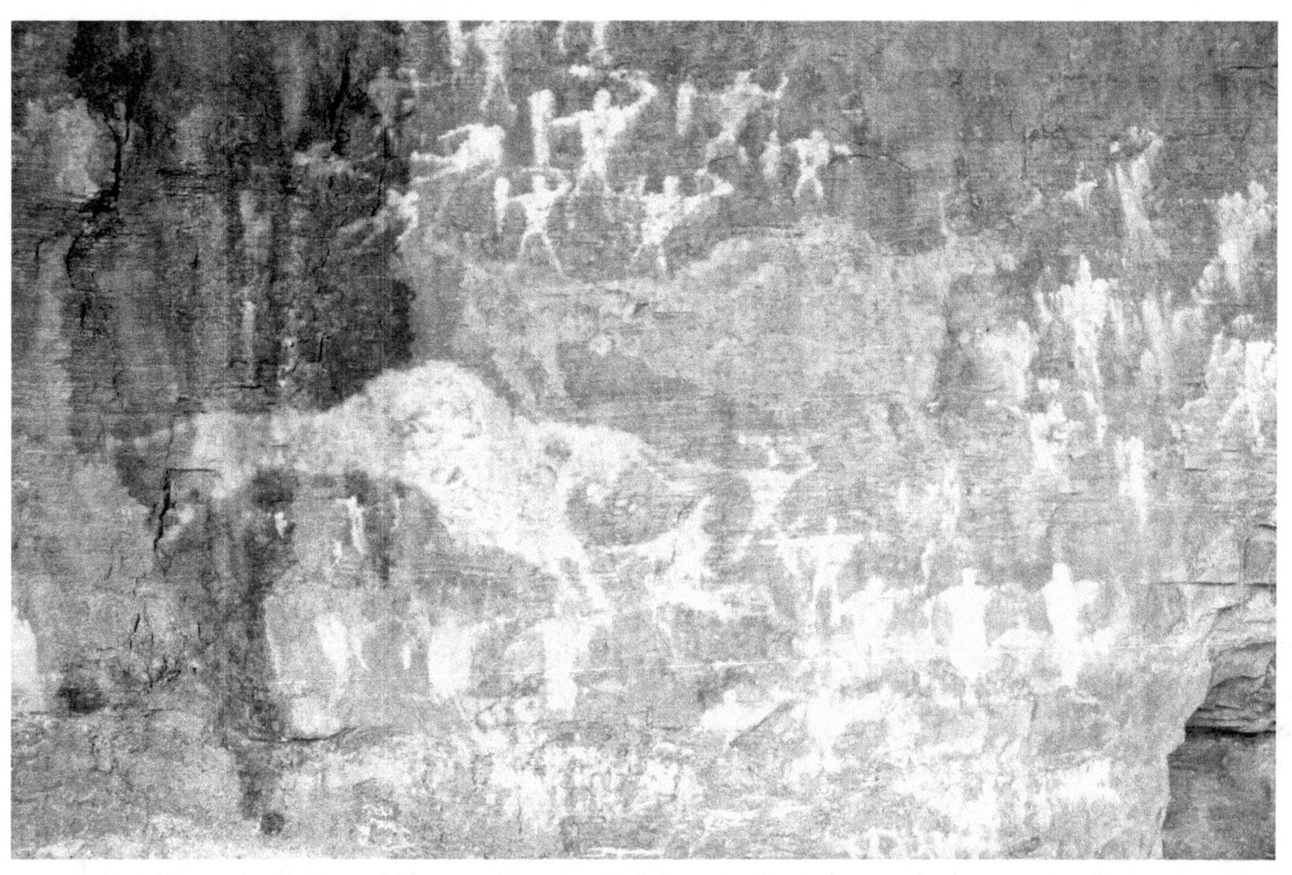

Rock painting, Hubei Province

Hunan (湖南): A Land of Rivers, Mountains, and Poetry

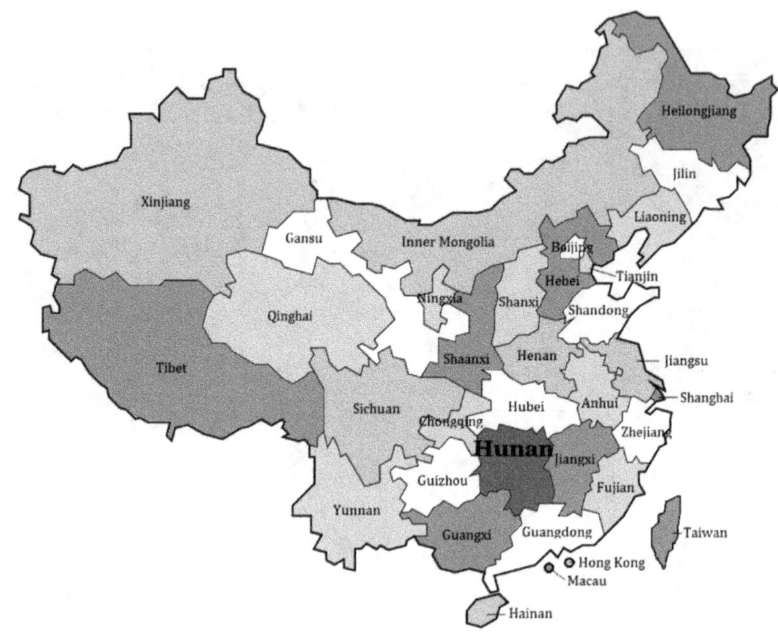

South of Lake Dongting, Hunan Province is defined by dramatic landscapes and fertile river basins. Most of its terrain lies within the watersheds of four major tributaries of the Yangtze River: the Xiang, Zi, Yuan, and Lishui Rivers, all of which flow into the lake. This intricate water network has sculpted Hunan's valleys, nourished its agriculture, and inspired its cultural soul.

Hunan's geology is as diverse as its history, from the karst pinnacles of Zhangjiajie—a UNESCO Global Geopark whose surreal quartz-sandstone pillars famously inspired the floating mountains in *Avatar*—to the sacred heights of Mount Heng, one of China's Five Great Mountains. The province's limestone caves, such as Huanglongdong (黄龙洞, "Yellow Dragon Cave"), and the terraced Longji Rice Fields further showcase its natural artistry.

Hunan was the heartland of the State of Chu (11th century–223 BCE), a kingdom renowned for its shamanistic traditions, lyrical poetry, and technological innovations in bronze and warfare. The Chu culture's reverence for nature and the supernatural permeated its music, spirit worship, and the earliest forms of Chinese romantic poetry, as seen in the Chu Ci (楚辞, *Songs of Chu*), an anthology dominated by the melancholic beauty of Qu Yuan (屈原, 340–278 BCE), Hunan's most celebrated poet and patriot.

The province's dreamlike scenery—mist-wrapped rivers, bamboo forests, and the towering peaks of Zhangjiajie—has long been a muse for poets. Du Fu (712–770 CE) wrote of Lake Dongting's "boundless waves" (*qizheng yunmengze*, 气蒸云梦泽), while Li Bai (701–762 CE) immortalized its waters in drunken verse. Later, the Hunan-born scholar Wang Fuzhi (1619–1692) fused philosophy with poetry, reflecting the region's enduring intellectual spirit.

Even today, Hunan echoes with literary history, from the Yuelu Academy (founded in 976 CE), a cradle of Confucian thought, to the hometowns of modern literary giants like Shen Congwen (1902 – 1988), whose works painted lyrical portraits of the Xiang River's folk culture.

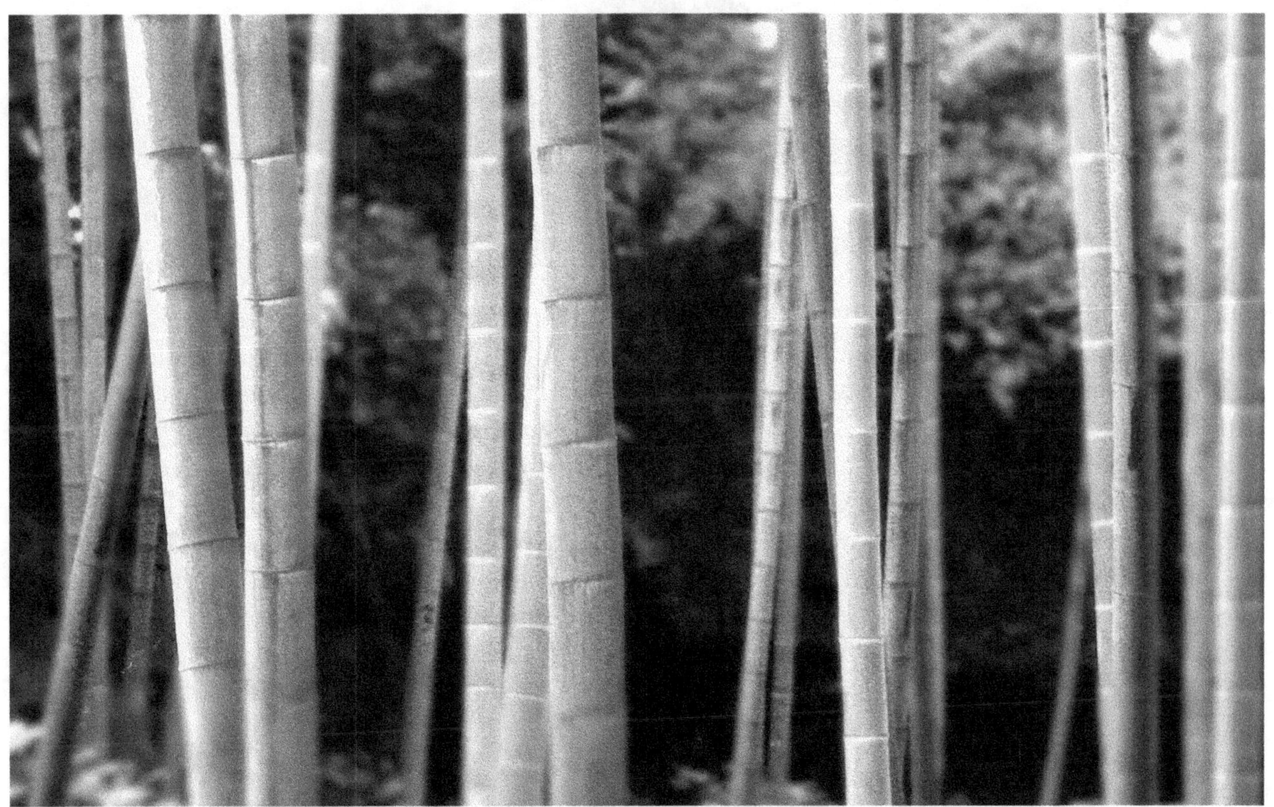

Bamboo forest, Hunan Province

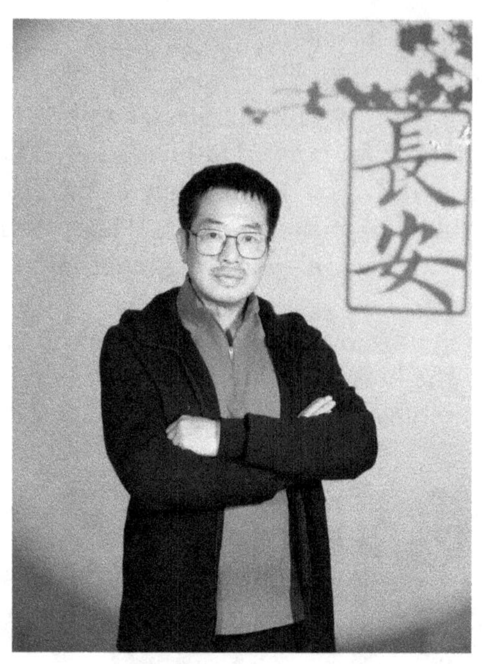

Caoshu (December 1964 –), born Tang Juliang, is a poet, critic, and a member of the Chinese Writers' Association. He graduated from Xiangtan University in 1985. His works have been widely published in journals such as *People's Literature, Poetry Periodical, October, Poetry Tide,* and *Yangtze River Poetry Journal,* and have been selected for various annual poetry anthologies. He is the author of five poetry collections, including *Reconstruction of Mawangdui, The Longevity Stele,* and *Son of the Mud,* as well as two collections of poetic essays, including *The Night Watchman of Civilization.* In 2012, he received a nomination for the 20th Rougang Poetry Award. In 2013, he won the inaugural International Chinese Poetry Award and the Contemporary New Realism Poetry Award. In 2019, he was awarded the Annual Critic Award at the 5th Lishan Poetry Conference. In 2023, he received a nomination for the Poetry Collection Award at the inaugural Li Shutong International Poetry Award, the first prize in poetry at the 2nd Cao Cao Poetry, Wine, and Culture Festival, the 6th Liu Bowen Poetry Award, and the Cultural and Art Award for Criticism at the 9th Hou Tian Biennial Award. He participated in the 12th Youth Retrospective Poetry Conference organized by *Poetry Periodical.* He is also an adjunct professor in the School of Liberal Arts at Hunan Normal University.

春钓湘江

树荫下，一个人垂钓湘江
这一带水阔天低，
空寂无人
水面静如镜子

我日日以词语垂钓虚无
春来江边垂柳泛绿
江面浮标看久了，出现幻觉
似乎沉下去了，细看
又矗立在水面

寂静的哗然。不是鱼而是
一些伟大的灵魂：老杜或船山先生
张栻或左宗棠大人
回声之骨闪亮

Spring Fishing at the Xiang River

Fishing alone under a willow
Wide river, low sky, I'm alone
In this empty space
Water flat like a mirror

Every day I fish the void with my words
Spring has come, willows turning green.
The buoys in the river appear
to have sunk, when I look again
They're standing erect

Noises break the silence, not from the fish
But those great souls: Du Fu, Wang Fuzhi
Zhang Shi, Zuo Zongtang
Their spirits shine with echoes

凤凰山

山洞清幽。囚禁过张学良将军
而有几分传奇的神秘
凤凰被拴住翅膀

那时没有谁能拴住我们
没等到一个雨雾天晨曦映现白塔
我们就动身去往远方

生活终究拴住彼此
过往之地：无论你的弗吉尼亚
还是我的凯里河池，无不凤凰山

Phoenix Mountain

The cave is quiet. General Zhang Xueliang
Was imprisoned here—the legend
Of a phoenix with chained wings

Nobody could chain our wings
We left for the north
Before rain and fog fell on the white tower

But in the end, life still got us
The Phoenix Mountain exists everywhere
Whether it's your Virginia or my Kaili Lake

凤滩行

沿着地图上没有的路径
我们前往凤滩

那时我们每个人都是
一座小水电站
两边立着画屏般的青山
崖壁上丛树，无数猴子跳跃

Journey to Phoenix Beach

We trekked to the Phoenix Beach
Along the unmapped road

Each of us was a mini-hydroelectric dam
Mountains stood like paintings
Monkeys leapt among trees
Hanging on cliffs

Wu Xiru (吴昕孺), originally named Wu Xinyu (吴新宇), is a contemporary Chinese poet and prose writer born in 1967 in Changsha, Hunan. He has established himself as a significant literary figure with a diverse body of work spanning poetry, essays, and other prose forms. Wu Xiru has published several poetry collections, including *Wildness* (野外) and *He Never Imitates His Own Loneliness* (他从不模仿自己的孤独).

In addition to poetry, he has authored over 20 books of prose, showcasing his versatility in essays, novels, and literary criticism. His works often explore themes of rural life, memory, and existential reflection, blending lyrical depth with philosophical inquiry.

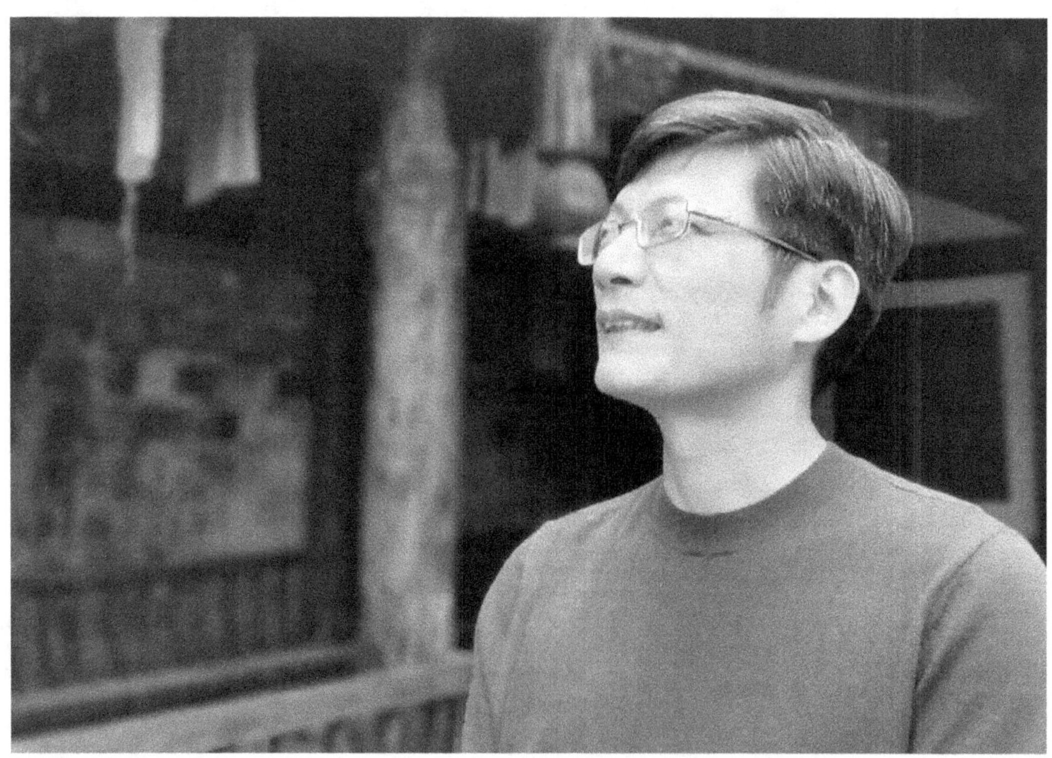

沩山，兼赠欧阳白

沩山似乎没有春天，既无喧闹之声
亦无俗艳之色。唯有那绿
深如碧潭，阔如大海
我们散落其间，仿佛几颗
圆润的水珠。突然有一株桃花
粉红地蹦出来
它将我们带到毗卢峰下的密印寺前

灵祐和尚站在门口。
一千二百多年过去了
他递给每位来访者的，依然是那把米
还有这句话——"米里有虫"
米在我们手里，时而只有一粒
时而有千百粒
但我们觉得没有任何不同
那一粒生千百粒，
千百粒又归于一粒

夜宿寮房。窗外月如银盘
盘里沏了一杯沩山毛尖。
我端着它
步出庭院，看见万物
都露出湛然明净的身体
交流着各自的静默与光芒。我们
慢慢走，慢慢啜饮
杯中水三分是茶，七分是禅

沩山主体部分在宁乡市境内，沩水自此发源。唐宪
宗元和末年，灵祐禅师在师父百丈怀海那里得道
后，前往沩山开辟道场，自立门户，成为禅门五宗
之一沩仰宗的开创祖师。"米里有虫"是灵祐在沩
山期间与弟子们机锋相接的著名公案。

Mount Wei

On Mount Wei, there's no spring, no sound
or color of the dust world. Only green,
deeper than a waterhole, vaster than a sea
We scatter in it like water drops
Suddenly a peach blossom leaps out
Its pink leading us
to the Miyin Temple on the summit of Pilu

Monk Lingyou stands at the door.
1200 years have gone by, still
handing out the same rice to every visitor with
the same Koan—"There's a worm in the rice."
We hold the rice, sometimes
Just one grain, sometimes thousands
But it's the same difference
One grain leads to thousands
Thousands of grains return to one

In the monk's shed we dwell
The moon shines like a silver plate
A cup of Mount Wei tea on the plate
I walk into the yard, tea in my hand
Everything reveals its clean face and body
Exchanging light in silence
We sip tea as we stroll
In our cups, 1/3 is tea, 2/3 is Zen

Mount Wei stands at the source of the Wei River. Wei
Temple founded one of the five Chan schools. During
the late Yuanhe period of Emperor Xianzong of Tang,
Zen Master Lingyou travelled to Mounta Wei to
establish his own school. He made the famous Koan
"There's a worm in the rice."

东洞庭观鸟

你曾经比所有的湖都大，坐落在天地中央
连接着东南西北
周围的人越来越多，你渐渐将自己缩小
小到正好可以放到
李白的诗中。你的波涛是最醇的酒
晃荡着氤氲的醉意
你的流岚和夕阳
是最美的汉语，铺陈在
二十多万只候鸟组成的秋天里

我叫不出它们的名字。你告诉我
也记不住。我走近其中一只
它淡红的喙，尖如钉子，却不传递敌意
一双细瘦的脚立在浅水
仿佛两根梦想发芽的枯枝。我慢慢蹲下
它扭头望过来，乌亮的小眼睛一眨
像按动快门　芦苇俯仰，麋鹿悠踱
一贯低调的江豚高高跃出水面……

风拂过头，水淌过脸，我的眉眼
浪花四溅。那只鸟
呼地展开翅膀，抻长脖颈
灰色身体腾跃而起，汇入
浩瀚无边的垂天之云——它会将给我拍的
那张照片带到哪里去？你的边界
又在哪里？我忽然明白
你比世界上任何一个湖都要大
自由翱翔的鸟群，让天空成为你的一部分

洞庭湖古称"云梦泽"，鸟如云，水似梦，吸引了
李白、杜甫、孟浩然、韩愈、刘禹锡、范仲淹等文
人墨客前来吟诗作文。东洞庭是生物多样性极为丰
富的国际要湿地，来此过冬的候鸟多达258种，被
誉为"中国观鸟之都"

Bird Watch on the East Lake Dongting

You were once the biggest lake, sitting between
sky and earth, connecting four directions
Populations grew and grew, and you shrank
To a size that could fit
Li Po's poems. You brew the best wine
Your waves shimmer with intoxication
Your mist and sunset becomes our most
beautiful language, decorating autumn with
two hundred thousand migrating birds

I can't name any of them, even if you tell me
one by one. I tiptoe close to a bird,
pink beak sharp as a nail, without hostility
thin long legs in the shallow water, like
withered branches dreaming of sprouting. I
squat slowly. It looks back, blinking eyes like
a camera's shutter. Reeds bend up and down
Deer pass through, dolphins leap from the river…

Wind blows past my head
Water flows down my face. Waves splash.
The bird opens its wings, its neck stretching
Gray body leaping into the clouds—
Taking my photo with it
I suddenly understand
The bird is bigger than any lake on earth
As it flies with its family
Turning the sky into part of its body

Lake Dongting was called *yunmengze*—"cloud dream
wetland." It attracts migrating birds and poets like Li Bai,
Du Fu, Men Haoran, Hanyu, Liu Yuxi, Fan Zhongyan,
and others. An international wetland with great varieties
of birds, it's known as China's birdwatching capital.

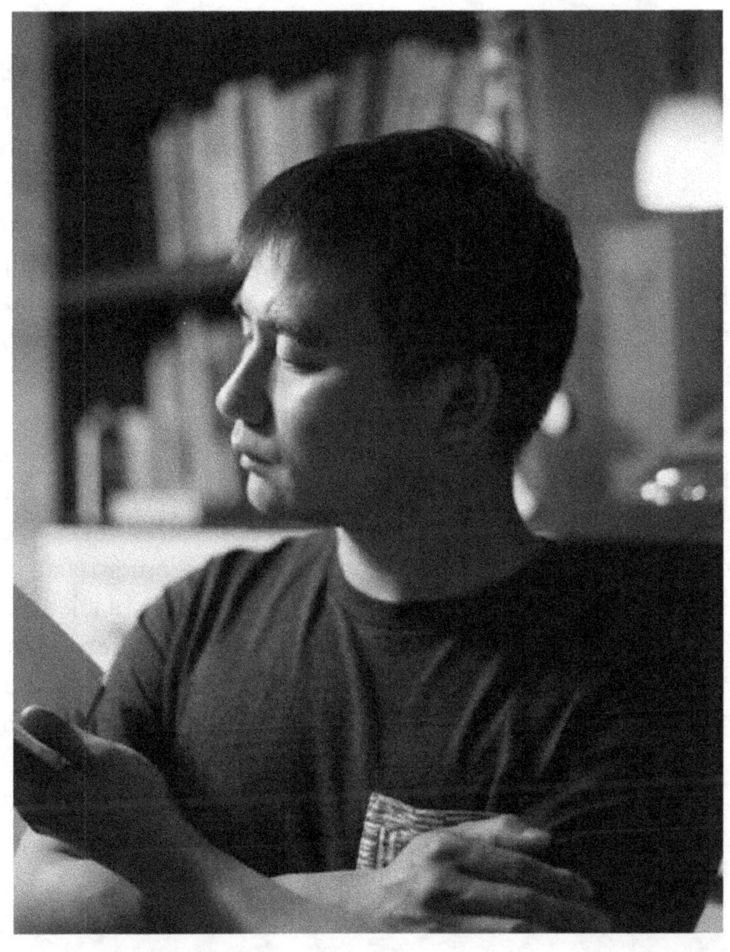

Xiao Shui (肖水), born in 1980 in Chenzhou, Hunan, is a poet, writer, translator, and professor of poetry at Shanghai University. He holds a PhD from Fudan University. His published works include *Lost and Found* (失物认领), *Chinese Lessons* (中文课), *Fishing Trout in America* (在美国钓鳟鱼), *Mugwort: New Quatrains* (艾草：新绝句集), *Tales of the Bohai Sea* (渤海故事集), and *Two Sunny Days: Yu Dafu* (两日晴, 郁达夫). His poetry explores themes of memory, cultural exchange, and the intersections of tradition and modernity.

富春行旅图

1

那次下黄山来，盛夏向我展露
群山的罅隙，所有绿色都褪去
容纳它们的外壳。我听见溪水
在耳边涨了起来，醒来的事物，
仿佛都努力拼合时间的碎片。
叶子和昆虫拨开身上纵横可见的界线
加入那些从山顶和田埂上
晃过来的远处的人影。

2

我们正与什么平行？此刻就在河的对岸：
阳光浅浅地斜射下来，被车外的一切翻动
的一天，又继续被翻动。即兴地，
需要一场出人意料的会面，打动你。
那些房子，弓紧黑白的背脊，
修竹也只像是被急耸的屋顶
推高的发冠。山的黛色潦草，
应和着廊桥灯笼里无可记数

Travel Map Along Fuchun River

1

That time I came down the Yellow Mountain
The mid-summer showed the mountains' cracks.
green shed its crust. I heard streams swelling, as if
all awakened things were piecing broken time together.
Leaves and insects brushed away borders
crisscrossing on their backs to join
the flickering shadows of humans
from the fields and mountaintops.

2

What parallel world are we traveling? Across the river:
the sun sets slantly upon us, the day continues
moving after disturbance. I need
a spontaneous meeting to surprise you.
Houses tighten their black and white spines,
Bamboos point like steep roofs,
heightened hairstyles. Mountain grass sways, white
dreams hidden in lanterns along a covered bridge.

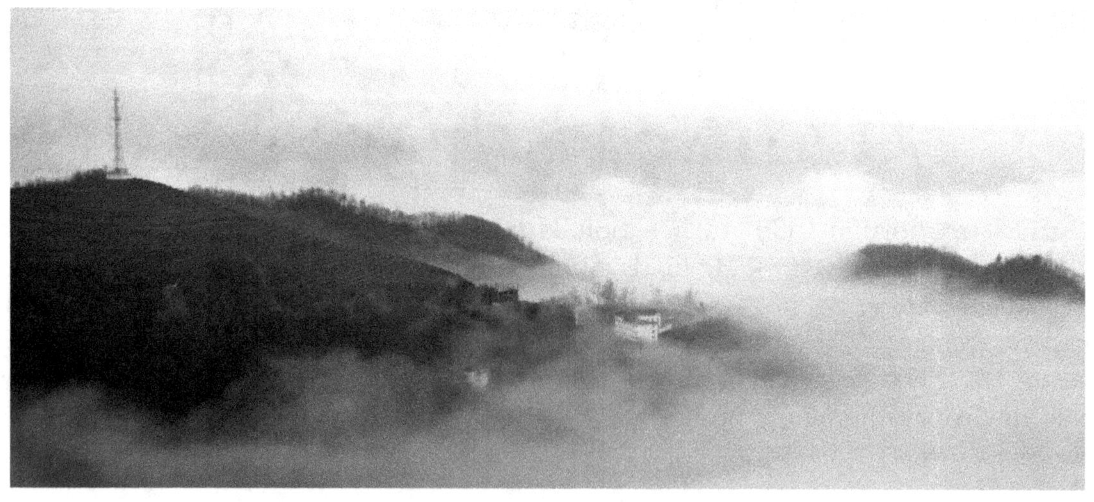

3.
忽然河面一动。桥墩的倒影
在无数波纹中，减损了鼻尖之上的温热。
坝顶的水草摆动，又像往足下的深渊，
捞取漂远的霞光。只有青苔，如翠绿的
舌尖，安然地，保有孤独的睡眠。
我不熟悉它们。我曾穿过漆黑小巷
就到达了五百公里外无人到达过的山巅。
在不知所措的困境中，我曾见金鱼在浴缸温
软的水流下产卵。那些咬我的事物，
仿佛不带入口的铁笼，而猛然惊醒我
的水鸟，在没有尽头的水线上
凫游。我的前面，就像多出来
一片空地。低头，藤蔓往胃管里
攀爬，呼吸散发着洗涤液的味道。
奇异的海底生物，在天空，只为
我一个人循回往复？我是一个
何时何地，被定义过的现代人？

4
从窗口，扔出来玩具娃娃。
铁匠铺的叮当声密密的，渐渐
雨也变得漆黑。酒储在竹节中，
像身体里裹进一截由粮食累积
的城墙。而只有它们，咬断
芦苇和苦草，在静静的波面上
推动着木色的浮巢。潮汐引来
整个星空，星空是宇宙战乱后
唯一的劫余，而我穿过纸上的
集市，恢弘的楼宇，在任意的
横线、竖线、斜线的交叠中，
看见结构简逊、没有灰瓦和
斗拱的家园。当视力抵达极限
我们还有耳朵？匍匐在水面，
如同在丝绸上不断摩挲。细腻

3

A shimmer on the river. In waves, the reflection
from the bridge lost heat on the nose.
Grasses sway atop the dam, the sunset drifts
away under my feet. Only the moss stays
Asleep like a green tongue. I don't know
The mountains well. I once walked 500 km
To reach the mountaintop that nobody ever
Touched. In difficult moments I once saw
goldfish lay eggs in a running bathtub.
Those who bit me are iron cages without gates.
Waterbirds startle me, diving in borderless
water. An empty field appears
in front of me. I bend, vines climb up my gut
Filling my mouth with the taste of detergent.
The sea is full of marvelous creatures.
Why am I alone, circling in the sky?
Who labeled me, where and when?

4

Toys thrown out of the window.
Clanking from the blacksmith's workshop. Slowly,
the rain becomes dark. Wine is stored in bamboo,
like a food wall inside the body.
Something bites off reeds and eelgrasses,
pushing a floating nest on the calm water. The
tide brings down the whole sky, the space war's
Only survivor. I pass through the market and
magnificent buildings on the paper.
In the pile of lines,
vertical, slanted, horizontal,
I see home, simple, no gray tiles, arched gates.
Do we still have hearing when our eyes
Can no longer reach? Something floats
On the water, as if stroking silk. Delicate

的声响已毫无韵味，比如汽车
发动，比如在亲密的关系中
放缓对另一个人的呼气。此刻，
所有人，都看见它们启动翅膀，
可它们并不飞往天空。

5.
潜鸟。我蹲在河岸的石头上。
金属光泽，使你像一枚迅速
翻转的硬币。你从此处消失。
你给水面上，吃稻谷和草料，
用照相机捕捉你陶瓷般尾翼
的人，哪种言外之意？

6
两年后，再从上海来，停车，
在河湾处张望，看见廊桥才
发现竟是重返。时已近寒冬，
雨水从电线杆顶端一直流到
草丛根部。路面水坑叠加了
密影与浓云。我想家乡的雪
已压断了许多枝条，裹雾的
雪松，像为自身建立路标。
湖山在简单情节里充满悬念
蓬松的鼓声只为那些冥冥中
要再次经历的人变幻。而我
再度站立大桥中央，往河面
搜索？我曾在常熟破山寺的
门外遇到有人贩卖露出新鲜
斫口的腊梅，而卧室铁瓶里
的蔷薇，你是否相信它已经
抽枝？河面没有薄冰，田野
太过平静。雨水收伏了万世
洞明的铃铛。莲子剥落盘里，
煮熟的老菱像锅里仰泳中的
一头水牛。

sounds have lost their rhythm.
Like the engine firing, like
blowing hot breath during sex. Right now,
everyone can see them open their wings,
But they don't fly into the sky.

5

Loon. I squat on the riverbank stones.
Your metallic color makes you look
Like a flipping coin. You disappear.
What meaning are you trying to grant me,
As I capture your porcelain tail with a camera
my stomach filled with vegan food?

6

Two years later, I returned from Shanghai, looked
around at the riverbend, saw the covered bridge,
then realized I was returning. It was winter,
Raindrops came from the electric posts
to the grass roots. Clouds reflected in the puddles
on the road. The snow in my hometown
must have broken many trees, snow-covered
pines stand like their own road signs.
Hushan suspends in simple stories
And the sparse drumming beats for those
Who'll go through another life in the netherworld. I
stand on the bridge, searching the river's surface
again. Outside the Temple of Broken Mountain,
I saw a child trafficker selling winter sweet freshly
cut from trees. Would you believe, the rose in the
steel vase in my bedroom is growing new
branches? No ice on the river. The fields are
too quiet. Rain has tamed the bells that have seen
centuries of history. Lotus seeds fall into the plate.
The cooked bat-nuts float like buffalos
Backstroking in the pot.

7

小鹠鹏，小鹠鹏。
小鹠鹏，小鹠鹏。

8

人们都降落在自己的生活中。
灵隐寺的枫香，植根在佛塔之巅。
只要放生桥的双臂探出水面，
一个秋天就挂满木瓜。就像迟来的
桂花，会落满陌生人的头顶。
在河边搭起小竹棚的人，注定
依次会在木板上，摆开苦笋、山茶
以及两丛带露、带刺的荷花。
而此刻，好生活之内确有无数
暗芽，在肉山上涌动。
时间并不在昏睡中匆匆流驶。
窗就像紧紧包裹一切的瓶盖
那些轮廓细致的山水在蒸腾
人影擦着车沿，呼啸而过。
但它们，似乎永不会挥发。
光圈在头顶，一漾，一漾
带锄头的人离开带尖顶的房子
风干肉挂在风干肉的上面。
铃声快速翻动学校操场上的
石头，三轮车穿过涵洞，就像
从容逃脱命运碾压的兔子。
而屋前的庭院里，广玉兰的
花瓣，像承担一切悲喜的瓢。

9

我想爬下河岸，鞠起的一捧清水。
可以有些许浮萍，可以在它的丝状
根上，拖曳一些别人的时光。
比如我们都经历过的贫穷，比如
那种被空间闭锁的想象力。我记起

7

Little loon, little loon.
Little loon, little loon.

8

We descend into our own life.
The maple from Linyin Temple has roots in the stupa.
Whenever the bridge emerges from the water
to release life, fall will have a good crop of papayas,
falling on people's heads like petals of sweet olives.
On the riverbanks the bamboo sheds' owners
display bitter bamboo shoots, mountain tea and
lotus flowers, fresh with thorns and dewdrops.
Meanwhile, young buds spring up on the
mountain of flesh, this is a good life.
Time never rushes by in your sleep.
The window wraps everything like a bottle cover.
The defined mountains and rivers are steaming.
Shadows whistle past the cars,
But never disappear.
Halos ripple over the head.
The man with a hoe leaves his steepled house.
The air-dried meats hang against each other.
The sound of bells turn stones on the sports field.
A tricycle runs through the tunnel like a rabbit
fleeing its crushing destiny. In the front yard,
magnolia blooms, its gourd shaped petals
holding all the joy and sorrow on earth

9

I want to climb down the riverbank to catch water
In my hands. There'll be some duckweed,
someone's life hanging on the roots.
The taste of poverty, for example, or
our imagination locked in space. I remember the

六岁时，在乡卫生院的大厅里，全镇
唯一的电视机，像一根银针，被无数
膨胀中的气球所簇拥。而父亲从城里
带来的录音机披着红绸，正穿墙透壁，
往我的放学之路，灌满无数高音。
还有母亲将麻鸭赶入沟渠的时候，
看见我赤足在砂石路上狂奔。而远处的
天空，一朵降落伞飘荡着，
仿佛影子此刻就落在我手心。
记忆中的时间，忽然有了粗糙的外形，
所有踏足过的地点，浓缩成
吞下热水时的喉音。我忽然想喊父亲、
母亲的名字，还有未曾谋面的祖母
和蔼然早逝的祖父。那些眼前的陌生人，
雨水冲刷着他们脸上的火焰。
我知道幸福在等待着暮色
即将笼罩的泥土，继续保有它们的温度。
幸福也让那些在自己新居里烤火的
人们偶尔走出屋外，往水面
多逡巡了一眼。

10

从下姜再到开化去。那里是钱江源。
柳浪闻莺婆娑的水杉，运河边的
一株鹅掌楸，或去往法镜寺途中的
小茶山，可能都有一条细小的暗道
连接那里的山林岩丛。又或，风在
彼地吹拂，西湖断桥下，每尾鲤鱼
都吐出绵长的气泡。又或，我还想起
开化失传的桃花纸，纯莹墨色在质地
细腻的白纸上铺开，有如无法安眠者
借阵阵松涛，传递虎王的咆哮。
而我站在南湖边旅店的窗口，望着
群山有如墨汁般，在雾气中化开。
马金溪两岸的楼群，似乎在堆叠它的

TV in the hospital hall, the only set in the county,
silver antenna surrounded by countless hot balloons.
The cassette Dad brought from the city, decorated
with red silk, blasted high songs through the walls,
welcoming me home from school.
Mom saw me run barefoot on the gravel road
as she herded her ducks into the ditch.
In the sky a parachute was floating,
descending into my palm like a shadow.
The memory suddenly forms into a rough shape,
all the places my feet once touched thickening into
hot water in my throat. I want to call the names of
my father and mother, my grandma I've never met,
met, my grandpa who passed so young. Rain washes
the fire on the strangers' faces in front of me.
I know happiness is waiting for the earth at dusk.
The earth will keep its temperature.
Happiness lets people out,
away from their fire and new house
To have another look at the river.

10

From Xiajiang to Kaihua, where the Qiantang
River begins, birds sing in willows and cypresses,
and a tulip tree stands on the canal bank. On the
tea hill to Fajing Temple, you may find a hidden
path leading to forests and rocks. The wind blows
under the broken bridge of the West Lake, the koi
blowing long bubbles. I remember
Kaihua's lost peach blossom paper, pure ink
spreading on pure white paper, as if insomnia were
sending tiger's roars through pines' whisper.
Standing by the window of South Lake Hotel, I
watch the ink-dark mountains disperse in the mist.
The buildings on the Majin Stream seem to pile on

堤坝，远处云雾缭绕中的茶芽也日益
肥厚。事物之间存在引力，也彼此照耀。
记得第二日去根官佛国，
心头陡然一震。那些树的躯干尚能
寄存它们的灵魂？那些树的灵魂
有轻轻对着我的灵魂触碰？
佛祖的目光在宽阔的厅堂里弥漫，
而建造它的人的灵魂仿佛借用过
木的质地和纹理？可是，我们在夺目的
造化之物中流连，要问：我为何而来？

11
我仿佛听见了某种声音，
它只是扑动了一下翅膀，
而在寒夜的微光中，水流
已经将很多人的梦推远。

12
金星村像薄雾中的一场山村电影。
我们沿着柏油路，走在光亮房子
中间的峡谷里。越来越宽，
泼洒开的河面成了幕布，回旋的
捣衣声仿佛为了点缀属于某个时代
的风格。而沉重的木舟在加宽河面，
挺身而出的黑鱼，再一次拨开水与水的
衣裳。等我要越过水面，去推开农人
的小院，去想象那光零零的无花果
树上的累累硕果，我忽然看见三五黑点
从水面悠悠而来。它们似乎在拖动
着整个水面，水面就像一张波光粼粼的
网，向那些注目的人，收拢世界的秘密。

13
我忽然觉得它们是从河的下游赶来，
与我相遇，或者我在听村中的老人

and budding tea leaves are getting thick in clouds.
Things attract and shine upon each other.
I remember visiting the Root Buddha Temple next day.
I was startled. How do trees keep their
souls in the roots? How do their souls
touch my spirits gently?
Buddha's eyes float across the big hall, watching
humans who used its wooden grains,
veins and texture to sculpt sacred souls.
Lingering in this wonder, we ask: Why am I here?

11
I seem to hear something,
But it just fluttered its wings.
In the dim cold night, water
Pushed away many dreams.

12
Gold Star Village is like a movie on a mountain.
We walk along the highway in a
brightly lit canyon. It becomes wider and wider,
till the river becomes a screen.
Sounds of laundry decorate the past epoch.
Heavy boats expand the river;
black fish leap to part the clothes of water and river.
Wait for me to cross the river, to push open the
farmer's yard, imagine fruitless fig trees
hanging with harvest. Suddenly I see dark spots
Moving towards me, as if pulling the whole river
behind them with a flickering net. Please keep the
world's secrets away from those who are looking.

13
Suddenly I feel those creatures have traveled
upstream to meet me. Am I just listening to elders

叙述过往的时候，我小心看了看门口
的桂树。它们尾随我，就停在上面。
它们翅膀扇动，我就明显感到了
一阵冷风吹动了一下我脸上的面具。
我羡慕那些幸福的人们，保留了山水
给予他们的原貌？那些邻水的人们
很容易就洗净尘世的虚妄？
我坐在陌生人家里，吃着薯干的同时，
我感觉裹挟杂质的甜蜜，
在缓缓地抬起，我并不用来写字的手。

14
即将返程，我回到河岸，
发现它们变成了更多的墨点。
它们在水面浮游，又消失。
那个夜晚，我回到上海，
我铺开一张纸，似乎看到
有什么突出了平面。手
抖动，房间里的空气摇晃，
又渐渐安静了下来。

reminiscing the past? I take a close look at the
cinnamon tree at the door. They followed me here
then stopped. Fluttering wings, and
I feel a cold wind lifting my mask. Am I jealous
of those who kept their happy countenance,
a gift from nature? Those who live by the river,
Can they cleanse the illusion from this dust world?
Sitting in a stranger's home,
I chew my yam jerky, a mixed sweetness
Lifts my hand, not yet writing.

14
Time to go home. I return to the riverbank,
and realize everything turns into ink spots.
They float on the water, then disappear.
That night, I return to Shanghai.
I open a sheet of paper. Something
seems to rise from the surface. Hands
shake. Air quivers in the room.
Then everything goes back to peace.

Zhang Zhan (张战) is a poet, essayist, and educator from Changsha, Hunan. An associate professor at Hunan First Normal University's School of Literature and Journalism, she specializes in children's literature research and teaching. A member of the China Writers Association, Zhang has published several acclaimed works, including *Poems by Zhang Zhan* (张战的诗, Winner of the First Ai Qing Poetry Prize Award in 2022), *Stranger* (陌生人, a collection exploring displacement and human connection), and *On the Ladder of Rain* (雨梯上, a lyrical prose collection blending memoir, literary criticism, and philosophical reflection, praised for its "pure, flowing language" and "literary clarity that carves a fresh stream for our times").

Her poetry, characterized by natural imagery and folk-inspired modernism, has appeared in *Poetry* (诗刊), *The Stars Poetry Journal* (星星诗刊), and *Furong* (芙蓉), with translations published in Romania. Notable honors include the Ding Ling Literary Award (2022) for *Snail and Me* (蜗牛与我) and the Xie Pu Children's Book Award. Zhang serves as Dean of the Hunan Democratic League Literature Academy and Vice President of the Hunan Poetry Society, actively promoting literary education.

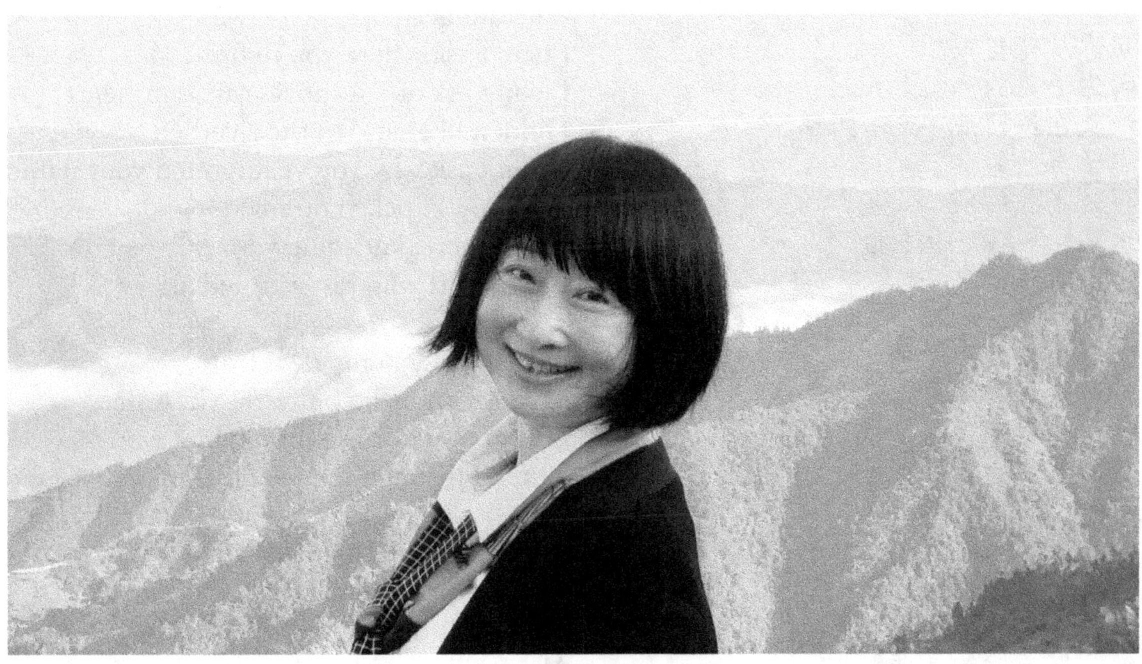

陌生人

这是我的厨房
这是我的餐桌
陌生人 我请你坐下
坐在这张老榆木桌旁
抽着烟　安心地等
我为你做一顿晚饭

洒些盐　滴两滴醋
煎几个鸡蛋
热油大火　我轻翻锅铲
把它卷得成一团鹅黄的云

清炒白菜苔　叶尖还带着露水
脆生生的秆　轻托着一簇绿火焰

啊陌生人
我不问你从哪里来
我不问你心里的恐惧
像河沙藏在深河底　我不问你
为何忘了自己姓名
为何会敲了我的门
坐在这里　你不安的手指
像刚逃出箭阵的哀鸟

我也不会说出我心里的怕
我的怕是水里的蝴蝶　石头里的鱼
我的怕是一根穿不过针孔的线头
我看着那些伤口　无法缝补

啊陌生人
你吃　你喝　然后你走
这样的日子　神仙都惶然失措
你也继续你踉跄的脚步吧

Stranger

This is my kitchen
This is my table
Stranger, please sit down
At my dining table made of old elm
Here's your smoke, please
Wait as I prepare your dinner

Sprinkle some salt, pour some vinegar
Fry some eggs in the hot wok
with a great fire. I stir gently
Till egg folds like a yellow cloud

The heart of napa cabbage, fresh with dewdrops
Its crispy stems turn to green fire

Oh stranger
I won't ask where you're from
I won't ask about the fear in your heart
Hidden like sand in the riverbed
I won't ask why you've forgotten your name
Why you knocked on my door
Sitting here, kneading your fingers
Like a bird who just escaped arrows

I won't tell you my own fear
My terror for the butterflies in water
Fish in rocks or the thread that won't
Thread through the needle to repair wounds

Oh stranger, please eat
Please drink, then leave
Even gods don't know what to do
About this world, so just continue

然后我关上门　我哭
哭那些被鸟吃掉了名字的人
被月亮割掉了的影子的人
被大雨洗得没有了颜色的人
那些被我们忘记了的人
那些和我一样
跪下来活着
却一定要站着仰望星星的人

清晰地喊出我们的孤独

呆呆站在树林里
我向你告别
我看着你的眼睛
好像我在用瞳孔呼吸

那条小路的尽头
栾树上挂满明灭的灯笼
一片树叶落下
树林悄悄发生了变化

一棵树把另一棵树拉进怀里
簌簌落下了露水
多凉啊
过些天，露珠会变成白霜
就像揉碎的月亮
突然一只鸟叫了
清晰地喊出我们的孤独

Your stumbling journey after food
Then I'll close my door to weep
For those whose names are eaten by birds
Whose shadows are cut by the moon
Who have lost their colors in the rain
Who have been forgotten
Who have been living on their knees
But like me still gaze at stars.

Crying Out Our Solitude

Standing in the woods
I say goodbye
I look into your eyes
As if I'm breathing with my pupils

At the end of the small path
Red lanterns hang on the golden rain tree
A leaf falls
The woods is changed quietly

One tree pulls another tree into its bosom
Dewdrops fall
How cool
Soon they'll turn into frost
Like the moon broken into pieces
Suddenly a bird calls
Crying out our solitude

Jiangxi (江西): Where Dinosaur, Porcelain and Poetry Gather

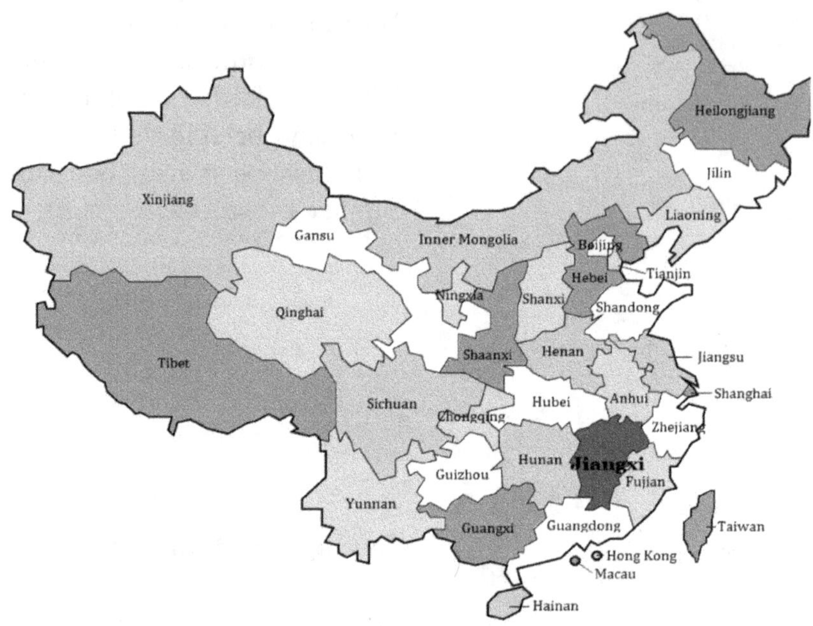

Jiangxi literally means "west of the Yangtze River." Poyang Lake, China's largest freshwater lake, is fed by five major rivers (Gan, Xin, Fu, Rao, and Xiu) and drains into the Yangtze here. Its size fluctuates dramatically between seasons, expanding to 4,000 km² in summer and shrinking to marshlands in winter, creating a dynamic ecosystem. The lake is a critical habitat for migratory birds, including 90% of the world's Siberian cranes, and is a Ramsar Wetland of International Importance.

Jiangxi's Zhoutian Formation is a fossil treasure. This Late Cretaceous geological formation (90–96 million years old) in Jiangxi's Ganzhou Basin preserves dinosaur fossils like the ankylosaur Datai and the titanosaur Gandititan, as well as abundant egg fossils.

Jingdezhen's porcelain thrived due to abundant kaolinite (porcelain clay) and water resources. Its kilns, active since the Han Dynasty, produced imperial-grade porcelain during the Song and Ming dynasties, earning it the title "Millennium Porcelain Capital" (*qiannian cidou*, 千年瓷都).

The Jiangxi School of Poetry was founded by Huang Tingjian (黄庭坚, 1045–1105). It emphasized meticulous craftsmanship, drawing from classical texts to create "thin and stiff" verse. It dominated Southern Song poetry, contrasting the Tang Dynasty's spontaneity.

Jiangxi nurtured China's literary giants, such as Tao Yuanming (陶渊明, 365–427 CE), a master of pastoral poetry. He's famed for his *Peach Blossom Spring*, a lyrical prose that envisions an idyllic utopia. It also birthed the great reformist statesman and poet Wang Anshi (王安石, 1021–1086), whose works reflected social ideals. Tang Xianzu (汤显祖, 1550–1616), playwright of *The Peony Pavilion*, has been a cornerstone of Chinese drama.

The Gan River valley was a cultural corridor, linking northern and southern China. Cities like Nanchang (site of the 1927 Communist uprising) and Jingdezhen became hubs of trade and artistry. Jiangxi's rivers and lakes not only shaped its geology but also nurtured its artistic soul. The Gan River's waters carried clay to Jingdezhen's kilns, while Poyang's wetlands inspired poets like Huang Tingjian. This interplay of land and literature makes Jiangxi a microcosm of China's natural and cultural heritage.

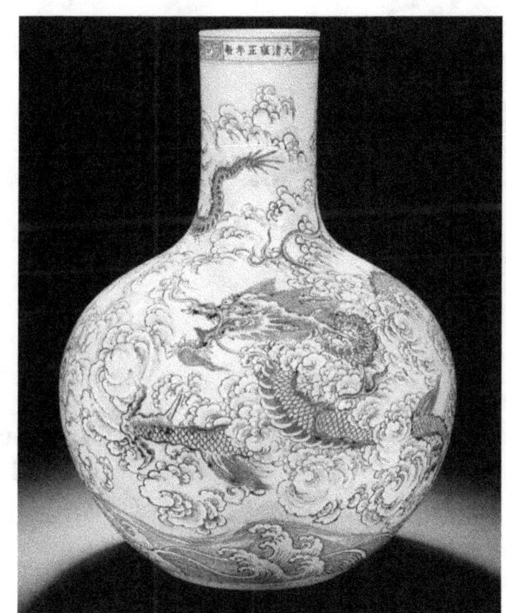

Jingde Porcelain

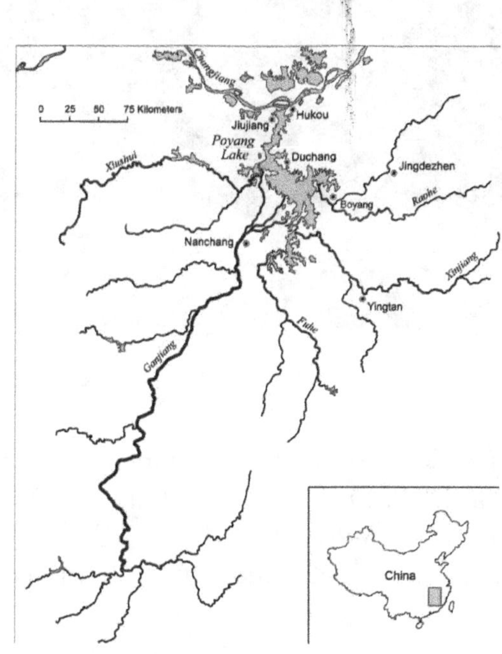

Jiangxi's Waterways

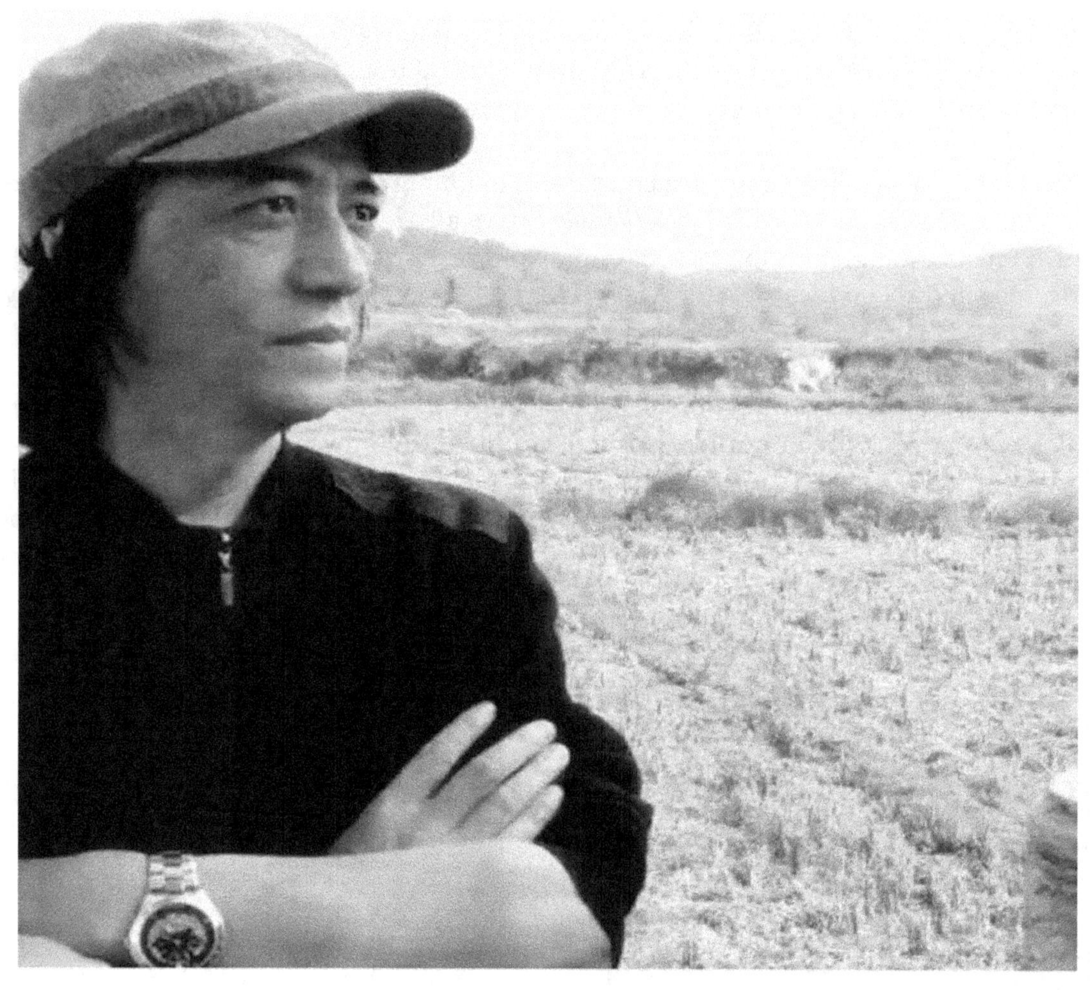

Lao De (老德), born in 1962 in Nanchang, Jiangxi, is the founder of the "Pseudo Avant-garde" (伪先锋) and "Writing Poetry is a Thing to Do After Drinking" (写诗是酒后的事) schools. He's the author of *The Natural-Born Actor* (本色演员), *You're My Wang Xiaomei* (你就是我的王小美), *Men's Bible* (男人的圣经), and many other poetry books.

我决定和你有点关系

1
其实 并不是我所能决定的
很多事情我都决定不了
这里有时间 环境与人物的原因
我所能决定就是今天晚上
好好地喝一杯 是不是喝第二杯
那要看当时的心情 还要看看
和我在一起喝酒的　都是些什么鸟人

2
她说　要喝　我喝一杯
你得两杯　我说
这是种什么逻辑
第一 我是女人
第二 我不胜酒力
第三 把我喝醉　你才有机会
在座的男男女女　一致同意
我喝了三杯　才知道今不如昔
我说 亲爱的　别喝了 我醉了
你也没有什么机会

3
机会无处不在
小东的机会就把握的很好
一个电话 就挣了一百多万
那天 他也喝多了
不停地拨着电话
我接到他电话 正好午夜十二点
我问他公司开得怎么样
他说 把公司关掉了
正坐在家里安心炒股
我说 有个股票很好
马上可能重组 半年以后

I Decide to Have a Relationship with You

1
Actually this is not what I can decide
In fact I can't make any decision
Due to time, environment and people
What I can do tonight is to drink
To my heart's desire　　should I have
another drink? That depends on my mood
Also who is there to drink with me?

2
Drink, she says, I want to have a drink
No, you need to have two drinks, I say
Nonsense, she says!
First, I'm a woman
Second, I can't tolerate alcohol
Third, you'll have a chance with me
Only when I get drunk. Everyone agrees.
So I drink three shots
Oh no, dear　　Stop drinking If I'm drunk
You'll have no chance with me either

3
Chance exists everywhere
Little Dong knows how to grab it
Once he made over a million yuan
With a phone call　　　He was drunk
That night　　kept dialing and dialing
Till I picked up　　　　at midnight
I asked him how his company was going
He said he had it shut down already
Now he's staying home buying and selling
Stocks. I told him about one stock
That looked promising　　six months later

他又给我打来电话 说
一定要好好请我喝一杯 我问
为啥 他报出了某某股票的代码
哦 那股票我也买过
挣了五角钱就跑掉了

4

我决定和你有点关系
并不是上帝安排好的
而是在中信银行的柜台前
你排在我前面 我发现
你的头发很飘 臀部还有点
微微的上翘　但你否定了这种说法
说是我们最初的相见
是在一个朋友的葬礼上
我穿着一件黑色的风衣
举手投足 与众不同

5

有关撒哈拉沙漠
我们并不知道很多
也许我们生活的太无聊了
对异域的风情充满着幻想
在撒哈拉酒吧 我们
习惯坐在窗口 边喝着啤酒
边看着窗外流动的风景
午夜十二点 我们走在
撒哈拉沙漠里 心太热
彼此都有些渴

6

没有阴谋 厄运也不曾出现
只是在某个瞬间 我们都有些疲软
沉湎往事 难以自拨

he called, inviting me for a drink.
For what, I asked? For the stock you told
me about, he said. I'm now rich.
Oh crap! That's the stock I had
Dumped after I made 50 cents

4

I decide to have a relationship
With you. This is not a decision
By God. That day you were standing
In front of me at the bank
I noticed your flowing hair
And full buttocks
But you told me I was wrong
We met at a friend's funeral
I was wearing a black coat
My manner was different from others

5

I know little
About Sahara
Maybe we just get bored
So we start imagining about deserts
In the Sahara Bar
We sit by the window as usual, drinking beer
Watching the scenery on the street
At midnight our hearts burn
From walking in the desert
So we both needed a drink badly

6

There's no conspiracy or bad luck
We just get tired and limp at that instant
We can't pull ourselves out of the past

7

有时我分不清白天与黑夜的关系
男人与女人的关系 这一个
和那一个的关系 对于这个世界
我是个不知道分子 而小露
知道得太多 爱滋病的形成
酒精肝医治的可能 她
还知道该怎样挣钱 那种男人最可信
但她对这个世界 也常常无能为力

8

有些关系 永远不能透明
它的背景有太多的阴影
就是走在香射丽谢大街上
也有那么一种暧昧的意味
虽然巴黎的阳光很好
抬头就能看见埃菲尔铁塔
可我们不是法国人 天生
一张中国人苦大仇身的脸

9

而西 你可能是个男人
也可能是个女人 我现在
和你没有一点关系 但说不定
那一天我们就会有点关系
前提是我不能死 而你必须是个
真实的人 那我们就发生一点关系吧
男女关系 同志关系 或者
作者与读者之间的关系 都可以
你有所不知
天色将晚 我心孤寂

7

Sometimes I can't tell the difference
between day and night, Between men and women
I know nothing about this world
But Little Lu knows too much
How one gets AIDS
How to find a cure for ALD
She knows how to make money, which men to trust
But she feels helpless about this world

8

Some relationships must stay in the dark forever
Their background has too many shadows
It feels suspicious and ambiguous
On Avenue des Champs-Élysées
Even though it's sunny in Paris
And Eiffel Tower is so visible
But we're not French   Our face
Looks Chinese, branded with suffering

9

Erxi, you might be a man or
A woman but I have nothing
To do with you   though
We may date someday
But I must stay alive and you
Must be real so let's have some
Relationship as lovers, comrades
Or as reader and writer   anything
You know it all
I'm getting lonely   As night falls

The Yangtze River Delta: Jiangnan (江南), Cradle of Culture and Power

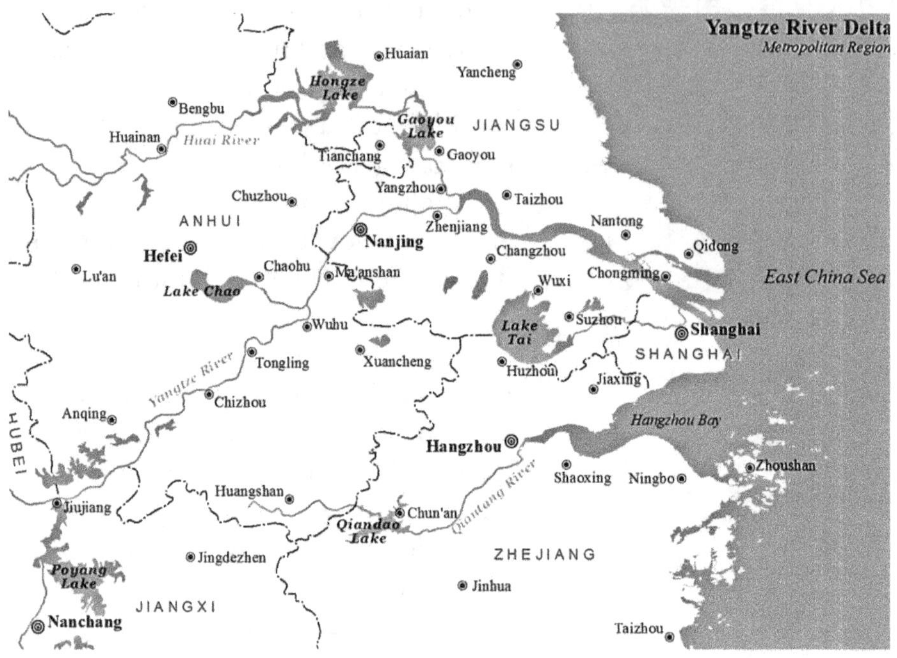

From Neolithic waterworks to the verses of its poets, Jiangnan's legacy flows as endlessly as the Yangtze itself. After traversing Jiangxi, the Yangtze flows eastward through Anhui, Jiangsu, Zhejiang, and Shanghai, forming the fertile and water-rich Jiangnan, a region stretching from the Yangtze's lower reaches to Hangzhou Bay.

This delta, one of China's most significant, is laced with a labyrinth of rivers, China's largest freshwater lake (Poyang), and the Grand Canal, the world's longest artificial waterway. Built over centuries (from 486 BCE onward), the Canal linked Jiangnan's agricultural wealth to northern China, transporting grain, salt, and even culinary traditions—giving rise to iconic dishes like Hangzhou's West Lake vinegar fish and Yangzhou's delicate steamed buns.

Jiangnan's landscape was shaped by millennia of sedimentary deposits from the Yangtze, creating a vast alluvial plain ideal for agriculture. Its hydraulic engineering heritage dates back to the Liangzhu Culture (3300–2300 BCE), whose advanced flood-control systems and rice paddies represent some of the world's earliest feats of water management. Later dynasties, particularly the Tang (618–907 CE) and Song (960–1279), expanded these networks, turning Jiangnan into

China's "Land of Fish and Rice" (*yumi zhixiang*, 鱼米之乡) and an economic powerhouse. By the Ming (1368–1644) and Qing (1644–1912) dynasties, Jiangnan produced over half of China's silk, tea, and taxes, fueling the empire's wealth. Today, Jiangnan remains central to China's economy, with Shanghai as its global face—a testament to the region's unbroken influence.

Jiangnan has long been the heartland of Chinese art, poetry, and scholarship. Its misty lakes, willow-lined canals, and monsoon-fed landscapes inspired countless poets: Tang Dynasty masters like Li Bai (who wrote of Jiangnan's "Sweet Osmanthus Blooms") and Du Mu ("Spring in Jiangnan," and "Rain on Apricot Blossoms") immortalized its beauty. The Song Dynasty saw the rise of Ci poetry, with luminaries like Li Yu (the last emperor of Southern Tang) penning melancholic verses about Jiangnan's lost splendor. In modern times, Bei Dao (b. 1949, lives in Beijing but has been shaped by Jiangnan's diaspora) and Xi Chuan (b. 1963, Jiangsu) carried forward this tradition, their poetry blending classical motifs with contemporary dissent, and Jiangnan's misty fragrance with the Yellow River's yang spirit.

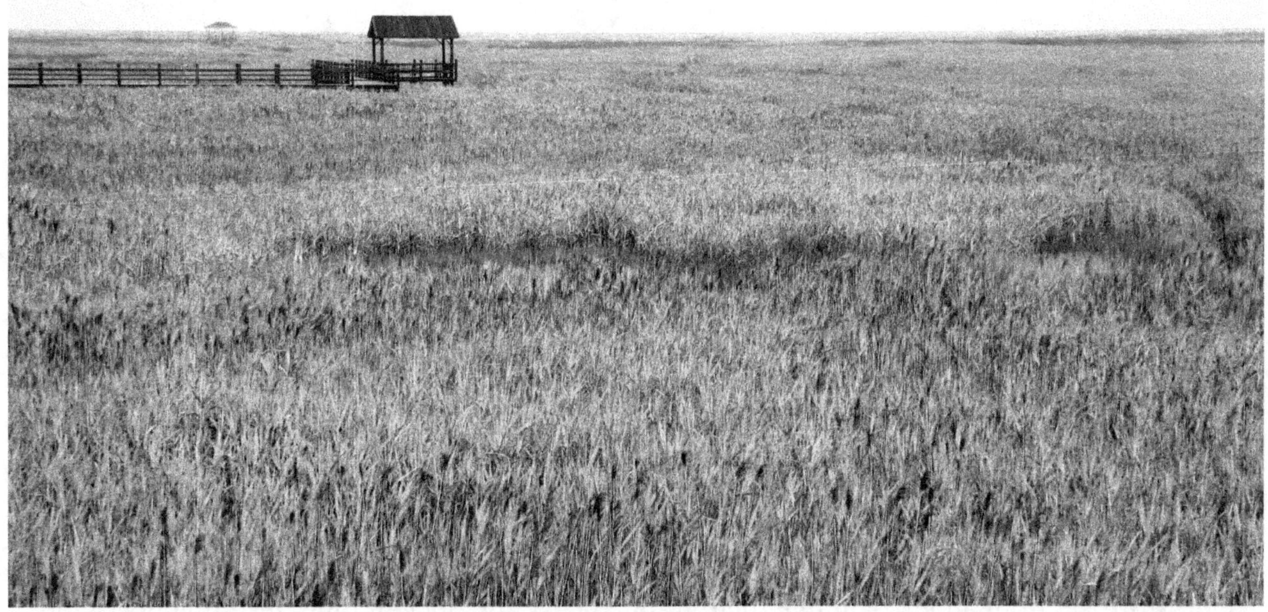

Chongming Island, Shanghai, the end of the Yangtze Delta

Anhui (安徽): A Land of Rivers, Mountains, and Timeless Legacy

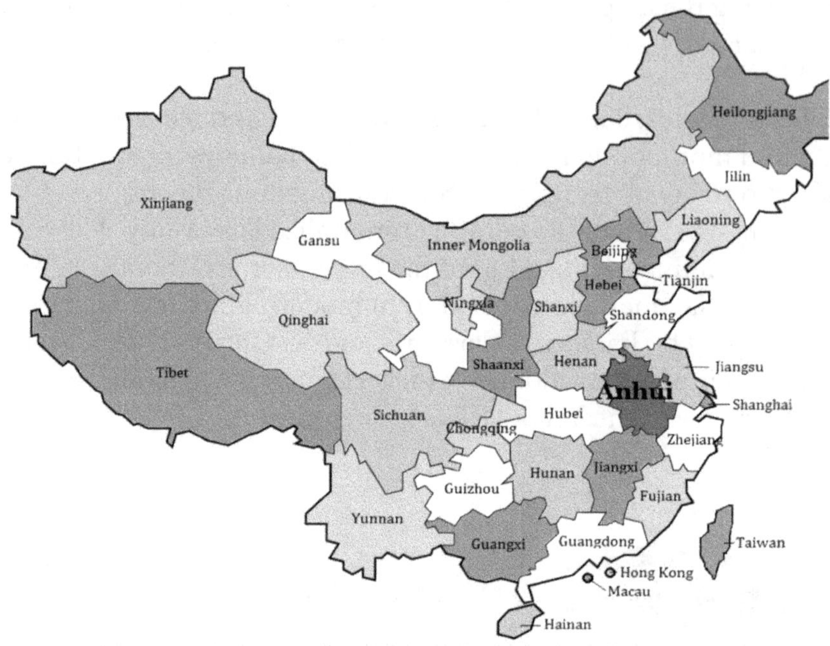

Nestled between the Yellow and Yangtze Rivers, Anhui has been a vital crossroads of water,
culture, and history for millennia. Human habitation here dates back 20,000 years, with
Neolithic settlements like Yangshao and Longshan (4,000–10,000 years ago) leaving traces of
early civilization. The region flourished from the Xia Dynasty (2070–1600 BCE) through
the Warring States period (475–221 BCE), its fertile plains and waterways shaping its destiny.

Anhui's landscape is defined by its two great river systems: the Huai River, linking the Yellow and
Yangtze, and the Qinling-Huaihe line, a climatic and geographical divide. This watery expanse
has brought both abundance and hardship—centuries of floods, famines, and wars tempered the
resilience of its people.

Geologically, Anhui is a marvel. The Yellow Mountains, a UNESCO World Heritage Site, rise
like brushstrokes from an ink painting, their granite peaks and ancient pines inspiring poets and
artists for centuries. Further south, Mount Jiuhua, one of China's Four Sacred Buddhist
Mountains, is carved from metamorphic rock, its temples clinging to mist-shrouded cliffs.

Anhui's legacy is etched in the lives of its most illustrious figures such as Yu the Great (2070–1600 BCE), legendary tamer of floods and founder of the Xia Dynasty; Laozi (6th century BCE), the sage whose Daodejing laid the foundation for Daoism; Cao Cao (155–220 CE), the cunning strategist and poet of the Three Kingdoms era; Ji Kang (223–263 CE), a Seven Sages of the Bamboo Grove philosopher-musician who championed individualism; Li Bai (701-762 CE), one of China's best poets who spent his late years in Anhui, till he died and was buried in Dangtu County; Zhu Yuanzhang (1328–1398), the rebel who became the Ming Dynasty's founding emperor; and Hai Zi (1964–1989), a modern poet from Huaining County, Anhui. Hai Zi (pen name of Zha Haisheng) is famed for his lyrical and melancholic verse, such as *Facing the Sea, with Spring Blossoms*. His tragic suicide at 25 cemented his legacy as a tortured genius.

Anhui's cultural soul thrives in its literary and artistic traditions. The Xinan School of Painting (late Ming Dynasty) was born here, blending poetry and landscape into ethereal scrolls. The Huizhou merchants of the Qing Dynasty amassed wealth but also patronized scholars, leaving behind exquisite ancestral halls and villages like Xidi and Hongcun (both UNESCO sites). In poetry, Anhui's rivers and mountains stirred the hearts of Li Bai, who wrote of the Yangtze's majesty, and Du Mu, whose verses captured the melancholy of its shores. The Huizhou dialect, a relic of Old Mandarin, still whispers in ancient villages.

Anhui is a testament to the harmony of water, stone, and human spirit.

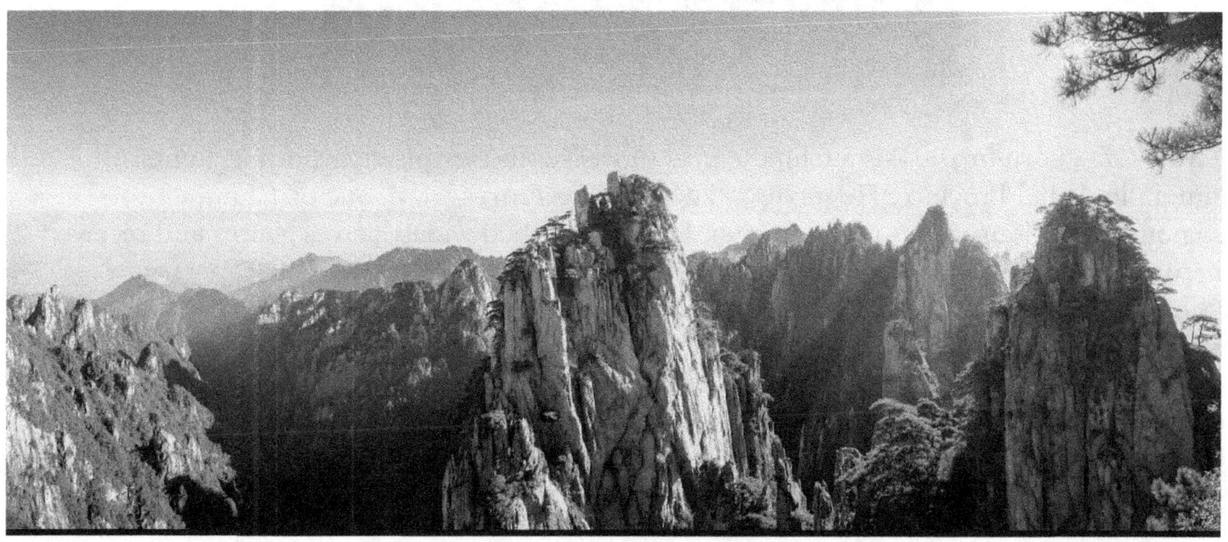

Yellow Mountain

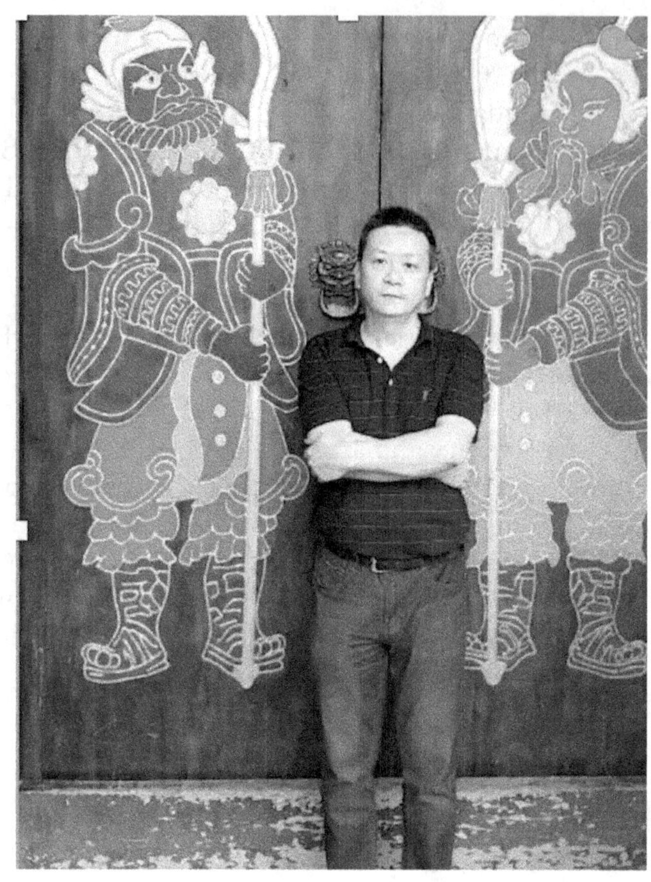

Li Yun (李云), born in 1964, is a Chinese poet, novelist, and scriptwriter born at Jiuhua Mountain in Anhui Province. He serves as an editor for *Poetry* (诗刊), one of China's most prestigious poetry journals. A prolific writer, Li has published widely across genres and received numerous literary awards. His works include *Big Fish in the Huai River* (淮河大鱼, poetry), *Waterway* (水路, poetry), and *Everything Comes from Sorrow and Joy* (悲喜皆由, poetry/prose).

Li Yun's writing often explores themes of nature, memory, and existential reflection, rooted in the landscapes and cultural heritage of his upbringing. His works blend classical Chinese lyricism with contemporary philosophical depth.

盒子

孩子，请不要打开盒子，无须看到全部
这世上所有事物真相你不该都弄清楚
盛在里面的东西不都是吉讯还有噩耗

在我最懵懂时，没恪守戒律
开口——说话
盒子被打开之际是阴霾沉寂的日子
请铭记这个教训

其实，盒子里是空的。其实，
盒子里是满的……

雷霆来了，藏宝图展开，秘密被泄密
阳光也会来，推启窗棂，万箭穿心
瘟疫接踵而至，密谋被暴露，腥风血雨
火星人来了吗？一颗流星悄然划过，
婴儿一声　啼哭

我是一只盒子，我是自己的破戒者
打开盒子，打开自己
放飞或存储什么
孩子，我唯一的不悔是——开口说话

Box

Child, please don't open the box, no need to see
everything. Not everything in this world needs to be
understood. The box brings good news, also death

I was too ignorant to follow the rule
I opened my mouth—I spoke
It was a grim day when I opened the box
Please remember the lesson

In fact, the box was empty. In fact,
The box was full…

Storm descended, treasures opened, secrets revealed,
sunlight broke the window, ten thousand arrows
through my heart, plagues came in waves,
conspiracy exposed, blood rained down.
Mars invasion? A comet through the sky, a cry of
a newborn

I was a box, I broke my own rule
I opened the box, I opened myself
To fly or stay put, but child, the only thing
I never regretted—opening my mouth to speak

水道—为心中的淮河

渡口

为了记住它
我得重新给它起个名字
就叫它桃花渡吧
其实，它有个更古老的名字
我恰巧是三月桃花开的时节
与它告别

这天一艘船载满红泥瓦的空花盆
（听说要驶向武汉的花鸟市场去卖）
这天一艘船装满晒干的毛花鱼
（听说要运到南京下关去批发）
这天有两艘船靠上渡口码头
船上卸下的货是芜湖的大米
义乌的小商品
这天我和镇里及村上
许多青葱年少的青年们
第一次扛着行李上轮船
去上海打工

这天我的心思比空花盆还空
情绪有着毛花鱼的咸腥味道
这天我希望有什么可以
栽满心里

就叫它桃花渡吧
谁让我和小镇的青年们眼睛都红如血桃

其实，渡口古名谓临淮镇
这是我故乡地理的名字
桃花渡
是我情感地理的名字
那年我十八岁
我起的名
我会终生牢记

Waterway — to Huai River in My Heart

Ferry

To remember this place
I gave it a new name
Let's call it Peach Blossom Ferry
I changed its name
For I said goodbye to that place
During the peach blossom season

That day a boat carried a load of red-clay pots
 (I heard it'd sail upstream to Wuhan flower market)
That day a boat was filled with dried Maohua fish
(I heard it'd sail downstream to Nanjing wholesale)
That day, two ships came into the port
They brought us rice from Wuhu
And all kinds of goodies from Yiwu
That day I boarded the boat with some youths,
tender like young scallions
We carried our luggage to sail to Shanghai for
work, for the first time

That day my mind was emptier than the red pots.
My soul tasted the fishiness of dried Maohua fish.
That day I wished I had something
to grow in my heart

Let's call it Peach Blossom Ferry
That day our eyes bled like the red peaches

The old ferry has a name—Linhuai Town
It's the name of my old home on the map
Peach Blossom Ferry
Is the name on my emotional map
That year I was 18
I gave the ferry a new name
to carry it in my heart forever

抛锚的锚

二十年后，我才来拜谒它
二十年前，我和一只貓在它身上爬来爬去

那时，锚也从船上到岸上爬上爬下
此时，它变成一只远古动物的标本
三棱骨角仰天无语
仿佛把蓝天系住
许多云朵都泊在那里
不动

在它的记忆里
自己牵挂的铁驳船
已被拆解为废铁
拆解那天
镇上一群被赶往屠宰场的牛
经过此地隆然地
集体下跪　　泪流满面

我摸着锚
如同抚摸当年那只貓的脊背
我好想让锚尖刺痛
我麻木的中年
如同那只貓挠破我的手背
我一直等了整整一下午

傍晚，城里来的孩子唤我
回家　　吃饭
我回答他的好奇提问
“这叫锚
抛锚的锚”

This is an Anchor

Twenty years later, I came back to see her
Twenty years ago, a cat and I climbed her up and down

The anchor also climbed up and down from barge
to shore. Now she's a specimen from an ancient time.
Her triangular bone faces the sky without a word
As if tying the sky together
Where many clouds park
Motionless

In her memory
The steel barge
Has been taken apart as scrap
That day cows on their way
to the slaughter house
knelt for no reason
Crying in unison

I stroke the anchor
As if stroking the cat's back in the old days
I long for her spikes to penetrate
My numbing middle age
Just the way the cat scratched my hand
But I wait all afternoon

Till dusk arrives, and my kids
from the city call me to go home for dinner. And I
reply to his curious question:
"This is an anchor you throw it into the sea
to keep the boat stand still"

Note: In Chinese, anchor (*mao*, 锚) and cat (*mao*, 猫) share the same sound. Different tones and contexts indicate different meanings.

Yang Jian (杨健), born in 1967, is a poet and artist from Ma'anshan (马鞍山, "Horse Saddle Mountain"), Anhui, a city on the banks of the Yangtze River. A Buddhist practitioner, his works include *Dust* (灰尘), *Shame* (耻辱), *Weeping Temple* (哭庙), and *On the Old Bridge* (古桥头).

Ma'anshan derives its name from a local legend: Xiang Yu (项羽), the fallen hegemon of Western Chu, ensured his beloved horse was safely ferried across the river before taking his own life. Overcome with grief, the horse leaped into the waters and drowned. A boatman buried its saddle on a nearby hill—hence "Horse Saddle Mountain." The area is also tied to the poet Li Bai, who is said to have drowned here while drunkenly embracing the moon's reflection.

In 2005, Ma'anshan hosted China's first poetry festival, cementing its place in the country's literary landscape.

I met Yang Jian in 2006, under the old Great Wall of the Ming Dynasty. We sat on the steps, watching the Yangtze River flow by, talking about poetry, life and philosophy till dawn. I've been translating his poetry since then.

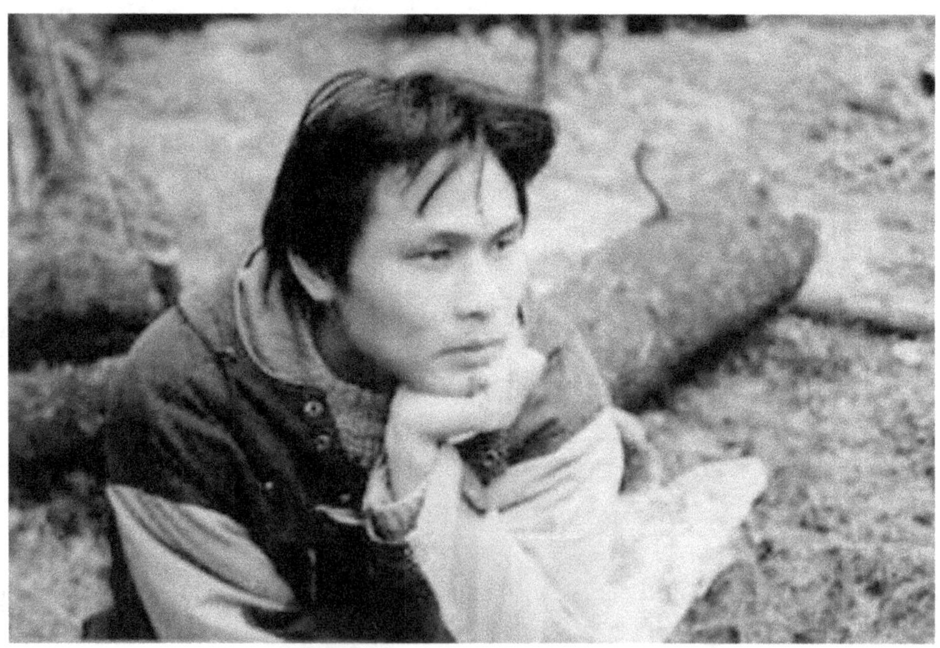

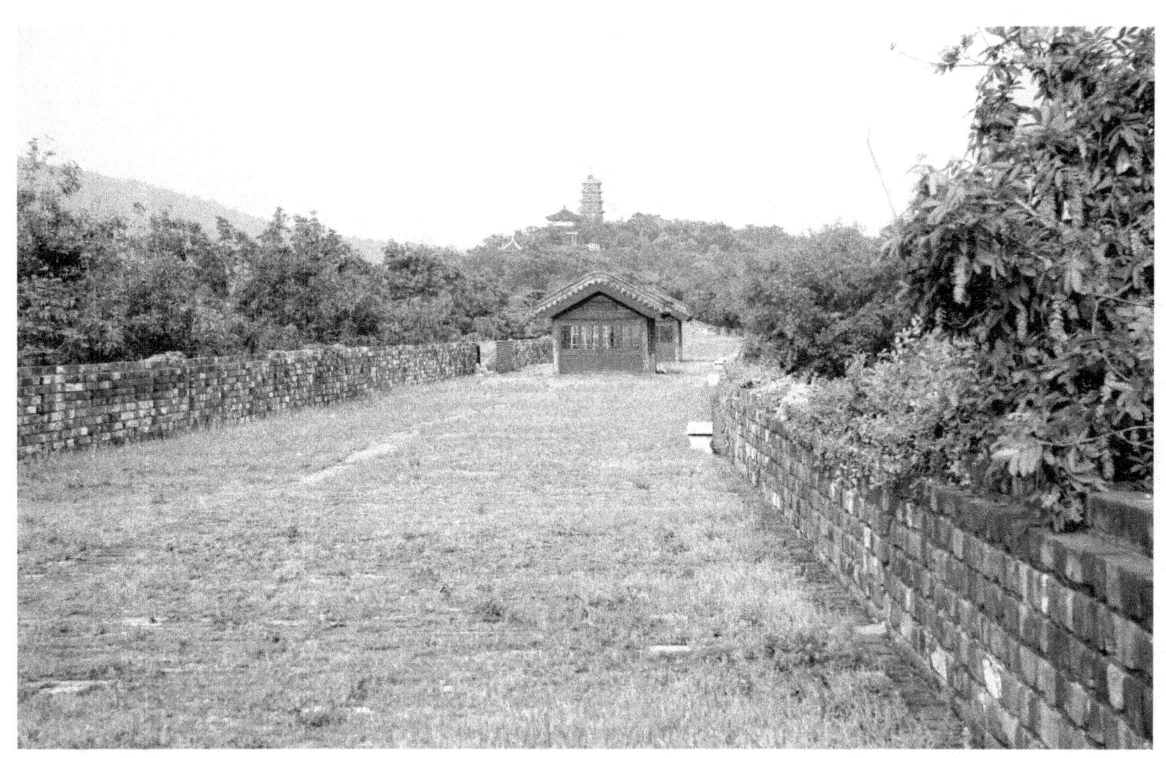

On top of the old Ming Dynasty wall

暮晚

马儿在草棚里踢着树桩
鱼儿在篮子里蹦跳，
狗儿在院子里吠叫，
他们是多么爱惜自己，
但这正是痛苦的根源，
像月亮一样清晰，
像江水一样奔流不止…

Dusk

Horses kick at tree stumps in the stall
Fish leap in the basket
Dogs bark in the yard
How they love themselves—
The source of all pain
Clear as the moon
Flowing like a river…

在悲痛里

光线洒下来，
像一阵阵细雨。
在棕榈树下，
请原谅我的黑暗，
像一条不净的小河，
在这里流淌，
玷污了我自己
轻柔的生命。
多少年过去了，
悲痛消磨着我，
仿佛爱情，
我一直就没有长大，
我的脑海里仍是那些石牌坊
倒下来时的轰响，
我还没有智慧去忘掉它们，
但我应当放下这些，
因为我的生命里，
没有石牌坊，也没有两只怒吼的狮子。
我的生命是轻盈的，
像傍晚时的落日给予人世的光辉。
可是我愚蠢地用痛苦惩罚自己，
仿佛只有跟痛苦对应才是正确的。
我就这样浪费了世上的光阴，
我的心是可以回应着夜晚
沉睡的群山的寂静，
回应着那些树木，在群山里的奥秘

Sorrow

Light pours
Like drizzle
Under the palm trees
Please forgive my darkness
That flows like a dirty stream
That pollutes
This fragile life
Years pass
Sorrow grinds me down
Like love
I have never grown up
My brain still shakes
With the sound
Of the falling steles
I'm not wise enough to
Forget them
But I must
There's neither stele, nor roaring lion in my life
So light and soft
Like the setting sun
But I foolishly punish myself with pain
As if it were the only way to feel
I've wasted my time on earth
Only my heart can answer
the silence of the sleeping mountains
Respond to the secrets in the trees, in the mountains

祖国

枯草上的绵羊默默无言地望着远方，
多美啊，摆在油菜花地里的蜂箱！

一头眼泪般的牛拴在石头上，
拖拉机来回运着稻草。

那叫不出名字的鸟，在蓝天，眼睛，
运河组成的灵魂里飞过，
晒在春天里的冬日身躯，
渗出幸福的汗滴！

我不了解运送石棉瓦的船工的苦水，
但是落在甲板，运河上的光，永存！
他们乌黑的眼圈，永存！

啊，枯萎的荷枝犹如古人残存的精神！
没有什么比看到倒塌的旧房子
更加令人难受。

姑溪河畔山顶的塔尖与江边码头的塔尖
同时，带着泥土的棕黄，刺向蓝天！

在车厢里，人们凝望着落日，
一件挂在桃树上的农民的蓝布褂！

Motherland

Sheep graze on the withered grass
How beautiful, beehives in the mustard flowers!

A tearful cow is tied to a rock
Tractors churn back and forth with straw

Nameless birds fly across the soul of the sky, eyes
and the canal, bathed in the
spring sun, winter bodies
sweating with joy!

I don't know the bitterness of boatmen shipping
asbestos shingles, but light on their decks lives forever,
dark circles around their eyes, live forever!

Withered lotuses stand like ancient spirits!
Nothing is more heartbreaking
than a collapsed house

On the hill above the Guxi River port, pagodas
and cranes thrust into the sky in mud colors!

On the train, we gaze into the sunset
A peasant's blue shirt on a peach tree

满月

1

孩子们在大树下睡着了，
儿子为衰老的母亲扣上扣子。

呵，满月的光辉，
瓦楞畅快的线条。

他吸收了柳树柔软的部分，
和露水里苍天的寥阔。

即将摆脱他的时代，
那种悲伤的局限。

2

柔和的傍晚又来临了
在悠远而凄怆的运河水上

那座古老的万年桥，
还是那么奥秘，灰暗

我爱它们
像未消的雪

在瓦楞上，
像满月和柳丝，在河湾上。

Full Moon

1

Children asleep under a big tree
The son buttons his aging mother's jacket

Full moonlight
The fluid lines of tiles

He becomes the willow
And the vast sky in dewdrops

Time is about to abandon him
A tragedy of limitation

2

Tender dusk arrives
Upon the distant canal of sorrow

That ten-thousand-year-old bridge
Still mysterious, still gray

I love them
As much as lingering snow

Upon tiles
Like the full moon and willow over the river

甄山禅寺

芭蕉的样子多么舒展，
狗跳着，咬身上的虱子。
当它叫累了，它会睡去。

小女孩翻看着睡莲叶子，
她的弟弟送一桶水去菜地，
在四周，群山像一件展开的僧人的架装。

几个农民刨开蒜苗地，
阳光涌入
死者正是这样得到幸福的。

池塘里掏出来的淤泥，
摆在路边
我们处在一个充分暴露的伟大时期

Mount Zhen Temple

How relaxed the banana tree is
A dog leaps, nipping at its fleas
It will fall asleep, exhausted from barking

A little girl turns lotus leaves
Her brother carries water to the garden
Mountains spread, like a monk's opened robe

Peasants dig in a garlic field
The sun pours in
This is how the dead receive happiness

The mud from the bottom of the pond
Piles on the road
We live in a great unfolding age

古别离

什么都在来临啊，什么都在离去，
人做善事都要脸红的世纪，
我踏着尘土，这年老的妻子
延续着一座塔，一副健康的喉咙。

什么都在来临啊，什么都在离去，
我们因为求索而发红的眼睛，
必须爱上消亡，学会月亮照耀
心灵的清风改变山河的气息。

什么都在来临啊，什么都在离去，
一个人情欲消尽的时候
该是多么蔚蓝的苍穹！
在透明中起伏，
在静观中理解了力量。

什么都在来临啊，什么都在离去，
从清风中，我观看着你们，
我累了，群山也不能让我感动，
而念出蓓日的人，他是否就是落日!?

Ancient Departure

Things come, things go
We live ashamed of our kindness
I walk in dust, this old wife
Still keeps her pagoda, her healthy voice

Things come, things go
Our eyes bleed from wanting
We must learn to love death, let the moon glow
Let the heart shape rivers and mountains

Things come, things go
When our passions dry
How blue the sky will be!
We rise and fall in transparency
To understand the power in stillness

Things come, things go
I watch you in the wind
I'm so tired, even the mountains can't move me.
The sunset singer, is he sunset himself?

黄昏即景

经历了火热的夏天
我安静地坐在山坡上，
多么美好，令人放松的荒凉！
山下抖颤的灯火，
像我们接近真理时不能抑制的心跳，
快变成灯吧，
我不想看了，
要让别人看，
我有过日落，
日出的痛苦，
整个白昼和将要黑夜的痛苦，
我悲怆的音调似乎来自余晖下的江水，
但我不想再唱了，
要让它们来唱，
灰蒙蒙的天，
苍茫茫的地，
树木、田野、小河……
样样都是心啊！

Scenery at Dusk

After a hot summer
I sit alone on this slope
How beautiful this desolation!
Below the mountain, lights flicker
Like the wild heartbeat when we near truth.
Let me turn into a light
I no longer want to look
Let others look
I've felt the pain
Of the sunset and sunrise
Pain of day and dusk
My sad calls come from the river
But I no longer want to sing
Let others sing
The gray sky
The endless land
Trees, brooks, fields . . .
Everything is heart!

Jiangsu (江苏): Link between South and North, Silk and Poetry

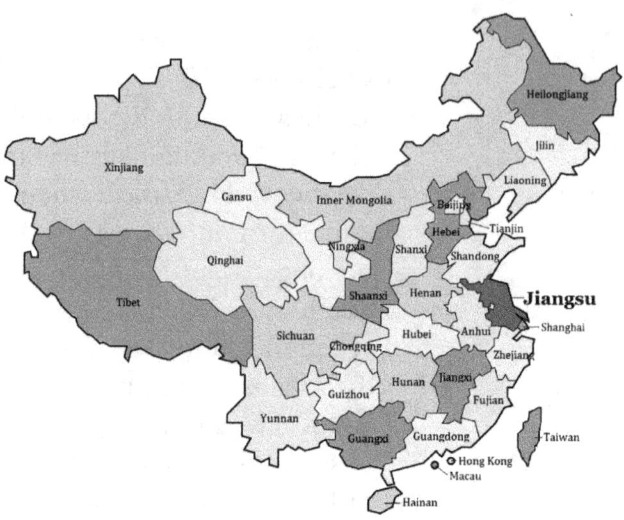

Jiangsu Province——where the Yangtze River surrenders to the sea, unfurling a fertile delta of water, silk, and poetry. A land of dualities, it is both China's flattest province and a realm sculpted by ancient geological forces—bedrock forged in the Proterozoic eon, iconic lowland plains shaped by millennia of sediment from the Yangtze and Huai rivers. Yet hidden in its northwestern reaches rise the weathered ridges of the Subei Hills, remnants of a far older landscape, while the karst limestone peaks of Tianmu Lake and Yuntai Mountain (a UNESCO Global Geopark) stand as silent witnesses to 2 billion years of tectonic drama.

In 1194, the Yellow River dramatically shifted its course, abandoning its northern path around the Shandong Peninsula to surge through Xuzhou, merging with the Huai River's old course at Qingjiang (modern Huai'an) before reaching the sea. This event reshaped the region's hydrology and left the region with a legacy of fertile loess plains and alluvial deposits, enriching its agricultural heritage.

Jiangsu's history runs as deep as its rivers. Neolithic Liangzhu culture (3400–2250 BCE) flourished here, crafting jade artifacts that predate dynasties. Later, the Grand Canal's lifeline linked the province to empires, turning cities like Yangzhou and Suzhou into glittering hubs of trade and scholarship. The Ming and Qing dynasties crowned Suzhou the "Venice of the East," its canals and scholar gardens inspiring poets for a thousand years.

This is a land of ink and lyricism. Jiangsu birthed the Jian'an School of poetry during the Han dynasty, and later nurtured Li Yu (937–978 CE), the melancholic poet-king of the Southern Tang, whose verses still echo in Nanjing's rain-soaked streets. The Yangzhou School of the Qing dynasty refined classical aesthetics, while Zhu Ziqing (1898–1948), a son of Jiangsu, penned modernist prose as delicate as the province's famed Suzhou embroidery.

From the mist-wrapped Slender West Lake to the tidal fury of the Qiantang River's northern reach, Jiangsu's landscapes have long been painted in verse. Even now, as the world's largest producer of silk hums with industry, the province remains a cradle of quiet contemplation—where scholars once gathered in Suzhou's Humble Administrator's Garden, and where the Yangtze's endless flow still murmurs the cadence of ancient poems.

Jiangsu also bridges the culture and history between the delta of the Yangtze and the Yellow River Basin. Xuzhou's cuisine, for example, blends northern robustness with southern refinement. Its distinct seasons—crisp autumns, icy winters, and humid summers—reflect its transitional climate, where the Qinling-Huaihe Line demarcates China's warm south from its arid north.

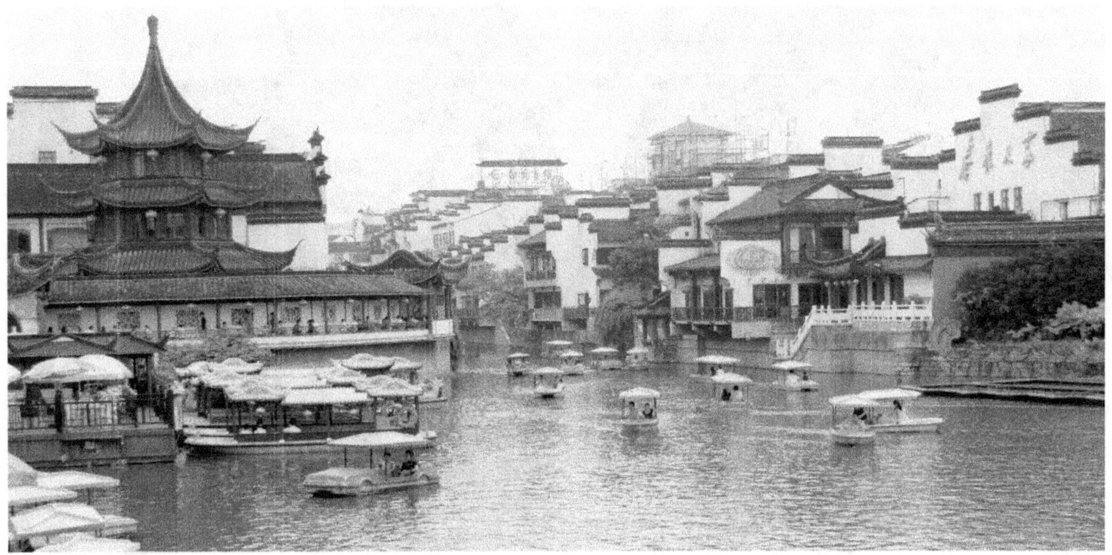

Suzhou, city in Jiangsu, the "Venice of the East"

Xi Chuan (西川), pen name **Liu Jun** (刘军), was born in 1963 in Xuzhou, Jiangsu Province. He's a celebrated Chinese poet, essayist, and translator, as well as a distinguished professor at Beijing Normal University. He is the author of ten poetry collections, two books of essays, three critical works, a play, and numerous translations of works by Ezra Pound, Jorge Luis Borges, Czesław Miłosz, Gary Snyder, and others. His accolades include the Lu Xun Literary Prize, the Swedish Cicada Prize for Poetry (2018), and the 1999 Weimar International Essay Prize Contest. His writing has been translated, anthologized, and published in nearly thirty countries.

His work *Notes on the Mosquito: Selected Poems of Xi Chuan* (translated by Lucas Klein, New Directions, 2012) won the 2013 Lucien Stryk Asian Translation Prize (ALTA) and was shortlisted for the 2013 Best Translated Book Award (USA).

Xi Chuan was a poet-in-residence at Macalester College in 2004, following his residency at the University of Iowa's International Writing Program. We were classmates in the English Department of Beijing University from 1981 to 1984.

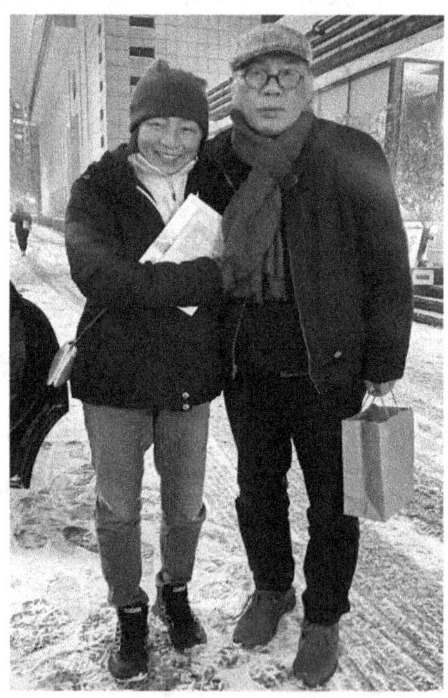
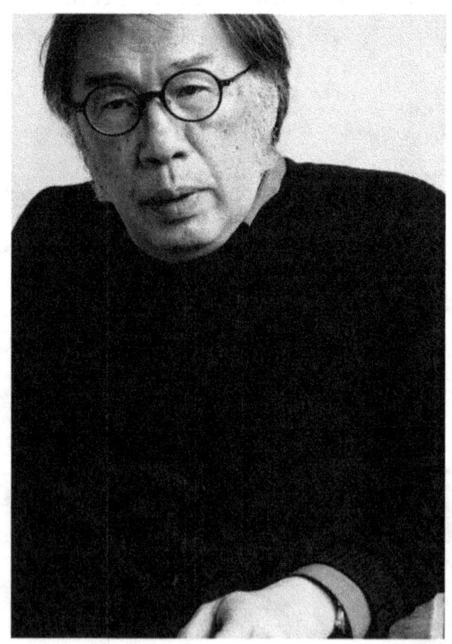

暮色

在一个幅员辽阔的国家
暮色也同样辽阔
灯一盏一盏地亮起
暮色像秋天一样蔓延

亡者呵，出现吧
所有的活人都闭上了嘴
亡者呵，在哪里?
暮色邀请你们说话
一些名字我要牢记
另一些名字寻找墓碑
无数的名字我写下
仿佛写出了一个国家

而暮色在大地上蔓延
伸出的手被握住
暮色临窗，总有人
轻轻叩响我的家门

Dusk

In a vast country
Dusk, too, is vast
Lamps light up one by one
Dusk spreads like autumn

Let the dead step out
And we, the living, seal our lips
Where are you, oh departed
Dusk is inviting you to speak
Some names will live in my memory
Some will search for a tomb stone
The rest will spill from my pen
As if making a new nation

Twilight on the horizon
Extends its hand to be held
When dusk arrives, someone
Will knock on my door

我的意识流

月亮就是那个样子麻雀就是那个样子但云彩永远没有完成的自己

所以我跳起来接近一块云时接近的是我自己的未完成就像我观察一片落叶时理解了另一个人的已完成

我也许在接近我自己也许在远离我自己我通过跟踪赵钱孙李周吴郑王兜一个大圈跟上我自己但我不认识我的影子他否定起自己来连我也否定了

我这自相矛盾自我怀疑自我高估的我自己啊一会儿大如恐龙一会儿小如恐龙蛋一会儿陷入火星往事一会儿学孟子说天时地利人和

仿佛这不是21世纪经过三年疫情之后而是公元前3世纪齐国的稷下学宫正欣欣向荣

从那时到现在我内衣外穿自我翻转识字量日益减少而垃圾信息居然已储满我脑子里60万个快乐的芯片

没办法 我即使有办法对付自己的退步也没办法对付夜晚的蚊蝇以及诡谲的星期一不确定的星期二以及星期三的套话和废话之海

以及不可逆转的昏昏欲睡进入噩梦的空间那里偶尔星光灿烂能看见蹦跳的小蓝人儿

我唠叨着沉默着开心着把自己变成一条空船顺流而下从A到B到C而能否再回到A这几乎不是我的问题

那是谁的问题呢那狗揽八泡屎的谁谁谁你站出来你跳个江给我看看

潮起潮落花开花落而天王老子的无为而治对称人间的有为而治却放任山洪冲走安全的昨日

再不归来的父亲再不闲暇的小鸟我忍不住喷嚏忍不住腰疼

忍不住看你一眼仿佛来了灵感两眼一黑跨上风的坐骑冲过臭鸡蛋烂菜叶的矩阵达成我自己的陌生人穿过彩虹的拱门

我站在陌生人一边顾不上再打一遍小算盘就对自己喊了一声喟

My Stream of Consciousness

The moon stays the same so does the sparrow but the cloud never completes itself

So when I chase the cloud I'm just trying to get close to my own incompleteness just the way I understand another person's journey through watching a falling leaf

Maybe I'm getting closer to myself maybe I'm getting further away I thought I've caught up after following zhao qian sun li zhou wu zhen wang and many others but I no longer recognize my own shadow which denies its own existence which makes me deny my own

I contradict myself doubt myself overestimate myself one moment I'm bigger than a dinosaur next I'm smaller than its egg one moment I sink into my past life on Mars then I study Mencius' yakety-yak about the harmony between time space and humanity As if this is not 21st century after a 3-year pandemic but the thriving Jixia Academy of Qi State in the 3rd century BC

Now I wear my underwear outside I turn myself inside out I'm losing my words every day my brain is piling up with garbage and 600,000 happy chips…What can I do

Even if I can do something about my digression I still can do nothing about mosquitoes or flies or tricky Monday malleable Tuesday or Wednesday filled with cliches

Or entering the space of irreversible nightmares to glimpse at stars and dancing blue things

I nag I stay quiet I turn myself into a joy boat flowing down from A to B to C I don't know if I can get back to A but that's not my problem

Whose problem then oh who dares come out say something show me how to jump into the sea

Tides come and go flowers bloom and fade gods do nothing humans do everything but floods continue washing away yesterday

My father no longer comes home birds are no longer free I can't stop sneezing my back won't stop hurting I can't stop looking at you as if the muse is visiting I leap on the back of the wind flying over the battlefield of rotten eggs and vegetables through the rainbow gate as a stranger

I stand by the stranger and shout Hey to myself without thinking

照镜子

照镜子偶然想到：都是眼耳鼻舌身意，我难看，大象不难看；

都是大鼻子，大象不难看，但某人的大鼻子在文革漫画中必须难看。

清朝的费丹旭赞赏小嘴巴。进入1950年代小嘴巴代表落伍的价值观。

而浓眉大眼适于地覆天翻，也就是适于牺牲，适于无私，适于奉献。

对此号称"新人类"者在2020年代都表示反对：先玩手机，先吃饭！

可生下来浓眉大眼却碌碌一生，让正能量公司大股东们情何以堪！

都属兔，有人活成老虎，有人活成大龙。我妈说：看看别人！

都膀大腰圆，有人活成圣人，有人活成保镖。我妈说：咱不攀高枝！

鸟叫，有人听进心里。雨落，有人避不开索性坦然地走在雨中。

平庸者也能诗意地行走于大地。遇上个疯子，血型相同怎么办？

菩萨没有血型，慈悲不论血型，但负责任地自我惩罚者毕竟是少数。

酒鬼以为天下人都好酒。破产者以为世界应在半小时内毁灭。

老板要求人人服从其癖好。猴子以为人人都爱孙悟空。

有人分发幸福像分发糖果，有人接住糖果以为接住了幸福。

Looking at the Mirror

It occurred to me one day in the mirror: we both have five senses, body and mind, why do I look ugly, but elephants look good?

We both have a big nose. It looks good on an elephant, but not on the man in the manga during the Cultural Revolution.

Small mouth is a sign for beauty in Fei Danxu's painting during the Qing. Since 1950, it represents only outdated value.

Big eyes with thick eyebrows fit better for revolution, for the selfless dedication and sacrifice.

These so called "new human beings" all objected in 2020, that we should play with phones and eat first.

Born in the year of the rabbit, some became tigers, others dragons. Mom said: look at them!

So big and strong, some living like saints, some working as bodyguards. "But we shall not climb the ladder!" said Mom.

Birds chirp, its sound reaching someone's heart. It's raining, someone is walking in the rain since getting wet is inevitable.

Even the mediocre can walk on the earth poetically. What shall we do if we bump into a crazy man with the same blood type?

Buddhas don't have blood type. Kindness doesn't have blood type. Only few of us will punish ourselves out of responsibility.

The drunk believe all alcohol is good quality. The bankrupt debtors believe the world should be destroyed within half an hour.

The boss demands all his employees to follow his obsessions. Every monkey thinks the world loves the Monkey King.

Some hand out happiness like candies. Some take the candy, thinking it contains happiness.

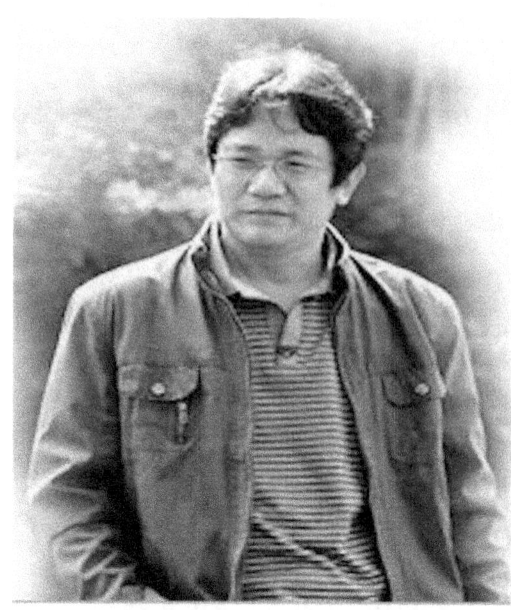

Hu Xian (胡弦) was born in 1966 in a rural village in Xuzhou, Jiangsu Province, near the historic Yellow River old course. A celebrated Chinese poet, essayist, and Editor-in-Chief of *Yangtze River* (扬子江), Hu Xian is renowned for blending China's layered history with lyrical introspection. His works reflect his rural upbringing and the landscapes of Xuzhou, where the "jumping rivers" and agricultural rhythms deeply influenced his poetic voice. After teaching in rural schools and working as a journalist, he moved to Nanjing in 2004, dedicating himself fully to poetry. His collections, such as *Sandglass* (沙漏) and *Empty Stairway* (空楼梯) explore time, memory, and displacement with metaphysical nuance.

Hu Xian insists on writing poetry by hand, finding inspiration in slow travel (e.g., old trains) and natural sounds like birdcalls. He rejects digital drafting, calling it "lifeless." His poems, such as *Longmen Grottoes* (龙门石窟) and *Ancient Bell* (古钟), weave historical trauma with everyday objects, creating "multi-layered time-space (*shikong*, 时空) collisions."

Other key works include the poetry collections *Rain* (雨) and *The Man Who Can Never Return Home* (永远无法回家的人), and the essays *Lake and River Vegetables* (江湖菜) and *Vegetable Notes* (蔬菜帖). Hu Xian is also the winner of the 2018 Lu Xun Literary Prize, the Xu Zhimo Poetry Prize, and the October Literary Award, among others. He is the first writer from Xuzhou to win the Lu Xun Prize.

醒来

我醒来时，你还在沉睡，
我独自听鸟鸣。
等你醒来，我已不是那个听鸟鸣的人，
只是一个陪伴着你的人，
把我区别开的是鸟鸣，
和你的睡眠，我却不能把它们
联系在一起，把一阵鸟鸣

带到你梦中，多么困难，
描述这一切，多么困难，
而如果把你提前叫醒，我将只是个
和你一起听鸟鸣的人，而非刚才
那个听鸟鸣的人。——还好，
除了我，世界并未曾有所改变

Awaken

When I woke, you were still sleeping,
I listened to birds singing alone.
Then you wake up, I'm no longer the man
 listening to birds, just someone
 accompanying you, what separated us
was the bird song and your sleep, and I can't
Connect them, or bring the bird singing

Into your dream, it's hard, so hard to
Describe all this, but had I woke you up,
I'd have been the man listening to birds
with you, not the man listening
to the singing, alone—fortunately,
the world hasn't changed, except for me

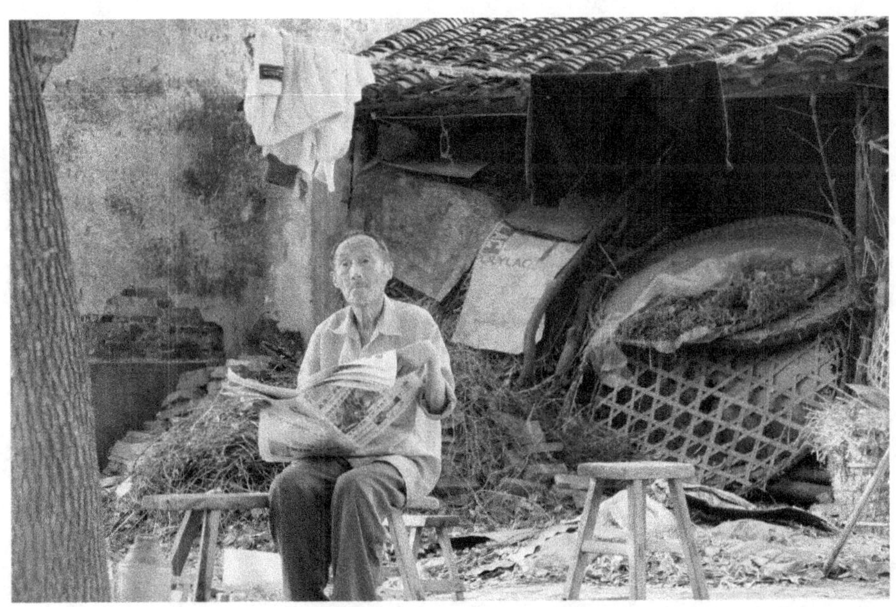

A village in the transition of China's modernization, 2006

树

一棵树如果看见了什么，
它的身体也不会有任何变化，
它总是站在事件之外。

一棵树对任何事物
都不会感到奇怪。
当它意识到要成为见证，
就长出了新的枝杈。

一棵树你已经看见它，
你却未必真的看见了它。
它不陪我们生，
也不陪我们死；
在它的内心，
有另外的事物在飞奔。

Tree

If a tree sees something,
Its body won't change,
As it stands outside the matter of things.

Nothing ever surprises
The tree. When it feels
It's about to become a witness
It grows new branches

You think you see the tree
But do you really see the tree?
It wasn't born for us,
It won't die for us;
Inside its heart,
Something else is running.

树木

老屋前后，杂树颇多，最老的
是一棵刺槐，心都空了，
可年年的白花开得满满。
门前栽过两棵白杨，亭亭如盖，
祖父和大伯曾坐在树下，商量
给大伯残疾的儿子讨个外地老婆。
后来伐倒了一棵，给祖父做棺木。
五年后，另一棵给了大伯。
再远一点的村外，曾经起过一片杏林，
又陆续砍去，只剩下
祖父坟边的一棵。
前些年我回了一趟村子，
老屋被侄儿翻盖成了平房，
拆下的房梁,椽子,
颜色黧黑，散落一地。
这些朽了的老木头，再也没有用了，
而村子里全是陌生的新绿，陌生的
柳树，楝树，梧桐……和沙沙声。

Trees

There were many trees around the old house, the
oldest one was a thorny elm, trunk empty inside,
but still blooming in white every spring.
Two birches in the front yard provided thick shade.
Grandpa and Uncle sat under the trees, discussing
how to find a wife from afar for the disabled son.
One birch was felled later, to make grandpa's coffin.
Five years later, the other fell for the uncle.
Outside the village, there used to be an
apricot orchard. All gone gradually,
except for the last tree, standing by grandpa's grave.
I visited my village a few years ago.
My nephew had turned my old home into a
new house, old beams from the old house
scattered around, black, rotten,
those old beams, all useless, unwanted.
The whole village is surrounded by a strange green,
new willows, bead trees, plane trees… rustling.

黑白石子

从前，西藏有个强盗
叫潘公杰，杀人越货多年后，
幡然醒悟，剃度礼佛。
他修行的法子是：
心有一善念，面前放一白石子，
心起一恶念，面前放一黑石子，
待石子尽白，他已被叫做
高僧潘公杰。
公元2015年，我来西藏，
见冰川、戈壁、河畔多石子，
大者如斗，小者如指，为风
和流水造就。
于是想起潘公杰，于是想起
以流水之慢，祛恶如剥皮，
以风沙之快，持善如诛心。
一双杀戮的手到最后
接受的竟是小石子的教育。
而黑与白，每次微小的移动，
宗教与人心中
都有雪崩生，有高原起伏。
指尖冷，天堂远，地狱
始终不远不近跟着。

Black and White Pebbles

Long ago, in Tibet, there was a bandit
Named Pangong Gya. After years of crimes
He repented, shaved his head, became a monk.
His practice was simple:
For each kind thought, a white stone was laid down,
for each bad thought, a black stone was laid down.
When all stones turned white, he became
The Venerable Lama Pangong Gya.
In 2015, I came to Tibet, saw many stones at
glaciers, Gobi Desert, riverbanks,
giant boulders, small pebbles, all ground down
by wind and water.
I remember Pangong Gya's story,
How slow the river flows, peeling evils like skin,
how fast the wind blows, holding kindness like punishment.
A pair of slaughtering hands finally
Received the blessing of little pebbles.
Black and white, each tiny move,
Could cause an avalanche in a faithful heart
Down the rolling steppe.
Cold fingers, distant heaven and hell follows,
not too far, not too distant.

井

村外的麦场边，当年
曾有两间破旧的土坯房，
那里住过三个外乡人：一对老夫妇
和他们漂亮的女儿。
麦场的南边有一口井，
那女儿常去打水，
拎着铁桶，乌黑的长辫子，
看人时，眼波流动。
哦，对于一个小学三年级学生，那是
我今生遇见的第二种光。
我一边趴在桶沿上喝水，一边
听她用低低的声音唱歌。
我听不懂那歌，只是感到忧郁，仿佛
歌声里也藏着一口深井。
据说，村子里和她相好的
不止一人……
哦，一个外乡人，她有过怎样的爱情，
其中，是否夹杂着对生活的恐惧？
就像那年秋天，她无法遮掩的
身体：肚子越来越大，最终，
在流言蜚语中跳进了井里。
派出所的人来过两次，事情
不了了之。
哦，这么多年了，悲伤
似乎从未消失，总在某些寂静的时候，
我体内会扑通一声，恍如
心脏落水。
——我一直记得那井水的清甜，
那脸，眼睛，难解的歌声，以及
在歌声深处晃动的，
铁皮水桶，和一口井
幽暗的凉意，苦腥。

Well

By the wheat square outside the village, there were
two mud huts, old, crumbling.
Three strangers lived there: an old couple
And their beautiful daughter.
There was a well on the southside.
The daughter went there to fetch water daily,
A metal bucket in her hand, black long braid, eyes
shining with light when she looked at you.
For a third-grade boy, the light
Felt like my second life.
I drank water from her bucket, listening
To her humming.
I couldn't understand her song, only felt its sorrow
as if the song had a well deep inside.
I heard she kept
more than one lover…
Oh, as a stranger to the village, what love did she
experience? Was it mixed with her terror for life?
Like her belly, getting bigger that fall,
Impossible to cover up, till finally
She jumped into the well—filled with rumors.
Cops came twice, but found
Nothing serious.
Oh, all these years, sorrow
never left me. In quiet moments something falls
inside me with a thump, as if my heart dropped
into the water.
——I remember how sweet the well water tasted,
and her face, eyes, songs,
the metal bucket in the heart
of her singing, and the cold, bitter taste
in the dark well

Nanjing (南京): A Capital of Dragons, Phoenixes and Poetry

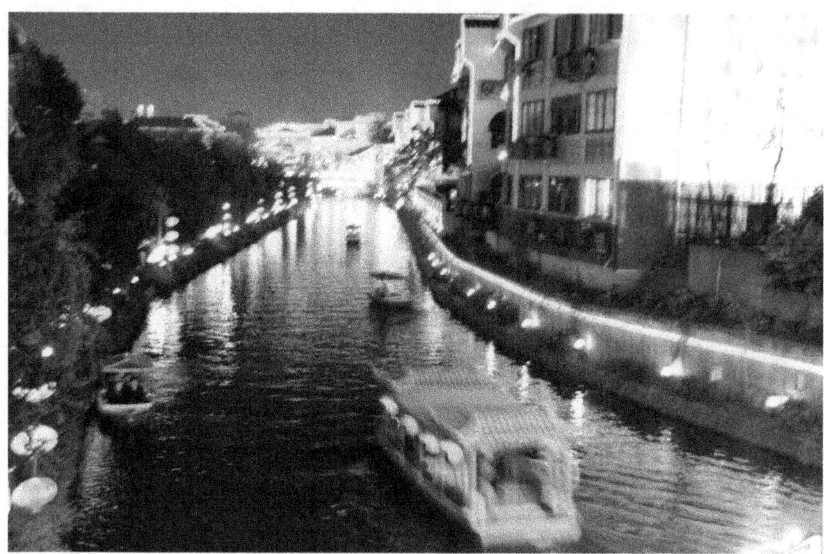

Qinhuai River—mother river of Nanjing

Nanjing, historically known as Jinling (金陵, "Golden Hill"), is a city where water, history, and culture intertwine. Approximately 11% of its area is covered by rivers, lakes, and streams, with the mighty Yangtze River and the poetic Qinhuai River flowing through its heart. The city's geological foundation lies in the Yangtze River Delta, with low-lying plains and rolling hills like Purple Mountain (Zijin Shan), a site of immense cultural and fengshui significance.

Nanjing's dragon-and-phoenix fengshui—marked by the protective curve of the Yangtze and the guardian presence of Purple Mountain—has made it a favored imperial capital. Alongside Xi'an, Luoyang, and Beijing, it served as the seat of power for six major dynasties, including the Ming Dynasty, when it became the launchpad for one of history's greatest maritime adventures.

Between 1405 and 1433, under the Yongle Emperor's patronage, Admiral Zheng He led seven epic voyages across the Indian Ocean, reaching Arabia and East Africa. His Treasure Fleet, constructed in Nanjing's Longjiang Shipyard, was a floating metropolis: 28,000 crewmen, 300 ships, including 60 colossal "treasure ships"—nine-masted behemoths stretching 120 meters (394 feet), dwarfing European vessels of the era. These voyages stand as a testament to Nanjing's maritime supremacy in the early 15th century.

Nanjing has long been a cradle of poets and scholars. The Six Dynasties (220–589 CE) saw the rise of "Jinling poetry," with luminaries like Li Bai and Liu Yuxi penning verses to its beauty. Today, the city nurtures a vibrant literary scene, centered around Xianfeng Bookstore (先锋书店, "Pioneer Bookstore"): a former bomb shelter transformed into one of the world's best bookstores. It serves as a hub for avant-garde poets like Huang Fan, Hu Xian, and Potato Brother who lead regular poetry workshops, keeping Nanjing's literary flame alive. In 2019, UNESCO designated Nanjing a City of Literature, honoring its 1,800-year publishing legacy—from China's first literary academy (438 CE) to the Ming Dynasty's *Yongle Encyclopedia.*

Nanjing's food mirrors its history: refined yet resilient. They include salted duck (*yanshui ya*, 盐水鸭), duck blood vermicelli soup (*yaxie fensi tang*, 鸭血粉丝汤), and stinky tofu (*chou doufu*, 臭豆腐).

Today, Nanjing's Confucius Temple lantern festivals and Plum Blossom celebrations coexist with Cloud Brocade silk-weaving (a 1,600-year craft) and bullet trains to Shanghai. As people walk along the Qinhuai's lantern-lit lanes, reflect at the Confucius Temple and Memorial Hall of the Victims in Nanjing Massacre, stand atop the Sun Yat-sen Mausoleum and the Great Wall of the Ming, enjoy Nanjing's silk and food, they will feel the weight of its 3,000-year history—a city of emperors, poets, and explorers, forever shaped by its rivers and its dreams. Here every duck dish, poem, and moss-covered wall whispers: *"We endure, we endeavor, we enjoy."*

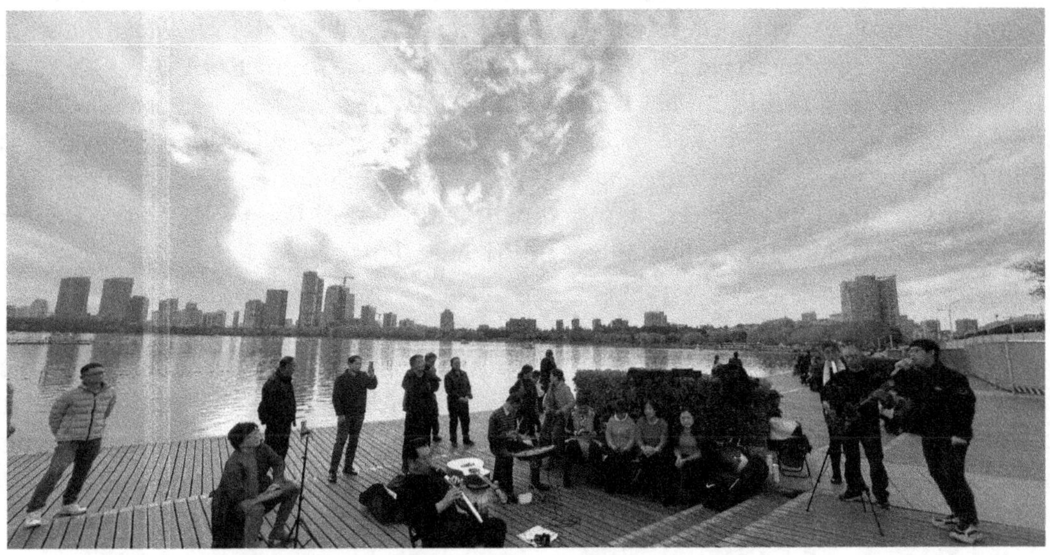

Xuanwu Lake—Pearl of Jinling, Nanjing

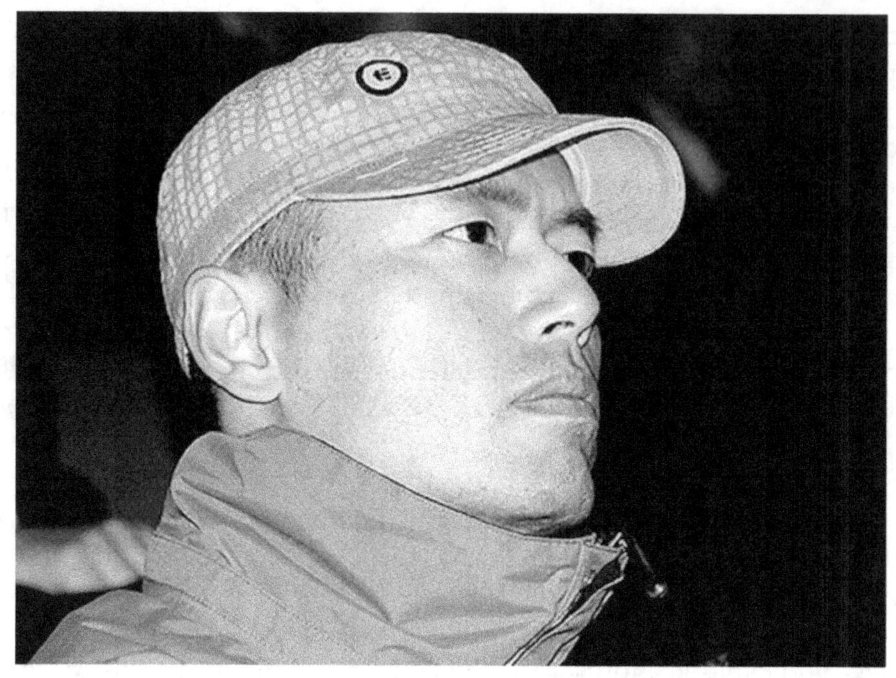

Huang Fan (黄梵) was born in rural Hubei and teaches creative writing at Nanjing University of Science and Technology. He is the author of three poetry collections, *The Plum Blossom's Whisper* (梅雨的消息), *Floating Island* (漂浮的岛), and *Rope* (绳索) from Roof Press, NYC (2025). His four novels—*The Tenth Day* (第十日), *Waiting for an Earthquake* (等待地震), *Southern Arrow* (南方邮站), and *The Age of Silver* (白银时代)—along with his short story collection *Woman in a Well* (井中女人) and essay *Notes of a Literary Layman* (文学闲话) have established him as a versatile voice in contemporary Chinese literature. His honors include the Good Poetry Prize, the Beijing Literary Prize for Poetry, and the Jinling Literary Prize for Poetry.

One snow-stormy night in St. Paul, I received a call from a stranger. It was Huang Fan, then a resident at the Vermont Arts Center. Vermont was also buried in snow. We spoke for three hours about poetry, translation, and life in China and America. After his return, I began translating his poems, culminating in *Midnight's Gate*. During the pandemic, he introduced me to Nanjing's Xianfeng Bookstore, where I taught a series of online poetry workshops. In 2023, we finally met in person, hosting a reading there for hundreds of young poets in Nanjing.

鱼

像灯一样的眼，为什么没有照亮？
像花蕾一样的眼，为什么没有盛开？
莫非你也像人一样，一直戴着面具？
为什么你有足够多的骨头
偏到死后才试图卡住人的喉咙？

我守着装你的盘子
守着怜你的假慈悲
你散发的浓香，来自你血腥的死亡
你一生的故事，我吃进嘴里还有用么？
你一生的视野，我用舌头也能继承么？

想到你是一个生命，甚至鱼里的先知
我不再是瞎子和聋子
一刹那，我成了
能听懂你遗言的罪人

Fish

Your eyes shine like lamps, why can't they see?
Bulging like buds, why don't they blossom?
Are you like humans, also wearing a mask?
With your abundant bones, why do you wait to
choke us after you're dead?

I guard the plate that holds your body
Guarding my fake compassion for you
You delicious smell comes from bloody death.
Who would tell your story once it enters my mouth?
How would my tongue inherit your vision?

Once I realize you are part of life, a fish prophet,
I'm no longer blind or deaf
Suddenly, I become a sinner
Who understands your last words.

水平仪

水平仪的眼睛，噙满泪水
谁是里面那个空虚的气泡
从不愿意坐在中央
宁愿水平仪，有一只俾倪的眼睛

当少年用木刨，刨出令人心动的桌面
他盼着水平仪，能正眼看他
但他不知，它的眼里只有空空的行囊
装满对大海起伏的向往

他也不知，水平仪无法闭眼的悲伤——
哪怕一只蚂蚁的苦难，也会涌入眼睛
甚至涌入中东枪弹呼啸的黑暗

就算盯着水平仪，他也不懂
俾倪，是它坚持了一生的宿命

The Spirit Level

Its eye is filled with tear
What's that empty bubble
Never willing to sit in the middle
Why does it look at us, always askance?

When the boy cut the table with a wood plane, he
wished the leveler would look straight at him.
He has no idea, this eye is empty of baggage
Filled with wonder, sailing in the sea

He doesn't know its sorrow, unable to close its eye——
even when an ant's pain seeps in
With flying bullets from the Middle East

He won't know, no matter how long he stares:
It lives because of its stance, askance

河蚌

用手掰开河蚌
这就是人主动上门的拜访？
读书人，已不上门找书

对着河蚌掰开的嘴
人要的，不是可以对话的舌头
人要的，是一场河蚌的苦难

人配得上河蚌的赴死？
配得上河蚌托付的未来？
人走得出河蚌闭眼的黑暗？

河蚌的余生，本该在流水潺潺的河畔
本该聆听，老人打盹儿的鼾声
春天的寂静，本来是另一场灾难

吞下河蚌的人，貌似慈悲
起身去禅寺祈福
学会遗忘的智慧

Clam

Opening the clam with my hands
Is this mankind knocking for a visit?
But intellectuals no longer seek books

Facing the clam's opened mouth
Mankind no longer wants its tongue for
A dialogue. They want its suffering

Is mankind worthy of the clam's martyrdom?
Are we worthy of the future it delivered us?
Can we walk out of darkness in its closed eye?

Clams are supposed to live in a running river
Supposed to listen to old men's snores
A silent spring is supposed to be another disaster

Those who swallowed the clams look
Kind-hearted as they pray in a temple
To learn the wisdom of forgetting

灯

你喜欢买灯，仿佛已厌倦太阳
喜欢灯在夜里，伸出黄皮肤的手臂
喜欢它抚摸，铺在床上的睡梦
唯有黑夜才让你看清，光线该有多干净！

灯的手，能被你回忆的泪打湿吗？
它用干净的手指，
要取出你揉进眼里的沙子？
你不敢正眼看灯，
是因为你有太多的愧疚？
灯把手伸向门缝，
是在操心门外的黑暗？

一整夜，灯用铜链，把你拴在桌前
你写下的每个字，都有春天的夜色
你甚至希望，白天与黑夜永远分居
直到天亮，你才看清
夜里的迷人光线，
原来都来自灯泡的灰头土脸

Lamps

You like to buy lamps, as if you're tired of the sun.
You reach out at night, yellow arms stroking dreams
Sprawled in bed. Only darkness lets you see
How clean the light can be

Would your memory's tears soak the lamp?
Could its clean fingers clear the dust
In your eyes? You will not look
At the lamp. Is it because
You carry too much guilt?
The lamp reaches into the door's crack
Is it worried about the night outside?

All night long, the lamp chains you
To the desk with bronze shackles
Every word you write carries the color of spring.
You hope to separate days and nights till dawn arrives.
You realize the shimmering beauty through the night
came from a dusty light bulb

姑姑的照片

姑姑扮青衣的照片，是我书房的装饰
她每天用戏装之美，给我的人生打气
那时，她的命运正在汉剧中高飞
家史还没有成为，一件刺向她的凶器

自从她被赶出剧团
悠长的唱腔是长巷，总把她引向戏台
直到砌墙的泥刀，在她手下铮铮
响成曲调，直到一代名旦，
变成炊烟中的巧妇

每个来书房的人，
都赞叹她的美
这样的美，能给中年人补钙
能让修行人，心里开一朵莲花
能给我书房的寂静，安上灯塔

一股秋风想用吟唱，引出她的唱腔
我试着用伤感的诗句，为她配词
仿佛催促她重登戏台，但生锈的
唱腔，已经适应安静
习惯让秋风做它的替身

My Aunt's Photo

My aunt's photo as a young woman hangs in my studio.
Her beauty in opera attire cheers my life. Her fortune
rose high in the sky of Han Opera at that time.
Her family history was not yet a dagger in her heart

Since she was tossed out of the opera house
The long lane sings like an aria, luring her back
to the stage. The knife to build walls becomes
melodies in her hands till a famous diva
turned into a good wife in the kitchen

Every visitor admires her beauty
Her face, like calcium, fortifies
the bones of a middle aged man
It opens a lotus blossom in a hermit's heart
It turns on the lighthouse in a silent studio

A gust of wind tries to bring out her song
I match her melody with melancholy poetry
As if it could push her back onto the stage, but her
rusty voice has settled in peace
Into the autumn wind as her replacement

老花之眼

书放得再近，字也看不清了
那些被黑夜染黑的字，仿佛提醒我
要离书中的苦难远一点，远一点才能看清
字的额头上，那些刚愈合的黑疤

我戴上老花镜，每个字都飘着乌亮的黑发
它们拔掉的岁月白发，早填满纸上的空白
也许字的每副黑棺里，都躺着好几条人命
我从小就用的字，里面的悲剧我能数清？

老花的眼，还会闪光
会把罚款五千，看成罚款五十万
那是暗示，老花的活着
已不怕讹诈、惊吓？
当我把111路，看成111111路
那是暗示，111111路曾在火星开通过？
当闪光，让所有的字都长出彗星的尾巴
那是暗示，我们的文明随时也会返祖吗？

五年了，看不清倒让我想得更清
看不清别人的皱纹
倒把别人都看成健身高人
每天在高人中跋涉
连念头也像高人的长跑
每天都留下一个奔向远方的公里数

Presbyopia

No matter how close I bring books to my face,
I can't read the words inked black by night,
    as if reminding me:
get away from the pain in the book, if you want
to see the black scar on the words' brow

I put on glasses, now black hair floats
across each word, pulling white hair from life
    to fill empty space on page
Maybe each word hides bodies in its black coffin.
How can I count all the tragedy?

My eyes also flash light, turning a
five thousand yuan fine into five hundred thousand
As if suggesting I no longer need to fear
extortion or scam in my blurry age?
When Highway 111 doubles into 111111
Is it saying this highway will take me to Mars?
When the flashing light gives each word
    a comet tail, is it saying our civilization is
regressing to a stone age?

Five years later, somehow my blurry
vision has cleared my thinking
so everyone becomes an athlete
Trudging among them, my thoughts start
running marathons, recording
how many miles left till the future

出血的眼睛

左眼出血，黑瞳仁
像架在火上烧的黑煤
右眼看着春天的灾难，仿佛说
是哭的时候了，请试着用泪
浇灭眼中的大火

医生叫我闭着眼。关上眼皮的炉门
炉火就不会灼伤内心？
眼里的红色，是想长成红玫瑰的红旗？
眼里的红灯，是想拦下不戴口罩的行人？
眼里的红火，是想把瞳仁的黑，
锻成淬蓝？

我的眼里，何尝不是火星的红尘？
那样的文明，早已下落不明
莫非，那样的红尘已盯上地球？
我闭上眼，宁愿让黑夜在眼里升起
宁愿让左眼的泪，在脸上修一条
绕开舌头的运河

Bleeding Eyes

My left eye is bleeding, black pupil
Burning like coal on fire
My right eye watches the spring's disaster, as if
saying it's time to cry,
to put out the fire with your tears

My doctor said close my eyes—the furnace door.
Would that prevent fire from scorching my heart?
Is the blood in my eyes trying to become a rosy flag?
Is the red light trying to stop maskless pedestrians?
Is the fire in my eyes trying to forge
the black pupil into blue?

My eyes contained red dust from Mars—
a lost civilization. Could it be true that
the red planet is eyeing the earth? I close
my lids, let night rise in my eyes
Let the tears run over my left cheek
to open a canal, away from my tongue

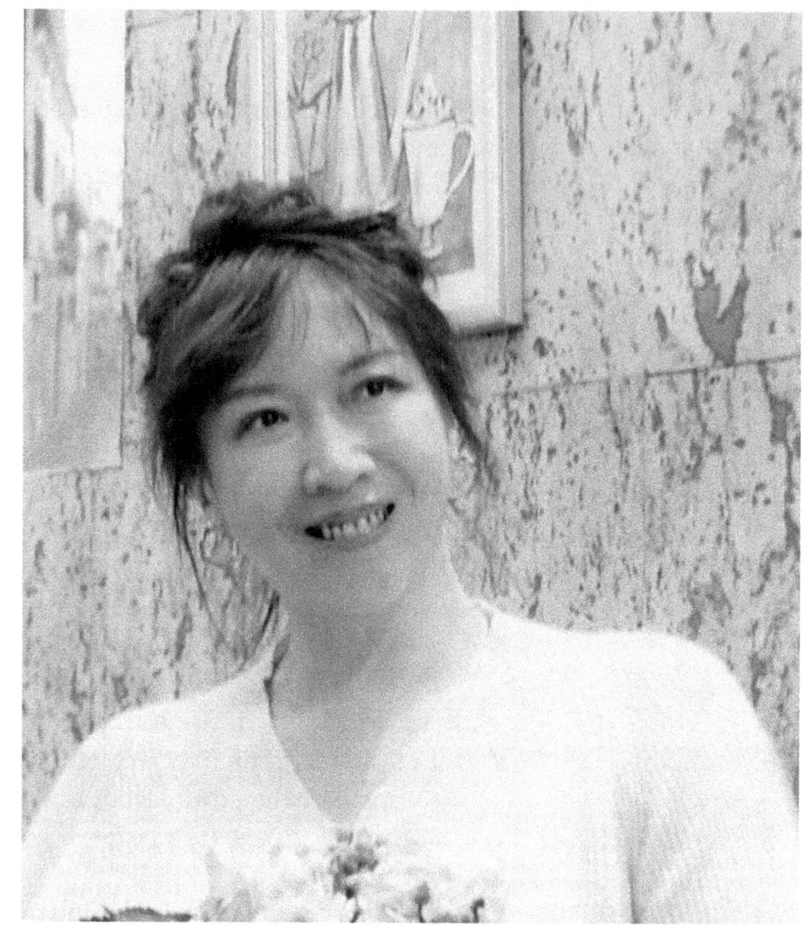

Fan Xiyu (范希予) is a poet, writer, critic, lawyer, and member of *Whistlers from Golden Hills* (金陵远啸). With Wang Ping, she co-translated poems and essays by Gary Snyder, Ron Whitehead, and other writers.

自画像

我选择你
因为你像童年
撕下作业本
偷偷摸摸画下的我
不时竖着耳朵听听
妈妈是否悄没声息接近我的房门
还好
就算来不及把你揉成一团
扔进纸篓
也没有什么大不了
我是可以抽烟的女孩
不是只能学书法的女孩
我是可以鼻孔朝天的女孩
不是顺着别人的言语喏喏而下的女孩
我有四条腿足以攀越星辰
不是只能用花裙子亭亭玉立
哦　　我想去闯荡的这个世界会到来吗
或者　你是五十岁时我的自画像吗

Self-portrait

I picked you
Because you look like my childhood
Tearing a page from the homework book
And painting yourself in secret
You listen from time to time
Is mommy tiptoeing to my door?
Not yet, that's good
Even if I don't have time to crumple you into a ball
And throw it into a trashcan
It's no big deal
I'm a girl who smokes
Not just someone who practices calligraphy
I like to stick my nose to the sky
Not just a demure, obedient girl
My limbs are strong enough to climb stars
Not just to stand like a flower in a skirt
I want to explore the world. Will it come my way?
Or are you just a portrait of me at 50?

Hai Yan (海燕) is the director and editor of Jiangsu Music Radio Station FM 97.5.

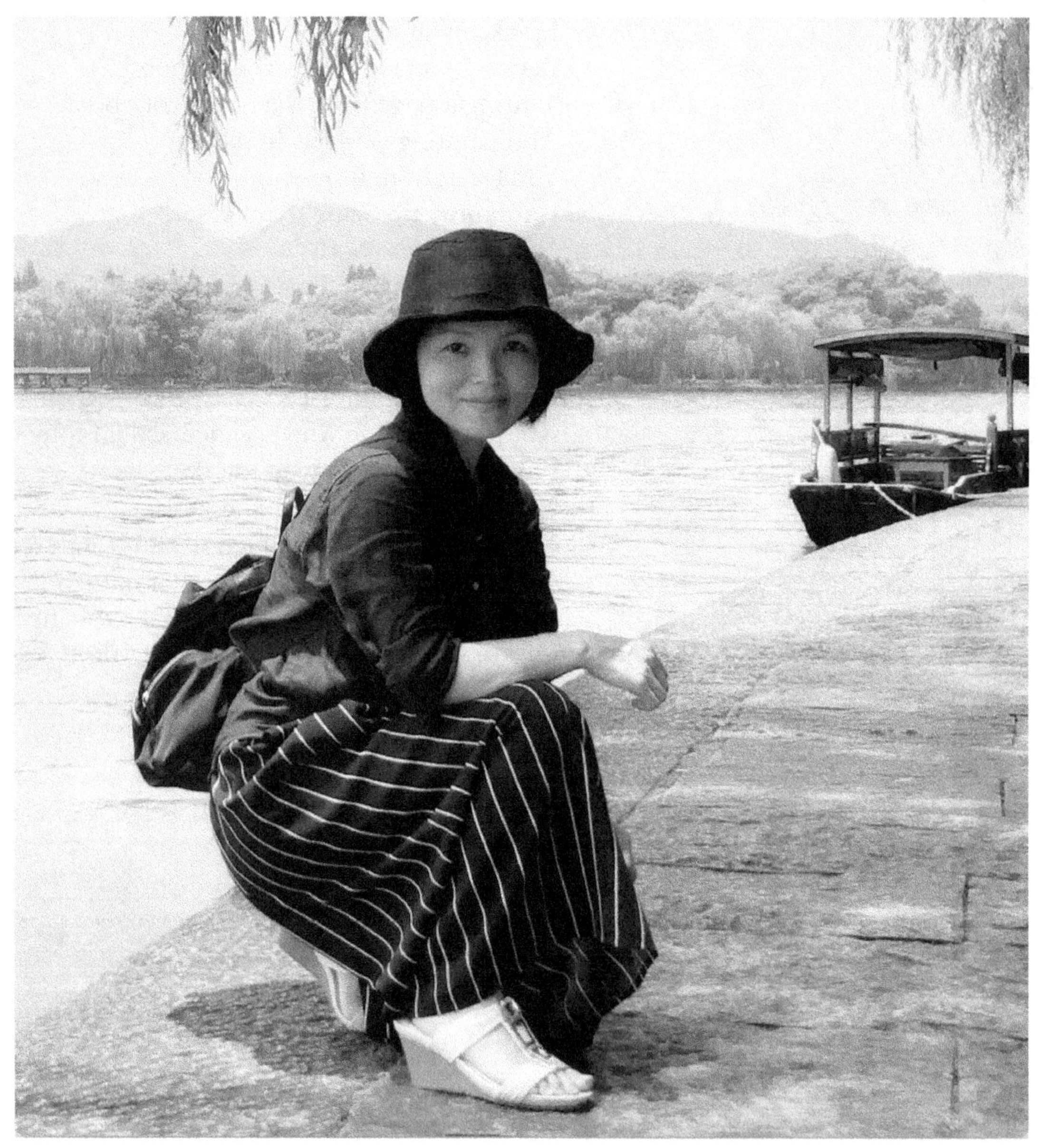

先锋书店（防空洞）

让我如何告诉你
四十年前它的模样？
一家书店，从前是一个防空洞
女诗人说这太有寓意

那些和小伙伴躲藏的游戏
还能再陪我玩一次吗？
五台山下弥散的槐树花香
我天真地以为　永远都不会消失

烈日下孩子在哭泣
暮春草丛间狸猫在欢歌
夜空的深海　坠满古老的故事

让我如何告诉你
四十年前它的模样？
年轻人说这是全世界最美的书店
只有我

只有我看见它远去的背影
盛满了童年的光线和无惧
只有我听见它空洞的回声
隐匿在文字的堡垒中
幻作大地上异乡者的布鲁斯
为我防守时间的塌缩

Xianfeng Bookstore—A Bomb Shelter

How can I describe
Its real face forty years ago?
A bomb shelter, transformed into a beautiful bookstore
Ping told me this is magic

Can I play the hide-and-seek there
One more time? I used to believe
The fragrance from the locust trees on Mount Wutai
Would never leave my childhood

A child is weeping under the noon sun
Bobcats are singing in late spring's tall grass
Ancient stories hang from the night sky

How can I describe
Its real face forty years ago?
Young people say it's the most beautiful place on earth
Only I

Watch it walking away
Carrying the light of my childhood
Only I can hear its echoes flow
Into the sound of blues from a strange land
Protecting me from the collapsing
Time and world

Han Qing (汗青), born in 1991 as Zhao Hanqing (赵汗青), is a poet, translator, and film instructor at Nanjing Film Institute, and a member of *Whistlers from Golden Hills* (金陵远啸). With Wang Ping, he co-translated Louise Glück, Paul Hoover and other American poets.

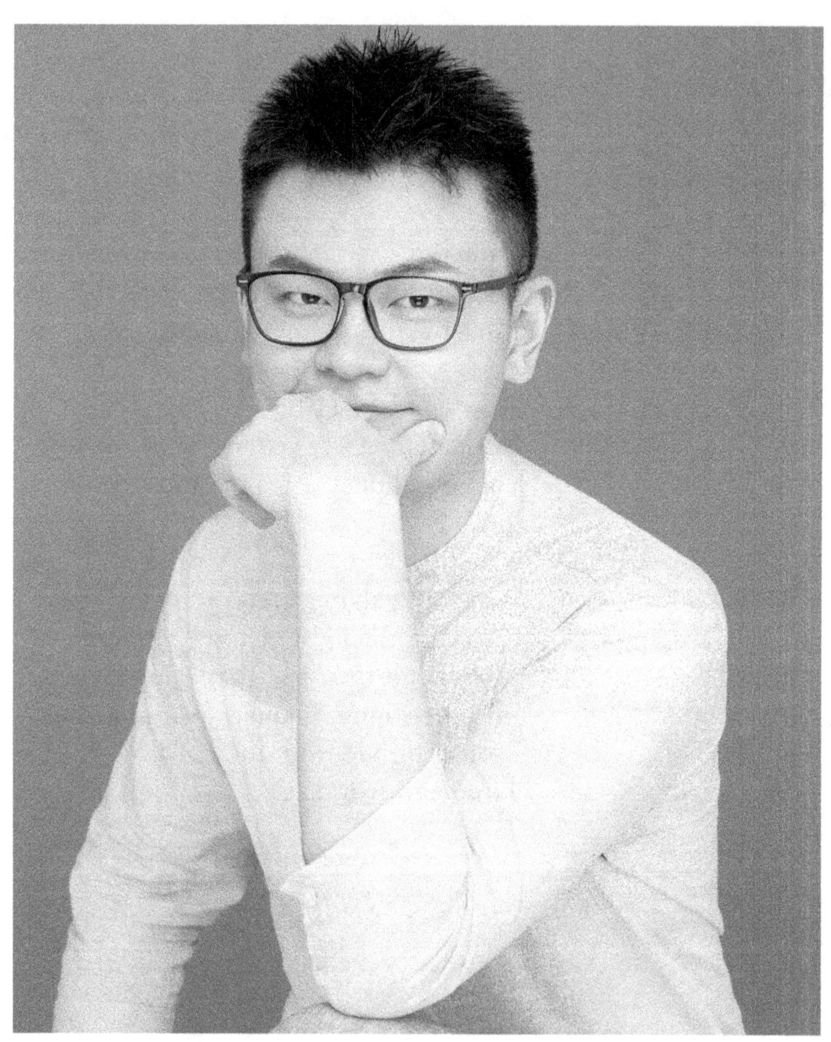

夜记

满是伤痕的手，抚琴 也抚摸城市。
城市的骨骼如此顺滑，
摸到哪里都一样
出租车里信号嘈杂
黑夜，是只对我嘶吼的公猫

六朝的事都在这儿了
千年前的和一年前的
我们却分辨不出。有的时候
还是不要和世界发生太多的联系

木抽屉的漆黑也是我们的漆黑
禁欲的拳击手，发出母兽般的嚎叫
抛弃一个玩具熊，跟抛弃一个婴儿
有什么区别？廉价的快乐如沙子
也会将人磨成工具.春天的手,将我撕成
柳絮.手机屏幕也是我的湖水。

童年时,我差点在池塘里淹死
可惜,被邻居救了上来.很多人觉得
最过瘾的,就是把下水的梯子拆掉

而我独喜欢深夜的耳鸣
提醒我还活着；我也喜欢安静
安静时才能听见　整个春天的耳鸣

Night Story

The hand, covered with scars, strokes
The city and strings. Its skeleton feels smooth,
wherever the hand touches
The signals in taxi are overwhelming
The night is a screaming tomcat

Everything about the Six Dynasties is here
Mixed from last year and a thousand years ago.
Hard to tell the difference. It's better to be cut off
from the world sometimes

The darkness in the drawer also belongs to us. The
celibate boxer howls like a she-beast
What's the difference between throwing away a
teddy or baby? Cheap happiness grinds us into
tools like sand. The spring hand tears me into
willow leaves. The phone screen becomes my lake

When I was young I almost drowned in a pond.
Unfortunately, my neighbor pulled me out. To some,
fun is destroying the pool ladder.

Yet I love the midnight ringing in my ears
It reminds me I'm still alive: I also love silence
where I can hear spring's tinnitus

褪色

记忆输球了，五官褪色了
肚子里的士兵们摇旗击鼓
我一无所知，只能看着。
天堂之光减弱，
逐渐变得暗淡，一束火光
穿过冷杉。
阳光晒不干胸中的卵石

帆船躲进大海的颜色里
风筝四处张望失散的孪生兄弟
我想如果我说得够久的话
我将说出答案
我将看见他们眼里的一切
我们的祖先也是年轻的
他和我们只隔了三千年
一个梯子，穿过冷杉
让他们去交换彼此的生命——
去思考我已领悟到的东西。

星球裂开后 静止了
静止之后 陨落
时间在老人的手里融化
转眼间就变成孩子最爱的糖稀

有蜡烛的时候，你问为什么点灯
岁月尽头，延龄草给你雕琢出答案
我耐心倾听
可我甚至感知不到这悲伤
直到一个词出现，直到我感觉
雨水从体内流淌而出
石头内无名君王的哀嚎
这次
我已不是正义的一方

Fading

Memory is lost, face faded
In the stomach, drum soldiers wave flags
I know nothing, can only watch
The sun from paradise weaken
Fading into a single light
Through the cool pines
The sun can't dry the pebbles in my chest

Sailboats hide in the color of the sea
Kites seek their twin brothers
In the sky. If I speak long enough
I think I can find the answer
I'll see everything in their eyes
Our ancestors are young
Separated from us by 3000 years
A ladder, through the cool pines
Let them exchange each other's life
To think over what I've understood

Stars break, then quiet down
Fall. Time melts through the old man's
Hands, turns instantly
Into children's soft candy

Why do I turn on the lamp
When candles are burning?
Trillium will give you the answer
I listen till the end of time
Yet I can't feel sorrow when the word appears.
I feel rain streaming from my body
Inside the stone, a king, nameless, howls
But this time
I no longer stand with the truth

Hui Linran (惠林然) is a poet and writer from Nanjing. Her work is widely published in China and Singapore. She's a member of *Whistlers from Golden Hills* (金陵远啸).

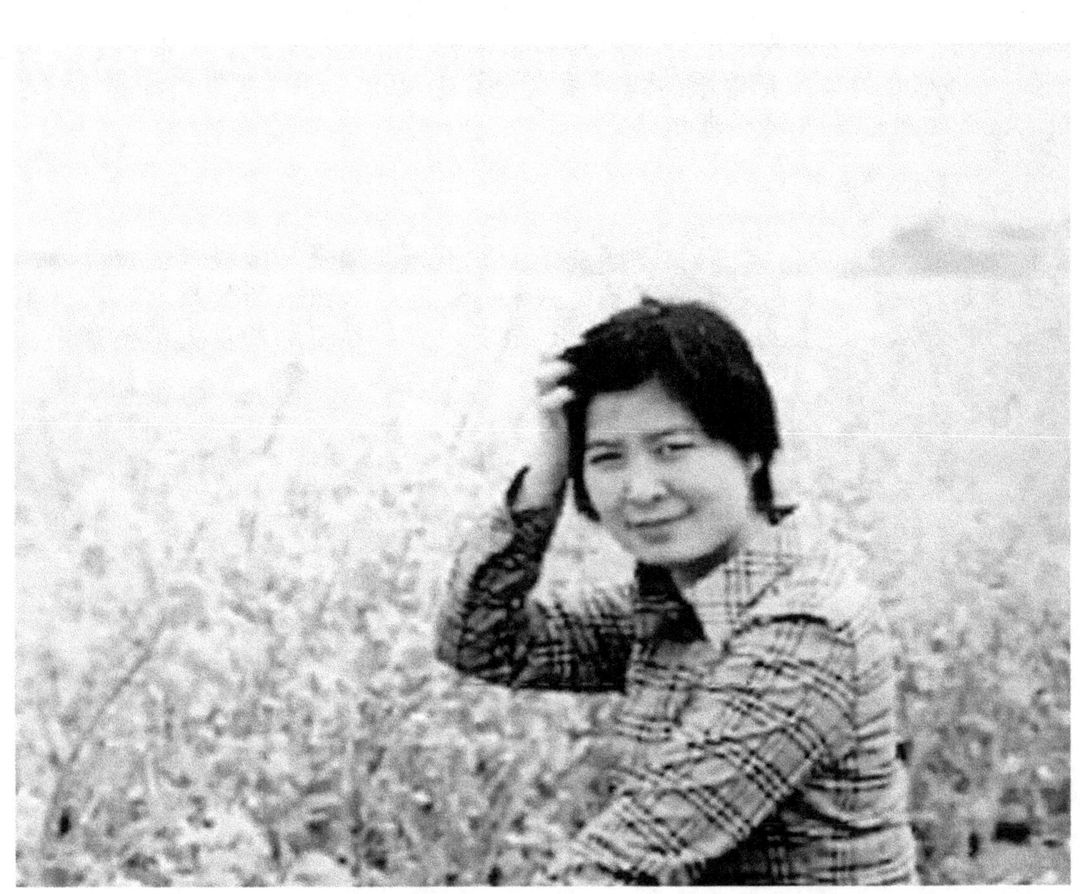

清明的馒头

小时候的柴门打开，一块白面馒头，叼走了姐姐的童年。小黑用它的血染红了外婆的榔头，榔头却弄丢了它的一生。母亲没有精湛的厨艺，只有手工馒头。一片油绿的棉花田，粉色和浅绿色的花朵闪烁，母亲背着农药桶，像在大海里潜泳。她是烈日下那朵最倔强的棉花。

父亲骑着他嘎吱作响的自行车从城里回来，一个大西瓜（有时候是摔破的）被孩子们簇拥到饭桌上。照例，第一块由我送给没牙的外婆。从来没有人反对过。"拉荆耙"的故事，我们都熟知:有个小孩的父亲把瞎眼的妈妈用荆耙拉进深山，小孩把荆耙挂在墙上准备给他父亲用。父亲后来也为外婆养老送终。

傍晚，晚霞翻过黝黑的山岗，我们扫干净院子，撒上一些清水。晚饭后，凉风吹起来，我们在院子里铺起竹席。外婆指着无数星星的银河，讲起牛郎织女的故事。我再没见过童年那么亮的银河，那么多的星星。虽然后来走过很多地方。难道那些星星都坠落了，变成树林里隆起的馒头？

母亲的馒头，已经长满青草。

Qingming Bun

The barn door opened. A dog stole a steamed bun and ended my sister's childhood. Little Black's blood splattered all over Grandma's hammer, and it shattered both lives. Mom was never a good cook, but great with making steamed buns. In the green cotton fields, pink and green flowers shimmered. Mom was spraying pesticide, as if swimming in the green sea. She was the most stubborn cotton plant in the hot sun.

Dad came home from town on his clanking bike, a giant watermelon on the back seat (sometimes it was already broken), and the kids carried it to the dinner table. As usual, the first slice was handed to our toothless Grandma. Nobody ever said no. We all knew the story of "Lajingba." A man carried his blind mother to the mountain in a vine basket, and left her there to die. His little boy cried and hung the basket on the wall, warning his dad that it would be for him when he became old and blind. My dad took care of his mother-in-law till her very end.

Twilight was crossing over the darkened mountains. We swept the yard, sprayed some water, and breeze started blowing after dinner. We spread bamboo mats on the ground. Grandma pointed to the Milky Way, told us the love story of Cowboy and Weaver Girl. I've never seen such a bright Milky Way since, or so many stars, no matter where I have traveled. Did all the stars crash, turning into the buns in the woods?

Mother's bun is now covered with tall grass.

Note: Qingming, the first day of the fifth Solar Terms, is the "Chinese Memorial Day," when Chinese people visit graves and offer food to the deceased.

Liu Qi (刘奇), born in 1996 in Xuzhou, Jiangsu Province, is a poet and event host for poetry and art at Xianfeng Bookstore, Nanjing. His poetry appeared in *Yangtze River* (扬子江) and other journals. He is a member of *Whistlers from Golden Hills* (金陵远啸).

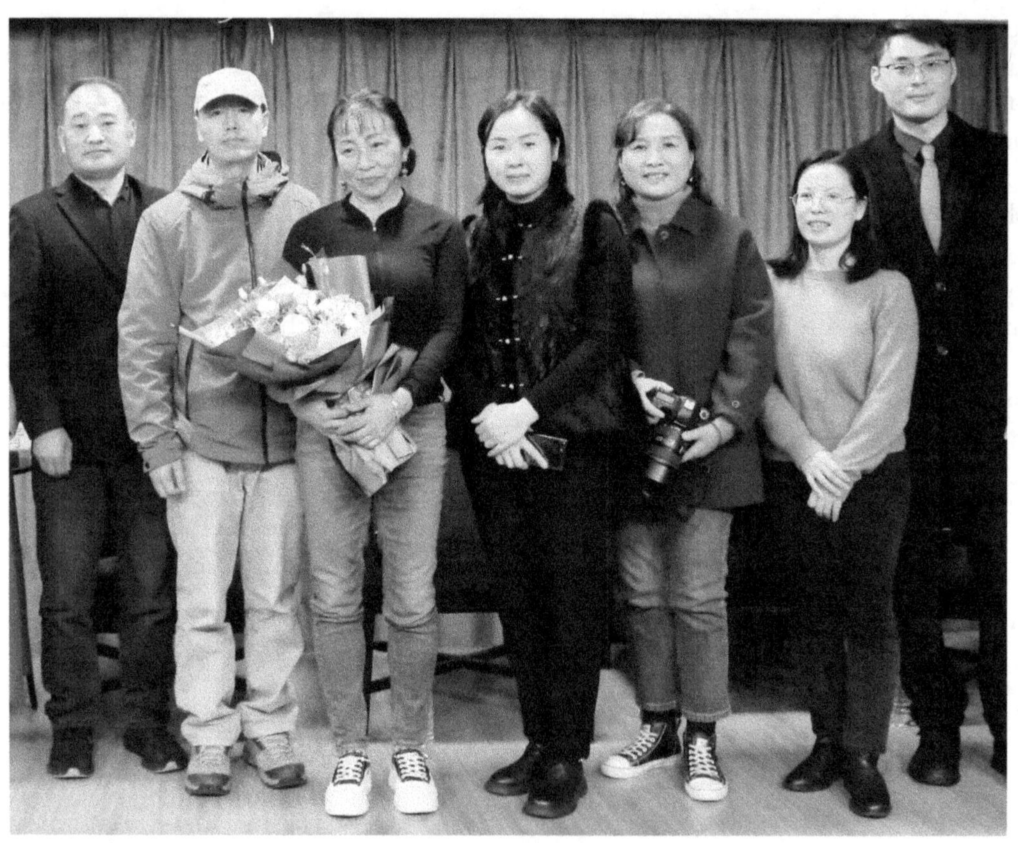

Liu Qi (right) with Wang Ping and others at Xianfeng Bookstore poetry event,
Nanjing, December 2023

长满刺的拳头

手指像玫瑰的根茎，
握拳时，常常刺伤掌心
再小心也无济于事，只要遇上
“生活”二字，就必然遍体鳞伤

雨后的脏水感染了伤口
化脓后长出新的疤痕
消失的刺头变钝，
连拳头都握不起来了

握不起来的拳头多像
玫瑰花呀，我双手举过头顶
向世人展示我的花，也炫耀那
越过头顶的一对镣铐

Fists

My fingers resemble the roots of a rose bush
When I clench my fist, it stabs into my palm
No matter how careful I am, I get hurt
from head to toe when I encounter "life."

The rain infects my wounds
Then scars grow over the puss
The vanished thorns get thicker
Till I can no longer clench my fists

My unclenched fists now look
Like roses, I raise my hands over my head
To show off my rose blossoms
And a pair of shackles

消逝的童年

有那么一点模糊
想起时，又覆盖了一个人的一生
在砖头缝里丢的鞭炮
炸出了人生仅有的金矿渣子
四处飞溅的泥土
像长大后，各自天涯的童年玩伴

其实，童年如布袋里的萤火虫
一点都不自由，烂漫是有限的
家长的许可，形成一种致命的弱
从小就落在孩子的心里
成年后，走向陌生的世界
沉默，延长了弱的期限

请善待每一个中年人
请不要忘记他们消逝的童年
——岁月的过道总是拥挤、堵塞
当父辈的小轮子抵达时
请为他们挪挪脚
即使这是很有限的座位

Vanished Childhood

It's a bit vague
But it covers my life when I think of it
Throw a firecracker into the cracks of bricks
It explodes, exposing what's left
Mud and rock splatter
Like scattered playmates from childhood

Childhood is not free at all
Like fireflies in a bag, with limited brilliance
Parental authority has planted the deadly
weakness in the child's heart
When he enters the strange world as an adult
His silence prolongs his weakness

Please be kind to every middle aged man
Please don't forget their childhood
—the passage of life is always jammed
When your father's cart arrives
Please make room for him
Even though the seats are limited

鱼缸

鱼缸的死是透明的
鱼的翻身 倒立 漂浮 下沉
像变戏法似的，轮番上演
沉的沉，浮的浮
死以各种姿势存在
如人以各种方式死去

鱼跳出鱼缸
在无人察觉的时间里
化成一条鱼干——
跳出时间之外
它有了缺水的自由

养鱼人是它的神明
网兜一捞，捞出一缸的活
活也在翻腾 倒立 漂浮 下沉
活着，正如同死去

Fish Tank

The fish tank dies in transparency
Inside, fish turn, summersault, float, sink
Like magicians, performing in turns
Some float, some sink
Dying in all manners
Like humans

When nobody notices
Fish leap out of the tank
And turn into dried fish—
The only way to gain freedom
Is to leap outside time

The fish keeper is their god
He catches the fish with his net, alive
Turning, somersaulting, floating, sinking
In the manner of dying

Sun Dong (孙东), born in 1969, is a professor at Nanjing University of Finance and Economics, as well as a poet and translator. Her poetry books include *The Broken Crow* (破乌鸦) and *Writing Animals* (书写动物). Her work has appeared in America, Canada, Australia, Turkey, Romania, and India. We met at Yanziji of the Yangtze, where Li Bai, Du Fu and other poets lingered.

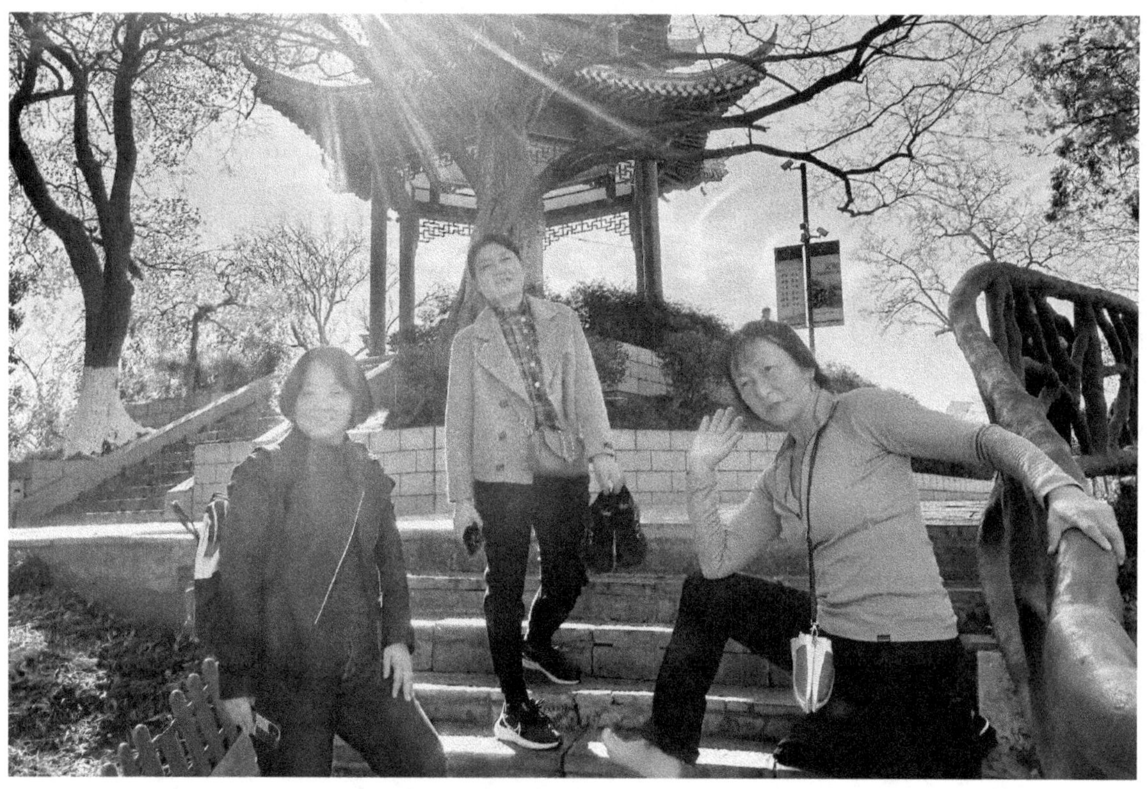

Sun Dong (left) at Yanziji, Nanjing

诗句不幸生于此地

句子本该是　羊齿类植物

紫色的拳头卷曲着
字里行间　　有细细的枝蔓
迴转　　却丝丝不入矩阵当中

句子本该珍惜自由
珍惜它和万物啃啮的
皮开肉绽的光晕
珍惜它边缘古老的病毒

在万物戴粉色
披针蕊帽的季节
反常的语法聚集
在万籁里打摆子

不像这里
词叶对生，诗句发端于
失语和多肉两个种子，
且一律一蒂两花，
在忍冬的季
从习惯的根系向上攀爬，
翻开土壤的正反两面而出的句子
不幸只能在此地开花.

This Poem Was Born Here

A sentence ought to be a fern

Its purple fists crooked and bent
Between lines   its slim cirrus
meanders   till it escapes the matrix of rules

A sentence should have cherished freedom
Cherished its bloody halo   cut and split
In this entangled world
Cherished its ancient virus at the edge

In the season when everything
Wears a pink lanceolate hat
The freak grammar trembles in malaria
Through sounds of all things

It's a different world here
Words and leaves are opposite phyllotaxis
A poem grows out of aphasia and succulent seeds
twin flowers on the same tray, a sentence climbs up
The winter habitat of honeysuckles
Piercing the toasted crust of earth
To reveal its positive and negative sides
Misfortune blooms only here.

Zhejiang (浙江): Where the Yangtze Meets the Sea

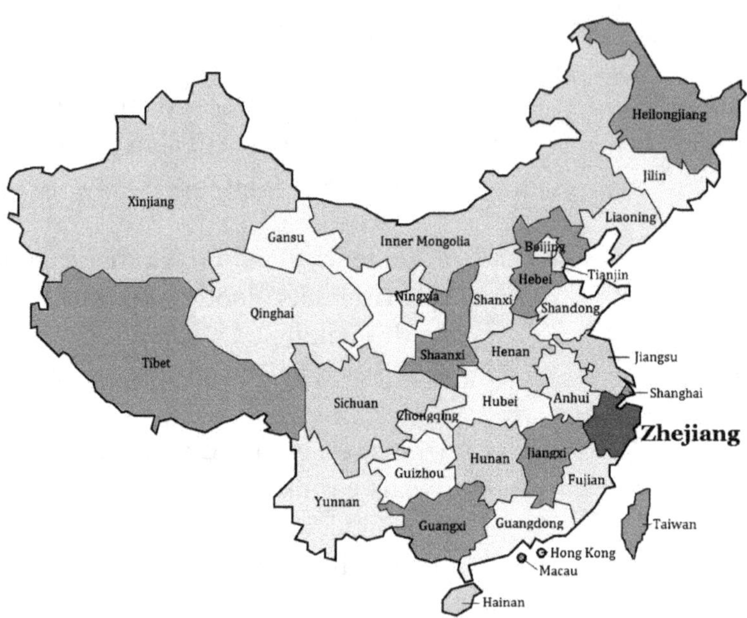

Zhejiang—the final province before the Yangtze River meets the East China Sea—is a land of timeless beauty, where fertile plains of fish, rice, and silk have thrived in the Yangtze Delta for millennia. Framed by rugged hills and a labyrinthine coastline, it boasts China's longest shoreline, dotted with over 3,000 islands, the largest being the Zhoushan Archipelago, a scattering of emerald peaks rising from the sea.

Zhejiang's landscape is a tapestry of contrasts: ancient Mesozoic volcanic formations shape its mountainous interior, while the Qiantang River's dramatic tidal bore—the world's largest— carves through coastal plains. The province's karst caves, like those in Jinhua, and the weathered peaks of Mount Yandang (a UNESCO Global Geopark) reveal a history etched in stone over 200 million years.

With roots stretching back to Hemudu Neolithic culture (6000 BCE), Zhejiang has long been a cradle of civilization. It was here that the Grand Canal's southern terminus linked the Yangtze to Beijing, reshaping China's economic and cultural destiny.

Nestled in Zhejiang's heart, Yiwu—a modest-sized city—dominates global small commodity trade, earning titles like "The World's Supermarket" and "Mecca of Retail Trade." Yet beyond its economic might, Yiwu harbors a Neolithic-era history (dating to 222 BC) and traditions like Wu Opera and martial arts. A linchpin of the Belt and Road Initiative, Yiwu bridges Zhejiang's ancient silk routes with modern globalization—where bargaining over buttons coexists with 1,000-year-old camphor trees.

A haven for intellectuals, the province produced luminaries such as Wang Xizhi (303–361), the "Sage of Calligraphy," Lu You (1125–1210), the patriotic Southern Song poet, Xu Zhimo (1897–1931), the romantic modernist, Lu Xun (1881–1936), the father of modern Chinese literature, and Bei Dao (b. 1949), the leader of the Misty Poetry movement.

From the misty tea fields of Longjing to the dreamy canals of Wuzhen, from Neolithic sites to the "World's Supermarket," Zhejiang's landscapes have inspired poetic imaginations for centuries—a legacy as enduring as the tides of the Qiantang.

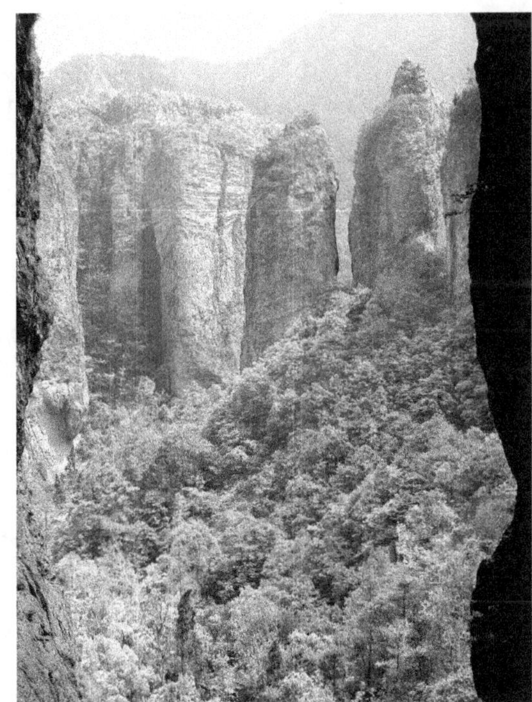

Mount Yandang, Zhejiang

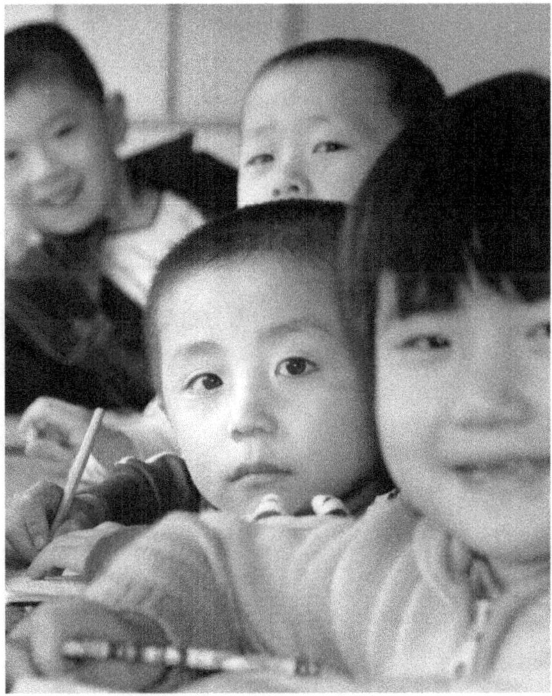

School children, Yiwu

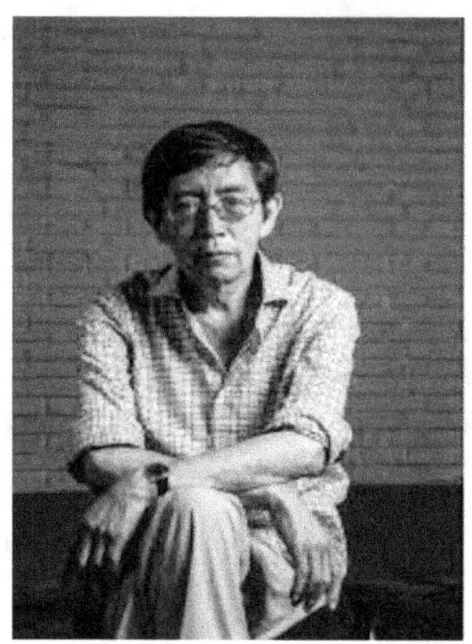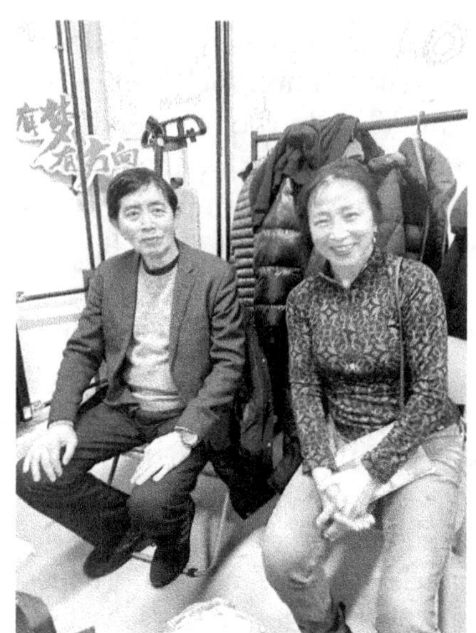

Bei Dao (北岛), pen name Zhao Zhenkai (赵振开), was born in 1949 in Beijing, though his ancestral roots trace back to Huzhou, Zhejiang—a region renowned for silk, ink brushes, and wonton soup dumplings. Founder of the Misty School and editor of the literary journal *Today*, he has lived in Germany, Norway, Denmark, the Netherlands, France, and the United States, where he taught poetry at UC Davis. His poetry has been widely translated, and he has received numerous awards, including a Guggenheim Fellowship and multiple Nobel Prize nominations.

His works include *Notes from the Sun City* (太阳城札记), *Bei Dao Selected Poems* (北岛诗选), *Bei Dao's Ancient City: Selected Poems* (北岛古城诗选), *Strange Beach* (陌生的海滩), *Midnight Singer* (午夜歌手), *Blue House* (蓝房子), *The Book of Failure* (失败之书), and *The Blue Lamp* (蓝灯).

I first met Bei Dao at the 1988 China-America Poetry Festival, organized by Allen Ginsberg. As the event's interpreter and translator, I worked with participating poets such as Gary Snyder, John Ashbery, Robert Creeley, Gu Cheng (顾城), Yang Lian (杨炼), and Shu Ting (舒婷). Later, in 2005, I invited Bei Dao and Eliot Weinberger to Macalester College as visiting poets and translators. The poems of Bei Dao in this anthology reflect his Jiangnan sensibility.

五色花

在深渊的边缘上，
你守护我每一个孤独的梦
---那风啊吹动草叶的喧响。
太阳在远方白白地燃烧，
你在水洼旁，投进自己的影子
微波荡荡，沉淀了昨日的时光。
假如有一天你也不免凋残，
我只有个简单的希望：
保持着初放时的安祥。

Five-Colored Flower

On the edge of the abyss
You guard my lonely dreams
——wind blows rustling grasses.
The sun is burning for nothing far away,
You throw your reflection into the puddle,
Its ripples drowning the past.
If one day you fade away,
I have one simple request:
Please keep the peace of your first blossom.

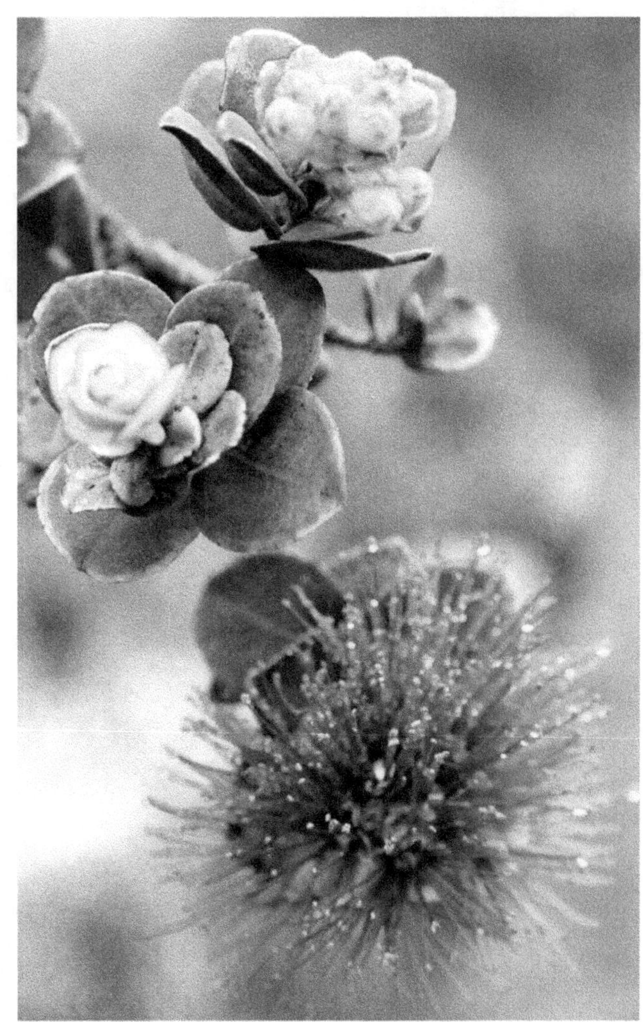

语言

许多种语言
在这世界飞行
碰撞，产生了火星
有时是仇恨
有时是爱情
理性的大厦
正无声地陷落
竹篾般单薄的思想
编成的篮子
盛满盲目的毒蘑
那些岩画上的走兽
踏着花朵驰去
一棵蒲公英秘密地
生长在某个角落
风带走了它的种子
许多种语言
在这世界飞行
语言的产生
并不能增加或减轻
人类沉默的痛苦

Language

Languages
Crash as they fly around the world
Sparks everywhere
Some carry hate
Some embrace love
The building of Reason
Sinks silently
Thoughts, thinner than bamboo strips
Weave a basket
To hold poisonous mushrooms
The animals on the rock painting
Have left us on flower petals
A dandelion
Grows secretly in a corner
Wind carries its seeds
Many languages
Fly in this world
Their births
Neither increase nor reduce
The silent pain of humanity

岸

陪伴着现在和以往
岸，举着一根高高的芦苇
四下眺望
是你
守护着每一个波浪
守护着迷人的泡沫和星星
当呜咽的月亮
吹起古老的船歌
多么忧伤
我是岸
我是渔港
我伸展着手臂
等待穷孩子的小船
载回一盏盏灯光

Shore

Accompanying today and the past
The shore looks around
A tall reed in its hand
You
Guard every wave
Their charming foams and stars
When the weeping moon
Sings an ancient song
Of sorrow
I am a shore
I am a port for fishermen
I open my arms
Waiting for poor children's boat
To bring back the lights

关于传统

野山羊站立在悬崖上
拱桥自建成之日
就已经衰老
在箭猪般丛生的年代里
谁又能看清地平线
日日夜夜，风铃
如纹身的男人那样
阴沉，听不到祖先的语言
长夜默默地进入石头
搬动石头的愿望是山
在历史课本中起伏

About Tradition

A wild goat stands on the cliff
The arch bridge starts aging
The moment it is built
Who can see the horizon
In the age of porcupines
Day and night, the wind chimes
Stay mute, like the tattooed man
No one can hear the ancestor's language
Long night enters rocks in silence
Only rocks wish to move the mountain,
rising and falling through the history books

真的

浓雾涂白了每一颗树干，
马棚披散的长发中，
野蜂飞舞。绿色的洪水
只是那被堤岸阻隔的黎明。
在这个早晨，
我忘记了我们的年龄。
冰在龟裂，石子
在水面留下了我们的指纹。
真的，这就是春天呵，
狂跳的心搅乱水中的浮云。
春天是没有国籍的，
白云是世界的公民。
和人类言归于好吧，
我的歌声。

It's True

Thick fog bleaches every tree,
In the long hair inside the horse stable,
Wild bees dance. Green flood
Is the dawn blocked by the other shore.
This morning
I forgot our age.
Ice is cracking, stones
Kept our fingerprints on the water.
True, this is spring,
My wild heartbeats disturb clouds in the water.
Spring has no border,
Clouds are citizens of the earth.
Let my songs reconcile
With humanity.

Shanghai (上海): The Shining Pearl at the End of the Yangtze

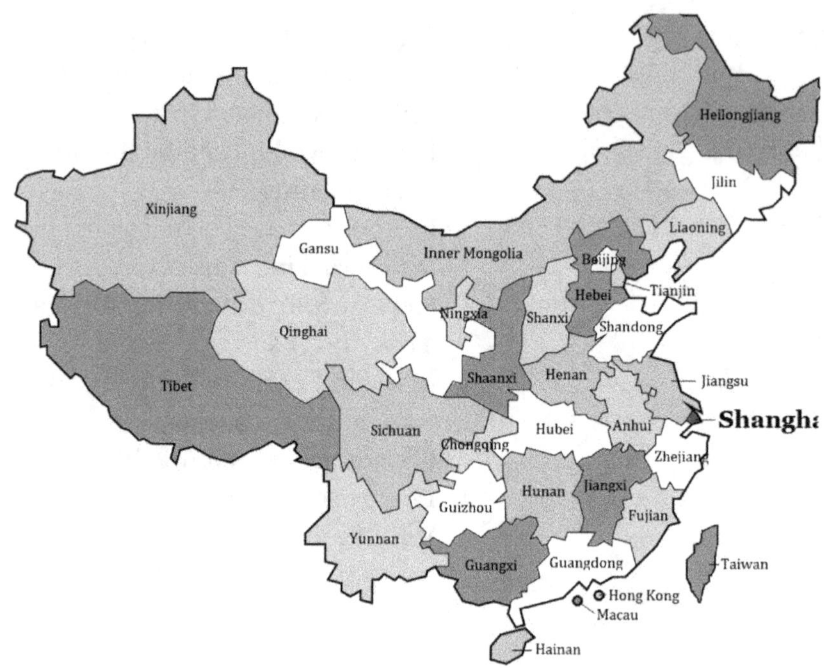

The Yangtze River, Asia's mighty dragon, ends its 3,915-mile journey here, spilling golden silt into the East China Sea. Over millennia, these sediments built the vast Yangtze Delta: a dynamic, ever-shifting landscape where land and water wrestle for dominance. Shanghai itself rose from this alluvial cradle, a city born of river and tide, its foundations pressed into soft clay and layered history. This newborn land became a beacon of trade, culture, and ambition, growing into China's most populous city—a roaring engine of finance and a crossroads of East and West.

Shanghai's soul lives in its art studios, where ink brushes meet avant-garde installations, and in its alleyways, where the scent of fried shengjianbao mingles with the bitter fragrance of freshly ground coffee. In the 1920s, modernist poets like Xu Zhimo wove verses between the city's jazz bars and lilong lanes, while writers Eileen Chang and Lu Xun captured its melancholy and glamour in prose. Even now, the M50 art district thrums with rebellious creativity, where graffiti and calligraphy share the same walls.

I was born here, in the heart of this shining pearl, in a building that still stands as the last witness of old Shanghai. My memory lingers in that cramped third-floor room, shared by three generations: grandparents, their five children, and seven grandchildren. That single space was our bedroom, dining room, study, bathroom, and storage—a microcosm of mid-20th-century Shanghainese life. From the 1940s until the turn of the millennium, this was middle-class existence. My grandfather, fluent in English, worked as an accountant for a British bank in the French Concession, where Art Deco façades whispered of a cosmopolitan past. Yet no one complained about the squeeze. Life spilled into the streets, where neighbors gossiped over majiang tiles, artists debated in shadowy tea houses, and lovers strolled the Bund, gazing at the Huangpu River's dance of freighters and neon.

Back then, as now, Shanghai was a universe unto itself—a place where people found magic in the mundane. Today, the city gleams with skyscrapers, luxury apartments, and Michelin-starred temples of cuisine. But some things endure: the thrill of window shopping on Nanjing Road, the timeless romance of a Bund rendezvous, the way a steamed crab dipped in Zhenjiang vinegar tastes like childhood.

Shanghai is more than a city—it's a living poem, written in river silt and oil paint, in steamed buns and jazz notes, in the laughter of generations who called it home.

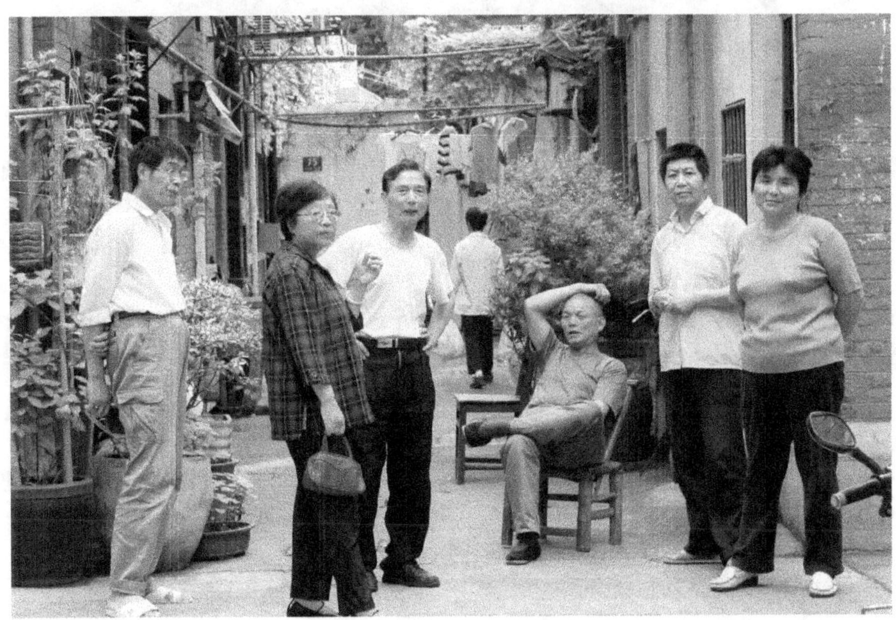

Neighbors hanging out after dinner, Yongjia Road, 2006

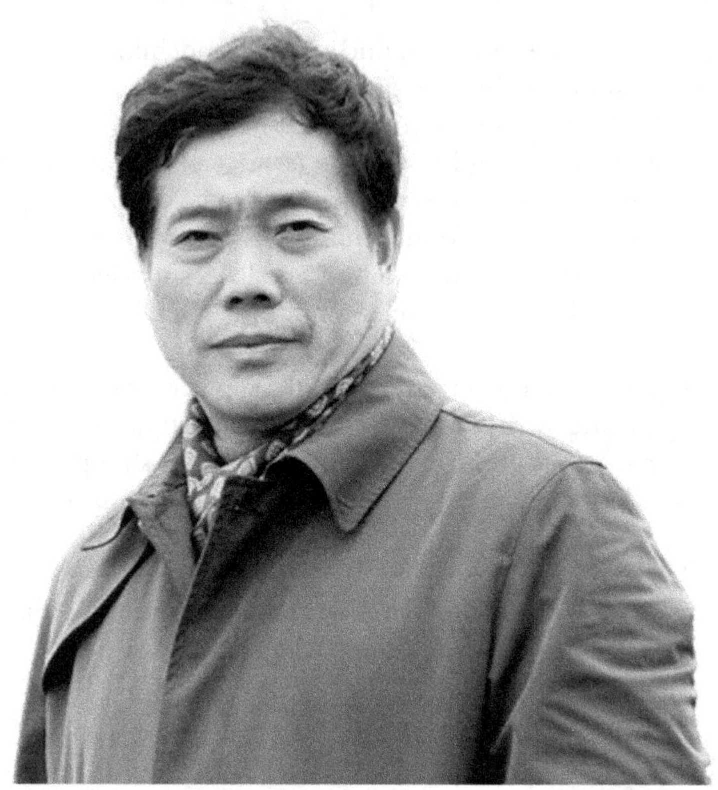

Zhao Lihong (b. 1952, Shanghai) is a celebrated Chinese poet, essayist, and children's author. A graduate of East China Normal University, he serves as vice-president of the Shanghai Writers Association and editor-in-chief of *Shanghai Poets*.

He has published over 90 books, and his essays are widely used in Chinese school textbooks. His works have been translated into more than 20 languages.

His poetry collection *Pains* (2017) is considered a landmark work. Major awards include the Smederevo Golden Key Prize (2013), the Mihai Eminescu International Poetry Prize (2019), and the Montale Literary Prize (2025), for which he was the first Chinese recipient.

联想

握着手中的铅笔
想起了变成铅笔的那棵树
那棵被砍伐的大树
一定还记得森林吧
记得森林里万类生灵的喧哗

喝着碗里微咸的汤
想起了被汤融化的盐
那些砂石一般的盐粒
大概还记得蓝色的大海吧
记得海里汹涌的浪涛和自由的鱼群

看着窗玻璃上千姿万态的冰花
想起了一夜呼啸的北风
在黑暗中四处奔走的寒风
想不到它粗犷的拜访
竟会在这里留下如此精致的脚印

望着远处天空飘舞的风筝
想起了大地上奔跑的孩子
那个欢呼着放飞风筝的孩子
想不到他手中那根细细的长线
正把一个白头人拽回到童年

摸着胸前的丝巾
想起了在桑树上吐丝的蚕
那些作茧自缚的蚕
曾经有过破茧飞翔的梦想
却不料被无情的沸水煎煮

听着一首凄婉的歌
想起了自弹自唱的歌者
那个忧伤孤单的歌者
曾经历尽人间的苦难和沧桑
却把辛酸化成了一缕温情

ASSOCIATION

Clutching the pencil in my hand
I remember the tree that birthed it
That fallen tree must still
remember the forest and
the buzz of life within its womb

Drinking a bowl of savory soup
I remember the salt melted in the broth
Those rocky grains, would they still remember the
blue sea, its high waves and schools of fish,
swimming free

Watching the icicles on the window
Blooming in infinite shapes
I remember the north wind howling all night
seeking a path in the darkness. I never thought its
brutal trail would leave such delicate footprints

Watching a distant kite in the sky
I remember children running in the fields
The boy who cheers for his flying kite
would never know that the thin long line
in his hands is tugging an old man
back to his childhood

Touching the silk scarf before my chest
I remember silkworms on mulberry trees
Those self-encased creatures
dream of bursting forth in flight
but were boiled for their silk instead

Listening to a tender lament
I remember a singer, sad and lonely
through this long bitter life
But turned his sorrow into love

Yan Li (严力) was born in 1954 in Shanghai. He is a poet, fiction writer, artist, and member of *The Stars Poetry Journal* (星星诗刊) and the Misty School of Poetry. In 1987, he founded *First Line (Yihang,* 一行) in New York, a quarterly journal featuring contemporary Chinese poets and translations of American poetry. His works have been translated into French, Italian, English, Swedish, Korean, and German. He has held numerous exhibitions and published many books, including *Poems* (诗选集), *Drinking Coffee* (喝咖啡), *Negative Proof* (负证明), *The Poem Impossible to Write* (不可能写的诗), and *The Unusual* (与众不同).

I met Yan Li in Chinatown, New York City in 1988. I had just begun writing in Chinese and English, and his journal *First Line* published my first Chinese poems. What was most precious was the artistic community in Chinatown, where I encountered extraordinary poets, composers, and artists from China, Taiwan, and Hong Kong—Yao Qingzhang, Peng Bangzhen, Tan Dun, Ai Weiwei, Xu Bing, Zhai Yongming…

At the same time, I was entering the American poetry scene, guided by Allen Ginsberg, Gary Snyder, John Ashbery, and Ed Friedman. I began the *New Generation: Poems from China Today* project (新一代：今日中国诗选, Hanging Loose Press, 2000), co-translating Chinese poets with American writers—both as an apprenticeship and as an act of gratitude.

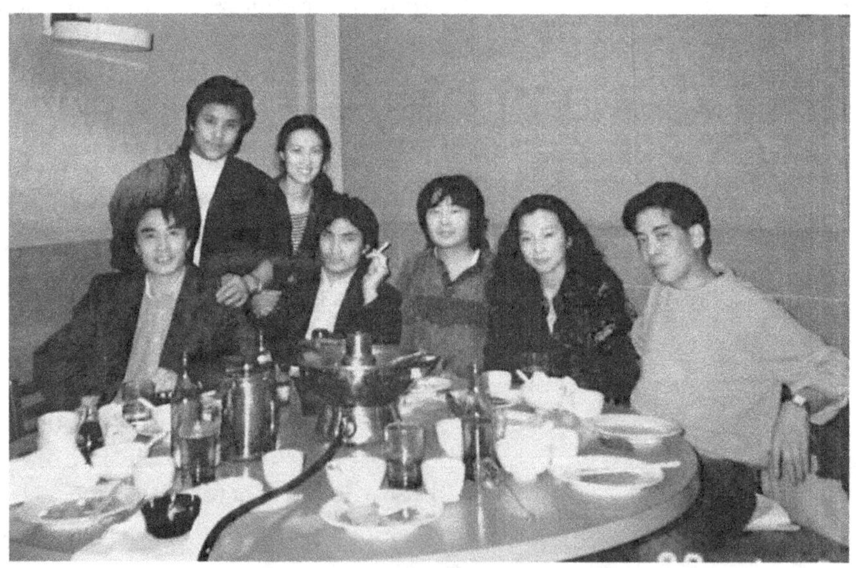

Yan Li (left)

梦

让梦和梦相爱
我们睡觉
睡到被梦和梦的婚礼吵醒
我们不吵
因为语言早就在公元前
列入了凶器的行列
所以
去看唇膏的广告

梦也曾是私奔的男女
留下衣架上的衣服一如我们
布在冬天的鼓舞中
也学会了生长
那就让布和布相爱吧
我们裸露着睡觉

梦也曾是蚊子
把我们叮醒之后就撒手不管了
连房子也浑身发痒
那就让消防队员来喷洒止痒水
但这是理想
其实我们每一次被梦叮醒
都发现
没地方可挠

Dreams

Let dreams fall in love with dreams
Let us sleep
Until awakened by dreams and its wedding
We don't fight
Because language was listed
as a lethal weapon before Christ
So
Let's go look at a lip balm ad

Dreams used to be eloping lovers
The clothes on the hangers—hang like us
Inspired by winter
Clothes have learned how to grow
So let cloth fall in love with cloth
Let's sleep naked

Dreams used to be mosquitos
They took off
After jolting us awake with their sting
Now the whole house is itching
Let the firemen spray some medicine to stop it
But this is just an illusion
Each time dreams sting us awake
We realize there is nothing to scratch

烂绳子

松开了！
你相信吗？
一条烂绳子松开的历史
定将被博物馆抱在怀里不放？！
松开了！
绳结像拳头一样松开了
没有骨节的烂绳子
松开了一捆出土的死亡
松开了祖先们系在绳子上的劲
那股劲
照遗传学讲
早已延伸到我们的手上
这手 正在把祖先们忘记告诉我们的
一些话挖出来
但这些话
被烂绳子松开了
这些话
再也系不成句子了
这些话使我们无法组成文章
也就是意味着
我们在二十世纪上了一个大当
啊　这烂绳子真他妈的烂！！！

Rotten Rope

It has come loose!
Can you believe it?
History has come loose from a rotten rope
Clasped forever in the museum's arms
It's getting loose!
Those knots are coming undone like fists
Loosen this bundle of excavated death
From the rope, spineless
Loosen the force tied inside
by our ancestors. The force
That passed into our hands
Through genetics
This hand is digging out the words
Our ancestors forgot to tell us
But these words
Have come loose from that rotten rope
These words
Can no longer be tied into a sentence again
Can no longer form another story
That means
The 20th century has fooled us completely
Damn! That piece of rope is truly rotten!

还给我

还给我
请还给我那扇没有装过锁的门
哪怕没有房间也请还给我
还给我
请还给我早上叫醒我的那只雄鸡
哪怕被你吃掉了也请把骨头还给我
请还给我半山坡上的那曲牧歌
哪怕已经被你录在了磁带上
也请把笛子还给我
还给我
请还给我爱的空间
哪怕已经被你污染了
也请把环保的权利还给我
请还给我我与我兄弟姐妹的关系
哪怕只有半年也请还给我
请还给我整个地球
哪怕已经被你分割成
一千个国家
一亿个村庄
也请你还给我

Give It Back

Give it back!
Please give me back the door without a lock
Even if it no longer has a room, I still want it
Give it back!
Please give the rooster
That wakes me in the morning
Even if you ate it, I want its bones back!
Please give the shepherd's song on the hill
even if it's only on tape, I want its flute back!
Please give me back
The space of love
Even if you've polluted it
I still want the right to protect our environment!
Please give me my relationship with my siblings
Even if it lasts just half a year
I still want it back!
Please give me the world, even if it's divided into
thousands of nations
hundreds of thousands of villages
I still want it back!

Yu Yu (郁郁), also known as **Yu Xiuye** (俞秀烨), was born in 1961, in Baoshan, Shanghai. He is a poet, essayist, and editor of influential poetry journals such as *Mourner* (送葬者) and *Continent* (大陆). His published works include *Holidays—1983* (假日—1983), *Poets: Angry Woodpeckers* (诗人：愤怒的啄木鸟), and *Dear Void Dear Meaning* (亲爱的虚空 亲爱的意义).

As He Zhong guided me into Tibet, Yu Yu was my guide to Chongming Island—where the Yangtze River meets the East China Sea. Like all poets of his generation in China, Yu Yu has lived through unimaginably tumultuous times, yet his faith in poetry remains unshaken. He and his peers are like battle flags along the Yellow and Yangtze Rivers—tattered, torn, but still standing, still fluttering in the wind…

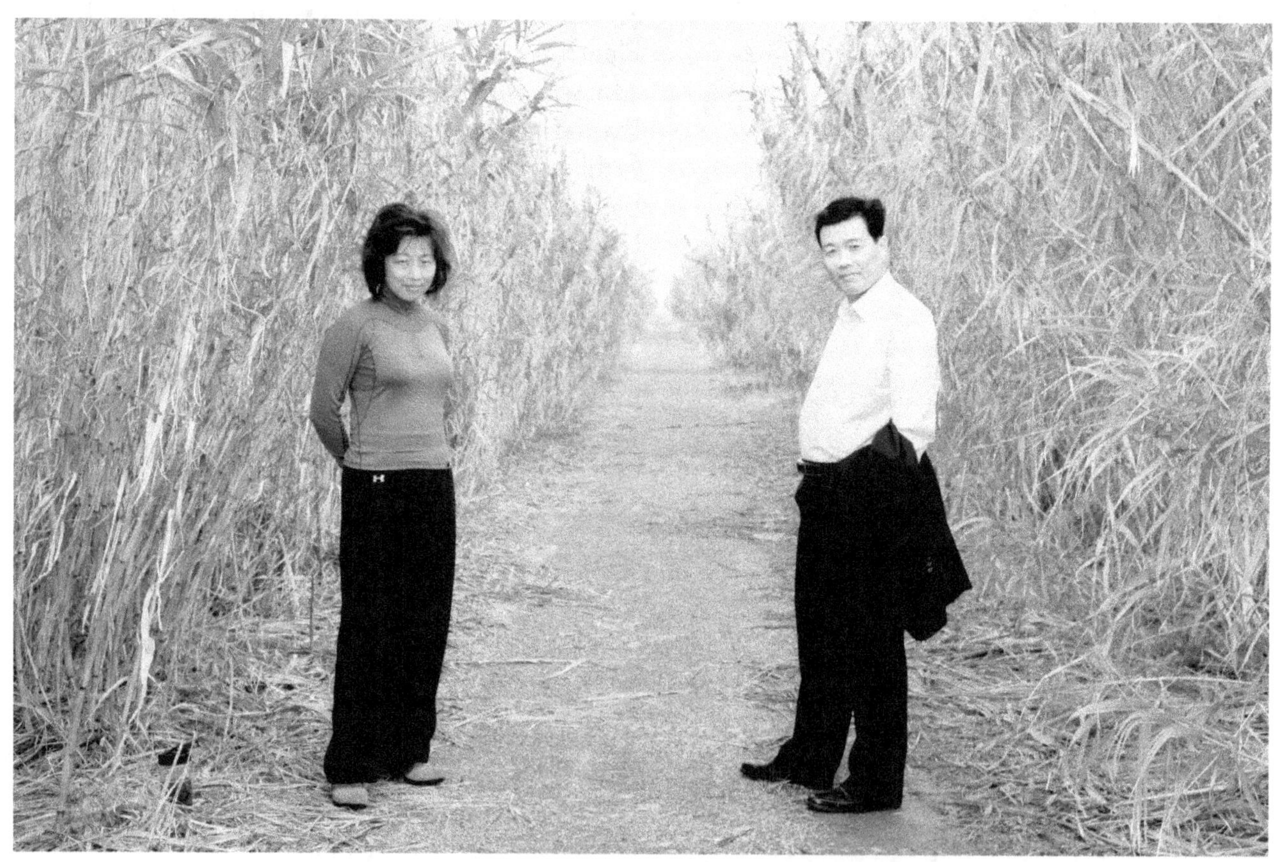

Yu Yu and Wang Ping, Chongming wetland, Shanghai

因为我爱你

因为我爱你，所以
就把尴尬当作苦涩的良药
以为从此就能健康崇高的胸怀

因为我爱你，所以
就把苦难当作理想的羁绊
以为从此就能质量道路的宽广

因为我爱你，所以
就把距离当作无限的空间
以为从此就能翱翔在甜蜜的思念

因为我爱你，所以
就把时间当作广阔的未来
以为从此就能舒心地款款散步

因为我爱你，所以
就把这一切当作了信仰
以为从此心里就会有一面面涌动的旗

Because I Love You

Because I love you
I take awkwardness as bitter herb
Believing I'd have a big healthy heart

Because I love you
I take pain for an ideal companion
Believing we'd have a wide open path

Because I love you
I take distance for boundless time
Believing we'd fly in the sweet memory

Because I love you
I take time for our wide future
Believing we'd take slow carefree walks

Because I love you
I take all of this as faith, believing
There'd be flags fluttering in our hearts

人是渺小的

听说那位经历过冷战的老政保
在长江中的一座岛上养病
和那个时代一样，他中风不轻
又听说那位官至处长的后生
入院一周便命下黄泉
尤为蹊跷　　医学上竟无此怪病
卷宗更不会记载家属的茫然

世事无常呀
我的感慨算什么
人是渺小的
历史上有许多手
抓人、打人，乃至杀人
还能若无其事地跟人民握手，留影

公正比真相更为重要
就像几十年来
这个国家的机器
习惯了敲敲打打
我所能证明的只是
我的渺小
衬托不了强大的规律

病榻上的转辗
孤岛上的张望
是渴望健康和极不甘心的挣扎
没用啊，上帝也伤痕累累
别了，去往天堂的魂灵
别了，生不如死的忏悔
我将继续在黑白之间搏弈
笑谈胜负　　包括生与死

Humans Are Specks

I heard the old veteran is recovering nicely from stroke
On an island of the Yangtze
He's been quite sick, like the epoch
I also heard that a young director
Died a week after he got into the hospital
Nobody knows how he died
The hospital won't record his family's doubt

Nothing is permanent
My emotions count for nothing
Humans are just specks
After arresting, beating, killing
Many people in history, can still
shake hands and take photos as if nothing happened

Justice is more important than truth
Like the state machine
Is used to beating around
All these years
I can only prove
How small I am
Against this powerful law

Tossing in the sick bed
Looking out from the island
We long for health; we refuse to give up
But it's useless; even God is full of injuries
Goodbye, spirits
Goodbye, regrets
I'll keep fighting between black and white
Laughing about loss and victory, life and death

十二月

十二月，你们终于把自己忙碌成蚂蚁，
而我，也必须在开始和结束之间寻找突破

十二月，我试图割断那些烦人的枝蔓
它们无法成为我生前的喝彩死后的花环

十二月，我总是会想起遥远的十二月党人
他们心爱的金发是俄罗斯上空的雪花

十二月，喜庆的习俗覆盖了深重的苦难
我悄悄地撤离不看最终的乐极生悲

十二月，老但丁为他心爱的贝德丽采点上
一生的蜡烛，然后神曲一样地合上眼睛

十二月，我零乱的诗篇堆成爱情的柴禾
一边燃烧一边朗读，温暖我自己的心绪

十二月，我回到因多愁善感而导致的心疼
意义喝光了，说什么也都适得其反

十二月，耶稣啊你的子民浑然不知
犹大流窜于人类的血脉已有二千年了

十二月，更多的时候一晃而过
如我长吁短叹的呼吸难敌风霜雨雪的弥漫

December

December, you turned yourself into an ant
I must find a break between origin and end

December, I sever the tangled twigs so they
Can't be my death wreaths for my past

You remind me of the December Party, their
Gold hair falls like snowflakes over Russia

December festivals cover deep pains. I flee
From the tragedy born out of too much joy

December, old Dante lit a candle for his
beloved Beatrice, before closing his eyes

December, my poems pile up for love, to be
Burnt to warm my heart, as I recite them

December, my heart aches with sentiments
I drank the meanings, nothing I say matters

Jesus, your children have no idea Judas' Blood
has run within us for 2000 years

December, you swing by in a flash.
My breaths can't combat wind or snow

Zhoushan Archipelago (舟山群岛): Rings of Pearls in the East China Sea

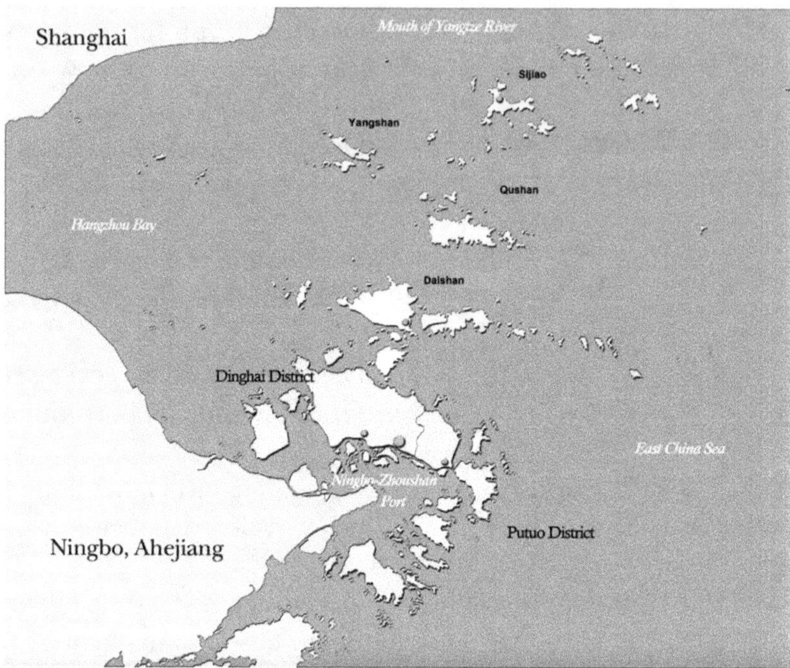

Here, where the mighty Yangtze River surrenders its waters to the East China Sea, the Zhoushan Archipelago rises like a scattered necklace of jade and pearl. These islands—over a thousand in number—are the drowned peaks of ancient mountains, sculpted by millennia of tides and tectonic shifts. This is where land, river, and sea converge in a dance as old as time.

Formed by the subsidence of the Yangtze River Delta and the uplift of the East China Sea shelf, the Zhoushan Islands are a living geological record. The archipelago sits atop the submerged remains of a prehistoric land bridge that once connected China to Japan and Korea. Fishermen still dredge up mastodon teeth and Neolithic tools from the seabed, silent witnesses to a time when these waters were plains and forests.

Here, the mysterious Japanese eel (*Anguilla japonica*) begins and ends its epic migration. Born in the dark depths of the Mariana Trench, the translucent larvae drift thousands of miles on ocean currents, drawn by instinct to the Yangtze's freshwater embrace. In Zhoushan's brackish estuaries, they transform—growing golden and pink, their bodies flushed with what Chinese fishermen call "marriage colors." After years in the river, they return to the sea, swimming back to their birthplace to spawn and die—a cycle unbroken for 70 million years.

For centuries, Zhoushan has been the heart of China's maritime culture. During the Tang and Song dynasties, it was a key hub of the Maritime Silk Road, where merchants traded porcelain, silk, and tea. In the Ming era, it became a stronghold against Japanese pirates (wokou), its jagged coastlines hiding secret coves and fortresses. Later, European traders—Portuguese, Dutch, and British—sought its harbors, drawn by the bounty of the sea.

Here is China's greatest fishing ground, where the cold currents of the East China Sea collide with warm Yangtze outflow, creating a paradise of marine life. For generations, fishermen have braved typhoons and treacherous tides to harvest yellow croaker, hairtail, cuttlefish, and the prized Zhoushan razor clams, known as "dragon's toes" for their tender meat.

The islands are also the birthplace of Putuo Maitreya, a Buddhist pilgrimage site where monks and fishermen pray for safe voyages. In the autumn, the Fishermen's Opening Festival fills the harbors with lantern boats, and pours rice wine into the waves to honor the Dragon King.

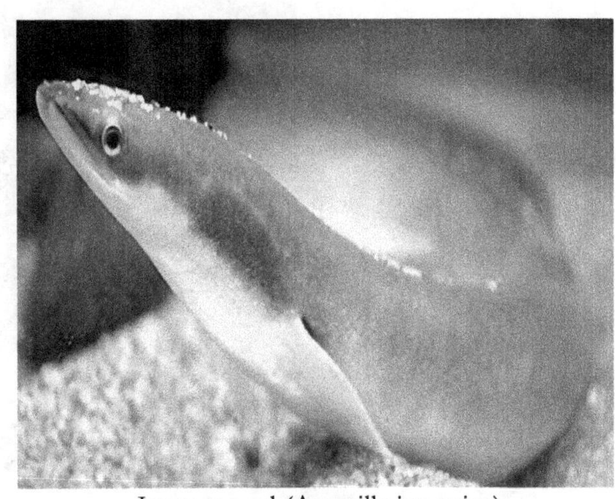
Japanese eel (Anguilla japonica)

I was born in Shanghai, and grew up on the archipelago. Here I dug shell fish on the mud beach for proteins. Here I learned how to grow rice, yam and wheat as an "educated youth." Here I heard the stories of *The Little Mermaid* and *Huckleberry Finn* from the radio in a sea cave. Here I found Whitman's *Leaves of Grass* buried under a chicken coop. Those stories and poems awakened my eel spirit, 70 million years old. On the islands of Zhoushan, my soul turned transparent like the fry, my spirit wild and untamable, my heart as colorful and passionate as the mature eel, my body free and nimble and regular like wind and rain. At 14, I left home, roaming the world till I reached the destination of poetry, living my life circling the sea and river, free, wild, fearless.

Such is the life for all Chinese poets. Such is the spirit of poetry.

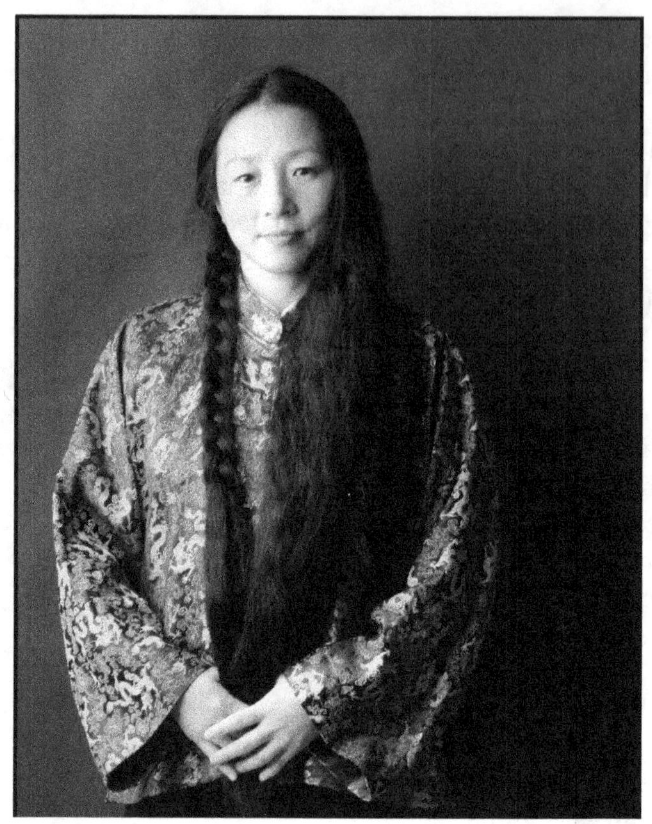

Wang Ping (王屏) was born in Shanghai and grew up on Zhoushan Island in the East China Sea before immigrating to the U.S. in 1985. She is the author of 15 books spanning poetry, prose, and translation, and has received numerous honors, including fellowships and awards from the NEA, Bush Foundation, McKnight Foundation, AWP, and others—notably the Midwest Distinguished Immigrant Award and the Venezuela International Poetry Prize. A Professor Emerita of Poetry at Macalester College, she is also a storyteller for *The Moth* and *Snap Judgement* (National Public Radio). In 2023, *The New York Times* featured her as a poet and athlete in the "Story of the Day." She is the founder and director of Kinship of Rivers, an ongoing project that fosters connections among rivers, mountains, and communities through poetry, storytelling, music, and food.

First Order of Things
For Gary Snyder

Today I rowed my first 12k in the Mississippi, and earned my first blisters.

The first shovel into the thawed earth, rich with compost from food scraps, bones, eggshells, leaves, worms, bacteria, rain, ice and patience.

The first planting of potatoes from last year's garden, pink sprouts and green skin, excited to re-enter the earth.

The first breaking of dirt in my hands, dark earth promising another year's harvest.

The first sprouting: garlic, leeks, dandelions, peonies, lilies, fiddleheads, creeping Charlie, all beautiful and delicious.

The first harvest from my garden, first sautéed egg with garlic leek, first robin's visit from Texas and old nest under my roof, asking why I'm not sharing food with her.

First filling of bird bath, after a long freeze, first line of chickadees splashing in ecstasy.

First meal under the sun, listening to Gary's" Long Hair" from 40 years ago, his fingers gnarly from fixing the generators for power and poetry, living off the grid in the Sierras, my fingers blessed with blisters and black earth, fingers that know how to dig, plant, nurse, cook, feed, write poetry, fingers that refuse to point, destroy, accuse, sow hate.

Fingers that vow to spread love and love only, through labor and devotion…intertwining west and east, mountain and prairie.

And then the deer runs inside me
The plants sprout inside me
The robin sings in chorus with chickadees
The garden blooms inside me
The Mississippi flows through me.

Dumpling 饺子: A Bite for Poetry

I listen to my vegetables, meat, fish and spices. They teach me what to do, how to sing and dance with them, how to make magic in the kitchen.

Food & poetry: we need both to live, especially when our tummy is full.

Gary Snyder picked a bowl from the sink, to make our granola breakfast. I wrenched it from his hands. "It has an inch of mold from the old yogurt," I told him.

"What's wrong with that?" he asked, laughing.

Many students came to my poetry workshops to learn how to keep living, and live well.

I started growing food when I was five, cooking and serving my parents, siblings, partner, children, students, former colleagues, and friends…

We laughed like crazy, as I washed the bowl and handed the clean one to Gary. Kai said he does that all the time, because of his eyes.

Kai is a foodie too. He made delicious lunches and dinners for us. We ate outside, in the "shop," under the prayer flags. The breeze and food brought yellow jackets, buzzing around my head.

"Don't pay attention to them," Gary told me.

"Don't mind the mosquito bites, because they need to eat, too."

Students don't remember what I taught, but remember the dumplings I made with them, 21 years ago.

I have tons of stories about food. I'm a big foodie, a fussy eater, especially eating out.

I get mad when I get overpriced bad food. Does it make me a bitch?

I have a hard time trusting people who dislike food.

If the food comes out bad for my guest, it's a warning sign.

You're too intimidating to cook for, people say, when I complain of not getting invited back.

Gary Snyder, 91 year-old-poet, brought the breakfast tray to my room: coffee with heated milk, granola with raisins and buttermilk.

I burst out in tears.

I wanted to make dumplings for Gary. I froze the marinated ground turkey and beef and flew to Sacramento. The airport security opened my bag, touched it, and waved me by, along with the garlic leek from my garden.

I took my poetry class to the reservation. For 3 days, we fished, swam, sang, sweated, and harvested wild rice. We ate what we gathered from water and soil.

We made the dumplings under the prayer flags, Gen, Kai and I. Gary drank beer, watching, smiling. He ate a huge plate, with bare hands.

Each dumpling is a little universe by itself: meat, vegetables, grain, love, friendship, family.

It tastes better from hand to mouth, as finger food, with a touch of black vinegar.

Chinese food is a way of living: art, joy, nutrition, medicine, friendship, love-making.

In the beginning, there's this silence: plates are passed around, food taken, smelled, tasted, chewed, savored…nobody says a word, then a collective sigh of happiness.

Good food flows from the heart to hand to mouth, a circle of joy and love, and the body churns it into blood, thoughts, emotions, words, till the mind opens like a summer melon.

Is this poetry? Like our daily life? Like our breath?

回家 **Circling Home**

Every Chinese belongs to lao jia 老家, our native land, ancestor, name, spirit, roots…

老 lao: old, origin…over the head is *tu* 土earth, a plough to dig a home.

Every Chinese wants to 回老家—*go back to old home*, or simply, *go home*, no matter how far we wander.

At 14, I left home on the big island of the East China Sea. I worked in a fishing village, for the one-in-a-million chance to go to college. I never returned.

3 years later, I left to study English in Hangzhou. I never returned to the island.

I left Hangzhou for Beijing University. My college dream came true at 22.

I left China in 1986, to pursue my PhD at NYU. I never returned.

"Go back home!" people scream at me. Still, I never went back.

I drift farther away from Weihai, my lao jia, carrying that old earth in my dreams.

Shanghai is my birthplace. Zhoushan Island is where I grew up till 17. I studied English in Hangzhou and Beijing. I earned two MAs and a PhD in NYC. I've settled in St. Paul for 20 years, raised my sons, taught poetry... My old home is still registered as Shandong, Weihai, my 老家, my earth, my heart and liver 心肝.

For Chinese, the liver stores blood, and the heart moves it, a circuit of paths leading to one destination--home. At night, the blood must go home to restore the soul and settle the spirit. If it can't go home, we have a problem: insomnia.

At 50, I took my sons to the Yellow Sea. It was our first time to see 老家.

Factories and buildings take over the land that my father talked about every day when he was alive. The wheat fields are gone. The village is gone. The sand beach is gone. My grandma's grave still stands in the yam fields. I sit down in front of her stone, and everything floods back: sorrow, joy, bitter, sweet, her stories, hand-made bread, noodles and dumplings, my father roaming on the island in search of the immortal mushroom reishi 灵芝, his longing to go back home 回家…

I watch my sons eating steamed bread, strung together like beads with a red thread. It is their first time to eat this traditional food, but they devour it as if it were their daily meal since birth, as if they were slurping Cheerios and milk. This is the bread my father craved while living on the island, while sailing East China Sea as a Navy commander.

回 hui: return, a mouth within a mouth. Is that why there is a Chinese restaurant wherever there's a Chinese? Just so we could go back home through our food?

Is that how my sons are tied to their lao jia in China, even though they were born in NYC and Minneapolis, love pizza, play hockey and baseball, speak English, Hebrew, and some Chinese?

I check the dictionary. 回 = 迴 = return = go home by walking, travelling, wandering on earth…

I remember my DNA test by National Geographic. 200,000 years ago, my ancestors walked out of Africa, crossing the land and sea, following food, hunting, gathering, making home along their paths, reaching South China after 100,000 years.

I remember my father: left home at 16 to fight the Japanese invasion, lived and died on an island of East China Sea, but in his heart, home is forever Weihai, Shandong, by the Yellow Sea.

Just like monarchs, geese, salmon, elephants, weeds and other life on earth, travelling thousands of miles to follow food, but always know how to go back 回老家.

Home is a transit word… 回 … 迴 … return … go home.

I keep digging. I need to find the origin.

What I found makes my hair stand. In the oldest version of Chinese, when words were carved on the bones of birds and whales, on the backs of turtles, 回 ☲ = water; 迴 彡☲ = water rippling, pushing, whirling, circling towards home.

Home is embedded in the water. Going home is embedded in running water. When Chinese see the word 回…迴, we've already arrived.

My heart feels at home, finally.

We are water, born to move, wander, migrate, whirl, circle…

No need to get mad when people shout "Go Home" at us.

We all carry home in our heart and liver, in our blood, in our DNA, as we flow from continent to continent, from sea to sea, to appease the soul, to circle back home…回…迴…

A Poem Is River Is Grass: An Afterword with Walt Whitman

The moment I found Whitman's *Leaves of Grass* in a sealed library on an island in the East China Sea, I felt its magic. It healed the wound in my heart and filled it with hope. I'd just been caught reading Pushkin and *Dead Souls*, and Mom had to punish me so I wouldn't read banned books again and endanger everyone around me. She broke her laundry bat, and Dad burnt those "poison books." That day I had just turned 12. I didn't speak English except for a few slogans like "Down with American Imperialism!" and "Long Live Chairman Mao." But I happened to know the words *leaves* and *grasses*, and I wondered: why this name for poetry—*leaves* and *grasses*, the most common things on earth, so cheap, so taken for granted?

I've been wondering ever since: why does *Leaves of Grass* fill me with delight and visions? Why does it pull me to its bosom, demanding my whole being to poetry, music, art, beauty, and truth?

> Not I, nor anyone else can travel that road for you.
> You must travel it by yourself.
> It is not far. It is within reach.
> Perhaps you have been on it since you were born, and did not know.
> Perhaps it is everywhere—on water and land.
>   —"Song of Myself," Walt Whitman

All my life, I have followed its calling, like birds, fish, and flowers following the sun and earth's magnetic pull—leaving home, leaving Zhoushan Island, leaving Hangzhou, leaving Beijing, NYU, Macalester College—always walking a path that seemed impossible and crazy, always following the breadcrumbs of beauty that is poetry, with translation as my guide and companion, a community of soulmates and comrades, with poetry as my courage, strength, and a goal to live.

Each poem is a leaf, a blade of grass, an earthling but blessed by the sun and stars.

"If you want me again look for me under your boot-soles." ("Song of Myself")

If you want to know who we are, please look for us in this collection of poetry, along the Yellow and Yangtze Rivers where the twin dragons of China soar.

Allow me to conclude this anthology with four of Mo Fei's poems that celebrate the winter and make way for a new season, new year, new era, new time from an ancient civilization.

听树叶

树叶的动静你听　仿佛隔窗
有耳．你听　山林随着季候
冒烟你继续

听树叶透过树叶的一阵光芒
树叶摇晃一棵大树的巅峰
雷那么响天那么空

被筛选的星星团团转
树叶一样闪烁你听
树叶一样听不清

风在开始的地方听
树叶在铺开的雨声里听
风雨交加忽近忽远你再听听

一片树叶奔跑你听
一片树叶紧紧跟你听
一片树叶撞到墙上你听见吗

扑腾扑腾的树叶
东躲躲西藏藏的树叶
树叶不听你的只听树叶

远处的惊魂之鸟　让萝藦绝对的
叶子　抖动荒凉的村庄羽毛的村庄

有时呼吸可以等一会儿
心跳怎么可以不跳
就好像树叶吹着树叶你听

Listening to Tree Leaves

Trees are whispering and you listen as if
someone hid behind the wall and you listen.
Forests burn with seasons and you keep

Listening to the light penetrating the leaves
Leaves are shaking the top of a giant tree
Thunders are rolling yet the sky is empty

The chosen stars are spinning
Tree leaves sparkle like stars and you listen
But like you the trees can't hear anything

Wind is listening to its origin
Tree leaves listen in the spreading rain
Listen again to the wind and rain dancing

One leaf is running and you listen
Another leaf is following and you listen
Do you hear a leaf fly into the wall

Leaves are flopping around
Leaves are hiding here and there
Leaves listen to leaves only

Birds startled in distance. Leaves confirmed
Moluo. Village fluffed its desolate feathers

Sometimes we can hold our breaths
But not our heartbeats   like the leaves
That can't stay still in the wind

听种子带着雪白的呼啸
听呼啸带着我们踉跄
听大地从来不怕野兽的嚎叫

怕的是人类细碎的脚步
仿佛世界的穿行漏洞百出
树叶碰到树叶一片叮当作响

听树叶说我爱你听
听说树叶照样千里万里听
听你说树叶全都来了那么寂静

Listen to the whistling of snow-white seeds
Listen how the whistling makes us stumble
Listen to the earth, never fear howling beasts

But terrified of the sounds of human steps
Breaking holes in the spinning world
Leaves bump against leaves, making noises

Hear the leaves say "I love you."
Hear them open their ears
to thousands of miles

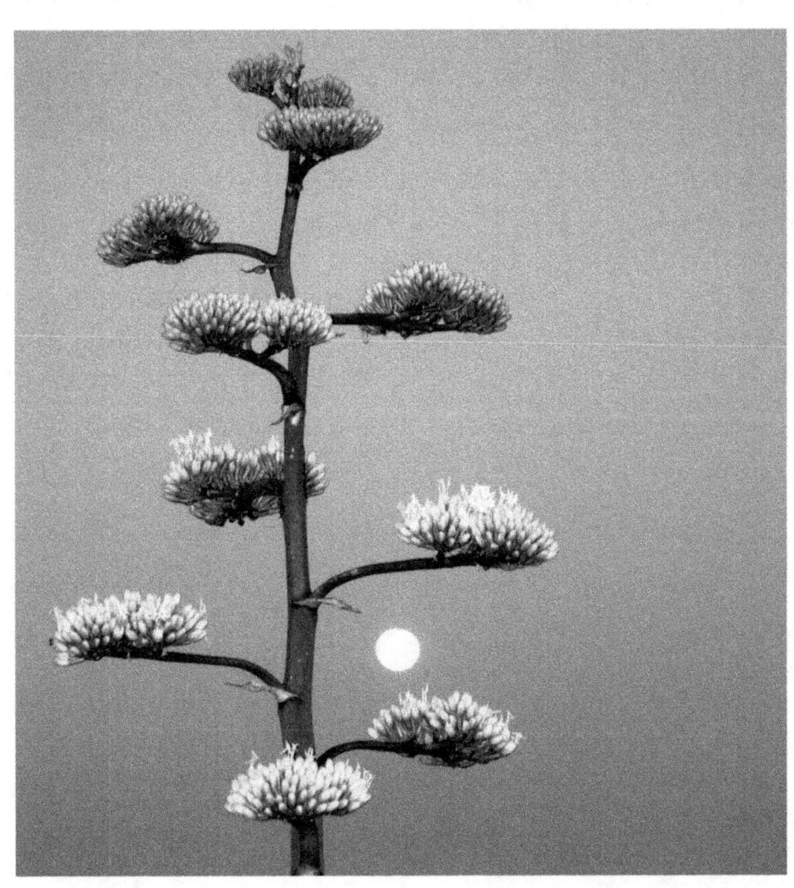

旧年

这一年分分秒秒数到今天
就算到头了，要另起一行。
生和死是最难的一副对子

上联写正了下联才好看。
在横批之上　有两个字叫当下
模模糊糊几近被人遗忘

喧声和无声的枝桠守护我们的安宁
我们的安宁，也是滚动的树叶继续滚动

大海在大雪围绕的地方依旧我行我素
一块石头推倒了，一块石头立起来

仿佛门外的人群散去仅仅是散去而已
云朵在低处但那是山的低处，无法借鉴

旧年的小板凳独自摇晃
叫着你的名字. 一棵梧桐树
结果了，却不知道花开何处

Old Year

Today the old year ends after I've counted
every minute and second. Time to start new
lines. But life and death are difficult to begin

The first line must be straight for the next
line. The top line has two smudged words
No one even remembers what they were

Noise and silent trees guard our peace
Our peace comes from rolling tree leaves

The sea keeps going despite the deep snow
One stone is toppled, the other stands up

Outside the crowd seems to have dispersed
Clouds hang low at the foot of the mountain

An old stool calls you from last year.
A plane tree is bearing fruit
Nobody knows where they blossomed

大拜年

旧年给辞了我给新年拜年。新年刮大风
我给窗外的桃树拜年。桃树等开花等你来

给我的春天拜年。那么多青草没人管过
却养育了肥沃的土地。我给土地拜年最多

拜年都跪在土地上。我给北方的麦田拜年
给土豆给辣椒给勺子拜年，然后溪水流淌

给我的冬笋拜年直到竹林七贤个个笑了
给我的魏晋拜年，在风骨上生出大好河山

我给羽毛干净的乌鸫，给乌鸫不吃的虫子
给虫子丢下的卵给槭树叶的绒毛，一一拜过

最后我给你拜年，萝藦都看见我哆嗦
大拜二拜之后，我拜倒在一粒种子的上面

New Year's Greetings

Say goodbye to the old year as I greet
the new year. Wind blows. I greet the peach
tree outside as I wait for the peach blossoms

I greet spring. Nobody pays attention to the
grass that keeps the earth fertile. I greet the
earth with the most devotion

Every year I kneel on her land. I greet the
wheat fields in the north. I greet potatoes,
peppers and spoons, then I greet creeks

I greet my bamboo shoots till the 7 Bamboo
Sages smile. I greet Wei Jing Dynasties that
kept rivers and mountains clean and straight

I greet crows with clean feathers, greet worms
that crows won't eat. I greet the worm eggs
and fuzzy skin on trees, I greet each of them

Finally I greet you, one kowtow, two
kowtows, till the luomo plants start to tremble
then I prostrate on a seed

幸福这件事

我想告诉你幸福这件事
特别啰嗦。很久之后
木头从木头里暴露出来

一片时间的水洼里
只有你没用过的时间

大地的风声和一串鸟鸣
分别给了我和黑夜
编织的技艺仿佛失传了

架上的葫芦和豆荚
带来满是瓜葛的事物
有结果的，有不结果的

星星看上去紧挨着
却漫无边际。你来了
那么远说话我都那么清楚

The Business of Being Happy

I want to tell you something about being happy
It'll take a while. Then the wood
Will finally reveal itself from the tree

In the pool of time
There's only time you've never used up

Wind and bird songs from the earth
Give me the night time
But I lost the skills to do needle work

The gourds and peapods on vines
Bring me entanglement of things
Some have results, some fruitless

Stars look all lined up, one by one
In reality, they're scattered everywhere. You're here
But I can't hear you, you're speaking so far away

About the Editor/Translator

Ping Wang was born in Shanghai, graduated from Beijing University in 1984, and received her PhD in comparative literature from NYU in 1999. She is the author of 15 award-winning books of poetry, translation, and prose, including *The River Within* (MadHat, 2023), *My Name Is Immigrant* (Hanging Loose, 2021), *Life of Miracles along the Yangtze and Mississippi* (University of Georgia, 2018), *Aching for Beauty: Footbinding in China* (Anchorage, 2001), *New Generation: Poems from China Today* (Hanging Loose Press, 2000), *Flashcards: Poems by Yu Jian* (Zephyr, 2010), *The Last Communist Virgin* (Coffee House Press, 2007), *Foreign Devil* (Coffee House Press, 1999), and *American Visa* (Coffee House Press, 1997). Her work has been featured by the *New York Times, PBS, BBC, The Moth*, and others. She is the recipient of fellowships and awards from the NEA, the Bush Foundation, the Lannan Foundation, the McKnight Foundation, AWP, and the Minnesota Book Awards, among others. She is the founder and director of the Kinship of Rivers project and a Professor Emerita of Poetry and Creative Writing at Macalester College.

王屏，山东威海，80级北大西语系，1999纽约州大学比较文学博士，出版了15部诗歌、翻译及小说，包括《心中的河流》（MadHat出版社2023年）、《我的名字叫移民（Hanging Loose出版社2021年）、《扬子江与密西西比河畔的奇迹人生》（佐治亚大学出版社2018年）、《为美而痛》（安克雷奇出版社2001年）。《纽约时报》、美国公共电视网、英国广播公司、《飞蛾》故事会等知名媒体曾专题报道并演出。王屏荣获美国国家艺术基金会、布什基金会、兰南基金会、麦肯奈特基金会等机构颁发的艺术奖项，以及美国最佳文化研究、美国文学、亚洲文学、明州最佳图书奖等诸多荣誉，马卡莱斯特学院终身教授，荣休诗歌教授＇现任＂;江河缘＂项目创始人兼艺术总监。